PURSUING THE AMERICAN DREAM

American Political Thought

EDITED BY

Wilson Carey McWilliams and Lance Banning

Cal Jillson

Pursuing the American Dream

OPPORTUNITY AND EXCLUSION
OVER FOUR CENTURIES

University Press of Kansas

Published by the University Press of Kansas (Lawrence,
Kansas 66049), which was organized by the Kansas Board
of Regents and is operated and funded by Emporia State
University, Fort Hays State University, Kansas State University,
Pittsburg State University, the University of Kansas, and
Wichita State University

Library of Congress Cataloging-in-Publication Data

Jillson, Calvin C., 1949–
   Pursuing the American Dream : opportunity and exclusion over
four centuries / Cal Jillson
      p. cm. — (American political thought)
   Includes bibliographical references and index.
   ISBN 0-7006-1342-0 (cloth : alk. paper)
   1. United States—Politics and government—Philosophy.
2. United States—Civilization. 3. National characteristics,
American.   I. Title.   II. Series.
   E183.J55 2004
   973′.01—dc22

                                        2004004568

British Library Cataloguing-in-Publication Data is available.

Printed in the United States of America

10 9 8 7 6 5 4 3 2 1

TO MY PARENTS

It helps to see character modeled.

Contents

Illustrations

Preface and Acknowledgments

> Our business is not to lay aside the dream, but to . . . drag
> dreams out into the light of day, show their sources, compare
> them with fact, transform them to possibilities.
> —Walter Lippmann, *Drift and Mastery*

"The American Dream" is one of the most evocative phrases in our national lexicon. Americans know instinctively what it means—a fair chance to succeed in open competition with fellow citizens for the good things of life. The grand promise of the American Dream has always been that those willing to learn, work, save, persevere, and play by the rules would have a better chance to grow and prosper in America than virtually anywhere else on earth. Still, as Walter Lippmann said nearly a century ago, dreams regularly need to be reexamined, questioned, and compared with reality, to insure that they still mark the way to a future that serves the real needs and interests of the American people. How has the American Dream informed and energized American life over the centuries, and how can we assure that it will do so for centuries yet to come?

John Winthrop, William Penn, Benjamin Franklin, Thomas Jefferson, Abraham Lincoln, Franklin Roosevelt, Lyndon Johnson, and Ronald Reagan all loom large in the American mind. But what ties them together? What skein runs through their contributions to American life? What instinct led them all to tack back and forth between liberty and equality, between freedom and the rule of law, between individual rights and the common good? I argue that the social instinct that guided the nation's great leaders and common citizens to move haltingly and often grudgingly toward a more open, diverse, and genuinely competitive society was the soft but insistent voice of the American Dream.

This book offers the fullest exploration yet of the origins and evolution of the American Dream. Literally hundreds of books have touched upon some aspect of the American Dream or explored some of its elements and themes, but no previous work has traced the idea to its origins and systematically pursued it forward into our own time.* This book demonstrates that a distinctive ideal, the American Dream, took shape very early in our national experience, defined the nation throughout its growth and development, and today remains central to our national ethos and collective self-image. Even the earliest versions of the Dream were premised on the assumption of "American exceptionalism"—that America offered opportunities for a good life that were simply unavailable in the Old World. Europe was dominated by hereditary monarchs, by aristocrats protecting wealth and privilege, and by national churches that limited the opportunities available to common people. Men and women in Europe, to say nothing of those wasting under the despotic regimes of Russia, Persia, and China, could rarely rise above the social station to which they were born.

America, on the other hand, offered the opportunity to build society anew. Even the Puritan worthies who envisioned a strict Bible commonwealth, a New Israel on the shores of Massachusetts Bay, gave way before religious diversity, economic opportunity, and a rising egalitarian ethic. Before long, America was known on both sides of the Atlantic, in the memorable phrase of Pennsylvania founder William Penn (1644–1718), as "a good poor man's country." For nearly four centuries, America has beckoned millions and offered them a breadth and depth of freedom, opportunity, and security distinctive in the world. For nearly a century, the American commitment to freedom, to democratic politics and free markets, has been the template from which the world has worked.

Yet we deceive ourselves if we imagine that American history has been an unambiguously uplifting story of opportunity, competition, and widespread

---

* The most recent burst of interest in the American Dream has brought forth two popular histories, Zachary Karabell's *A Visionary Nation* and Jim Cullen's *The American Dream: A Short History of an Idea that Shaped a Nation.* Both books suggest that there are multiple American dreams that evolve and shift over time, hence they organize their narratives thematically. Karabell views American history as a "cycle of vision giving way to vision" (214), and Cullen describes competing American dreams that include religious purity, political freedom, upward mobility, equality, home ownership, easy living, and immigrant aspiration. These presentations drift toward the idea that any American's dream is an instance of the American Dream. I describe an American Dream that is broader and more basic and that has been remarkably stable since well before the American Revolution. That dream was of an America that offers citizens and immigrants a better chance to thrive and prosper than any other nation on earth. Our national history, and the story told between the covers of this book, is of a bold promise made early and the struggle of the excluded to share fully in it.

success. Truth requires that we remember, acknowledge, and explain the fact that full, free, and unquestioned membership in the American society has always been more readily available to white men of a certain level of wealth and status than to others. For most of American history, some poor white men and virtually all women, blacks, American Indians, Asians, and others were barred from effective pursuit of the American Dream. This book is about how both the content of the American Dream and our broad sense of who has the right to pursue it have evolved and expanded over the course of American history.

This telling of the American story charts a middle course between the "triumphalism" that sees American history as the march of freedom in the world, and a "multiple traditions," or "collision of histories," perspective that sees it as an insupportably immoral aggression against Native Americans, minorities, and women. No doubt there are multiple traditions in American public life, and no doubt some of their elements have fostered oppression and exclusion throughout American history. Yet the best of America's values, grounded on the Declaration of Independence's promise of "life, liberty, and the pursuit of happiness," have empowered the excluded and acted as levers to help them pry open American society.

The basic structure of our story is broadly historical; describing the evolution of the American Dream from first settlement to the dawn of the twenty-first century. Chapter 1 describes the American Creed and the American Dream and the shaping role that these seminal ideas and ideals have played in American history. Chapters 2 to 8 divide American history into seven familiar periods and answer four questions about each period. The first major section in each of these chapters, always entitled "Young Dreamers and the World Before Them," asks how the social landscape looked and how it was evolving during the era under consideration. To understand the hopes and dreams of each generation of Americans and each new wave of immigrants, we must understand the world before them as they set out to pursue the promise of American life. The young dreamer of 1800 looked out on a very different society, a very different set of social and economic opportunities, than did the young dreamer of 1900 or of 2000.

The second major section of each chapter asks how the American Dream was articulated, how it was voiced, what it envisioned and hoped for, in that period of our history. In general, the dream has always been that education, hard work, and a little luck will lead to success. Yet when we look more closely, we see that Winthrop's Puritan saint, Jefferson's sturdy yeoman farmer, the industrialist of the late nineteenth century, the middle-class suburbanite of the

1950s, and the young entrepreneur of this new century dreamed different American Dreams. Even when the words seem the same—freedom, autonomy, opportunity, and work are good examples—what these words refer to in the world has evolved continuously and sometimes changed entirely.

The third section, always entitled "The Dream Embedded in Institutions, Law, and Policy," asks what society and government have done at each stage of our national history to define and structure the American Dream. What were the legal principles and public policies that facilitated or hindered access to the dream? For example, how did homestead, immigration, tariff, transportation, and Indian suppression policies interact to facilitate or hinder individual opportunity and economic growth in the mid-nineteenth century? How did the GI Bill, the FHA, the interstate highway program, the space program, and the civil rights revolution interact to facilitate or hinder opportunity and growth in the mid-twentieth century?

The concluding section of each chapter, until Chapter 6 always entitled "The Faces of Exclusion," asks why exclusion from the dream left only nightmares for many. When Jefferson penned the famous declaration that "all Men are created equal," he simply did not mean it as broadly as most of us mean it today. Yet between Jefferson's day and ours, poor white men, minorities, and women have been admitted, usually grudgingly and often by degrees, to the right to dream the Dream. At each stage in American political history, we ask not just who was excluded from the American Dream, but on what grounds, by what means, and over what objections.

Finally, Chapter 9 asks how the American Dream stands today and what we must do to insure that it is real and meaningful for all of our children and grandchildren. Some contend that opportunity is so constrained in modern America that the dream is slipping away for all but a privileged few. It has seemed so before; one thinks of the Gilded Age, the Roaring Twenties, perhaps the 1980s and 1990s. Yet America in the twenty-first century is a radically different and better place than it was in the early twentieth century, let alone in the early seventeenth, eighteenth, or nineteenth centuries. And it is not just a wealthier and more comfortable place; it is more just, fair, open, and tolerant. The concluding chapter explores the kind of educational, health care, job training, entrepreneurship, and quality-of-life initiatives that might best renew, rejuvenate, and expand the American Dream for the twenty-first century.

The health of the American Dream is defined by the interaction between individual preparation and effort and the structure of social and economic opportunity. Individuals must prepare themselves well and work hard when they get the opportunity, but only government, through well-designed law and policy, can insure that social and economic opportunities are available for Americans to compete over. Government creates, maintains, and updates the legal and political structures that define opportunity and how it is pursued within American society. The triumph and the tragedy of American history is that for nearly four hundred years, the nation's dream has drawn it forward to a fuller and fairer future than it has ever quite been able to realize. America enters a new century, as it has entered other new centuries, challenged to make the dream real in every American life.

Fortunately, I have not confronted the challenge of telling the story of the American Dream alone. Many people, over many years, in ways large and small, have contributed to the birth of this book. Although I am the book's father, the matchmaker that brought me together with the idea for the book was Fred Woodward, editor of the University Press of Kansas. Over beers in the fall of 1997, I told Fred that my next book would treat one of the key ideas of American life—liberty, equality, opportunity, responsibility, or some such—but that I had not settled on a topic. Fred said, "How about the American Dream?"—and we were off to the races. The race became a marathon, and many have been generous with help and encouragement.

Some—my wife Jane and my students—have had little choice but to run alongside me. These ongoing conversations have buoyed my spirits and sharpened my ideas. Many others have read drafts, listened to musings, and responded to queries along the way. I am grateful to all of them, especially Phil Abbott, Joe Cooper, Cecil Eubanks, Ruth Grant, Jennifer Hochschild, Mike Lienesch, and Jeff Stonecash, as well as the series editors, Lance Banning and Carey McWilliams, for helpful comments and astute guidance. As always, librarians, curators, and other angels of the world of letters, deserve special praise. I am exceedingly grateful for the support of Southern Methodist University, first for a research leave during 2001–2002, but also for support and assistance from the Political Science Department, the John Tower Center for Political Studies, the libraries, and the Digital Commons. The Library of Congress, the Massachusetts Historical Society, the Gilder Lehrman Collection, the Democratic Leadership Council, the William J. Clinton Presidential Library, the Woolaroc Museum, the Lyndon Baines Johnson Library, and the Ronald Reagan Library were endlessly responsive.

As always, perfection eludes, and the faults that remain are mine.

The American Dream and Its Role in American History

The new world . . . once pandered in whispers to the last and
greatest of all human dreams; for a transitory enchanted moment
man must have held his breath in the presence of this continent. . . .
face to face for the last time in history with something
commensurate to his capacity for wonder.

—F. Scott Fitzgerald, *The Great Gatsby*

No phrase captures the distinctive character and promise of American life better than the phrase "the American Dream." As former President Bill Clinton said in his 1997 State of the Union address, "America is far more than a place. It is an idea." There are other beautiful lands, other free societies, and other wealthy nations, but America is "exceptional" because it is the home of an idea—and that idea is the American Dream. But ideas have to be realized, they have to be embodied in the lives of real people, before they have weight and substance.

Has the American Dream been embodied in the lives of real Americans? Has the American Dream even been open to all Americans? If not, how should we think about equality and opportunity, about gender, race, ethnicity, and achievement as these ideas relate to the American Dream? How these questions are answered will determine how Americans think about themselves and their history, whether with undiluted pride, with deep shame and remorse, or with some complicated and evolving mix of pride, shame, and hope.

The answer, as we shall see, is hope. Hope is justified, indeed required, because a society born in hierarchy and exclusion has become dramatically more free and inclusive. How did this happen? What were the forces of exclusion that barred some Americans from full access to the American Dream, and what were the social, economic, and political processes that promoted, often only partially, equality and opportunity for the formerly excluded? To answer these questions, we must first explore two related ideas: the American Creed and the American Dream.

The American Creed

Louis Hartz, one of the leading American historians of the mid-twentieth century, described colonial America as a "fragment society."[1] Hartz meant that the Englishmen and women who immigrated to America in the seventeenth century did not represent the full range of English, let alone European, political, social, and religious opinion. The fragment of English society that fled the tensions and conflicts of the Old World to seek a better life in the New World was composed mostly of middling men, small landowners, artisans, and tradesmen. In the political battles of the 1620s, these men placed their hopes with the reformers in Parliament and the Church of England. When King Charles and Archbishop Laud began to resist reform with force in the 1630s, John Winthrop, John Cotton, and more than twenty thousand of their followers removed to North America.

The liberal fragment of English thought that wave after wave of settlers carried to the New World drew heavily but selectively on the Old World. First, the seventeenth-century Protestantism that the Puritans and Quakers shared, even when leavened by the Anglicans in Virginia, Catholics in Maryland, and a thin smattering of Jews and others throughout, stressed covenanted communities, Christian millennialism, and a consuming sense of God's immediate presence in the world. Second, the early eighteenth-century focus on Enlightenment ideals highlighted the individualism latent in Protestantism while bringing increased attention to natural rights, popular sovereignty, and limited government. And finally, throughout the colonial period, most Americans maintained a deep reverence for English political and legal traditions. For example, the English Common Law tradition lay behind American reverence for ideas, phrases, and themes like a government of laws, not men; law and order; the rule of law.

Colonial Americans drew on this cultural and intellectual heritage to create communities that then developed and evolved in interaction with the continent itself. By the late eighteenth century, America's self-image, its political creed, was set. Thomas Jefferson, Benjamin Franklin, John Adams, and their revolutionary colleagues in the Congress of 1776 grounded the new nation's independence on the declaration that "all Men are created equal, that they are endowed by their Creator with certain unalienable Rights, that among these are Life, Liberty, and the Pursuit of Happiness." Although Jefferson was immensely proud of his primary authorship of the Declaration of Independence, the ideas to which he gave voice belonged to a generation. In fact, nearly fifty years after the Declaration was written, Jefferson told Henry Lee that the Declaration was intended "to be an expression of the American mind, and to give that expression the proper tone and spirit called for by the occasion."[2] The luminous phrases of the Declaration of Independence put liberty, equality, and opportunity at the core of the American Creed. Jefferson's words have been a standing challenge to each new generation of Americans to do well, to do right, and always to do better.

Nor is the importance of the Declaration to the American Creed simply American mythology. A long line of foreign observers has pointed to the Declaration as the definitive summary of American values. The British sage G. K. Chesterton, in his 1922 classic *What I Saw in America,* declared that "America is the only nation in the world that is founded on a creed. That creed is set forth with dogmatic and even theological lucidity in the Declaration of Independence."[3] Another prominent foreign observer, the Swedish sociologist Gunnar Myrdal, also beautifully captured the central ideas of the American Creed. Writing during World War II, Myrdal argued that the American Creed was grounded on "the essential dignity of the individual human being, of the fundamental equality of all men, and of certain inalienable rights to freedom, justice, and a fair opportunity. . . . For practical purposes the main norms of the American Creed . . . are centered in the belief in equality and in the rights to liberty."[4]

Moreover, contemporary analysts still point to the same familiar ideas and concepts as fundamental to the American Creed. Two prominent American scholars provided nearly identical descriptions of the fundamental principles on which our polity, economy, and society rest. Samuel Huntington concluded his study of the American Creed by declaring that "the same core values appear in virtually all analyses: liberty, equality, individualism, democracy, and the rule of law under a constitution."[5] Seymour Martin Lipset concluded that "the American Creed can be described in five terms: liberty, egalitarianism, individualism, populism, and laissez-faire."[6] Both Huntington and Lipset high-light liberty, equality, and individualism. These are the Jeffersonian core of the American Creed. Lipset's reference to populism is probably preferable to Huntington's to democracy, at least for the founding and early national periods. American politics was populist; that is based on popular sovereignty and active citizenship, before it was recognizably democratic. Finally, Lipset's laissez-faire (by which he means a dedication to capitalism, markets, and competition) and Huntington's rule of law under a constitution draw attention to our base commitments to free markets and limited government. Hence, a general description of the fundamental values of the American Creed would include liberty, equality, individualism, populism, laissez-faire, and the rule of law under a constitution.

Yet even as we define the American Creed, we know that the pride that we feel is not fully justified. Consider three of the authors and books referred to in the immediately preceding paragraphs. Myrdal's famous book, *An American Dilemma: The Negro Problem and Modern Democracy,* is a landmark study of the continuing presence of racism in a society that boasts of its commitment to liberty, equality, and opportunity. Moreover, Huntington's study of the American Creed is entitled *American Politics: The Promise of Disharmony,* while Lipset's study is entitled *American Exceptionalism: A Double-Edged Sword.* All three titles exude ambivalence about the state of our national life. The source of this ambivalence is not hard to find. America has never fully lived up to its Creed.

The best recent analysis of the conflicting strains of thought and action in American public life is Rogers M. Smith's *Civic Ideals* (1997). Smith described the American civic culture as comprising "multiple traditions," including the liberal individualist tradition that Hartz highlighted, as well as a republican communitarian tradition, and an exclusivist (nativist, racist) tradition. In Smith's description of American history, the hierarchical influences of republicanism and the exclusivist strains of nativism and racism are woven throughout American culture, thought, and action; they are always present, and they often triumph. Scholars and analysts also are keenly aware that the ideas that form the American Creed are both complex and at least potentially incompatible. Isaiah Berlin's famous "Two Concepts of Liberty," in which he distinguished between negative liberty, described as freedom from, and positive liberty, described as freedom to, still sparks heated debate. Equality has been variously argued to mean equality in the eyes of God, before the law, of opportunity, and of outcomes. Moreover, liberty can conflict with equality, constitutionalism can constrain democracy, and laissez-faire competition can conflict with the rule of law. Each new generation of American citizens and leaders has struggled to find a healthy balance in law and policy between and among the disparate elements of the American Creed.

The American Dream

So how have we found the right balance between the component ideas, even the conflicting shards, of the American Creed? We have been guided by the American Dream. The American Dream has always been, and continues to be, the gyroscope of American life. It is the Rosetta stone or interpretive key that has helped throughout American history to solve the puzzles of how to balance liberty against equality, individualism against the rule of law, and populism against constitutionalism. The American Dream demands that we constantly balance and rebalance our creedal values to create and preserve an open, competitive, entrepreneurial society in which the opportunity to succeed is widely available. Despite the many conflicting strands of the American Creed, the American Dream insists that this must, and must increasingly, be a country in which opportunity is available to all and honest hard work yields the chance to succeed and thrive.

At the dawning of the eighteenth century, decades before American independence, Virginia planter Robert Beverly (1673–1722), building on William Penn's description of America as "a good poor man's country," described America as "the best poor man's Country in the World." Benjamin Franklin made a similar point in assuring immigrants that though many arrive in America as poor "servants or Journeymen, . . . if they are sober, industrious, and frugal, they soon become Masters, establish themselves in Business, marry, raise families, and become respectable Citizens."[7] Penn, Beverly, and Franklin were at the head of a long line of commentators that have seen America as holding out a distinctive promise of opportunity to citizens and immigrants alike. Throughout the nineteenth century, Franklin and his literary creations, Poor Richard and Father Abraham, were the most widely cited exemplars of opportunity and success in the society. One nineteenth-century orator lauded Franklin as "a man who rose from nothing, who owed nothing to parentage or patronage, who enjoyed no advantages of early education, which are not open,—a hundredfold open,—to yourselves, who performed the most menial services in the business in which his early life was employed, but who lived to stand before Kings, and died to leave a name which the world will never forget."[8] By the end of the century, Emma Lazarus's famous lines, "Give me your tired, your poor, your huddled masses yearning to breathe free. . . . Send these, the homeless, the tempest-tost, to me," adorned the new Statue of Liberty. To Lazarus, as to so many before her, America was a vast continent of enormous potential with open land and opportunity for all that would come.

Although the idea of a distinctive American Dream has been central to our national history, the precise phrase did not come into common use until the twentieth century. Still, both J. Hector St. John de Crevecoeur, the author of *Letters from an American Farmer* (1782), and Henry Adams, the grandson and great grandson of presidents, in his magisterial *History of the United States During the Administration of Thomas Jefferson* (1889), described the powerful American ethos of freedom and opportunity as a "dream."[9] The young Walter Lippmann used the phrase "the American dream" in *Drift and Mastery* (1914) to condemn as unconscionable drift the Jeffersonian localism that had so dominated the nineteenth century. Lippmann called for a new dream worthy of the new century.[10] James Truslow Adams's classic *Epic of America* (1931) popularized "the American dream, that dream of a land in which life should be fuller for every man, with opportunity for each according to his ability or achievement."[11] While the exact phrase "the American Dream" may have been coined by Lippmann and popularized by Adams, the idea, the insight, and the feeling have been present from first settlement.

Moreover, contemporary analysts describe the American Dream in terms almost identical to those used by Franklin, Lazarus, and Adams. Jennifer L. Hochschild's prominent book, *Facing Up to the American Dream* (1995), said, "the American Dream . . . promises that everyone, regardless of ascription or background, may reasonably seek success through action and traits under their own control."[12] John Schwarz wrote that the promise of the American Dream is that "everyone who steadfastly practices certain practical virtues will find a place at the table. . . . These virtues—self-control, discipline, effort, perseverance, and responsibility—stand at the core of our . . . idea of good character. . . . The notion that people do have a capacity to control their own destinies is an enormously strong, almost insistent feature of our American culture."[13]

Not surprisingly, then, modern cultural and political icons, from Bruce Springsteen to Bill Clinton, have appropriated the idea of the American Dream. Rocker/balladeer Bruce Springsteen reminded his listeners: "I don't think the

American dream was that everybody was going to make . . . a billion dollars, but it was that everybody was going to have an opportunity . . . to live a life with some decency and some dignity and a chance for some self-respect." In a 1993 speech to the Democratic Leadership Council, Bill Clinton reminded his listeners: "The American Dream that we were all raised on is a simple but powerful one—if you work hard and play by the rules you should be given a chance to go as far as your God-given ability will take you."[14]

The American Dream is the spark that animates American life. It is the promise that the country holds out to the rising generation and to immigrants that hard work and fair play will, almost certainly, lead to success. All who are willing to strive, to learn, to work hard, to save and invest, will have every chance to succeed and to enjoy the fruits of their success in safety, security, and good order. Education (physical and intellectual skills), good character (honesty, cleanliness, sobriety, religiosity), hard work (frugality, saving, investing), and a little luck form a broad pathway to the American Dream. Some start life with more wealth, more prominence, and more influence, but the opportunity to rise in society is promised to everyone. And it's not just rise—if the breaks go right, everyone has a shot at the top. If Abraham Lincoln and Bill Clinton can become president and Andrew Carnegie and Bill Gates can become the world's richest man, then others can reasonably seek to rise as well.

This promise of opportunity and sense of possibility has quickened the national pulse from the beginning and has tied each generation to those that came before and, just as importantly, to those that will come after. CBS News anchor Dan Rather made this point in a recent book, entitled *The American Dream: Stories from the Heart of Our Nation* (2001). Rather reported that all of the people he interviewed have a "sense of the dream's presence, and importance, and feel that America has made their own dreams possible. This commonality, this interconnectedness between our own dreams and a national ethos of aspiration may be the dream's most important contribution to the America of today and tomorrow."[15]

So that's the dream—a shimmering vision of a fruitful country open to all who come, learn, work, save, invest, and play by the rules. The reality, as we all know, has had darker dimensions. The continent's original inhabitants were slowly but inexorably dispossessed by a rising tide of alien settlement. Of the new arrivals, not all came in any meaningful sense; some were brought, held, and used. Others were barred. Only America's most fortunate sons, and few, if any, of her daughters, were allowed, at least initially, to compete for her accolades and prizes. What influences and forces limited the application of the dream to some Americans while barring others? What claims were made, what arguments offered, what principles advocated to explain and justify the inclusion of some and the exclusion of others from the promise of American life—the right to pursue the American Dream?

Patterns of Exclusion

The American Dream has always been more open to some than to others: it has been more open to wealthy white men than to women and people of color. In fact, Howard University's Jane Flax argued that "the normative American citizen has always been a white man and, though others have won rights, he remains so."[16] Moreover, when immigrants, minorities, and women achieved new rights, these usually amounted to the right to compete against well-entrenched white men in a matrix of established law and policy that they had developed to protect their current interests and future prospects.

At every stage of American history, ours has been a more or less hierar-chical society. Only some—initially white, male, Protestant, property holders—were entitled to full and unfettered participation. Their advantages were written into colonial charters and later into state constitutions. American Indians were removed, slaves were imported, women were legally subordinated, and the federal constitution acknowledged and entrenched these patterns of privilege and exclusion. Harvard political scientist Jennifer Hochschild reminds us that throughout American history, "the emotional potency of the American Dream has made the people who were able to identify with it the norm for everyone else. . . . Those who do not fit the model disappear from the collective self-portrait."[17]

Others might have a place in society, but it was a limited and subordinate place. Race, gender, wealth, ethnicity, and religion have all been used to exclude persons and groups from the community of American citizens.[18] The reasons offered to justify these exclusions have included the will of God, innate psychological differences, lack of social and economic independence, lack of physical and intellectual ability, and familial and societal requirements. That many were excluded is well known, but the arguments used, how and why they worked, and how ultimately they were overcome, is neither well known nor well understood.

The treatment of blacks has been the most glaring deviation from the American Creed. Although a few blacks entered early Virginia as indentured servants and some apparently gained their freedom after serving out their indenture, blacks were first brought to Virginia and sold as slaves in the mid-1620s. The Virginia House of Burgesses formalized chattel slavery in 1661, Maryland followed in 1663, and over the remainder of the century, the "peculiar institution" spread throughout the South. During the eighteenth century, slave codes were strengthened to grant masters overwhelming power over slaves; education was prohibited, manumission was made more difficult, and the rights of the small class of free blacks were restricted. The Constitution recognized slavery, without ever mentioning the word, in its provisions on continued importation, representation, and taxation, and in subsequent legal guarantees concerning the return of fugitive slaves. Although the slave trade formally ended in 1808, slavery continued to expand right up to the outbreak of the Civil War. Moreover, throughout the nineteenth century, even after the end of slavery, most blacks continued to live in the agricultural South, and most were tied to the land almost as effectively by the sharecropping and crop-lien systems as they had been by slavery. Early in the twentieth century, black social scientist and social activist W. E. B. Dubois declared that the movement to erase the "color line" from American society would be the defining struggle of the new century. As America entered the final decade of the twentieth century, the legal scholar Derrick Bell declared that "racism is permanent."[19] Although Americans can hope that Bell is wrong, we must admit that racism has, so far, been a prominent part of American life, law, and policy.

Women's struggle for equality in America, while less overt and less obviously intense than the struggle of blacks, has, in its own way, been just as difficult. Blacks were held in slavery by force, and their white masters often declared them to be and treated them as if they were less than human. Women, on the other hand, were held in subjection at least partially by religious and cultural assumptions in which they shared. The Christian teaching that wives were to love, honor, and obey their husbands was powerfully reinforced by the common-law principle of "coverture." Coverture held that women were subsumed, or covered, by the legal personality of their father until marriage and their husband after marriage. With limited exceptions prior to 1850, a woman's property went to her husband at marriage, as did any wages or income she might earn after marriage. She could not sue in court in her own name, serve on juries, vote, or otherwise assume a posture of equality in the public sphere. Divorce was rare, but when it did occur, property and children remained with the husband. Although women could not be bought and sold, only in unusual circumstances did they possess or control significant property of their own. Not until the middle of the twentieth century did growing movements for racial and gender equality gain traction in America.

Despite the presence of inequality and discrimination, the dream made America a magnet for immigrants. Throughout the colonial and early national periods, most Americans saw immigrants as important to settlement, defense, and economic development. But when too many immigrants arrived too quickly, concern grew that the fundamental nature of the country might be submerged in a sea of unacculturated newcomers. Whether they came for religious freedom or economic opportunity, they came in waves that alternatively thrilled and frightened those already here. The first major nativist reaction against immigrants began in the mid-1790s with federalist concerns over Irish and French radicals. That crisis passed with Thomas Jefferson's election in 1800, and immigration remained manageable through the 1830s. However, when Irish Catholic immigration picked up substantially in the 1840s, nativist reaction produced the Know Nothing movement. Several northern and midwestern states elected Know Nothing, or American Party, governors and state legislatures, though their power generally waned before they could pass the anti-Catholic agenda upon which they had campaigned. Nativism generally subsided from the Civil War into the 1880s. Again, an upsurge in immigration and a change in the sources of immigration heightened nativist concern. Between 1880 and 1920, about 25 million immigrants came to the United States. Among the new immigrants were 4 million Italians, mostly Catholic, and 4 million Eastern European Jews, mostly from Russia, Germany, and the Austro-Hungarian empire. These new immigrants aroused widespread suspicion and a wave of discrimination ensued that lasted through World War II. For more than half a century beginning in the early 1880s, most Asians were simply excluded from immigration and from eligibility for citizenship. Moreover, Jews "were at first kept at the margins of 'white' America simply because they were not Christians."[20] Over the course of the twentieth century, economic integration and intermarriage blurred the lines between old immigrants and new immigrants, but the color line between whites and blacks remained stark.

Finally, the relationship between American Indians and later settlers remains a deeply tragic story. From the first appearance of Europeans in the Americas at the end of the sixteenth century to the last Indian wars of the late nineteenth century, native American peoples declined due to war and disease from perhaps 10 million to a mere quarter of a million. For nearly three centuries, colonial and later state and federal government policy was to remove Indians from the advancing line of white settlement. By the closing decades of the nineteenth century, Indians had been subdued and restricted to reservations. Throughout the twentieth century, with brief interludes in the Franklin Roosevelt and Lyndon Johnson administrations, national policy was to wean Indians from federal protection and support and to immerse them in mainstream society and economy. Some even envisioned the dismantling of the Bureau of Indian Affairs and the reservation system and, ultimately, the disappearance of Indians qua Indians within the American society. As the twenty-first century dawned, Indian reservations still existed, and despite the glitz of the occasional casino, they were among the bleakest and most impoverished places in America.

Processes Leading to Inclusion

Exclusion has been a persistent and destructive fact of American social life, but it has not been a permanent and unchanging fact. Over time, the right to dream the American Dream has been opened, at least formally, to new and increasingly diverse groups. Critically, the intellectual case for inclusion was always present. The core ideas of the American Creed—liberty, equality, opportunity—were always available to be claimed by the excluded. Not every claim was honored or even acknowledged immediately; resistance was continuous and often tenacious, but the claimants had Mr. Jefferson's words and America's best sense of itself on their side. Their opponents frequently knew it or ultimately came to see it. In addition, broad-scale social processes, including democratization, westward expansion, the rise of markets, urbanization, industrialization, education, and the transition from physical to mental labor, have steadily carried yesterday's others closer to the center of American life. Great differences in status, wealth, and opportunity still remain, but over time, new groups of contestants entered the great game, learned its rules, and began to take home at least some of the prizes.

Vernon Parrington, a prominent historian of the early twentieth century, explained the power of the American Creed as an inclusionary vehicle. He wrote, "The humanitarian idealism of the Declaration has always echoed as a battle cry in the hearts of those who dream of an America dedicated to democratic ends. It cannot be long ignored or repudiated, for . . . It is constantly breaking out in fresh revolt."[21] Later generations of Americans added to the Declaration of Independence, the U.S. Constitution and Bill of Rights, the Gettysburg Address, the Pledge of Allegiance, and the "I have a dream" speech of Martin Luther King. These sacred texts evoke the central tenets of the American Dream in each new generation. Hence, Dan Rather, an American icon in his own right, concluded his recent investigation of the contemporary American Dream with the observation that it is still the best foundation "on which to build the American future. As an idea, it is inherently inclusive, and it has the power to strike a chord in all of us. It defines us as a people, even as we add to its meaning with each new chapter in our national experience."[22]

Yet we all know that the implementation of these luminous ideas—that all men, all people, should enjoy legal, political, and social equality—is incomplete even now. So how are we to understand the place and role of the American Dream in American history? Should we exult with Louis Hartz that "since the first sailing of the *Mayflower*," American history has been "a story of new beginnings, daring enterprises, and explicitly stated goals."[23] Or should we sigh with Samuel Huntington, that "the history of American politics is the repetition of new beginnings and flawed outcomes, promise and disillusion, reform and reaction"?[24] Neither, fortunately. Reality is more complex and interesting. The view of American history that sees an endless and nearly futile cycle of reform and reaction misses the incremental advance of the formerly excluded toward a fuller share of American life. Poor white men, women, and minorities achieved rights incrementally and over time as they doggedly pressed for the opportunity to fairly measure themselves against the Dream. Poor white men won legal and political equality during the Jacksonian era but have continued to struggle for economic opportunity, labor rights, workplace safety, and social equality. Women claimed legal equality, property rights, employment opportunities, and educational access throughout the nineteenth century. Political rights were achieved in 1920, and attention turned to economic and social equality later in the twentieth century. The movement to abolish slavery in the middle of the nineteenth century was followed by battles throughout the twentieth century to secure educational, economic, political, and social equality. Paul Berman makes the critically important point that all of these movements were long-term "campaigns to lead one sector of society after another upward from the gloom of bottom-place standing in the social hierarchy into the glorious mediocrity of the American middle."[25]

The long and winding spiral staircase that leads to "the glorious mediocrity of the American middle" is well worn because, as Pauline Maier has observed, "the ultimate authority of the Declaration," and of the American Creed and Dream more generally, "rests, as it always has, . . . in the hearts and minds of the people, and its meaning changes as new groups and new causes claim its mantle, constantly, reopening the issue of what the nation's 'founding principles' demand."[26] But in a free society, governed more by norms and values than by law and force, one must often wait for what seems a painfully, even embarrassingly, long time for the hearts and minds of the people to change. Moreover, hearts and minds do not change mysteriously; there is no shower of moral clarity that leaves them pure and new. Usually, society must evolve and change in ways that draw old ideas, or at least their existing institutional embodiments, into question. Nobel Prize–winning economist Robert William Fogel has described this process, arguing, "there has been a recurring lag between the vast technological transformations and the human adjustments to these transformations. It is this lag that has provoked the crises that periodically usher in profound reconsiderations of ethical values, that produce new agendas for . . . social reform, and that give rise to political movements that champion the new agendas."[27] Socioeconomic change can so reconstitute American society that its political structures no longer seem to promote the fundamental principles of equity and justice that Americans believe is their birthright.

Key dynamics creating change within the American society have been westward settlement, economic growth and development, the consequent evolution of work, and the increasing importance of education. The easy availability of land, the presence of a whole continent to conquer and tame, created a powerful and enduring sense that America was the land of opportunity. The images of the woodsman, the mountain man, the wagon master, the trail boss, the '49er, and the riders lined up for the Oklahoma land rush, suggest the importance of the westward migration in search of opportunity, success, and wealth. The frontier required that people be judged on results, not status, which produced a strong commitment to equality of opportunity, competition, and achievement. J. Hector St. John de Crevecoeur, Alexis de Tocqueville, Frederick Jackson Turner, and many others have been eloquent on this point.

In 1800 nearly 95 percent of adult white men were farmers, and as late as 1820 only six American cities had populations over 25,000. But the rapid urbanization, industrialization, and economic growth of the nineteenth century created tremendous opportunity and expansion. By 1900 New York was the second largest city in the world, and Chicago, which had not even existed in 1800, was the fifth largest city in the world, with a population of 1.7 million. By the end of the nineteenth century, only 45 percent of the workforce was still in agriculture, leaving 55 percent for the new industrial and service occupations of the burgeoning cities. As the economy evolved, so, obviously, did the nature of work and the skills and qualifications that workers needed to be successful.

Over the course of the nineteenth century, as the American economy modernized, families evolved from units of production to units of consumption. The evolution of economic activity from family production into increasingly large, bureaucratic, and corporate entities changed the role and place of women in society. Once husbands abandoned self-employment for wage labor—in other words, once they gave up the farm or the downstairs craftsman's shop—the only way that a wife could add to the family resources was to work for wages herself. Moreover, the evolving economy increasingly created jobs that both men and women, appropriately trained, could perform. In fact, by 1930 more Americans were working in white- and pink-collar service jobs than in either agriculture or manufacturing. Services employed more than 50 percent of workers for the first time in the 1960s, and by the end of the 1980s, more than 70 percent of workers were in services.[28]

Robert Max Jackson described the forces that produced new roles and opportunities for women in *Destined For Equality: The Inevitable Rise of Women's Status*. His conclusion was that "the structure and integral logic of development within modern political and economic institutions . . . eroded gender inequality." Modern jobs more often require and reward strong minds than strong backs. When you are hiring brains, being distracted by the gender packaging is inefficient and costly. "Ultimately," Jackson reasoned, "the logic of modern state organization has simply proved inconsistent with the needs for maintaining gender inequality."[29] Moreover, Jackson pointed to the U.S. educational system as "a defining institution of modern life" in which individualistic assumptions relating to promotion through successive grades, competitive exams, achievement, and the importance of intellectual capability are "wedged . . . between the private world of the family and the public world of the economy and the political order."[30] As the economy's preference turned from strong backs to strong minds, an increasingly egalitarian educational system was expected to assure that young minds, male and female, black and white, Christians, Jews, and more, would be ready when the market summoned them.

How, then, has American society and the opportunities that it provided to citizens, whether the "normative" white male or the once marginalized and excluded, evolved and changed over four centuries? This book tells that story.

American Dreams: The Promise of Life in the New World

> We shall be as a City upon a Hill, the eyes of all people are upon us; so that if we shall deal falsely with our god in this work . . . we shall be made a story and a by-word through the world . . . till we be consumed out of the good land whether we are going.
> —John Winthrop, aboard the *Arabella*, bound for North America in 1630

The American Dream includes images both of the nation within the world and the individual within the nation. The vision of America's place in the world that still defines the American Dream has deep roots in John Winthrop's promise to his Puritan brethren that they would be as "a City upon a Hill." Winthrop reminded his colleagues that their reason for leaving England to settle in the howling wilderness that was then North America was to build a society that the world could emulate. Later generations of Americans have been just as certain that the world would do well to follow their example. Hence, presidents from Washington to Lincoln to Reagan and beyond have reminded Americans of their role in the world by using the image of the United States as, in Ronald Reagan's formulation, "a shining city on a hill."

Although we still hold John Winthrop's elevated view of America, we do not recognize his Americans. Winthrop's vision had little room for the individual and less for individualism, choice, and diversity. But to be fair, Winthrop led English Puritans, not Americans, and their dream was to construct a holy commonwealth, to raise up a New Israel within a New Eden on Massachusetts Bay. In this holy commonwealth, the saints, excluding others by force if necessary, would form covenanted communities to live in harmony with God and nature. John Winthrop and his fellows had a dream, but it was not yet an American dream, and certainly not the American Dream.

The image that we now think of as central to the American Dream, the individual as an independent, hard-working entrepreneur, did not come to North America with the earliest settlers. Rather, it emerged over the course of the seventeenth century in an ongoing confrontation between the early visions of leaders like John Winthrop, John Cotton, William Berkeley, and William Penn, dissenters like Roger Williams, Anne Hutchinson, and Nathaniel Bacon, and the fruitful and robust vastness of the continent itself. Over the course of the eighteenth century, the American Dream that we know in our bones assumed its familiar shape. In fact, one might almost say that it took a human form in the person of Benjamin Franklin. Benjamin Franklin (1706–90) was the central figure of the American eighteenth century. He was a printer, investor, politician, scientist, diplomat, and philanthropist. More importantly, Benjamin Franklin was what America and Americans were becoming. His was the story on everyone's lips; a century before Horatio Alger, Ben Franklin was America's first rags-to-riches hero.[1] Both as author and exemplar, he consciously molded and shaped the broad outlines of the American Dream.

Young Dreamers and the World Before Them

The first settlers into North America came either for quick wealth or to live in ways not permitted them at home. If they came as adventurers in search of quick wealth, they were almost invariably disappointed. Most adventurers died anonymously or returned home without leaving much of a trace. But if new settlers came as covenanted communities, sharing a vision of social and religious life, they usually survived, and then thrived, and ultimately laid the foundation on which later generations built. How did these first settlers understand God, religion, churches, and their religious obligations and responsibilities? And what did their religious views tell them about the purposes of society and how it should be organized politically and economically to support true religion best?

The enthusiasts, entrepreneurs, and politicians planning colonies in North America began with related, though quite distinct, visions. Most envisioned reproducing some, but not all, of English life. To avoid the effort of going colony by colony, I focus on Massachusetts, Pennsylvania, and Virginia as representative of the social visions of New England, the middle states, and the South. The Puritans envisioned the village culture and organization of rural England before the enclosures; the Quakers envisioned an urban commercial culture; and the Virginians envisioned the life of the landed gentry. Initially, each regional vision rested on a strong sense that God approved a certain order in the world and that that order should be adopted and defended. The tighter and more integrated the vision, the longer it held together, but each had to counter the ever-present allure of open land to the west.

Social conflicts in England, and in Europe more generally, sent wave after wave of immigrants crashing ashore on the American coast. Among these conflicts, none was more fundamental than the religious upheaval of the Protestant Reformation. Much of Europe was involved in intermittent religious warfare from the early sixteenth century through most of the seventeenth century. Reform currents in England were diverted when Henry VIII (reigned 1509–47) rejected Catholicism without fully embracing Protestantism. Henry declared the Catholic Church in England to be independent of Rome and renamed it the Church of England. Having established his royal control over the church, Henry saw little need to tinker with church vestments, liturgy, and doctrine. Mary's bloody reign (1553–58) highlighted the destructive power of religious divisions in Britain, but Elizabeth (1558–1603) was masterful at keeping the religious peace within a broad Protestant dispensation. Nonetheless, festering tensions built toward civil war after Elizabeth's death.

Puritans were English Protestants who thought that the Church of England needed to be thoroughly reformed and purified. Low church Anglicans agreed with the Puritans that the hierarchy and Latin liturgy of the Church of England should be reformed, whereas high church Anglicans cherished the traditional liturgy as a bulwark of social stability. Catholics awaited the return of the true faith. The seventeenth-century civil wars that wracked England pitted a rising Puritan middle class against the traditional Anglican elites and their resurgent Catholic allies. Once Charles I (1625–49) suspended the Puritan-dominated Parliament in 1629 and instructed Archbishop William Laud to suppress Puritan dissenters within the Anglican Church, many despaired both of political revolution and church reform in England. During the 1630s and 1640s, Puritan leaders organized an exodus of 21,000 faithful out of England to New England, where they vowed to live a revolution in religious and secular affairs. The Puritans withdrew to New England to build a "holy commonwealth" that could serve as an example and an encouragement until their coreligionists across Europe could transform and purify their own societies.

John Winthrop, the first governor of the Massachusetts Bay colony, reminded his colleagues that they had bound themselves formally to God for performance of this critical task and that they would be judged on their faithfulness. "Thus stands the cause between God and us," Winthrop dramatically reminded his Puritan brethren aboard the *Arabella,* "we are entered into a Covenant with him for this work, . . . if we neglect the . . . ends we have propounded, . . . the Lord will surely . . . be revenged on such a perjured people and make us know the price of the breach of such a Covenant."[2] Fortunately, what the covenant required of the faithful was quite clear. John Cotton, the Massachusetts Bay colony's most prominent minister, explained, "the word, and scriptures of God do contain . . . not only of theology, but also of other sacred sciences, (as he calleth them) . . . which he maketh ethics, economics, politics, church-government, prophecy, academy . . . for the right ordering of a man's family, yea, of the commonwealth too, so far as both of them are subordinate to spiritual ends."[3]

Puritans believed that God ordered the world to its right end and that the role and place of every man was set by God from the beginning of time. Though man could know God's intention only vaguely, his every effort was to be expended in understanding it better. Each person could best praise and serve God by hard work in the social and economic role to which he or she was called. "The idea was simple: if the Puritans worked on their own purification and sanctification, then God would grant them peace, security, and material bounty . . . While the point of this life was to prepare for the next, material prosperity was seen as God's gift in return for fulfilling the covenant with Him."[4] Failure and poverty suggested the absence of God's favor, usually as a punishment for sloth and ignorance.[5] Hence, Puritans valued hard work but not individualism. They worked to serve God, their communities, and their families, never, at least never overtly, to serve their own desires, needs, and interests.

Through most of the seventeenth century, the Puritans formed small, tight-knit, rural communities that faithfully replicated the village culture and structure of their native East Anglia. Kenneth Lockridge's fascinating study of the founding of Dedham, Massachusetts, described the reaction of thirty Puritan families awarded a tract of 200 square miles in the summer of 1636. Instead of dividing the land into large private farms, they laid out a village with a town commons, a church, a school, and a town lot for every family. They then allocated scattered plots of farm and woodland in 2- to 12-acre strips, depending on each man's status, usefulness, and family size. Each family's strip of arable land was embedded in a larger field, and the colonists made joint decisions about what crops to plant in the field. Lockridge explained that these Puritan families "turned their back on the wilderness" to concentrate on the communal social and religious life of the village.[6]

The Quaker settlements in Pennsylvania were just as God-centered as the earlier Puritan settlements in New England. The Quakerism that arose in England in the middle of the seventeenth century was a utopian variant of the dominant Puritanism of the age. Quakers eschewed a formal ministry out of reverence for the inner light that illuminated the heart and soul of every man and woman. No church hierarchy, as in the Catholic tradition, or covenanting congregation, as in the Puritan tradition, could interpret the scriptures, ordain a liturgy, or intercede with God for the individual Christian. Yet because God was eternally one, the inner light kindled in each soul was expected to yield the same broad counsel to every Friend.

Like the Puritans before them, the Quakers that followed William Penn to Pennsylvania in the early 1680s believed that religion should give form and direction to politics and economics so that life in this world might simply be a well-marked path to life in the next. Quaker theology attended principally to the New Testament, and within the New Testament to the Sermon on the Mount. The Sermon on the Mount presented to Quakers a mandatory ethic of peace, love, and charity. Following this ethic constituted walking with Christ and living in the inner light of the Holy Spirit. Frederick Tolles, the leading historian of colonial Pennsylvania, described a shared confidence between the Quaker and God: "If one kept one's inner eye to the Lord and labored diligently in one's calling, one could expect that God would show His favor by adding His blessing in the form of material prosperity."[7] Puritans and Quakers brought religious fervor to their work in the world that produced security and even prosperity for most of them.

Penn was just as keenly aware as the Puritan saints of Boston and Dedham that community required proximity. The Quaker meeting, like the Puritan congregation, was intended to be the center of social and religious life. Hence, Penn encouraged equality and community by declaring that anyone owning 100 acres, or 50 acres if they had begun as an indentured servant, was a freeman entitled to vote and hold office. Leading Quakers tended to be urban merchants rather than landed gentry, although successful Quakers did build impressive country homes once their commercial success was established.

Massachusetts and Pennsylvania were settled by families and sometimes even whole communities that shared religious goals and were willing to sacrifice greatly to achieve them. Puritans and Quakers dreamed of peaceful, prosperous communities in which they might tend the inner plantation of the soul and walk humbly with their God. But England was home to other men as well—noble men, men who contested for royal favor and sought to expand the monarch's and their own lands and riches. These men followed an ethic most baldly stated by the poet and essayist Ben Jonson (1573–1637); "Get place and wealth—if possible with grace; . . . If not, by any means get wealth and place." Although Massachusetts and Pennsylvania warned such men away, Virginia offered them an open field upon which to pursue their dreams of wealth and glory.

Virginia was born in a rush of adventurers out to make a quick fortune, either by discovering gold or easy passage to the Indies. Historian T. H. Breen writes, "early Virginians were ambitious, self-confident men. . . . They were extraordinarily individualistic, fiercely competitive, and highly materialistic . . . by establishing economic privatism as the colony's central value the Virginia Company of London spawned . . . a society based upon the expectation of almost unlimited personal gain."[8] Even after the gold fever subsided and the search for commercially viable crops began, Virginians kept their individual interests in clear view. The discovery that tobacco grew well and enjoyed a steady demand in Europe set off an intense scramble for prime land along the York and James Rivers. A decade before the Puritan saints at Dedham began to plant their communal fields in potatoes, corn, and squash, Virginia Company investors had established private hundreds, separate plantations often miles from their nearest neighbor, to own and work for private profit.

Virginians wanted the freedom to contest for wealth and status and to enjoy what they won. Individualism, competition, and luck played a distinctive role in the Virginians' view of the world. "In public these men determined social standing not by a man's religiosity or philosophic knowledge, but by his visible estate—his lands, slaves, buildings, even by the quality of his garments."[9] Although Puritans and Quakers fought hard to limit drinking, gambling, laxity, and public display, Virginia gentlemen reveled in them all. Hence, unlike the Puritans and Quakers, "seventeenth-century Virginians never succeeded in forming a coherent society . . . they lacked cohesive group identity; . . . voluntaristic associations remained weak; education lagged, churches stagnated, and towns never developed."[10]

Institutions and rules, to the extent that they are honored and enforced, set the structure and dynamics of a society, and thereby set the balance between liberty and order, competition and cooperation, individual and community. The covenanted communities of New England believed that social order required the support of institutions, law, and policy to survive and thrive in a dangerous world. Even before the Puritans stepped ashore at Massachusetts Bay, Governor John Winthrop was careful to stress that the covenant they had entered into with God was to establish "a due form of Government both civil and ecclesiastical."[11] The Puritan's "due form of Government" was to be a "holy Commonwealth," a true Bible polity, where piety lived under the protection of a strong and watchful secular authority. Winthrop reminded his fellow voyagers that the magistrates, called to their offices by God through the suffrage of the people, were responsible for maintaining the covenant and implementing the mandates that flowed from it. The people's responsibility, once they had chosen good men to be magistrates, was to honor and obey them. Winthrop explained, "when the people have chosen men to be their rulers, and to make their laws, and bound themselves by oath to submit thereto, . . . the people . . . are to be subject." Further, Winthrop contended, to resist or disobey laws "savors of resisting an ordinance of God."[12]

The Puritans who founded Massachusetts thought that the Bible described the due form of church and state and traced out the separate but closely related and mutually supportive responsibilities of each. John Cotton explained, "God's institutions (such as the government of church and of commonwealth be) may be close and compact, and co-ordinate one to another, and yet not be confounded."[13] The church held the keys to salvation and eternal life, but because God's kingdom was not of this world, church discipline extended only to expulsion. The state, on the other hand, was decidedly of this world, and it could draw upon force, even deadly force, to maintain good order in the community. To the Puritan mind, it was not mixing church and state to recognize that one of the state's key responsibilities was to enforce the laws of God. As Perry Miller observed nearly fifty years ago, "the unity of religion and politics was so axiomatic that very few men would even have grasped the idea that church and state could be distinct."[14]

The Quakers, like the Puritans, viewed government as hierarchical, general, and intrusive. William Penn reminded his fellow Quakers of the appropriate relationship between magistrates and subjects in the preface to his famous *Frame of Government of Pennsylvania* (1682). Penn wrote, "This the Apostle teaches . . . 'Let every soul be subject to the higher powers; for there is no power but of God. The powers that be are ordained of God: whosoever therefore resisteth the power, resisteth the ordinance of God.'"[15] Proprietor Penn also agreed with Governor Winthrop and Reverend Cotton that the separate provinces of church and state were closely related and even intertwined. Again in the preface to the *Frame of Government,* Penn wrote, "government seems to me a part of religion itself, . . . sacred in its institution and end. For, if it does not directly remove the cause, it crushes the effects of evil, and is as such (though a lower, yet) an emanation of the same Divine Power, and is both author and object of pure religion; the difference lying here, that the one is more free and mental, the other more corporal and compulsive in its operations."

The broad shape and feel of public life was the purview of both church and state. Initially, because the state was small and its compulsive power was rarely needed in early Pennsylvania, the Quaker monthly meeting handled questions and disputes touching upon the full range of human interaction. Moreover, like the Puritans, Quakers believed that any action that compromised "the good name of Truth" and might bring the wrath of God down upon the community was the business of every member of the meeting. Hence, such matters as property rights, labor disputes, interpretation of contracts, settlement of debts and estates, marital issues, and discipline for immoral conduct formed the main business of the monthly meeting.

The Puritan and Quaker sense that government, working closely with the church, was an institution authorized by God to combat evil and do good in the world held weaker sway in Virginia. The intensely competitive individualism that characterized Virginia society throughout the seventeenth century "poisoned political institutions. Few colonists seemed to have believed that local rulers would, on their own initiative, work for the public good. Instead, they assumed that persons in authority used their offices for political gain. . . . In fact, Virginia planters seem to have regarded government orders as a threat to their independence, almost as a personal affront."[16] As the British colonies in North America grew and prospered, both the tight communalism of Boston and Philadelphia and the unconstrained individualism of the Virginia tidewater would leave their marks, but each would be shaped and molded by new immigrants, future generations, and the call of the continent itself.

Virginia and Massachusetts remained the main centers of North American population throughout the seventeenth century, with Virginia always slightly more populous and considerably wealthier. Although immigration continued to be an important supplement to population growth throughout the colonial period, natural increase outstripped immigration by 1650. Between 1650 and

1775, the total population of the colonies grew very rapidly, at a rate of slightly over 3 percent per year, doubling and a bit more every twenty-five years. Hence, total population was about 50,000 in 1650, 250,000 in 1700, 1.2 million in 1750, and 2.6 million in 1775. The slave population stayed small until the eighteenth century and then exploded. Fewer than 30,000 slaves in 1700 became 236,000 by 1750 and nearly half a million by 1775.[17]

Economic output grew even more rapidly than population, about 3.2 percent per year. While England's population expanded by just over 50 percent between 1650 and 1775, the population of the colonies expanded fiftyfold. By 1775, the colonies had about one-third of England's population and more than 30 percent of her national wealth, and the colonies' growth showed no signs of slowing. Hence, on the eve of the Revolution, the average American lived better than the average man in any other country in the world. About 90 percent of freemen were farmers, and about 70 percent of these worked their own land. The rest were artisans, laborers, seamen, lumber men, merchants, clergymen, lawyers, or planters. Though the first settlers came to North America for a variety of reasons, virtually all believed that the new land was uniquely capable of fulfilling their dreams.

The Emergence of an American Dream

America seemed to hold out unlimited promise to its first settlers. They knew the difficulties they would face from Indians, from nature, and most importantly from their own shortcomings; but if these could be overcome, the New World promised everything that the Old World had denied them. Religious authority, economic opportunity, and social status were available in the New World. There were no guarantees, and the threats were great and the dangers many, but the possibilities were evident, and they meant to realize them (Figure 2.1).

In those first days of danger and privation, the promise of America was both singular and multidimensional. Its core was always the chance to live well. Its elements were always the chance to live rightly and to prosper. To live rightly, at least for seventeenth-century Englishmen, was almost always to live rightly in the eyes of a Protestant God by praising His name, expanding His kingdom, and praying for signs of His grace in your life. In so doing, they

Figure 2.1. "Pocahontas Saving the Life of Captain John Smith," 1607. This famous lithograph vividly depicts the vulnerability of the earliest settlers in North America. Here Pocahontas pleads with her father, Chief Powhatan, to spare the life of Smith. (Library of Congress, Prints and Photographs Division, reproduction LC-USZ62-5254)

believed that they would be rewarded with eternal life, as well as earthly security and success. To live well required good land and hard work. The earliest settlers believed that God had created a particularly rich and receptive land for them. In 1624 John Smith wrote in his famous history of Virginia, "The mildness of the air, the fertility of the soil, and the situation of the rivers are so propitious to the nature and use of man, as no place is more convenient for pleasure, profit, and man's sustenance."[18] Francis Higginson, a Puritan minister who arrived with the first ships in 1629, observed that "The Temper of the Air of New England is one special thing that commends this place. Experience doth manifest that there is hardly a more healthful place to be found in the world that agreeth better with our English bodies."[19] How could it be otherwise in a New Eden?

Andrew Delbanco, in a book entitled *The Real American Dream,* calls Puritanism "the first American form of hope."[20] What Puritans hoped for, what they dreamed of and strove mightily to achieve, was to make the word of God live in their lives. Israel had faltered, Peter's church at Rome had fallen into corruption, and England's church was hostile, so the Puritans determined to make their stand with God in New England. The Puritans' decision to leave England was not simply to flee the king's oppression, but to fly to a promise land. Puritans lavished special attention on Bible passages in which God promised to protect and watch over his flock. No promise spoke more directly to Puritan hopes and dreams than God's promise to Abram in Genesis 12:1–2. God said to Abram, "Get thee out of thy country, and from thy kindred, and from thy father's house, unto a land that I will shew thee: And I will make thee a great nation." John Cotton chose a related text, God's promise to Israel in 2 Samuel 7:10, to hold up to the faithful aboard Winthrop's tiny fleet as it prepared to depart England for Massachusetts in June 1630: "Moreover I will appoint a place for my people Israel, and will plant them, that they may dwell in a place of their own, and move no more; neither shall the children of wickedness afflict them any more, as beforetime." Cotton and his listeners were certain that just as God had called Israel out of Egypt to the promised land; he had called them out of England to be a New Israel in a New England (Figure 2.2).

John Winthrop described the Puritan vision in detail in his *Model of Christian Charity,* written in 1630 aboard the *Arabella* during the voyage to North America. Winthrop concluded the *Model* with his famous declaration that the Puritan experiment would be an example for good or ill to all the world. Winthrop wrote, "we must Consider that we shall be as a City upon a Hill, the eyes of all people are upon us; so that if we shall deal falsely with our god in this work we have undertaken and so cause him to withdraw his present help from us, we shall be made a story and a by-word through the world."[21] Winthrop's "City upon a Hill" imagery of America as an example to which all of mankind should attend has been central to the American Dream since the day Winthrop penned the words. Less than a decade later, at the height of the Great Migration of Puritans out of England, Thomas Tillam saluted his new country: "Hayle holy-land, wherein our holy lord hath planted his most true and holy word . . . methinks I hear the Lamb of God thus speak. Come my dear little flock, who for my sake have left your Country, dearest friends, and goods, and hazarded your lives o'er the raging floods, possess this Country."[22] Tillam's words, so similar in spirit to the poem that would grace the Statue of Liberty almost 250 years later, is one of the first classic calls to Europe's oppressed to find peace and security in America.

The Puritan city on a hill was not a collection of isolated individuals; it was

Figure 2.2. "Puritans Leaving for the New World," 1630. Puritans seeking religious liberty in the New World entreat God's blessing on their endeavors. (Corbis/Bettmann, image PG1994)

the Lord's "dear little flock," a community with interests and goals to foster and defend. Perry Miller made this point in writing: "The theorists of New England thought of society as a unit, bound together by inviolable ties; . . . functioning for a definite purpose, with all parts subordinate to the whole, all members contributing a definite share, every person occupying a particular status."[23] The communitarian, even anti-individualist, character of Puritan social theory is clear in Winthrop's *Model of Christian Charity.* Winthrop explained that God created difference and hierarchy in the world so, "that every man might have need of [each] other, and from hence they might all knit more nearly together in the Bond of brotherly affection." Later he reminded his fellows, "we must be knit together in this work as one man, . . . we must love one another with a pure heart fervently, we must bear one another's burdens, we must not look only on our own things." The purpose of Puritan communalism, as Winthrop explained, was "to improve our lives to do more service to the Lord, . . . increase of the body of Christ whereof we are members, . . . and work out our Salvation under the power and purity of His holy Ordinances."[24] The Puritan improved his life to be of more service to the Lord, his church, and his community by dedicating himself to that place in the world for which God prepared him and to which God called him.

The Puritan vision of America had little to do with the individualism, freedom, and entrepreneurship that ultimately became so central to the American Dream. Through most of the seventeenth century, Puritans wanted each other's close support and fellowship. Perry Miller expressed this idea by noting, "The lone horseman, the single trapper, the solitary hunter was not a figure of the Puritan frontier. . . . Neither were the individualistic businessman, the shopkeeper who seized every opportunity to enlarge his profits, the speculator who contrived to gain wealth at the expense of his fellows"[25] Nonetheless, as the eighteenth century progressed, community ties loosened, the frontier pushed west, and open land beckoned to each new generation of Americans. The solitary pioneer, the sharp-eyed shopkeeper, and the entrepreneurial merchant emerged in New England as the Puritan saint slowly faded into history.

The Quakers, like the Puritans, assumed from the beginning that they would only realize their fondest dreams if they stuck together, advising, counseling, and correcting one another where necessary. George Fox, the leading Quaker in England, reminded "friends, that are gone, and are going over to plant, and make outward plantations in America, keep your own plantations in your hearts, with the spirit and power of God, that your own vines and lilies be not hurt."[26] Similarly, William Penn wrote to remind Pennsylvania Friends, "truly blessed is that man and woman who, in the invisible power, rule their affections about the visible things, and who use the world as true travelers and pilgrims, whose home is not here below"[27] (Figure 2.3).

Frederick Tolles's important history of colonial Pennsylvania quoted extensively from an anonymous 1684 *Planter's Speech to His Neighbors* concerning Quaker motives for leaving England. Two reasons—peace and prosperity—predominated. First, the planter noted, was the hope "That we might here, as on a *virgin elysian shore,* commence . . . such an innocent course of life, as might unload us of those outward cares, vexations and turmoils, which before we were always subject unto, from the hands of self-designing and unreasonable men." In the wake of peace would come prosperity, "as *trees* are transplanted from one soil to another, to render them more thriving and better bearers, so . . . in peace and secure retirement, under the bountiful protection of God, and in the lap of the least adulterated nature, might everyone the better improve his talent, and bring forth more plenteous fruits, to the glory of God, and public welfare of the whole creation."[28] Quakers continually

Figure 2.3. "William Penn's Treaty with the Indians, When He Founded the Province of Pennsylvania in North America," 1681. (Library of Congress, Prints and Photographs Division, reproduction LC-USZ62-2583)

reminded themselves that to prosper in the outer plantation of the world, while withering in the inner plantation of one's heart and soul, would be to lose all. Hence, the *Planters' Speech* continued, "Our business . . . here, in this *new land,* is not so much to *build houses,* and *establish factories,* that may enrich ourselves (though all these things, in their due place, are not to be neglected) as to erect temples of *holiness* and *righteousness,* which God may delight in; to lay such lasting frames and foundations of *temperance* and *virtue,* as may support the superstructures of our future happiness, both in this, and the other world."[29]

Although Quakers were keenly aware of the priority of the inner plantation and the need to employ the outer plantation only in its service, many came in the hope of doing better in the world than was possible at home. In 1685, one Thomas Ellis wrote to George Fox in the still-quavering voice of the European peasant, uncertain of his right to reach out and partake of the bounty before him, saying, "I wish that those who have estates of their own and leave fullness to their posterity, may not be offended at the Lord's opening a door of mercy to thousands in England . . . and other nations who had no estates either for themselves or children."[30] Many walked, hesitantly at first, but then with an increasing sense of right, through the "door of mercy" that God had opened for the poor in Pennsylvania.

The Advice of William Penn to His Children is the Quaker patriarch's justly famous injunction to tend first the inner plantation of the heart and soul. Penn's third letter to his children, written around 1699, but published posthumously in 1726, was organized in twelve numbered paragraphs. Each presents, explains, and grounds in scripture a virtue that Penn admonishes his children to attend. Penn advised: "(1) Be humble . . . (2) From humility springs meekness . . . (3) Patience is an effect of a meek spirit and flows from it . . . (4) Show mercy, when ever it is in your power . . . (5) Charity is a near neighbor to mercy . . . (6) Liberality or bounty is a noble quality in man . . . (7) Justice or righteousness, is another attribute of God . . . (8) Integrity is a great and commendable virtue . . . (9) Gratitude or thankfulness is another virtue of great luster . . . (10) Diligence is another virtue . . . (11) Frugality is a virtue too . . . (12) Temperance I must earnestly recommend to you."

Good Quakers, like good Puritans, living humbly and working diligently in their callings, almost inevitably accumulated wealth. Penn described explicitly and in some detail the kinds of virtues he believed made for success in the world. In his second letter, Penn advised his children, "If God give you children . . . Teach them also frugality, and they will not want substance for their posterity. A little beginning with industry and thrift will make an estate." In the third letter, as noted above, Penn praised diligence and frugality at length. "Diligence," he said, "is a discrete and understanding application of one's self to business; . . . it loses no time, it conquers difficulties, recovers disappointments, . . . it is the way to wealth . . . Frugality is a virtue too, and not of little use in Life, the better way to be rich, for it has less toil and temptation, . . . for this way of getting is more in your own power, and less subject to hazard."[31] Working, saving, and investing led to prosperity and enhanced one's role in the community because thriving was taken to be a visible sign that one was living in the light of the Lord's grace. With disconcerting regularity, those who worked hard, saved, and invested became comfortable, and not a few became wealthy.

Material success and social mobility eroded the dreams carried to America by the early settlers, especially the tight communalism of the Puritans and Quakers. Alan Simpson declared, "the history of the New England Way is the history of a losing struggle to preserve the intensity of the experience of the saints and his authority over society."[32] The struggle was lost, somewhat incongruously, if not tragically, because, Perry Miller explained, "pious industry wrecked the city on a hill . . . The more everybody labored, the more society was transformed. The more diligently the people applied themselves, . . . the more they produced a decay of religion and a corruption of morals."[33] Frederick Tolles told a very similar story about the Quakers. He asked, "what happened to a religious group . . . with a pronounced mystical and perfectionist outlook in the presence of material prosperity, social prestige, and political power"?[34] He answered that Quaker society gave way to a broadly entrepreneurial culture because "there was a conflict implicit in the Quaker ethic . . . On the one hand, Friends were encouraged to be industrious in their callings by the promise that God would add his blessing in the form of prosperity; on the other hand, they were warned against allowing the fruits of their honest labors to accumulate lest they be tempted into luxury and pride."[35]

Before long, the social hierarchy that both Puritans and Quakers thought necessary to assure order and stability was compromised because wealth often seemed to flow toward new men rather than the traditional elite. Each year, new men arrived, others served out their indentures or took up their first small plots of land, and still others increased their holdings and began to rise in society. The Puritan and Quaker elites could not miss the success of ordinary men in wrestling the necessities and even the comforts of life from the wilderness. America offered special opportunity to the man who earned bread by the sweat of his brow. Moreover, as the eighteenth century opened, the frontier line began to push back from the coast, and the western counties of Massachusetts, New York, Pennsylvania, and Virginia began to fill. The westering spirit that Frederick Jackson Turner and so many others credit with nurturing the love of liberty, individualism, and opportunity in America became more insistent. Land of one's own, to support one's family and pass onto one's children, was the proximate goal of every free immigrant. As James Truslow Adams wrote, "it was . . . 'land in the woods' as a possibility for almost every inhabitant of America that was to prove one of the most powerful forces which worked toward democracy of feeling and outlook, toward the shaping of our American dream."[36] Opportunity also beckoned in America's cities and towns. Rapid economic and demographic growth transformed the colonies from the fairly static, inward-looking, traditional village cultures of the seventeenth century to the more dynamic, expansionist, and entrepreneurial cultures that were evident on the eve of the revolution.

No man more clearly embodied America rising than Benjamin Franklin.

Franklin's life, as well as his ideas and writings, came to define the American Dream. Benjamin Franklin was born in Boston on January 17, 1706, to Josiah and Abiah Franklin. Josiah's first wife Anne bore him seven children, and Abiah gave him ten more. Benjamin was the tenth son and third youngest of seventeen children. Josiah, a dyer by trade in England, became a soap and candle maker in Boston. Although he was a solid and respectable member of the community and of Boston's South Church, his work kept him too busy to participate actively in town affairs and too poor to educate his children beyond the basics of reading, writing, and arithmetic.

Ben, initially seen by his father as a "tithe" to the church, being the tenth son, was enrolled in one year of grammar school at age eight. However, when the grammar school proved too expensive, Ben was given one more year of basic school, focusing on writing and arithmetic, before attention was turned to finding him a trade. Ben's obvious disinterest in the candle shop led his father to apprentice him at the age of twelve to his older brother James, a printer. The print shop fed Ben's interest in reading, writing, editing, and persuasive argument. Ben read widely, experimented with various styles of oral and written argument, and practiced long and hard to improve his skills. In 1721 James started a newspaper called the *New England Courant* and was soon embroiled in a fierce battle with the magisterial and ministerial authorities of Boston—led by John Cotton's grandson, the formidable Cotton Mather. Ben's confidence and pride swelled when, at 15, he joined this battle as the author of an anonymous series of letters published in the *Courant* under the name "Silence Dogood." Silence Dogood strongly defended freedom of speech and conscience, saying, "it has been for some Time a Question with me, Whether a Commonwealth suffers more by hypocritical Pretenders to Religion, or by the openly Profane? But some late Thoughts of this Nature have inclined me to think, that the Hypocrite is the most dangerous Person of the Two, especially if he sustains a Post in the Government."[37]

As Ben matured physically and intellectually, tensions arose between Ben and his brother and master James. A few months after his seventeenth birthday, in one of the most richly symbolic events in American history, Benjamin Franklin fled the personal, political, and religious constraints of Puritan Boston for New York and then Philadelphia. Like the Horatio Alger heroes of a century later, Franklin made some missteps and saw others falter as well. Several of his close friends succumbed to alcohol, and although Franklin did not, he joined them in "going to plays and other places of amusement." The result was that, his money gone, he "just rubbed on from hand to mouth."[38]

Franklin's missteps, which he called "errata," provided the occasion for explaining how he mastered the talents and virtues that allowed him to overcome, correct, and avoid them in the future.

One of the key lessons taught in Franklin's *Autobiography* was the value of education. Franklin explained that he worked hard to perfect a limited formal education. For example, as soon as he reached Philadelphia in 1723 and settled into a printer's job, he organized a club "among the young people of the town that were lovers of reading." When somewhat better established, Franklin gathered his most "ingenious acquaintances into a club of mutual improvement, which we called the JUNTO; The rules . . . required that every member . . . once in three months produce and read an essay of his own writing, on any subject he pleased. Our debates were . . . conducted in the sincere spirit of inquiry after truth."[39] Franklin saw writing, like carpentry, as a skill that one had to practice to improve.

Franklin worked just as hard on his personal habits and character as on his intellectual skills. Franklin's remarkable dedication to self-improvement was reflected in a *"plan* . . . for regulating my future conduct in life" that he devised at eighteen and pursued the rest of his life. Franklin concluded that though scholars and sages seemed to define the virtues differently, a review of their work suggested that thirteen virtues were most important. These virtues were temperance, silence, order, resolution, frugality, industry, sincerity, justice, moderation, cleanliness, tranquility, chastity, and humility. Franklin planned to make these virtues, as much as possible, a permanent and habitual part of his character and conduct. First, Franklin tried for a full week to do nothing that was intemperate. Then, while trying to hold to what he had learned about temperance, he moved on to "silence" and tried to speak only "what may benefit others or yourself; avoid trifling conversation." Then, trying to hold to temperance and silence, he dedicated a week to "order" and so on through all thirteen virtues before beginning the cycle again.[40] Although Franklin had something of a sense of humor about all of this, he believed that there was an "art of virtue" that one had to study and practice, just like any other art.

Franklin's program for self-improvement was cast into a social philosophy and elaborated for public edification in "The Way to Wealth" (1758). Franklin chose his title from *The Advice of William Penn to His Children,* wherein the Quaker patriarch advised his children that diligence and frugality point "the way to wealth." In Franklin's clever hands, "The Way to Wealth" became a long parable featuring a character called "Father Abraham." Father Abraham was a wise old man who came upon a group of his fellow citizens complaining about the difficulty of their lives. The old man reminded his listeners that the road to success was well marked and "God helps them that help themselves." In general, Franklin advised, "Early to Bed, early to rise, makes a Man healthy, wealthy, and wise." Concerning preparation, Franklin taught, "He that hath a Trade hath an Estate," and "Keep thy Shop, and thy shop will keep thee." Concerning hard work, he enjoined, "Industry need not wish" and "Sloth makes all Things difficult; but industry all easy." Frugality was crucial to Franklin's counsel. He said, "Beware of little Expenses; a small Leak will sink a great Ship," and "If you would be wealthy, think of Saving as well as Getting." And in regard to perseverance, Franklin reminded his readers that "Little Strokes fell great Oaks" and "Diligence is the Mother of Good luck." Franklin concluded "The Way to Wealth" with an injunction that is oftentimes overlooked but that was central to his vision of social responsibility. After all the advice about hard work, frugality, and perseverance as the keys to getting on in the world, Franklin advised men not to "depend too much upon your own Industry, and Frugality, and Prudence, though excellent Things, for they all be blasted without the Blessing of Heaven ... and be not uncharitable to those that at present seem to want it, but comfort and help them." Franklin's own life was evidence of how seriously he took the counsel to serve God by serving one's fellow men.

Franklin was the moving force behind a remarkable number of public projects in Philadelphia. He initiated a fire company, a hospital, a philosophical society, and what became the University of Pennsylvania. He gained international fame as the inventor of the "Franklin stove," refusing a patent that was offered, and the lightning rod to draw lightning away from homes and other buildings. Franklin focused on civic activities and practical workaday inventions because, he believed, "Human felicity is produced not so much by great pieces of good fortune that seldom happen, as by little advantages that occur every day."[41] Franklin taught personal virtues, but men were to use them in the service of the community.

Hence, Franklin's specifically religious views were practical, focused on this world, and on immediate improvement in people's lives rather than on theological doctrine and otherworldly visions. In his eminently practical way, Franklin undertook to distill the fundamental tenets of every major religion while avoiding particular doctrinal points to which some might object. Franklin concluded that six tenets might form the religious core of an "Art of Virtue." Adherence to these tenets would support personal morality and the public good: (1) That there is one God, who made all things. (2) That He gov-

erns the world by His providence. (3) That He ought to be worshipped by ado-
ration, prayer, and thanksgiving. (4) But that the most acceptable service of
God is doing good to man. (5) That the soul is immortal. (6) And that God will
certainly reward virtue and punish vice, either here or hereafter.[42]

Benjamin Franklin, Poor Richard, and Father Abraham taught that self-control and self-improvement led to sufficiency, security, and respect. Respecting
the persons and property of others led to community, peace, and order.
Franklin and his surrogate voices recommended and even celebrated a char-
acteristically middle-class set of virtues that was both practical and democratic. Anyone could adopt them, practice them, benefit by them, and improve his
lot in life. And many did. Poor Richard and Father Abraham, taken up in
McGuffy's *Readers,* were taught and recited as the nation's common wisdom
throughout the nineteenth century and into the twentieth. They were and are
the moral core of the American Dream: education, work, thrift, dedication, and
a dash of good fortune will put an honest man in a position to thrive and prosper. Fate may determine otherwise at first, but probably not forever.

The Dream Embedded in Institutions, Law, and Policy

How were the evolving visions of American life embedded in
institutions, law, and policy from first settlement to the eve of the American
Revolution? Initially, a close collaboration of ministers and magistrates seemed
necessary to sustain and protect the early settlements from privation, danger,
and backsliding. Safety and well-being were enhanced by the arrival of more
settlers, the establishment of new towns, and settlements further out, all of
which meant more demand, higher land prices, more wealth, and greater
opportunity. As the colonies grew and the economic pulse quickened, the
early intensity, the first assumptions, and initial institutions and rules began to
constrain and then to chafe. Grudgingly, authority and hierarchy made way
for freedom and equality.

Most members of the early New England churches were committed
Puritans who had made the wrenching decision to leave all that they knew in
England to build their lives around their religious beliefs. Among persons of
such obvious motivation and conviction, church membership was open to all
men and women of good reputation and decent behavior. Since church mem-

bership opened the door to civil and political rights, most adult men enjoyed a full role in the religious and political life of their community. Nonetheless, early Boston was vulnerable to Indian attacks, starvation, and the intrusion of political and religious authorities back home, so unity seemed a prerequisite to safety. Moreover, Winthrop and the ministers believed that the covenant between God and New England was that He would bring them safe to the New World and protect them there if they would erect a "holy commonwealth." If they faltered, if they violated the covenant, He would withdraw His protection and they would surely perish. Unity, order, and discipline were the keys to their survival.

But dissent is hard for dissenters to forebear. Soon tender consciences like Roger Williams and Anne Hutchinson were raising questions that threatened to undercut the whole enterprise by creating divisions in the community and drawing the unwelcome attention of authorities in England. Williams questioned the very idea of an exclusive covenanted church, arguing instead for religious liberty. Anne Hutchinson went even further, arguing that God was not bound by the minister's cramped and impoverished understanding of His will and grace. Each individual ultimately had to listen for the voice of God in his or her own soul. Winthrop and the ministers responded not just by expelling the dissenters, but also by tightening the requirements for church membership. By 1640 almost every church in New England required a candidate for membership to testify to the assembled congregation about the nature, character, and timing of his or her conversion. Moreover, the aging saints of the first generation remembered their "soul-shattering" conversion experiences more and more gloriously as years passed. The sons and daughters of the saints, many born in England but raised in the peace and increasing prosperity of the New World, knew that they did not feel the religious intensity that their fathers and mothers described. Fewer young adults offered to appear before the assembled saints to present their conversion experiences, and fewer still were convincing when they did.

Church membership was required for participation in congregational affairs and for political participation, including both voting and office holding. With the religious and political rolls narrowing steadily, the churches of New England convoked a synod in 1662. This authoritative ecclesiastical policy-making body announced the Half-Way Covenant. The Half-Way Covenant allowed the children of full church members to attend services and bring their children for baptism by "owning the covenant." This kept the halfway congregants within the church community, but not as saints eligible for the Lord's

Supper. For the next quarter century, theory and practice continued to diverge. Extended baptism, mass covenant renewals, and a looser Half-Way Covenant admitted to partial membership all who would come while maintaining the ideal of testified regenerate church membership. Alan K. Simpson's memorable description of the ebbing of Puritan religious enthusiasm still resonates: "Everywhere the taut springs relax, the mass rebels, and compromises eat away at a distinction on which the whole system is based."[43]

Puritan divines sought to stem the rising tide of secular individualism by booming jeremiad after jeremiad from the pulpits of New England. Finally they were all but swept away as a major evangelical revival inundated the English-speaking world in the late 1730s and 1740s. In America, Jonathan Edwards, the leading New England minister of the mid-eighteenth century, further blurred the distinction between saints and sinners by declaring that though salvation was by the grace of God alone, it could occur in an instant in anyone of any age. It was never too late. A bad beginning did not preclude a glorious end for those whose hearts had truly changed. The "New Light" message of the Great Awakening was a rousing, often boisterous, emotional appeal that promised a spiritual rebirth to all who would accept Jesus as their Savior.

Quaker history presents a remarkably similar picture, including a compromise like the Puritan's Half-Way Covenant. The Quaker meeting distinguished between "consistent or strict Friends and those who tended to give way . . . The latter, who came to be known as 'wet Quakers,' were . . . allowed to attend meeting for worship, but not Monthly or Quarterly Meetings for discipline."[44] Like the Puritan saints, the consistent Friends were intensely aware that later generations had fallen away from the faith of their fathers. In 1764, John Smith, an elderly Quaker who had been witness to much of Penn's "holy experiment," spoke to the annual meeting of Quaker elders in Philadelphia. Smith observed that although the original "Friends were a plain lowly minded people," within two generations, "many of the Society were grown rich, that wearing of fine costly Garments and with fashionable furniture, silver watches became customary with many of their sons and daughters. And as these things prevailed in the Society and appeared in our Meetings; . . . the weakness amongst us in not . . . supporting the Testimony of Truth in Faithfulness was a matter of much Sorrow."[45] Increasingly, wealthy Quakers found the monthly meeting's focus on "plainness" and "simplicity" in manners and dress too constraining. They tended to disappear from the meeting and to reappear in the more comfortable pews of the Anglican church. Religious fervor did not disappear, but it did become more private, while the public sphere became the forum for addressing secular issues. As had long been true in the Anglican South, a gentleman's report of his deep religious conviction came to be accepted easily.

Magistrates and citizens negotiated new rules of access and influence in government as well. In Massachusetts, magistrates made and implemented law until 1634, when they were forced to share legislative authority with deputies elected by the freemen. Governor Winthrop initially resisted this intrusion on the magistrates' prerogatives and later insisted that while the deputies might participate in law making, the judicial power to apply law in individual cases was part of the magistrates calling and should be left to their discretion. The deputies generally respected the priority of the magistrates and allowed them to lead. The "due form of Government" that Winthrop and early saints had erected to protect peace, order, and true faith worked largely as intended through the middle decades of the seventeenth century.

In 1635 the General Court defined the powers and responsibilities of local governments in Massachusetts. The court gave the towns broad powers to elect local leaders and enact ordinances consonant with the general laws of the colony. Most Massachusetts towns authorized a town meeting to set general policy and an elected board of selectmen, or town council, to do the daily business of the town. For most of the next half century, town meetings were pleased to meet a couple times a year, to stay close to the agenda prepared by the selectmen, and to defer to their judgment and experience on most business. Still, hierarchy and deference needed support, and liberty needed to know its limits.

Winthrop, Cotton, and many others made the point that religious liberty was obedience to the law of God, and political liberty was obedience to legitimate political authority. What, then, the freemen wished to know, were the rights and liberties of the people? In 1635 the General Court first charged a committee, led by the Reverend John Cotton, to recommend "a draft of laws agreeable to the word of God, which may be the Fundamentals of this Commonwealth." In 1636 Cotton, ever the biblical literalist, presented to the General Court a document entitled *A Model of Moses His Judicials.* The General Court respectfully set Cotton's *Judicials* aside as to exclusively Mosaic and insufficiently reflective of the common law rights and liberties of English freemen. In 1639 a committee led by the Reverend Nathaniel Ward reported a document that was circulated to all of the towns for comment, debated further in the General Court, and in 1641 approved as the *Massachusetts Body of*

Liberties. This fascinating document is widely accounted to be the first Bill of Rights in American history.

The *Massachusetts Body of Liberties* was composed of a preamble and a list of one hundred liberties. Many of the Liberties are familiar because they were drawn from the English common law, but many are not because provisions accord different rights by social class, gender, and race, and include biblical prohibitions and punishments. The first liberty shows how Puritan ministers and magistrates sought to buttress secular law with religion. "No man's life shall be taken away, no man's honor or good name shall be stained, no man's person shall be arrested, restrained, banished, dismembered, nor any ways punished, no man shall be deprived of his wife or children, no man's goods or estate shall be taken away from him, . . . unless it be by virtue of equity or some express law of the country . . . or in case of the defect of law in any particular case by the word of God." Magistrates were to draw on the laws of man and God to create equity and do justice in Massachusetts Bay.

Among the *Liberties* are several that have come forward into modern American law, including the right to post bail, the right to a speedy trial, the right against double jeopardy, and the right against cruel and unusual punishment. Others, although perhaps distant relatives of modern rights, are harder to recognize. For example, the right against self-incrimination was attenuated as follows: "No man shall be forced by torture to confess any crime . . . unless it be in some capital case where he is first duly convicted . . . after which if . . . it is very apparent there be other conspirators, . . . then he may be tortured, yet not with such tortures as be barbarous and inhumane." The "liberties" also approved variation in punishment by social rank: "No man shall be beaten with above forty stripes, nor shall any true gentlemen, nor any man equal to gentleman be punished with whipping, unless his crime be very shameful, and his course of life vicious and profligate." Finally, true religion was to be protected by punishments ranging up to death for worship of false gods, witchcraft, and blasphemy.

Governor Winthrop was concerned that the people understand the true nature and limits of their liberties. Winthrop's famous *Little Speech on Liberty,* recorded in his *Journal* under May 1645 but argued and defended throughout the previous decade, warned that "There is a twofold liberty, natural (I mean as our nature is now corrupt) and civil or federal. The first is common to man with beasts and other creatures. By this, man . . . hath liberty to do as he lists; it is a liberty to do evil as well as to do good. This liberty is incompatible and inconsistent with authority. . . . The other kind of liberty I call civil or federal, it may also be termed moral, in reference to the covenant between God and man, in the moral law, and the politic covenants and constitutions, amongst men themselves. This liberty is the proper end and object of authority, and cannot subsist without it; and it is a liberty to that only which is good, just, and honest. . . . This liberty is maintained and exercised in a way of subjection to authority; it is the same kind of liberty wherewith Christ has made us free."[46]

Winthrop was by no means alone in believing that natural liberty, the liberty that man has in common with beasts to do as he lists, promised disorder and even destruction. If God punished whole communities for the misbehavior of some of their members, then whole communities had to monitor the behavior of each of their members. With typical Quaker thoroughness, William Penn made this point at wonderful length in his *Frame of Government of Pennsylvania:* "That as . . . the wildness and looseness of the people provoke the indignation of God against a country: therefore, . . . all such offenses against God as swearing, cursing, lying, profane talking, drunkenness, drinking of healths, obscene words, incest, sodomy, rapes, whoredom, fornication, and other uncleanness (not to be repeated) all treasons, misprisons, murders, duels, felony, seditions, maims, forcible entries, and other violences, . . . all prizes, stage-plays, cards, dice, May-games, gamesters, masques, revels, bull-baitings, cock-fightings, bear-baitings, and the like, which excite the people to rudeness, cruelty, looseness, and irreligion, shall be respectively discouraged, and severely punished." Despite the obvious misgivings of colonial elites, individual liberty was on the rise.

The 1680s brought massive political change both to England and to her North American colonies. New England's stubborn support for Parliament in its struggle with the King led him in 1684 to revoke their generous colonial charters and impose royal governments. Colonists rejoiced in 1688 when the English civil wars culminated in the fall of Stuart absolutism and the rise of parliamentary supremacy. They thrilled to John Locke's *Two Treatises of Government,* which found the natural and secular origins of government in the consent of free men. Arguments for equality, individual rights, and popular sovereignty were in the air, and Americans felt empowered and energized by them. Yet Parliament did not see fit to restore colonial autonomy.

If little could be done about London, men could apply these new ideas to their own communities. Early in the eighteenth century, town meetings began to assert their primacy over boards of selectmen and town councils. Town meetings began to meet more frequently, to elect constables, treasurers, and other key officials, and to acquire and use power in their communities. Freemen were taking their local governments into their own hands, debating important issues, and learning that difference, even conflict, need not threaten the peace and good order of a community. Men began to think about the origins, purposes, and conduct of government in new ways. Three changes were most profound. First, the origins of government came to be seen as secular and rational, rather than religious. Second, the purposes of government came to be seen as peace and order—the protection of life, liberty, and property, rather than an all-encompassing effort to recreate Eden. And third, with the origins and purposes of government lowered and limited, public officials came to be seen as accountable to the people, rather than to God.

John Wise, minister to the congregation in Ipswich, Massachusetts, drew heavily on European social contract theorists, especially John Locke and Samuel Pufendorf, to argue for the rational and secular origins of government. In 1717 Wise wrote in his famous *Vindication:* "It is certain Civil Government in General, is a very Admirable Result of Providence, and of Incomparable Benefit to Man-kind, yet . . . not of Divine Institution, . . . there is no particular Form of Civil Government described in God's Word, neither does Nature prompt it . . . it is the Produce of Man's Reason." The eighteenth century also brought new views of the nature and origins of rights and liberties that highlighted civil equality and looked to nature and reason as the source of civil liberties. John Wise reasoned that "since no man can live a sociable life with another that does not own or respect him as a man, it follows as a command of the law of nature that every man esteem and treat another as one who is naturally his equal or is a man as well as he is." Nonetheless, that all men were equal did not mean that each man was free to follow his own nature, instincts, and will. Throughout the eighteenth century, liberty was seen as action in concert with reason and law. Wise observed, "liberty does not consist in a loose and ungovernable freedom or in an unbounded license of acting. . . . So that the true liberty of man, . . . is guided and restrained by the ties of reason and laws of nature; all the rest is brutal, if not worse."[47] Increasingly, however, men began to see how liberty could still mean abiding by law, even while, even especially while, the scope of government was closely defined and clearly limited. In 1764 James Otis explained that "the end of government being the good of mankind points out its great duties: it is above all things to provide for the security, the quiet, and happy enjoyment of life, liberty, and property." Here was a vision of secular life in which a distinctively American Dream might arise and thrive. Before long, it did.

Practical considerations—the need to attract settlers and enhance economic activity—also spurred political change. Immigration was a constant source of tension between London and the colonies. English leaders were always willing and sometimes eager to see orphans, paupers, criminals, and dissidents take ship for North America. Emptying the orphanages, almshouses, and prisons reduced the burdens on English churches and communities and provided indentured servants to North America, where more labor was always needed. On the other hand, English officials were reluctant to lose skilled workers and artisans and unwilling to see Catholics from Europe immigrate to America. Colonial leaders always wanted more settlers to expand the domestic market, drive up the price of land, and settle the backcountry. But they wanted useful citizens rather than the paupers and criminals that the English authorities wished to send. Most were willing to take good Protestant immigrants, but different colonies used different screens to sift for the immigrants they most desired. Massachusetts and all of New England, save Rhode Island, wanted good Puritans who could join the covenanted communities already in place. Pennsylvania wanted good and sober men and women and was less concerned about religious orthodoxy or national origin. Virginia and the South wanted tractable labor, and as much of it as they could get.

Colonial officials sought to encourage immigration from Europe by offering easy citizenship and generous civil and political rights to newcomers. However, English authorities denied that naturalization procedures in the colonies automatically awarded full British citizenship, particularly the right to engage in the colonial trade, arguing instead that any citizenship rights awarded in the colonies applied only in the colonies.[48] Not until the Plantation Act of 1740 did English officials create a mechanism by which English citizenship could be conferred by act of the colonial legislatures. The act made anyone eligible for English citizenship that had lived in any American colony for seven years, belonged to a Protestant church, and swore allegiance to the king. Immigration surged between 1750 and 1775 as thousands arrived each year to take up land and opportunity in America. Competition for immigrants among the colonies, complete with offers of free land, tax abatements, economic opportunity, religious toleration, if not full religious freedom, and easy citizenship was common.[49]

Finally, colonial governments also engaged in a wide range of activities designed to support and promote economic development. Colonial governments allotted lands to settlers or arranged land sales, laid out highways and kept them up, improved harbors and wharves, supported churches and schools, operated loan offices, and coined and printed money. Moreover, they promoted particular enterprises by "grants of land and money, bounties, monopolies of local markets, tax incentives, freedom from military obligations for workers, and even a relaxation of religious regulations" when these seemed necessary.[50] Naturally, defense also fell under the government's purview.

The key resource that colonial governments had to spur economic activity was land. Free land brought immigrants faster, while the reasonable sale of land filled government coffers and allowed improvements and services such as roads, harbors, schools, and churches. With growth, dynamism, and expansion came greater opportunities in agriculture, commerce, the artisan trades and crafts, and legal and related services. In a secularized version of Winthrop's "city on a hill," Jonathan Mayhew captured this confident sense of America's future in 1759 when he predicted "mighty cities rising on every hill and by the side of every commodious port . . . happy fields and villages . . . through a vastly extended territory."[51] As the revolution approached, nearly two-thirds of white men worked on land that they owned or were buying, and their families enjoyed the most widespread economic security and comfort in the world.

The Faces of Exclusion

Seventeenth-century England, from which most of the early colonists came, was a monarchical and aristocratic society. A titled nobility, an established national church, and a mercantilist economic policy produced a sense of social order in which estates were separate and men were called to positions within their estate. Most common men did not and could not expect to own their own land, and only about 5 percent of the adult male population had the right to vote for members of Parliament. Most laborers were bound to their employer by legally enforceable service contracts, and vagrants were subject to being swept up and consigned to a poorhouse or a jail. Hence, most of the early colonists brought with them the conviction that hierarchy was the best guarantee of social order. In fact, throughout the colonial period, American society was shot through with myriad forms of subordination and dependency that most of the population, even many of the excluded, thought natural. Andrew Burstein says baldly, "American society prior to the Revolution was predicated on human inequality."[52] Although that statement is probably always true of society, it is important to understand how true it was of the

American society during the colonial period. Nature and nature's God were thought to authorize exclusions and preferences based on class, religion, gender, race, and ethnicity.

A deep conviction held on both sides of the Atlantic was that any form of social and/or economic dependence precluded political and civil equality. Even among adult white men, apprentices, indentured servants, paroled convicts, and wage laborers were seen as dependent on the will of their employer. Because they had no will of their own, they were seen as too vulnerable and unstable to participate in governance by voting or holding office. The best available estimates suggest that half to two-thirds of white immigrants arrived in America under some form of service contract. Usually when dependent white men achieved independence, they gained civil and political rights, but they were still expected to show the deference due their betters.

Religious exclusions also were prominent in colonial America. Governor Winthrop, after reviewing appropriate scripture, assured both the General Court and his diary that "we may lawfully refuse to receive such whose dispositions suit not with ours and whose society (we know) will be hurtful to us." Perry Miller, the great historian of colonial America, declared, "the government of Massachusetts, and of Connecticut as well, was a dictatorship, and never pretended to be anything else; it was a dictatorship, not of a single tyrant, or an economic class, or of a political faction, but of the holy and regenerate."[53] Even the more secular Virginians used religious exclusions. The first thing that Governor Berkeley did when the civil wars erupted in England in the 1640s was to expel the Puritans from Virginia. Anti-Catholic sentiment was especially widespread during the colonial period. Though the middle colonies often welcomed Catholics, most American colonies followed the English example of excluding or restricting non-Protestants. The Puritans, of course, were particularly watchful for any sign of the "pernicious" doctrines of Catholicism.[54]

Religion, law, and circumstance all made clear to women that they were subordinate to and dependent on their fathers and husbands. The theologian John Calvin (1509–64), fountainhead of English Protestantism, said, "Let the woman be satisfied with her state of subjection, and not take it amiss that she is made inferior to the more distinguished sex."[55] John Cotton taught that God thought it "good for the Wife to acknowledge all power and authority to her Husband, and for the Husband to acknowledge honor to the Wife."[56] Finally, by 1660, the great English Puritan poet, John Milton, in his classic *Paradise Lost,* defined gender relations in the famous epigram, "he for God only, she for

God in him." Most women, in deference to these and so many other authorities, gave the obedience expected and hoped that honor would be their reward.

Anne Hutchinson discovered what happened to women who defied male authority in the public sphere. She challenged the political and religious authorities of Massachusetts Bay, charging that they valued a covenant of works over a covenant of pure grace. They responded with a withering attack designed to intimidate and silence her. When she rose to defend herself before the General Court, Governor John Winthrop called her a most "disorderly woman" and informed her that "we do not mean to discourse with those of your sex." Reverend Hugh Peter warned Mrs. Hutchinson, "[you have] stepped out of your place, you have rather been a Husband than a Wife and a preacher than a Hearer; and a Magistrate than a Subject."[57] All of this, they were clear, was unbecoming to and unacceptable in persons of her sex. When she persisted, she was excommunicated by the church and exiled by the government.

Although a husband's honor might bring love and safety to a woman in her normal social roles, her civil due was to be somewhat less. English common law made women dependent on the male who was legally responsible for them. The legal principle of "coverture" made daughters and wives the wards of their fathers and husbands. Married women, *femme covert,* were subsumed within the legal personality of their husband; they could not vote, represent themselves in court, claim property, and sue for divorce, or claim children if their husband sued for divorce. Although unmarried adult women, *femme sole,* did have an independent legal position in society, their economic circumstances were often dire indeed.[58] *Provisions of the Massachusetts Body of Liberties* define the role of women in colonial society. Adult men were free to buy and sell property, but "any Conveyance or Alienation of land or other estate what so ever, made by any woman that is married, any child under age, idiot or distracted person, shall be good if it is passed and ratified by the consent of a general Court." Men could buy and sell property as they saw fit; married women, children, and idiots needed the permission of the General Court. Nonetheless, other provisions allowed women to appeal to the General Court if their husbands did not provide for them in their will and stood between wives and husbands who wished to administer "bodily correction or stripes."

Even in the absence of fear and physical vulnerability, the day-to-day lives of colonial women were hard and often bleak. Absent dependable birth control, women tended to be either pregnant or breast-feeding throughout their fertile years. Families with ten children, even fifteen or more, were not uncommon, and the average woman had eight children.[59] Few colonial women received any formal education, and their days were generally spent in a dawn-to-dusk round of cooking, cleaning, gardening, tending animals, and caring for children. Although life was arduous all around, women living in towns had sources of consolation and support that were unavailable to their sisters on isolated frontier farms. The further out the farm and the younger the woman, the more likely she was to work beside her husband in the fields. On the other hand, white women were the wives and daughters of white men. Although they were by no means the social and economic equals of their husbands and fathers, they did live in the same houses, share the same food and drink; in fact, they participated in, even if they did not fully share in, the social position and priority of white men. Others, including blacks and Indians, were far less fortunate.

During the colonial period, almost no one thought Africans could or should have the same rights as independent, freeborn Englishmen. In fact, most Englishmen thought that Africans had so little sense of liberty, reason, and responsibility that they did not feel the lack of them. Moreover, the wild appearance and degraded behavior of many slaves were widely attributed to their nature rather than to the effects of slavery itself. Although the Quakers stood firmly against slavery on religious and humane principles, the Puritans were more ambivalent, and the South saw only the need to secure a stable and compliant workforce. The Quakers thought that slaves were clearly human and, as creatures of God, deserving of some care and respect. Although slavery was not unheard of in Philadelphia, it was uncommon and subject to negative social sanction. Puritans, as always, thought the Bible covered this matter. *The Massachusetts Body of Liberties* declared: "There shall never be any bond slavery, villeinage, or captivity amongst us unless it be lawful captives taken in just wars, and such strangers as willingly sell themselves or are sold to us. And these shall have all the liberties and Christian usages which the law of God established in Israel." With the door thus open, Yankee traders became the main carriers of slaves from Africa and the Caribbean during the eighteenth century, although the number of slaves in New England was never large.

The first Africans arrived in Jamestown aboard a Dutch vessel in 1619. Although their initial status remains unclear—they were probably somewhere between indentured servants and slaves—they were always treated differently than indentured whites. White indentured servants served out their time and left to take up their own land. Blacks were more vulnerable, and by the early 1660s, both Virginia and Maryland had enacted chattel slavery. Slavery as a full-blown legal system was worked out over a period of decades but was largely in place in the South by 1700. Slaves were denied all but the thinnest legal existence. They could hold property only as the master allowed, and they could not legally marry, inherit, sue in court, or even appeal to authorities against heinous abuse. Individual slaves could be sold away from those they considered to be family at the discretion of their masters. Male slaves could protect neither spouses nor children, and no slave could protect him- or herself. Slaves were universally barred from congregating or moving about freely. Once the black codes were securely in place early in the eighteenth century, even free blacks were denied most civil protections. Free blacks could not vote or hold office, testify against a white man in court, serve in the militia, or marry across racial boundaries. Like a single white woman, free blacks had a cramped and restricted legal personality. Their interests might be considered and even protected in court, but not on a footing equal to white men. They did, on the other hand, have an obvious and ongoing economic use to white men (Figure 2.4).

American Indians were of no use to the white settlers. Hence, no numerous people over such an extensive territory as the Americas has ever been so thoroughly decimated as the Indian populations between 1492 and 1750. Estimates suggest, and we can do no better than estimate, that the Indian population declined, mostly due to infectious diseases, but to war as well, by up to 90 percent. Indians could not account for the deadly plagues, while many whites thought they saw the hand of God clearing the continent for their settlement. Where disease did not sweep the Indians from the land, as in early Virginia, colonists were often hard-pressed to prevail over tribes protecting their ancestral lands. Devastating Indian attacks shook Virginia in 1620 and 1640 before the superior firepower of the colonists began to tell. Conflict meant that the initial goal of converting the Indians to Christianity soon gave way to a determination to push them west by force, treaty, or other stratagem. For many whites, extermination became the preferred stratagem.

Indians understood quite well the threat that white settlers posed to them, no matter what the settlers said about their intentions. The dreams of some men, no matter how attractive or how confidently held, are nightmares for those who do not share them. In the 1760s, when the English defeated the French to take control of the Ohio Valley, "a Delaware chief named Shingas observed to an English missionary . . . 'We have great reason to believe you

Figure 2.4. "Disembarkation of Slaves," 1860. This image represents the endless stream of slaves led ashore in North America between 1619 and 1860. (Corbis, image BK001442)

intend to drive us away, and settle the country; or else, why would you come to fight in land God gave to us.'"[60] The missionary, one assumes, offered assurances that Shingas, like so many of his brothers over the centuries, found unconvincing.

3

The Dream Defined: The Founding Visions of Crevecoeur, Jefferson, and Hamilton

Welcome to my shores, distressed European; . . . If thou wilt work,
I have bread for thee; if thou wilt be honest, sober, and industrious,
I have greater rewards to confer on thee—ease and independence.

—Crevecoeur, *Letters from an American Farmer*

All the pieces of the American Dream were in place by the 1780s.
Benjamin Franklin, both in his own remarkable life and in the pages of *Poor Richard's Almanac,* had been defining the core of the dream for decades: pre-pare, work hard, save, invest, catch a break, and success will be yours. J. Hector St. John de Crevecoeur promised that the American Dream belonged to the immigrant too; if they would come, learn, work, and save, they too could prosper as they never could in Europe. But precisely how government policy should be designed to promote freedom, prosperity, and security remained uncertain. Two visions predominated. One was the liberal, egalitarian, agrarian vision of Thomas Jefferson, and the other was the individualistic, competitive, commercial vision of Alexander Hamilton.

The Jeffersonian vision was a calm, almost sedate, promise of equality, sufficiency, and security. It was a rural vision of slow but steady accumulation, natural growth, and competition restrained by community. The big gain was unlikely, but the steady application of effort could lead to larger and more secure holdings each year. The Hamiltonian vision was more aggressively entrepreneurial; it envisioned a rising commercial and manufacturing economy guided by an elite of talent, wisdom, and wealth. In the new nation's first half century, although the Hamiltonian vision predominated for a time, the Jeffersonian vision effectively shaped the new nation because it comported so well with the hopes and aspirations of the westering agricultural multitudes.

Still, most Americans remained outside the civic ken of the Founding generation. Their sense that "all men are created equal" was the fairly narrow sense that all adult, white, male, property owners were citizens and therefore members of the governing class. Poor white men, women, blacks, American Indians, the physically and mentally deficient, all lacked the independence that flowed from male strength, reason, and judgment. Hence, many believed that it was in the interest of society and all of its members that free white men should lead. The Revolution shook these convictions; they cracked, but they did not give way for more than half a century.

Young Dreamers and the World Before Them

The United States has been called the "first new nation" because it was the first nation in modern history to emerge from colonial dependence to national independence.[1] Wars for independence always produce tumult, and the American Revolution was no exception. Traditional republican norms and influences, with their stress on continuity, order, hierarchy, and deference, continued to exercise great influence in the small and homogeneous rural communities of the nation. Nonetheless, the transition from colonial status to independence fostered the rise of new ideas, like liberty, equality, and popular sovereignty.[2]

Independence gave new momentum to intellectual forces that had been on the rise in Europe and America for more than a century. Sir Isaac Newton (1642–1727), father of modern empirical and experimental science, had sought to explain the natural world as the interplay of physical forces, gravity being the most prominent, acting according to universal laws of motion. Newton demonstrated that the balance, symmetry, and harmony of the universe, variously described as "celestial mechanics" or the "harmony of the spheres," operated according to natural, and therefore discoverable, general laws. Men thought of their world differently when they accepted that the heavens were held in place by gravity, rather than hung in place for all eternity by the hand of God.

The search for balance and harmony guided the social sciences too. Within the social sciences, students of human motivation adhered to a perspective called "faculty psychology." Faculty psychology highlighted three human faculties: reason, passions, and interests. Each had a legitimate and even critical role to play in human life, but the relationships between and among them varied. In some people, they were in harmonious balance, whereas in others, they were in perpetual conflict. The ideal interaction of the human faculties was for reason to direct the proper, healthy, and measured pursuit of the passions and interests. Unfortunately, for most men most of the time, and for virtually all women, children, and nonwhites, passions and interests overwhelmed reason. Disorder and conflict were the inevitable result.

The best minds of the eighteenth century thought that the uniformity of human nature described by faculty psychology made history a storehouse of empirical data, of natural experiments, showing what worked and what did not work in human political organization. If human nature was uniform and unchanging; like the matter in Newton's universe, then well-built institutions, like well-built machines, might order the world to the benefit of man. John Adams wrote that "the systems of legislators are experiments made on human life, and manners, society and government. Zoroaster, Confucius, Mithras, Odin, Mohamet, Lycurgus, Solon, Romulus, and a thousand others may be compared to philosophers making experiments on the elements."[3] Similarly, as General George Washington resigned his military commission to return to civilian life in June 1783, he observed that "the treasures of knowledge, acquired by the labors of Philosophers, Sages, and legislators, through a long succession of years, are laid open for our use, and their collected wisdom may be happily applied in the Establishment of our forms of Government. . . . At this auspicious period, the United States came into existence as a Nation, and if their Citizens should not be completely free and happy, the fault will be entirely their own."[4]

Clearly, the Founding generation believed that great things were possible. But they also knew that achieving great things, particularly in the disorderly wake of war and revolution, was difficult. Many pieces of a new and potentially transformative order were present, but no one claimed to know exactly how all of the pieces fit together to assure peace and prosperity. Monarchy was discredited, democracy was still thought dangerously unstable, and between them lay a disconcertingly wide spectrum of political regimes called republics. John Adams reflected the sense of many that republicanism provided a direction in which to search, but not a destination. Adams observed that while "there is no good government but what is republican. . . . Of republics there is an inexhaustible variety, because the possible combinations of the powers of society are capable of innumerable variations."[5]

What the Founders were looking for was what Aristotle had called a *polity,* a balanced government in which the disparate interests of the few rich and the many poor were carefully balanced to produce security and prosperity. However, scholars and theorists had long taught that governments in which the many poor played a prominent role had to be small so that the people could come together to discuss issues, vote, and work their will. Larger, wealthier, more powerful republics tended to be governed by elites. The most authoritative presentation of this view came from the French scholar, Charles Secondat (1689–1755), the Baron de Montesquieu, in *The Spirit of the Laws* (1748). Still, new insights were working their way into the public consciousness.

David Hume (1711–76) offered a dramatic new perspective on the relationship between state size and regime type. In a beautifully titled essay, "The Idea of a Perfect Commonwealth" (1741), Hume rejected "the common opinion that no large state . . . could ever be modeled into a commonwealth." In fact, he declared, quite the opposite was true. "In a large government, which is modeled with masterly skill, there is compass and room enough to refine the democracy, from the lower people who may be admitted into the first elections . . . , to the higher magistrates who direct all the movements. At the same time, the parts are so distant and remote that it is very difficult, either by intrigue, prejudice, or passion, to hurry them into any measures against the public interest."[6] A constitution "modeled with masterly skill," the Founders came to believe on their reading of both Newton and Hume, might "check interest with interest, class with class, faction with faction, and one branch of government with another in a harmonious system of mutual frustration."[7]

In addition to intellectual ferment, the American society experienced tremendous, even explosive, growth and expansion in the half century between 1775 and 1825. Well before talk of independence was heard, thoughtful men on both sides of the Atlantic were aware that the balance between England and her North American colonies was shifting ominously. Britain was deeply concerned about the exodus to America. *The London Chronicle* of July 19, 1773, warned readers: "every sensible person must foresee that our fellow subjects in America will, in less than half a century, form a state much more numerous and powerful than their mother-country. . . . Thousands . . . fly every year to that happy country, where they can live with freedom and get their bread with ease." The *Nova Scotia Gazette* of August 9, 1774, quoting a dispatch from

London, reported: "The emigration of people from all parts of England is very amazing indeed, and if no stop is put to it England will really be drained of multitudes of mechanics of all sorts, ships are daily taken up for this purpose, and the spirit of emigration daily increases—America that land of promise is their cry."[8]

Americans worried about how the British government would react to their rapid growth. Charles Carroll observed to William Graves in a letter of September 7, 1773, that "the growing population of the colonies, increased by such a considerable annual influx of newcomers, bids fair to render British America in a century or two the most populous and of course the most potent part of the world. I fancy that many in England begin to entertain the same opinion."[9] In February 1775, Alexander Hamilton's "The Farmer Refuted" blamed England's oppressive policies on "a jealousy of our dawning splendor." He wrote, "the boundless extent of territory we possess, the wholesome temperament of our climate, the luxuriance and fertility of our soil, the variety of our products, the rapidity of our population, the industry of our country men and the commodiousness of our ports, naturally lead to a suspicion of independence."[10]

When American independence did come, it served merely to inflame European imaginations. The *Belfast News-Letter* of April 18, 1783, reported that "more than 13,000 Emigrants have already gone from the north of Ireland. The Stop that was put to it by the War being removed, they fly thither, with an eagerness never known before." Later that same year, the *Leeds Mercury* of August 12, 1783, reported, "All Europe seems now to fix its views on the States of America. . . . The Emigrations there from all parts of Europe . . . augment daily; so that this rising republic, situated on a soil favorable in all respects, will, according to all appearance, soon become one of the best peopled and most flourishing countries of the globe."[11]

Within America, both native-born citizens and immigrants were on the move. After the Revolution, settlers poured over the mountains, first into western Pennsylvania and the Carolina backcountry, and then into the territories of Kentucky and Tennessee. The census of 1790 showed a total U.S. population of 3.9 million, with about 170,000 living west of the mountains, 73,677 of them in Kentucky and 35,691 in Tennessee. Kentucky was admitted to statehood in 1791 and Tennessee in 1796. Total population in 1800 approached 5.3 million (a ten-year increase of 36 percent), and more than a million settlers were in the western country. The populations of Kentucky and Tennessee had tripled (to 220,955 and 105,602, respectively), 45,365 people were in Ohio, and

5,641 had pushed the settlement line into Indiana. Ohio became a state in 1803, and settlement spread north into Michigan and Minnesota and south into Missouri, Louisiana, Arkansas, and Alabama. Between 1800 and 1810 total population expanded another 36 percent (from 5.3 million to 7.2 million). Ohio's population expanded fivefold (45,365 to 230,760) and Indiana's expanded four-fold (5,641 to 24,520). Between 1810 and 1820 total population increased by another third (from 7.2 million to 9.7 million), and by 1820 more than 2.5 million Americans were over the mountains, and a hundred thousand more followed each year during the 1820s. New states were added to the union almost every year: Louisiana in 1812, Indiana in 1816, Mississippi in 1817, Illinois in 1818, and Alabama in 1819 (Figure 3.1).

As Americans spread out and took up the land in the backcountry and deep into the Ohio and Mississippi River valleys, they had to be connected so they could exchange goods and information. Hence, western settlement was followed and facilitated by improved transportation and communication systems. Stagecoaches bumped and rattled between Boston and Baltimore, but went no further south. By 1800 three wagon roads, the Old Walton Road, the Wilderness Road, and the Knoxville Road, connected the east to the Ohio River. The Ohio and Mississippi Rivers connected the West to the South. A gentle current unobstructed by narrows, rocks, or rapids allowed a heavily burdened raft to float from Pittsburgh to New Orleans in 20 days. Steam power came to water transportation "when Fulton and Livingston ran the *Clermont* on the Hudson in 1807, and sent their steamboat the *New Orleans* on a successful round trip between New Orleans and Pittsburgh in 1817."[12] Moreover, several thousand miles of canals were built by the states to connect various internal waterways, culminating in the opening of the Erie Canal in 1825. Midwestern canals connected the Ohio and Mississippi basins through the Great Lakes to the Erie Canal, the Hudson River, and New York City. Settlers and manufactured goods going west and agricultural products going east moved at about 4 miles per hour over the nation's roads, rivers, and canals.

The half century between 1775 and 1825 witnessed a tremendous expansion of the American population and territory. Just as importantly, growth meant opportunity in the burgeoning cities of the Atlantic coast as well as on the distant reaches of the Ohio and the Mississippi. Every new immigrant was a potential customer, and every new village and town needed a general store, a blacksmith's shop, a tin smith, and a carpenter. Doctors, lawyers, preachers, and undertakers were always in short supply. The new nation was booming, and opportunity was everywhere.

Figure 3.1. "Pioneers Traveling Down the Ohio River by Flatboat," undated, circa 1810, woodcut by Felix Octavius Carr Darley. Note the Indian canoe in the left foreground and the village on the shore in the right background. (Corbis/Bettmann, image BE023669)

The American Dream in the Founding Period

Americans were convinced that God had set aside the new nation for a special experiment in human freedom. Even before independence, Philadelphia's leading physician, Dr. Benjamin Rush, was urging Americans to "Remember the eyes of all Europe are fixed upon you, to preserve an asylum for freedom in this country, after the last pillars of it are fallen in every other quarter of the globe."[13] Tom Paine's *Common Sense*, a call for independence that hit the colonies like a thunderclap in January 1776, declared that "the cause of America is in a great measure the cause of all mankind." Paine challenged Americans and Europeans alike, saying "O! ye that love mankind, . . . stand forth! Every spot of the old world is over-run with oppression. Freedom hath been hunted round the globe. Asia and Africa have long expelled her. Europe regards her like a stranger, and England hath given her warning to depart. O! receive the fugitive, and prepare in time an asylum for mankind."[14]

By war's end, most Americans were convinced that freedom's home was now secure. Yale University President Ezra Stiles declared in 1783 that the new nation, which he called "God's American Israel," had combined faith, freedom, and opportunity to create "a most amazing spirit" among the people. "Never before," he declared, "has the experiment been so effectively tried, of every man's reaping the fruits of his labour, and feeling his share in the aggregate system of power."[15] Benjamin Rush agreed, declaring: "America seems destined to exhibit to the world the perfection which the mind of man is capable of receiving from the combined operation of liberty, learning, and the gospel upon it."[16] In June 1793, as the French Revolution engulfed Europe and the United States seemed secure behind President Washington's neutrality policy, the *New Hampshire Magazine* published a poem simply entitled "America":

> O ye oppress'd! who groan in foreign lands,
> No more submit to tyrants' vile commands,
> While here a calm retreat from all your woes,
> Invites to freedom, joy, and blest repose.[17]

Finally, Noah Webster again highlighted the difference between America and Europe in a 1798 Fourth of July oration. Webster declared, "America alone seems to be reserved by Heaven as the sequestered region, where religion, virtue, and the arts may find a peaceful retirement from the tempests which agitate Europe. If, in the old world, men are . . . perpetually shedding each other's blood, . . . we have the more reason to cling to the constitution, the laws, to the civil and religious institutions of the country, and to cherish the pacific policy which doubles the value of those blessings."[18] Americans shared a widespread sense of what made their new nation distinctive. First, separation from Europe and its traditional conflicts allowed peace, order, and security to reign. Second, American society offered its members freedom to believe, strive, and achieve as they thought best. Hence, and third, not just liberty and property thrived and grew, but so did human intellect and character—learning, the arts, morality, and religion.

J. Hector St. John de Crevecoeur (1735–1813) assured immigrants that the American promise belonged to them too. Crevecoeur was born in the Normandy region of France, came to America about 1760, and, after serving France in the Great Lakes and the Ohio Valley, settled on a comfortable farm in Orange County, New York. His *Letters from an American Farmer* (1782) provided the first full articulation of the American Dream from the immigrant perspective. Crevecoeur was concerned both to praise the benefits of life in America to potential immigrants and to assure native-born Americans that it was reasonable to continue welcoming strangers to the newly independent nation. Some Americans were concerned that immigrants carried monarchical and aristocratical ideas, attitudes, and habits that might pollute republican America. Crevecoeur argued that immigrants came not to recreate their past, but to find their future. He asked, "what attachment can a poor European emigrant have for a country where he had nothing? . . . Can a wretch who wanders about, who works and starves, . . . call England or any other kingdom his country? A country that had no bread for him, whose fields procured him no harvest, . . . who owned not a single foot of the extensive surface of this planet? No!"

Rather, Crevecoeur assured his native-born countrymen, in choosing America, the immigrant becomes an American. "[H]is country is now that which gives him land, bread, protection, and consequence." Crevecoeur drove home his point by asking a justly famous question: "What then is the American, this new man? . . . He is an American," Crevecoeur answered, "who, leaving behind him all of his ancient prejudices and manners, receives new ones from the new mode of life he has embraced, the new government he obeys, and the new rank he holds."[19] In America, Crevecoeur reminded his readers, "the bright idea of property, of exclusive right, of independence. . . . Precious soil . . . constitute the riches of the freeholder." Opportunity encouraged the freeholder's hopes and molded his behavior. All Americans, old and new, are "animated with the spirit of industry which is unfettered and unrestrained, because each person works for himself."[20]

Like Franklin, Crevecoeur reminded his readers that opportunity had to be grasped and not everyone would succeed, even in America. Crevecoeur explained, "it is not every immigrant who succeeds; no, it is only the sober, the honest, and industrious. . . . If he is a good man, he forms schemes of future prosperity . . . ; he thinks of future modes of conduct, feels an ardor to labor he never felt before." Crevecoeur hastened to say, "I do not mean that everyone who comes will become rich in a little time; no, but he may procure an easy, decent maintenance, by his industry."[21] Crevecoeur was so dead-on the sense and feel of the American Dream that he described the immigrant's opportunity to work, save, and invest in their own land as "a dream." Crevecoeur highlighted the Germans as particularly effective in studying and pursuing the opportunities available in America. He said of that "absolute property of two hundred acres of land. . . . What an ephoca in this man's life. He is become a freeholder from perhaps a German Boor—he is now an American. . . . by dint of sobriety, rigid parsimony, and the most persevering industry, they commonly succeed. Their astonishment . . . is very great—it is to them a dream."[22]

Finally, like Thomas Tillam more than a century before, Crevecoeur developed themes that Emma Lazarus would enshrine on the Statue of Liberty a century later. Crevecoeur recommended that those who would be Americans listen closely to their new nation's promise, lest they miss the fact that it is a conditional promise. "After a foreigner from any part of Europe is arrived, and become a citizen; let him devoutly listen to the voice of our great parent, which says to him, 'Welcome to my shores, distressed European; bless the hour in which thou didst see my verdant fields, my fair navigable rivers, and my green mountains!—If thou wilt work, I have bread for thee; if thou wilt be honest, sober, and industrious, I have greater rewards to confer on thee— ease and independence. . . . Go thou and work and till; thou shalt prosper, provided thou be just, grateful, and industrious.'"[23]

By the early 1780s, Franklin and Crevecoeur had described the two main pathways to the American Dream in terms that have stood in broad outline for well over two centuries. Franklin described and exemplified the American Dream that has shimmered before each new generation of Americans: learn, work, save, invest, keep an eye out for the main chance, and success will follow. Crevecoeur described and exemplified the dream that has beckoned the immigrant: get here any way you can, learn a skill or trade, study her ways, work hard, save, and America will make a place for you. Thomas Jefferson added the poetry, the uplifting, future-oriented, intergenerational promise of opportunity and prosperity that has been central to the dream from his day to ours.

Students of Jefferson have long noted that his was a distinctly positive and uplifting view of human nature. Richard Hofstadter, no idealist himself, wrote that "through all of Jefferson's work there runs like a fresh underground stream the deep conviction that all will turn out well, that life will somehow assert itself."[24] Joseph J. Ellis has recently written that "the most visionary version of the American Dream" derived from Thomas Jefferson.[25] Jefferson himself simply said, "I am among those who think well of the human character generally."[26] Jefferson's hope for and trust in the future became a steady breeze beneath the wings of the American Dream.

Thomas Jefferson's vision for America was encapsulated in the Declaration of Independence. Although the Declaration was the work of a committee, further amended on the floor of the Congress, Jefferson's vision of an egalitarian individualism lived out in the context of peace and plenty, shone through.[27] Jefferson put human rights, the right of individuals to security, honor, and self-development, at the core of the American promise. The justly famous second paragraph of the Declaration reads, "We hold these truths to be self-evident, that all men are created equal, that they are endowed by their Creator with certain unalienable Rights, that among these are Life, Liberty, and the pursuit of Happiness.—That to secure these rights, Governments are instituted among Men, deriving their just powers from the consent of the governed,—That whenever any Form of Government becomes destructive of these ends, it is the Right of the People to alter or to abolish it, and to institute new Government, laying its foundation on such principles and organizing its powers in such form, as to them shall seem most likely to effect their Safety and Happiness" (Figure 3.2).

The opening sentence of that paragraph makes several points that are foundational to the American Dream and to our national sense of self. First, it defines as "self-evident," that is, beyond demonstration and dispute, "certain unalienable Rights," "among" which are "Life, Liberty, and the pursuit of Happiness." The idea of self-evidence is a wonderful way of saying, despite all the evidence of difference and inequality that you see around you, a free society must see men as fundamentally equal. These words have proven to be so alluringly open that each succeeding generation has understood the "all Men" who are "created equal" and "endowed" with the "unalienable Rights" of "Life, Liberty, and the pursuit of Happiness," more broadly. Moreover, the simple phrase "among these" suggests that there may be, and probably are, more self-evident and unalienable rights.

Second, John Locke's identification of life, liberty, and property as fundamental rights was significantly softened, broadened, and enriched by Jefferson's substitution of "pursuit of Happiness" for property. Life and liberty remain foundational for Jefferson, as for Locke, and there is no doubt that Jefferson valued property, but "pursuit of Happiness" is forward-looking, egalitarian, and aspirational, while "property" is conservative, defensive, and exclusionary. The Founding generation believed that property supported security, independence, and autonomy, but Jefferson's "pursuit of Happiness" suggests a goal well beyond security that we might call human fulfillment and thriving.

Third, widespread happiness or fulfillment is made a defining purpose of

Figure 3.2. "Declaration of Independence, July 4, 1776." This classic painting by Jonathan Trumbull depicts Thomas Jefferson and his committee colleagues delivering the Declaration of Independence to the Second Continental Congress. (Library of Congress, Prints and Photographs Division, reproduction LC-USZ62-3736)

government. The second paragraph of the Declaration, quoted above, mentions happiness twice, once in the list with life and liberty, and once later in the paragraph. The second reference to happiness came as Jefferson explained that people have a right to change a government that does not suit their needs, laying the foundation of the new government "on such principles and organizing its powers in such form, as to them shall seem most likely to effect their Safety and Happiness." *Effect* means *realize,* so that seldom-noted phrase means that people empower government in the expectation that it will help them realize or achieve security and happiness.[28] Jefferson defined the goals of American public life—the promise of life, liberty, and the pursuit of happiness—in positive and expansive language that has thrilled and challenged every subsequent generation of Americans.

Jefferson believed that society and government should act to maximize individual liberty and then help people take advantage of the opportunities available to them. His broadest insight was that freedom and education make democracy possible. To Jefferson and the Founding generation, freedom meant individual autonomy and independence. In a nation of small villages and farms, independence meant land and the means to work it. Jefferson famously thought that the agrarian life encouraged and sustained personal virtue. In *Notes on the State of Virginia,* he wrote, "those who labor in the earth are the chosen people of God, if ever he had a chosen people, whose breasts he has made his peculiar deposit for substantial and genuine virtue."[29] Jefferson believed that the new nation's social health and character depended upon the widespread pursuit of agriculture. In 1787 he wrote, "I think our governments will remain virtuous for many centuries; as long as they remain chiefly agricultural; and this will be as long as there shall be vacant lands in any part of America."[30]

Jefferson was also committed throughout his life to assuring that common people were educated for their roles and responsibilities as free citizens.[31] Writing to Abbe Arnoux in July 1789, he said, "We think in America that it is necessary to introduce the people into every department of government as far as they are capable of exercising it; and that this is the only way to insure a long-continued and honest administration of it's powers."[32] He wanted the common people to have choices and to have the wherewithal to make them well. In December 1789, Jefferson wrote to Madison, saying, "above all things I hope the education of the common people will be attended to; convinced that on their good sense we may rely with the most security for the preservation of a due degree of liberty."[33] Jefferson wanted every citizen to receive enough education to "enable them to read and understand what is going on in the world, and to keep their part of it going on right: for nothing can keep it right but their own vigilant and distrustful superintendence."[34] Jefferson thought that when free men were well educated, they could and should run their own lives. Jefferson's security as the foundational theorist of the American Dream rests on the close connection he made between freedom, education, and democracy.

As Jefferson entered upon the presidency early in 1801, he expressed deep satisfaction in a nation and people that were free, prosperous, and secure. His goal was to defend and expand the agrarian simplicity that he saw around him. Jefferson used his first inaugural address to promise the nation "a wise and frugal government, which shall restrain men from injuring one another, shall leave them otherwise free to regulate their own pursuits and shall not take from the mouth of labor the bread it has earned. This is the sum of good government."[35] A free people needed no more, and in fact, more would be both expensive and dangerous.

Alexander Hamilton did not believe that social order was simply an emergent property of human nature or that men could simply be educated to civility. As Bernard Weisberger has recently observed, "Hamilton saw society as a theatre of perpetual conflict rather than cooperation for security."[36] A light touch from government would more likely produce chaos than order. Public order, whether in the market place or the public square, had to be created, enforced, and protected. Hamilton began from a skeptical view of human nature and concluded that an authoritative and powerful national government was required to secure and maintain peace and prosperity. "Mankind in general . . . are vicious—their passions may be operated upon," Hamilton warned his fellow delegates to the Constitutional Convention. "One great error is that we suppose mankind more honest than they are. Our prevailing passions are ambition and interest . . . these ever induce us to action."[37] Hence, Hamilton refused to idolize or flatter the people. Though "the voice of the people has been said to be the voice of God; and however generally this maxim has been quoted and believed, it is not true in fact. The people are turbulent and changing; they seldom judge or determine right."[38]

Nonetheless, like others of his generation, Hamilton believed that well-built institutions could secure and defend social, political, and economic order. Madison followed this insight to his historic place as "Father of the Constitution." Hamilton could as justly be called "Father of the American Economy." Hamilton envisioned a national economy designed, organized, and regulated by government to develop the human and natural wealth of the new nation. Even more importantly, Hamilton saw a healthy, vibrant economy as eliciting and even shaping good character among citizens. Although Jefferson thought education and the security of agricultural independence promoted good character, Hamilton thought that agriculture permitted a certain laxity, while manufacturing encouraged determination and innovation. Hamilton noted in the "Report on Manufactures" that "the labor employed in Agriculture is in a great measure periodical and occasional, depending on seasons, liable to various and long intermissions; while that occupied in many manufactures is constant and regular, extending through the year, embracing in some instances the night as well as the day." Hence, Hamilton concluded, "minds of the strongest and most active powers" thrive in a diverse economy. "When all the different kinds of industry obtain in a community, each individual can find his proper element, and can call into activity the whole vigour of his nature."[39]

Hamilton believed that involvement in markets encouraged regular and predictable behavior; "a general habit of punctuality among traders is a natural consequence of the necessity of observing it with the Bank . . . from the very nature of things, the *interest* will make it the policy of a Bank, to succor the wary and industrious; to discredit the rash and unthrifty." In fact, in a well-ordered entrepreneurial environment, Hamilton argued, "there is good reason to believe, that while the laws are wise and well executed, and the inviolability of property and contracts maintained, the economy of a people will, in the general course of things, correspond with its means."[40]

Nonetheless, market incentives to good and wise conduct might sometimes be insufficient. Then the appropriate source of constraint on the human passions and interests, in Hamilton's view, was government and law forcefully applied. Hamilton said, "Government supposes control. It is that POWER by which individuals in society are kept from doing injury to each other and are brought to cooperate to a common end."[41] Some of Hamilton's strongest statements on the nature and authority of government came during the controversy over the Whiskey Rebellion in 1794. A tax on domestically distilled spirits, enacted by Congress in 1791 on Hamilton's recommendation, sparked rebellion in western Pennsylvania. From Hamilton's perspective, the tax on whiskey was part of a well-balanced fiscal program in which everyone paid their share. From the farmers' perspective, their grain was distilled to alcohol for ease of transport rather than simply for consumption, and should therefore be viewed as crops rather than hit with a sin tax. Jefferson counseled restraint in the application of government power lest the public spirit be cowed and broken. Not Hamilton. Hamilton declared it *"inherent* in the very *definition* of government . . . that every power vested in a government is in its nature sovereign, and includes, by the *force* of [that] *term,* a right to employ all the means requisite."[42]

Hamilton was convinced that people only had meaningful rights under a strong government. "The rights of government are as essential to be defended as the rights of individuals. The security of the one is inseparable from that of the other."[43] If government was weak or its legitimacy questioned, people's rights were at risk. Hence, Hamilton used the setting of a cabinet discussion about how to deal with the whiskey rebels to warn Washington that unless checked "the spirit of disobedience . . . will naturally extend and the authority of the government will be prostrate."[44] Jefferson liked a little rebellion now and then. Hamilton definitely did not.

Jefferson depended on security, peace, and plenty to make citizens calm, kind, and generous. Free men, working their own land and guiding their own local affairs, confident that they and their families were secure and that hard work would produce a sufficiency and perhaps prosperity, required little governing. Hamilton thought that men were naturally fractious and that various incentives and pressures, including force, were required to elicit predictable and productive behavior. Jefferson depended on local democracy and schools to guide men's choices and behavior; Hamilton depended on markets and law, with the strong arm of government ever ready to shape and enforce both. Jefferson saw the American Dream as widespread, comfortable security; Hamilton saw it as a fair competition for society's best places. The 1790s belonged to Hamilton, but the first quarter of the new century belonged to the Virginia triumvirate of Jefferson, Madison, and Monroe.

The Dream Embedded in Institutions, Law, and Policy

How and how well was the American Dream, described so beautifully by Crevecoeur and Jefferson and so practically by Franklin and Hamilton, embodied in the institutions, law, and policy of the new nation? The new political order, anticipated in the Declaration of Independence and embodied in the Constitution, highlighted limited government and the protection of individual rights and liberties. In the half century after the American Revolution, the new national government developed policies to balance human rights and property rights, promote economic development, define and monitor immigration, naturalization, and citizenship, and open the western lands to sale and settlement.

Independence required that early attention be given to state political institutions and practices. The need to rewrite state constitutions and to place them before the people for ratification raised the issue of suffrage—of who would have the right to vote and to play a full role in the new political order—immediately. The traditional English rationale for limiting the suffrage to property holders was famously laid out in William Blackstone's *Commentaries on the Laws of England,* published in England in several volumes during the late 1760s and immediately available in the colonies. Blackstone's "stake in society" argument was that only those owning sufficient land to give them a stake in the future stability and prosperity of the society should be allowed to participate in the governance of the society. Although suffrage in the colonies was far broader than in England, about 60 percent of white men in the colonies compared to 5 percent in England, the dominant rationale for excluding some potential voters was similar. Hence, before the Revolution, most colonies restricted voting to adult, white, male, native-born or naturalized citizens, owning 50 acres or more of real property. Most colonies explicitly barred servants, women, blacks, including free blacks, and Indians from the electorate. Moreover, six colonies employed viva voce voting, oral voting in public, to reinforce elite control and lower class deference.

As resistance became rebellion, the rhetoric of the Revolution veered hard toward popular sovereignty. In the summer of 1776, the Continental Congress instructed the former colonies to revise their charters to remove all suggestions of British sovereignty. Although about half the states loosened their requirements for voting, all stopped short of universal white manhood suffrage. For example, Pennsylvania's constitution of 1776 eliminated property qualifications but replaced them with a taxpaying requirement that still excluded dependents like paupers and domestic servants.[45] Virginia's constitutional convention of May and June 1776, even though under the leavening influence of Thomas Jefferson, did not remove the land requirement for voting. Jefferson instead proposed that Virginia meet the property qualification for all white men by granting 50 acres to all who did not already have it.[46] His conservative colleagues blocked the proposal. Nonetheless, many revolutionary leaders realized that the payment for the common man's support would be a more egalitarian society. By the time independence was assured in the early 1780s, the idea of property was broadening beyond land, and even urban property, to include each man's rights, liberties, and future opportunities. The spread of the idea of self-ownership steadily broke down traditional systems of indentured servitude and apprenticeship and offered the first tools to challenge exclusions based on class, race, and gender. Other democratic reforms brought debtor relief, increased western representation, and improved access to free or cheap land for those lacking it.

Before long, conservatives became concerned that liberty was tending toward license. They worried that free citizens, absent strong and stable political institutions, might create little more than disorder and injustice. Several state constitutions were revised and strengthened during the 1780s, but Shays Rebellion, a conflict between the hard-pressed debtor farmers of western Massachusetts and the state authorities in Boston, convinced conservatives throughout the nation that a more powerful national government was required to guarantee security and justice in states and communities. A federal convention met throughout the summer of 1787, initially to consider amendments to the Articles of Confederation, but eventually it offered a new Constitution for the United States. The opening paragraph of the Constitution restated the Declaration's goals of ordered liberty based on popular sovereignty, declaring; "We the people of the United States, in order to form a more perfect union, establish justice, insure domestic tranquility, provide for the common defense, promote the general welfare, and secure the blessing of liberty to ourselves and our posterity, do ordain and establish this Constitution for the United States of America." How was the Constitution expected to produce justice, liberty, and the general welfare of the American people?

The Founders believed that a carefully constructed constitution might divert human ambition toward the public interest and the common good. The wisdom of the ancients, as well as the best physical and social science of the day, suggested a way to secure both human rights and property rights in a structure of freedom, liberty, and order. Following David Hume, James Madison argued that thoughtfully "contriving the interior structure of the government" would make men and institutions check and balance each other. In the *Federalist Papers* number 51, Madison explained: "Ambition must be made to counteract ambition. The interests of the man must be connected with the constitutional rights of the place." Though ambitious men might govern; "This policy of supplying, by opposite and rival interests, the defect of better motives," promised good government even when good men did not rule.[47] Written constitutions allowed well-defined executive, legislative, and judicial powers to be placed in separate hands. Beneath the broad separation of powers might be constructed an intricate machinery of checks and balances that would permit self-interested officeholders to employ and protect their powers and responsibilities over time. Indirect and mediated elections of presidents and senators, for differing terms, by differing constituencies, were designed to "extract from the mass of society the purest and noblest characters; such as will at once feel most strongly the proper motives to pursue the end of their appointment, and be most capable to devise the proper means of attaining it."[48]

The Constitution defined the powers of government and sought to protect against their ill use by a complex system of separation of powers and checks and balances, but the debate over ratification made it clear that many Americans worried that their individual rights and liberties were at risk. Even Jefferson, on diplomatic service in France when the Constitution was drafted, wrote to Madison expressing concern over the absence of a bill of rights. Madison became concerned that a cloud of doubt would hang over the Constitution if more protections for individual rights were not added. He ushered the first ten amendments to the Constitution, which came to be known as the Bill of Rights, through Congress and the ratification process. The Bill of Rights, broadly conceived, accomplished two things. First, it defined a preserve of personal autonomy, choice, and expression where government power should not intrude. The First Amendment offered the expansive assurance that "Congress shall make no law respecting an establishment of religion, or prohibiting the free exercise thereof; or abridging the freedom of speech, or of the press; or of the right of the people peaceably to assemble, and to petition the government for a redress of grievances."

Second, the Bill of Rights defined how persons would be subject to the power of government. Isolated individuals, especially common people, must quake before the concentrated power of a national government unless that government is required to proceed slowly, carefully, and according to well-known rules and procedures. Hence, the Bill of Rights confirmed the rights to a speedy trial before an impartial jury, to confront witnesses, and to have the aid of counsel (Amendment 6). The Bill of Rights protected citizens against "unreasonable searches and seizures" (Amendment 4), double jeopardy and self-incrimination (Amendment 5), and excessive bail or cruel and unusual punishments (Amendment 8). The Ninth Amendment, like the Declaration of Independence, suggested that citizens, as human beings, have more rights than those specifically listed in the Constitution and its amendments. The Declaration said that "among" the unalienable rights that the Creator gave men were life, liberty, and the prospect of happiness. The Ninth Amendment said, "The enumeration in the Constitution, of certain rights, shall not be construed to deny or disparage others retained by the people." These reassuring commitments encouraged citizens to give the new Constitution a chance. Just as Madison had hoped, support for the Constitution increased to near unanimity within a few years.[49]

The Constitution checked government, and the Bill of Rights emboldened individuals. But even more importantly, these documents put a foundation under the American Dream. Their commitments to individual liberty and limited government left a broad social space for variety, choice, and competition. Dan Rather recently noted that the "First Amendment is more than a set of limitations on state power; it is a sort of guide to living the American life. . . . The freedom to speak, to practice one's religion freely, to peaceably assemble— all of these are at the very core of the American dream. So is the freedom to go beyond the circumstances of your birth."[50]

After 1790, with a new federal Constitution securely in place, democratization continued apace. Delaware expunged its property qualification for voting in 1792, Maryland did so in 1802, both Massachusetts and New York followed suit in 1821, and Virginia finally abandoned the property-holding requirement for voting in 1829. Moreover, most states admitted to the union after 1790 entered with universal white manhood suffrage or easily met taxpayer or residency requirements in their constitutions. Congress responded to the suffrage issue in regard to the West by adopting the traditional 50-acre freehold requirement in most early territorial acts. However, by 1811, Congress eliminated the property requirement in favor of the more permissive requirements of taxpaying and residency. Other reforms made voting easier and less intimidating. County polling places were broken up into smaller districts to make it easier to vote without losing a full day's work. Paper ballots replaced viva voce voting. Formerly appointive offices were made elective to broaden popular influence and enhance political accountability. Not surprisingly, turnout rose as more people became eligible and elections became more important.

Convinced that the structure of a Constitution and the substance of the Bill of Rights would protect individual rights and liberties, the Founders turned their attention to protecting property rights and facilitating economic activity in the new nation. The Constitution envisioned a national commercial system, free from state interference, in which uniform laws and regulations concerning coinage, weights and measures, postal communication, patent protections, and bankruptcy law facilitated entrepreneurship, opportunity, and wealth-getting. President Washington's new government sought to design policies that would foster a freestanding American economy that could compete internationally while providing independence, security, and opportunity to citizens at home. The role of government in the economy became the subject of heated debate. Two broad views—one Hamiltonian and the other Jeffersonian—clashed.

Hamilton believed that Britain's rise to European and then global supremacy began with the founding of the Bank of England in 1694. The Bank both fueled the Industrial Revolution in England during the middle decades of the eighteenth century and provided a source of credit that the government could draw upon to expand its navy and civilian marine beyond what other nations in Europe could afford. Even the tremendous national debt that hung over England in 1763 at the conclusion of the Seven Years' War was politically beneficial because it tied the English landed and commercial elites to the government. Hamilton wished to reproduce the political economy of England in America. He advocated a Bank of the United States to facilitate commercial and manufacturing activity, provide a source of public credit to the government, and manage the currency and credit of the private economy. He also sought to define and control the postwar public debt, whether owed by the national or the state governments, to create a consolidated national debt. The revenue required to fund the debt would come principally from tariffs on imported goods. This tariff wall would also serve to protect nascent American manufactures from foreign competition until they could get established.

Jefferson envisioned an agrarian republic in which the vast majority of men worked their own land and others engaged in supportive commerce and artisanship. A bank to facilitate large-scale commercial and manufacturing endeavors, a tariff to protect domestic manufactures, and a national debt to tie a privileged elite to a powerful national government all seemed not just bad policy, but destructive of the social and moral fiber of the country. Jefferson envisioned a nation of agriculturists, secure in self-governing local communities, free from the tyranny of concentrated wealth and power. These deep differences over how national policy should direct and shape the American economy and society caused unremitting conflict within the Washington administration.

Unfortunately for Jefferson, he was secretary of state and Hamilton was secretary of the treasury, so the economic portfolio was Hamilton's. Congress asked the treasury secretary how an efficient national economy might be organized, and he answered over the course of nearly two years in three brilliant state papers. The first dealt with the means of establishing the nation's currency and credit markets, the second dealt with the need for a banking system, and the third discussed how to stimulate manufacturing in the new economy. These three reports to the Congress provide the foundation for Hamilton's lasting reputation as the father of the American economy. As Bernard Weisberger has recently written, "Hamilton . . . had an uncanny anticipation of a national economy in which encouragement of the investing classes, a numerical minority, would generate productivity that would enhance everyone's well-being—but it necessarily meant allowing room at the top for fortunes to be made by the few."[51]

Hamilton sought to lift and energize an American economy that had recently been prostrate. War and its attendant economic dislocations left the American economy bereft of specie, currency, and credit. These lubricants of economic activity had to be created or viable substitutes had to be found in the short term. Hamilton's wizardry was not simply to create a currency, but to conjure one out of debt. Approximately $80 million in debts incurred by Congress and the states remained from the war. During and after the war, doubts about American military success and about any new government's ability to redeem the debt sapped confidence, and some types of debt traded in the marketplace at pennies on the dollar. Much of the debt gathered in the vaults of wealthy speculators betting that the new government would provide for the war debt, perhaps not repaying it at par, but at levels higher than the speculators had paid for it.

Heated policy debate arose over how to treat this debt. Everyone recognized that debts owed to foreign governments and banks had to be honored or the nation's future credit would be compromised. But some, Jefferson and Madison most prominently, argued for "discrimination" among various domestic debt holders. They called for original recipients of the debt, such as soldiers and suppliers to the army, to be paid all that they were owed, but speculators who had bought the debt at steep discounts should, they argued, be paid only the discounted rate commanded in the market when they bought it. They argued that discrimination would reward the original holders of the debt for their direct contribution to the war while denying speculators an illegitimate windfall.

Hamilton's great insight was that funding the debt at par would create pools of active capital in a nation that had little. Hamilton began his famous "Report on Public Credit" by coolly observing that "in a country, which, like this, is possessed of little active wealth, or . . . little monied capital, the necessity of that resource, must . . . be proportionately urgent." Rather than wait for capital to accumulate slowly over time, Hamilton proposed to use the debt as a substitute for capital and currency. He noted "that in countries in which the national debt is properly funded, and an object of established confidence, it answers most of the purposes of money."[52] With the English model in mind, Hamilton proposed to reconfigure the debt as interest-bearing bonds that might be held for the interest payments, like modern treasury bonds, or traded in the marketplace like modern currency.

The English model also envisioned a national bank. Stable and well-managed banks, Hamilton argued, "increase the active capital of a country . . . and keep the money itself in a state of incessant activity." Moreover, "banks in good credit can circulate a far greater sum than the actual quantity of the capital . . . two and three to one." Hence, Hamilton assured the Congress, "by contributing to enlarge the mass of industrious and commercial enterprise . . . banks become nurseries of national wealth."[53] Hamilton's goal was to raise the discounted value of the debt by promising secure government funding, thereby creating new wealth, new mobile capital, and then leveraging the economic impact of the new capital by a factor of two or three through the creation of a national bank.

Hamilton understood that markets were not naturally occurring phenomena, but were, in fact, created by law and policy. He knew that government set the rules of the marketplace through initial legislation, ongoing regulation, and investigation where appropriate. In regard to banks, Hamilton declared, "public utility is more truly the object of public Banks, than private profit. And it is the business of Government, to constitute them on such principles, that while the latter will result, . . . the former be not made subservient to it." Once established, Hamilton expected the bank directors' "keen, steady, and, as it were, magnetic sense, of their own interests" to guide the institution. Nonetheless, oversight remained a right and obligation of government. Hamilton reminded Congress that "Government owes to itself and to the community . . . a right of ascertaining, as often as may be necessary, the state of the Bank, excluding however all pretensions to controul."[54]

Finally, Hamilton differed from Jefferson in believing that government, especially the government of a developing nation, should nurture, encourage, and direct economic development. Manufacturing stood in particular need of protection and support. Hamilton argued that "cautious and sagacious capitalists" might not undertake new and uncertain initiatives without "a degree of countenance and support from government." Even more obviously, Hamilton argued, new American businesses might not rise to challenge established European businesses without the "extraordinary aid and protection of government."[55] Hence, Hamilton favored aggressive use of tariffs and bounties to protect and foster the rise of manufactures in America. Jefferson opposed all of this as an unnecessary tax on southern and western agriculture in favor of northern commercial and manufacturing interests. When Washington regularly sided with Hamilton and he would not relent, Jefferson left the government so that he could more effectively oppose it.

Once Washington decided to retire from the presidency in 1796, Jefferson emerged from retirement to challenge Vice President John Adams for the presidency. He lost narrowly, continued to mold opposition sentiment into a more stable party structure, and defeated Adams to win the presidency in 1800. Still, Jefferson understood that his presidency did not begin from scratch; rather, he took over a government and economy already in operation. Soon after his inauguration, Jefferson wrote, "When this government was first established, it was possible to have kept it going on true principles, but the contracted, English, half-lettered ideas of Hamilton destroyed that hope in the bud. We can pay off his debts in 15 years; but we can never get rid of his financial system. . . . What is practicable must often control what is pure theory."[56] Jefferson believed that by displacing the Federalists, he had won the opportunity to revise their policies and programs, but not to replace them wholesale. Still, the Jeffersonian displacement of Hamiltonian policies was a transformative event in the early development of the American state. Federalist congressman Fisher Ames clearly understood that Jefferson's ascendancy was "no little cabinet scene, where one minister comes into power and another goes out, but a great moral revolution proceeding from the vices and passions of men, shifting officers today, that measures, and principles, and systems, may be shifted tomorrow."[57] Ames was absolutely correct. Jefferson allowed the charter of the Bank of the United States to lapse, paid off the national debt, reduced the tariff, and shrunk the national political and military establishments.

Once Jefferson had revised and limited Hamilton's fiscal, banking, and commercial programs, he turned his attention to the interests of agriculture. Land in the woods represented independence and opportunity for most Americans during the colonial and early national periods. Nonetheless, speculator influence and the government's need for revenue had led to adoption in 1785 and again in the famous Northwest Ordinance of 1787 of a policy which required the public domain to be surveyed and divided into townships of 6 square miles each. Each township was then divided into sections of 640 acres and sold at public auction for not less than $1 per acre. Congress knew that the large plot size of 640 acres meant that most sales would be made to wealthy speculators and land companies. The hope was that the initial purchasers would repackage their large tracts into smaller units, provide credit, and sell them to individual farmers, thus saving the government the administrative burden of overseeing small sales and time payments.

The Land Law of 1800 was more flexible, but just slightly more friendly to small purchasers. The government offered sections for $2 per acre, but allowed purchasers to put one-quarter down and pay the balance in equal installments at the end of the second, third, and fourth years. A total of 19.4 million acres of public lands was sold under these terms, although most of the prime land was bought in blocks of up to 500,000 acres and sold to settlers on credit at inflated prices. Even at the government price, default was common, and in the end, almost one-third of the land originally contracted for was returned. Cash purchases in an economy that was still largely subsistence and barter were hard to manage, especially for the poor families that looked to the

West as a place to get started. These policies remained in force throughout Jefferson's and Madison's administration and into Monroe's.

President Jefferson soon faced new opportunities in the West. In 1802 Spain ceded the Louisiana Territory to France. Spain's control of the Mississippi River and the key port of New Orleans had been troublesome throughout the 1780s, but Spain was a declining European power and not a serious land threat in North America. Napoleon's France, on the other hand, was a great power. Its control of the Mississippi might well make that river the permanent western boundary of the United States. Jefferson sent special envoy James Monroe to Paris to assist Ambassador Robert Livingston in procuring Louisiana from Napoleon. Napoleon was pressed for cash to prosecute his European wars and put little value on what was widely reported to be the desert of central North America. In less than three weeks, Monroe and Livingston secured title to a million square miles from the Mississippi to the Rockies and from Texas to the Canadian border for $15 million (Figure 3.3).

Geographical expansion and economic growth steadily drove Jefferson, Madison, and Monroe to reconsider their aversion to Hamiltonian principles and methods. Jefferson came to realize, under the tutelage of Secretary of the Treasury Albert Gallatin, that American security required a balance of agriculture, commerce, and manufacturing. He continued to believe that the balance should favor agriculture, but as the national economy developed and New England's commerce increasingly carried the products of its shops and factories, Jefferson declared, "manufactures are now as necessary to our independence as to our comfort."[58] In 1816 President James Madison, Jefferson's chosen successor, chartered the Second Bank of the United States, enforced a protective tariff, and recommended a constitutional amendment to permit federal spending on internal improvements such as roads, harbors, and canals. With a more balanced economic program in place, President Monroe secured the Land Act of 1820, which abolished the credit system and reduced both plot size and price to facilitate the needs of small purchasers. Settlers could get as little as 80 acres at $1.25 an acre. Earlier purchasers who had defaulted on part of their payment were given clear title to the portion paid for, and the remainder reverted to the government. Jefferson's heirs warily recognized that economic growth required the assistance of an active, if not quite an activist, government.

Finally, as an independent nation, the United States had to define in law and policy what kinds of immigrants it would welcome and on what terms. U.S. immigration, naturalization, and citizenship policies were set and reset over

Figure 3.3. "Sacajawea Guiding the Lewis and Clark Expedition," 1806. This Alfred Russell drawing depicts Sacajawea, the young Indian wife of a member of the "Corps of Discovery," guiding the Lewis and Clark Expedition west. (Corbis/Bettmann, image BE060143)

the course of the 1790s, but by 1802 the nation arrived at a set of policies that it would maintain with little change for nearly a century. Through most of the new government's first decade, Thomas Jefferson was ambivalent about immigration. He worried that new immigrants might disrupt or endanger the rural, participatory village culture that he envisioned. He asked, "may not our government be more homogenous, more peaceful, more durable, without large-scale immigration?"[59] Alexander Hamilton and the Federalists were more comfortable with immigration. The Federalists envisioned a commercial society governed by social and economic elites. Hence, new immigrants would expand the labor force while being kept well away from meaningful political power.[60]

The Naturalization Act of 1790 was the first attempt to codify how immigrants would move toward citizenship. This act came early in the first Washington administration and reflected the Federalist's sense of social and political control. Hence, the act leaned decidedly toward openness for European white men but exclusion for others. The Naturalization Act of 1790 made eligible for U.S. citizenship any "free white person" who had been a resident of the United

States for two years (and one year in the state in which the petition was submitted), could prove "good character," and was willing to take an oath to "support the Constitution." However, once the French Revolution began to spread radicalism through Europe, the conservative Federalists and the more liberal Jeffersonians swapped views on immigration. Soon Alexander Hamilton was arguing that "the influx of foreigners must . . . tend to produce a heterogeneous compound; to change and corrupt the national spirit; to complicate and compound public opinion; to introduce foreign propensities. In the composition of society . . . whatever tends to a discordant intermixture must have an injurious tendency."[61] The Federalist's Naturalization Act of 1795 increased the residency requirement from two years to five and required resident aliens to declare three years in advance their intention to apply for citizenship. By 1798, the Federalists, now quite convinced that foreign radicals were a danger to national security and to their political control of the national government, secured provisions that required aliens to register their arrival in the United States and increased the residency requirement for citizenship from five to fourteen years. Simultaneously, the Alien and Sedition Acts allowed President John Adams to bar dangerous aliens and to limit speech and press to protect public peace and stability.

The Republicans protested the Federalist initiatives of 1798 and made them a major issue in the presidential election of 1800, in which Thomas Jefferson defeated incumbent President John Adams. Jefferson, once an opponent of easy immigration, warned in his annual message to Congress in early December 1801, "Considering the ordinary chances of human life, a denial of citizenship under a residence of 14 years is a denial to a great proportion of those who ask it." He closed by asking, "shall we refuse the unhappy fugitives from distress that hospitality which the savages of the wilderness extended to our fathers arriving in this land? Shall oppressed humanity find no asylum on this globe?"[62] The Jeffersonian Congress of 1802 responded by reducing the residency requirement from fourteen years back to five years. Congress retained the three-year declaration of intent, the renunciation of all foreign allegiances, and the requirement that prospective citizens swear allegiance to the Constitution. These requirements remained the foundation of U.S. naturalization policy throughout the nineteenth century. The whites-only restriction was removed in the immediate wake of the Civil War, but within just a few years, new provisions were in place that kept nonwhite immigration small into the mid-twentieth century.

The Faces of Exclusion

The fight for liberty is the dominant theme of the nation's early history. Yet those who participated directly and benefited fully were a growing but initially narrow band of propertied white men. Others were excluded for reasons that the Founding generation thought obvious—even "self-evident." The Founders' survey of history showed that no republic in the ancient or modern world had ever been equally free to everyone. Defining freedom and equality in terms of economic independence—the possession of sufficient property to attest an ongoing stake in the community—drew a sharp line between citizens and mere inhabitants. The vast majority of white American men of the revolutionary generation thought that members of dependent classes lacked property because they lacked the requisite characteristics and virtues to compete successfully for it. They thought that women, children, slaves, idiots, and propertyless white men all lacked the capacity for independent judgment and rational planning that led to property, autonomy, and security. Hence, half a million slaves, virtually all women, and many poor and dependent white men were outside the "imagined community" of American citizens at the Founding.

Few white voices were raised against slavery in America before the 1770s. Perhaps the most principled opponent of slavery among the revolutionary generation was Philadelphia's Benjamin Rush. Rush was a prominent physician, an intimate of Franklin, and a wide-ranging intellect. As the debate over American liberty raged in the Philadelphia press, Rush challenged the patriots, saying; "Ye men of SENSE and VIRTUE—Ye ADVOCATES for American liberty, rouse up and espouse the cause of Humanity and general Liberty." Rush argued that the patent differences that white men thought they saw between themselves and their black slaves should be attributed to the effects of slavery rather than to permanent natural endowments. "Slavery is so foreign to the human mind," Rush declared, "that the moral faculties, as well as those of the understanding are debased, and rendered torpid by it. All the vices which are charged upon the Negroes, . . . such as Idleness, Treachery, Theft, and the like, are the genuine offspring of slavery."[63] Yet Rush's was a lonely voice.

Thomas Jefferson best reflected the terrible ambivalence that pervaded the American mind as it confronted the issue of slavery during the Founding and early national periods. Jefferson was never with Rush in believing that the differences between blacks and whites were simply a reflection of slavery, but he did think that the ideals of the Revolution were incompatible with slavery and that slavery should therefore be reassessed. His reassessment of the place of slavery in America reached emancipation, but the idea of a peaceful, prosperous, biracial society seemed inconceivable to him. Unless the freed slaves could be sent out of the country—Africa or South America were likely destinations—he could see no way to proceed. Hence, he slowly backed away from emancipation. Given Jefferson's commitment to liberty and equality, and given the wide respect in which he was held, his rejection of black freedom and equality reverberated for decades.

In *Notes on the State of Virginia* Jefferson drew on faculty psychology to offer tentative but stark observations that summed to black inferiority. He compared blacks to whites on emotions, passions, and intellect. Jefferson reported the universal sense—including among blacks, he said—that whites were more beautiful, elevated, and refined. Jefferson thought blacks "dull, tasteless, and anomalous" in imagination and emotion, and hence less capable than whites of love of family and community. As regards intellect, he thought whites well superior to blacks in reason, and hence in the powers of foresight, reflection, and planning. He concluded that whereas whites, or at least the best among them, responded to reason, blacks were governed by "sentiment and sensation."[64]

Moreover, Jefferson thought that events had long since moved beyond the possibility of a multiracial society in America. More likely, he thought, force would decide the fate of blacks and whites. Jefferson's sadly observed, "Nothing is more certainly written in the book of fate than that these people are to be free. Nor is it less certain that the two races, equally free, cannot live in the same government. Nature, habit, opinion has drawn indelible lines of distinction between them."[65] Elsewhere he concluded, "Deep rooted prejudices entertained by whites; ten thousand recollections, by the blacks, of the injuries they have sustained; . . . will divide us into parties, and produce convulsions which will probably never end but in the extermination of the one or the other race"[66] (Figure 3.4).

Nonetheless, American independence did bring some progress for blacks, although mostly where it made the least difference. In 1780 blacks made up less than 3 percent of New England's population, about 8 percent in the middle states, and nearly 40 percent in the South. In the northern and middle states during the 1780s and 1790s, courts and legislatures tentatively embraced emancipation. A few slaves won their freedom by arguing before the Massachusetts Supreme Court that the provision of the Massachusetts Constitution of 1780 declaring that all men were born free and equal made slavery illegal. More

Figure 3.4. "To Be Sold, Negroes," 1780s. Advertisement from a Charleston, South Carolina, newspaper reports a slave sale to be held at nearby Ashley Ferry around 1780. (Library of Congress, Prints and Photographs Division, reproduction LC-USZ62-10293)

generally, every state from Pennsylvania north initiated gradual emancipation by passing laws that declared that all children born to slaves after a certain date (the dates varied by state) would be free at maturity. But emancipation did not mean equality. States frequently denied free blacks civil, economic, and social equality. Every state that entered the union after 1800, except Maine, limited the franchise to white men, and many of the original states, including Connecticut, New York, New Jersey, Pennsylvania, and Maryland, moved in the early decades of the nineteenth century to bar free blacks from voting. Free blacks were commonly denied the right to serve in the militia or to sue or testify in court, and most libraries, schools, and professional training and licensing programs were closed to them.[67]

Like blacks, women were thought to differ from men in natural capacity. While men were equipped for the public marketplace and forum, the natural talents and instincts of women fitted them for domestic life. Still, women found it hard to avoid politics as war loomed. John Jay's wife, Sarah, deeply concerned about the growing tumult around her, was also aware that politics and war were not women's traditional business. When her correspondence first turned to politics, she pulled back, asking, "But whither, my pen, are you hurrying me? What have I to do with politicks? Am I not myself a woman, and writing to Ladies? Come then, the fashions to my assistance." As the conflict grew, the wall that stood between women and the political world began to crack. In subsequent correspondence, Sarah Jay became somewhat less inhibited, saying, "I've transgressed the line that I proposed to observe in my correspondence by slipping into politicks, but my country and my friends possess so entirely my thought that you must not wonder if my pen runs beyond the dictates of prudence."[68]

The most famous exchange of the Founding period over the relations between the sexes occurred between John and Abigail Adams in the spring of 1776. John had been in Congress off and on for almost two years, the British had occupied Boston and now held New York City, and Abigail had been managing the family's affairs in Boston and Braintree. Abigail Adams, it must be said, was intelligent, articulate, and engaged well beyond the expectations of her time. She opened her letter of March 31, 1776, by scolding John for not sending more political news and saying, "I long to hear that you have declared an independency." Abigail then went on to remind her congressman husband to "Remember the Ladies" when it comes time to write "a new Code of Laws." She asked John to see that America's lawmakers "be more generous and favorable . . . than your ancestors. Do not put such unlimited power into the hands of the husbands. Remember, all Men would be tyrants if they could . . . but such of you as wish to be happy willingly give up the harsh title of Master for the more tender and endearing one of Friend. Why then, not put it out of the power of the vicious and Lawless to use us with cruelty. . . . Regard us then as Beings placed by providence under your protection and in imitation of the Supreme Being make use of that power only for our happiness." Abigail's letter is a wonderful mix of the assertiveness of an intelligent woman, the plaintiveness of one who knows that the operative cultural assumptions are not on her side, and resort to arguments from utilitarianism and traditional religion for whatever they might be worth.

John's reply of April 14, 1776, is the classic evasion of justice by power. Rather than confront Abigail on the merits, he sought refuge in levity, saying, "As to your extraordinary Code of Laws, I cannot but laugh. . . . We have only the Name of Masters, and [to] give up this . . . would completely subject Us to the Despotism of the Petticoat." Only in a separate letter of May 26, 1776, to John Sullivan, did John Adams adopt the standard defense for the legal subjection of women to men. The common sense of the matter was that women's "delicacy renders them unfit for practice and experience in the great businesses of life, and the hardy enterprises of war, as well as the arduous care of the state. Besides, their attention is so much engaged with the necessary nurture of their children, that nature has made them fittest for domestic care."[69]

Although we might expect the conservative Adams to laugh away the demand for greater rights, the liberal Jefferson was just as determined to maintain the traditional homebound role of women in the American society. As late as 1788, Jefferson found the comparison of French women to American women to be between "Amazons and Angels." He criticized French women for neglecting their domestic duties and "hunting pleasure in the streets." He praised American women for being "contented to soothe and calm the minds of their husbands returning ruffled from political debates." American women had "the good sense to value domestic happiness above all other, and the art to cultivate it beyond all others."[70]

Traditional male attitudes, such as those displayed by Adams and Jefferson, did not go unchallenged. The strongest challenge came from Judith Sargent Murray in a 1790 essay "On the Equality of the Sexes." Murray adopted the dominant social science theory of her day, faculty psychology, to question the basis of male superiority. Murray argued that although women were thought to have weaker powers of reason and stronger emotions than men, this was a function of nurture, education, and clearly communicated social expectations, rather than permanent differences of nature. Murray asked, "Is it upon mature consideration we adopt the idea, that nature is thus partial in her distributions? Is it indeed a fact, that she has yielded to one half of the human species so unquestionable a mental superiority?" "Are we deficient in reason?" She answered, no, women were equal in reason, imagination, and memory and would be equal in wisdom and judgment if appropriately trained and educated. "We can only reason from what we know, and if opportunity of acquiring knowledge has been denied us, the inferiority of our sex cannot fairly be deduced from thence." Boys are early "taught to aspire" while girls are "confined and limited." The *apparent* superiority" of men comes from the better education of boys. Thorough education of boys and girls would result not in women becoming more like men, more aggressive, competitive, and demanding, but in being more fulfilled and satisfied women and, hence, better homemakers and better mates for men. "Yes, ye lordly, ye haughty sex, our souls are by nature *equal* to yours."

Under the pressure of events and of arguments like Murray's that drew on the dominant social science of the day, the general understanding of women's role in society slowly evolved from subject to limited partner. Public life, the rough and tumble of politics, business, and war remained the purview of men due to their natural capacities for planning, competition, and conflict. But women's role and responsibilties in the home took on new social and political import. "Republican motherhood" suggested that the future of the republic depended on the effectiveness with which wives provided sterling examples of virtue to their husbands and mothers instilled religion, good habits and manners, knowledge, and patriotism in their sons and daughters. Although women's role was to remain within the familiar confines of the home, it was nonetheless critical to the nation's future, and to fulfill it well required hard work, dedication, intelligence, and importantly—education. Still, women's legal position changed little between 1775 and 1825. Women remained *femme covert* in law. They were legal appendages of their superintending male, their father before marriage and their husband afterward, which meant that absent special arrangements, they could not own property, earn wages, or appear in court on their own behalf. Property-owning women, usually widows, who had been allowed to vote in New Jersey since 1776, were barred from voting in 1807. On the other hand, legal provision for divorce became more common, although the grounds for divorce were usually limited to adultery and long-term abandonment.

Finally, the spreading market economy and the rise of manufacturing in the early decades of the nineteenth century presented both difficulties and opportunities for women. Hard-pressed New England farmers could often support a hard-working son, but daughters could best help the family by leaving, at least until marriage, for paid work in town. Most women still did piecework in the home, but by 1816 the textile industry in New England employed "66,000 women, 24,000 boys, and 10,000 adult men."[71] Although jobs open to women involved long hours and low pay, they did promise some autonomy and independence.

While women and slaves both provided services that white men could appreciate, Indians did not. The Declaration of Independence's reference to "Indian savages" was warning enough that Native Americans stood in the way of America's advance. Most white Americans believed that the only way to protect frontier settlements was to remove Indians from the path of progress. William Henry Drayton, leader of the revolutionary forces in South Carolina, encouraged his state's militia to clear Indians as well as the British from the state. Drayton reminded his commanders: "It is expected you will make smooth work as you go—that is you cut up every Indian cornfield, and burn every Indian town—and that every Indian taken shall be the slave and property of the taker; that the nation be extirpated, and the lands become the property of the public." Drayton assured his troops that he would never agree to peace with the Indians "upon any other terms than their removal beyond the mountains."[72]

The settlers that poured west in the wake of the Revolution were in constant conflict with the Indians and looked to the new government for protection. The federal government made literally dozens of treaties with the various Indian tribes to gain access to new land, but it was never enough. Settlers inevitably sought out the best land, whether the Indians had given up title to it or not, settled on it, came into conflict with the offended Indians, and called for government aid. Jefferson initially hoped that Indians could be assimilated into the white population by adoption of a settled agricultural life, education, and intermarriage. If Indians chose not to adopt white ways and join the general culture, they were to be expropriated and removed in favor of white cultivators. Most Americans were unwilling to leave Indians the option of retaining their lands. Jefferson soon concluded that Indian removal beyond the Mississippi was the only viable solution.

By the time Jefferson left the presidency in 1809, settlers, soldiers, and treaty negotiators had forced Indians off 48,000,000 acres in the east, and fewer than 4,000 Indians remained in what had been the Northwest Territory. Further south, the Indians were still numerous enough to consider resistance. The Shawnee war chief, Tecumseh (1768–1813), sought to rally the southern tribes and lead them into coalition with the British in the war of 1812. Tecumseh warned the council called to consider war that they could fight for their traditional lands and freedoms or become the white man's slaves: "Do they not even kick and strike us as they do their black-faces? How long will it be before they will tie us to a post and whip us, and make us work for them in their corn fields as they do them?" To warriors who would not choose slavery, Tecumseh offered a stark choice: "let us by unity of action destroy them all . . . War or extermination is now our only choice."[73]

White leaders saw the ongoing conflict in equally stark terms. Andrew Jackson, major general of the Tennessee militia and soon to be commanding general of the Southern Division of the United States Army, rallied whites to the defense of the frontier. General Jackson warned readers of the *Nashville Tennessean* on September 29, 1813, "Your frontier is threatened with invasion by a savage foe! Already do they advance toward your frontier, with their scalping knives unsheathed, to butcher your wives, your children, and your helpless babes. Time is not to be lost! We must hasten to the frontier, or we will find it drenched in the blood of our fellow-citizens."[74]

With these fierce warriors, Tecumseh and Jackson, both convinced that the future of their people hung in the balance and that only war could decide the issue, the fate of the Indians was sealed. Jackson defeated the southern Indians, negotiated the forfeiture of most of their lands in the east, and limited them to narrow tracts among the white settlers. Tecumseh was killed in battle near Thamesville, Ontario, on October 5, 1813, while in command of the right wing of a British force facing an American army led by Jackson's northern counterpart, another future president, General William Henry Harrison. Soon Jackson would be a national hero, victor in the Battle of New Orleans, and in little more than a decade, the Indians would be facing Andrew Jackson as president. President Jackson, long an advocate of Indian removal beyond the Mississippi, made removal national policy.

The Dream Expanded: The Democratizing Visions of Jackson and Lincoln

Society is full of excitement; competition comes in place of monopoly; and intelligence and industry ask only for fair play and an open field.
—Daniel Webster, in Congress, 1823–24

The middle decades of the nineteenth century, from the rise of Andrew Jackson to the assassination of Abraham Lincoln, spanned the boisterous adolescence of the American Dream. Andrew Jackson promised that every white man willing to earn bread by the sweat of his brow would enjoy a full and honorable role in the civic life of his community. Government was to clear the field for competition and ensure that neither privilege nor prejudice affected the results as men pursued their dreams. Although land in the woods was still the dream of most, the sense of agrarian limits began to fall away as men looked to new opportunities in business, trade, and manufactures. Americans saw an endlessly promising future in a nation that was both pushing steadily west and pulling the three great regions—North, South, and West—together with bands of water and steel. Young Abraham Lincoln's progress from rail splitter, to store clerk, to reading law and standing for office, on his way to becoming a successful railroad lawyer and candidate for the nation's highest offices, seemed a glowing vindication of Jackson's promise. But the mature Lincoln saw further than Jackson and sought to use government to expand opportunity into new realms. Lincoln believed that men and women who sweat for bread, irrespective of their color, deserved the full benefit of their labor. Yet even Lincoln was not yet ready to endorse social equality for blacks.

Despite Jackson's fight for white equality and Lincoln's for black freedom, most white men in antebellum America were referring only to themselves when they talked about freedom and opportunity. American Indians were driven beyond the Mississippi during the 1830s. Slavery's grip was tightened as the Civil War approached, and every social, political, and legal effort was made to teach free blacks, northern and southern, that they were not Americans in any meaningful sense of the word. Women, though, were permitted a few legal gains beginning in the late 1830s, mostly on property rights, only to be denied full civic and suffrage rights when these were granted to black men in the wake of the war. The broad achievement of freedom and opportunity for white men made the exclusion of women and minorities even more glaring as Lincoln rose to the herculean task of redefining human rights in America. How did Americans view their changing world in the years between Jackson's rise and Lincoln's tragic fall?

Young Dreamers and the World Before Them

John Adams and Thomas Jefferson, the second and third presidents of the United States, died within hours of each other on July 4, 1826. The symbolism of these two great men succumbing together on the fiftieth anniversary of the nation's independence produced a sustained period of national introspection and analysis.[1] Massachusetts congressman, soon to be senator, Daniel Webster spoke for a national consensus that the Founders had done their work well. Like so many American leaders, before and after, Webster was certain that the world was watching: "The world turns hither its solicitous eyes. . . . It cannot be denied . . . that with America, and in America, a new era commences in human affairs. . . . If we cherish the virtues and the principles of our fathers, Heaven will assist us to carry on the work of human liberty and human happiness."[2]

Jefferson and Adams passed from a world that had become increasingly foreign to them. Just eighteen months before his death, Jefferson had lamented in correspondence with another old friend, "All, all dead, and ourselves left alone amidst a new generation whom we know not, and who knows not us."[3] Jefferson still viewed the world through the lens of faculty psychology, which held that only a few superior men were guided by reason while most were at the mercy of their interests and passions. Hence, he was particularly dismayed at the rise of a raucous partisan politics that seemed to deny the very existence of a common good or a public interest. Jefferson believed that his Democratic-Republican Party had been necessary only to defeat and guard against the resurgence of the Federalist faction of the New England commercial elite. Martin Van Buren and those around him in the Jackson movement were the first to understand that well-organized political parties could be permanent vehicles for contesting elections, winning office, and enacting the views of the majority, even a narrow partisan majority, into law. The Whigs found that they had to match the Democrats' party organization and electoral techniques if they were to compete with them in the electorate.

Alexis de Tocqueville (1805–59), widely acknowledged to have been the most insightful and prescient foreign observer ever to study the American society, declared equality to be America's "ruling passion." In Jacksonian America, Tocqueville declared, "equality is the distinguishing characteristic of the age . . . it creates opinions, gives birth to new sentiments, founds novel customs, and modifies whatever it does not produce."[4] Tocqueville also coined the word *individualism* to help describe what he saw in America. He defined individualism as "a mature and calm feeling, which disposes each member of the community to sever himself from the mass of his fellows and to draw apart with his family and his friends, so that . . . he willingly leaves society at large to itself." Individualism produced in Americans "the habit of always consider-ing themselves as standing alone, and they are apt to imagine that their whole destiny is in their own hands."[5] Americans also saw their society as egalitar-ian and individualistic. The poet Ralph Waldo Emerson (1803–82), in an essay entitled "The American Scholar" (1837), declared that a leading "sign of our times . . . is the new importance given to the single person. Every thing . . . tends to insulate the individual,—to surround him with barriers of natural respect, so that each man shall feel the world is his."[6] William Ellery Chan-ning's famous essay, entitled "Self-Culture" (1838), declared, "men are now learning to . . . determine for themselves . . . and the results must be, a delib-erateness and independence of judgment, and a thoroughness and extent of information, unknown in former times."[7] American men thought they knew more and could see further and deeper into their world than men had known and seen before; their chests swelled with confidence, pride, and determina-tion. The world seemed to welcome their efforts.

The energy pulsing through the American society was palpable throughout the antebellum period. Total population continued to expand at a remarkable rate of 35 percent per decade from 1830 to 1860.[8] Thirteen million inhabitants in 1830 became more than 31 million by 1860. Population growth drove further expansion during the second quarter of the nineteenth century. Texas declared its independence from Mexico on March 2, 1836. President Jackson recognized Texas as a free republic in March 1837, but it was not until 1845 that Texas was admitted to the union and President Polk sent troops to secure disputed territory along the Rio Grande. The ensuing war with Mexico resulted not only in the acquisition of Texas but also in the conquest of what is now the southwestern United States and California. Almost simultaneously, Polk secured clear title to the Oregon Territory from Britain. The acquisition of Texas and all of the territory from the Rocky Mountains to the Pacific filled out the United States to its current continental boundaries. The westward population flow that pushed through Kentucky, Tennessee, and Ohio into Indiana and Illinois in the early decades of the century spread to the northwest and southwest after 1830. Michigan grew sevenfold in the 1830s, Wisconsin grew tenfold in the 1840s, and Minnesota grew thirtyfold in the 1850s. The old southwest grew rapidly too, but not as rapidly as the old northwest. During the 1830s, the population of Alabama doubled, that of Mississippi almost tripled, and that of Arkansas tripled. Missouri's population nearly doubled in both the 1840s and 1850s, Arkansas's population more than doubled in both decades, and that of Texas tripled in the 1850s.

Americans became movers and searchers in the eighteenth century, but the distances over which they ranged expanded dramatically as the nineteenth century reached its midpoint. The discovery in 1845 that wagons could cross the Rockies at South Pass turned a trickle of settlers beyond the Mississippi into a flood. Beginning in 1846 huge wagon trains formed up at Independence, Missouri, to follow the Platte west to South Pass and then on to the Oregon Territory or south at Fort Hall, Idaho, to northern California. Other wagon trains headed south into southern California by way of Santa Fe. Then in 1848 gold was discovered near San Francisco, and 100,000 farmers, day laborers, and storekeepers dropped what they were doing to pursue their dreams of adventure and riches in the West. California's Anglo population exploded from a few thousand in 1848 to nearly 100,000 in 1850 and then quadrupled during the 1850s. Further discoveries a decade later in Nevada and the northern Rockies brought hundreds of thousands and then millions more into the far west. The discovery of oil at Titusville, Pennsylvania, in 1859 drew a few back east, but by that time, the United States bestrode the continent.

Immigration also fueled population growth, economic development, and westward expansion. Immigration averaged only about 8,000 per year from 1775 to 1825 before expanding rapidly in the late 1820s. The 1830s brought an average of 54,000 each year, the 1840s brought 143,000 each year, and the 1850s brought 281,000 each year. Almost 5 million immigrants came to America between 1830 and 1860. Most of the new immigrants, like those that had come before, were from England, Ireland, and Germany. The English and the Irish settled in the eastern cities, with the English integrating easily and the Irish often forming an urban underclass subject to considerable discrimination. The Germans usually passed through the eastern cities on their way to take up land in the Midwest. Fully 85 percent of immigrants chose the North or West, with just 15 percent settling in the South.

Free white men in the age of Jackson, native and immigrant, saw opportunity everywhere. Just as important, opportunity took a modest scale that common men approached with confidence. The scale of economic opportunity was set by the speed and efficiency of transportation and communication. Raw materials and finished goods had to be moved by wagon or water and advertisement was limited to letters, handbills, and newspapers. Hence, early nineteenth-century businesses were sole proprietorships, or partnerships, and the owners provided the capital. Proprietors were usually merchants or master craftsmen, and their employees were, formally or informally, apprentices learning the business or trade before launching out on their own. The proprietor and the business were very closely identified, and his reputation depended equally on his personal and business integrity. But unprecedented change was looming on the horizon. The second quarter of the century brought technological developments that allowed businesses that had been local, or at most regional, to move goods more cheaply, at greater speeds, over longer distances, and to communicate instantaneously with distant suppliers and buyers. Bigger businesses required more capital and new forms of organization. The corporation became the dominant form of business organization, first in banking and insurance, then in shipping, canals, and railroads, and finally in capital-intensive businesses such as iron and steel manufacturing. The corporate form allowed multiple investors to pool their capital for a particular business endeavor without encumbering all of their assets or being fully and personally responsible for the conduct or financial fate of the business.

In 1825 the Erie Canal opened, linking the Great Lakes to the Hudson River and New York City. By 1827 the Ohio Canal system was pushed through to Lake Erie, connecting the agricultural Midwest to the commercial and manufacturing East. Railroads were chartered in New York, Maryland, and South Carolina, and by 1830 steam locomotives were carrying freight and passengers on regularly scheduled runs. The first miles of track connected city harbors to nearby warehouse districts, then to nearby waterways to serve barge traffic, and finally overland to connect cities and compete directly with the canals.[9] The rail network was 23 miles in 1830, 2,818 miles by 1840, 9,021 by 1850, and 30,626 by 1860. The railroad reached Pittsburgh by late 1852 and the Mississippi River by 1857. The thickening network of turnpikes, barges, steamships, and railroads dramatically reduced transportation costs and expanded business opportunities. Canal and railroad building and the commerce that followed slowly shifted the focus of the economy from agriculture to manufacturing and from dependence on Europe to the development of the domestic economy. Urbanization accompanied this process as the migration from the countryside to the cities got underway.

Railroads epitomized the new "machine age," but mechanization spread throughout the economy. For example, the McCormick reaper, developed in the 1840s, reduced the time required to harvest an acre of wheat from twenty hours to one. Similarly, the Singer sewing machine, introduced in the late 1850s, reduced the time required to make a shirt from twelve hours to less than one. The $65 for the sewing machine and the $100 for the harvester were big investments in an era when a prosperous farm might clear $300 a year, but the gains in productivity were immense, and few who could manage the payments were willing to do without them.

Fundamentally, life sped up in antebellum America, and the forces active in society got bigger, stronger, and more complex. To some, the new size and speed spelled opportunity, but for many it was disturbing, even threatening. Farmers and craftsmen who had worked on their own account, owned their own tools, and set their own schedules were proud of their independence and autonomy. They felt a threatening loss of control when shops and factories set their hours, owned the machines on which they worked, paid them a fixed wage, and fired them when they were no longer needed. To many, the very equality that characterized the age of Jackson seemed endangered by these developments. It was not just that the nation was booming, but the scale of business, the ferocity of competition, and the rewards of winning were all burgeoning. Hence, equality of opportunity came under pressure from the growing inequality of results. Everyone dreamed big, a few won big, and many, if not most, worried that they might be left behind.

The American Dream from Jackson to Lincoln

The Jeffersonian dream was of a bountiful country that would provide sufficiency and even plenty to all who were willing to work. A productive agricultural economy, in which land was cheap and easily available, also ensured high wages for young laborers and a market for the goods of village craftsmen and urban merchants. Once Jefferson made peace with the idea that manufacturing, as well as trade and agriculture, was required to make America a self-sufficient society, his domestic vision became one of a balanced and diversified economy of competitive small producers. The character traits most admired in Franklin's tradesman and Jefferson's farmer were hard work, honesty, frugality, and resilience. Decentralized competition between small producers promised widespread opportunity without runaway jealousy, competition, and greed. Foresight, planning, and careful accumulation might lead beyond sufficiency to comfort and even plenty, but sufficiency was the promise and the general expectation.

The Jacksonians tried to hold to these traditional Jeffersonian ideals, but they were overwhelmed by the onrush of a vastly more competitive and entrepreneurial age. Antebellum America was a place of immense energy, movement, and optimism. *Exuberance* seems like the best word to describe the confident assertion that the day of the common man had arrived, that the world was new, and that the opportunities for growth, improvement, and achievement had no limits near enough that a man need worry about them. Encomiums to the boundless optimism and enthusiasm of the age filled the popular press as well as the elite opinion and literature of the day. A long article published in the *New York Sun* in 1838 celebrated the new age of equality and individualism: "Boys . . . are educated in the belief that every man must be the architect of his own future. . . . Dreams of ambition or of wealth" danced in the head of every young American. "There is scarcely a lad of any spirit who does not, from the time he can connect the most simple ideas, picture to himself some rapid road to wealth."[10]

Andrew Jackson shared fully in the excitement and enthusiasm of the day. Jackson rose from obscurity. Orphaned early and thinly educated, he arrived in Nashville at 21 and immersed himself in the western scramble for wealth, prominence, and prestige. Although the economic turmoil of the frontier left Jackson in debt well into his 40s, prominence and prestige came early. He was a congressman, federal judge, and senator in his 30s and the architect of the smashing American victory in the Battle of New Orleans in his 40s. Thereafter, he was simply known as "the hero" by his friends and supporters. As the revolutionary generation passed from politics in the 1820s, the nascent democratic forces of the day rallied around Andrew Jackson.[11] Richard Hofstadter described "the typical American" of the second quarter of the nineteenth century as "an expectant capitalist, a hardworking, ambitious person for whom enterprise was a kind of religion, and everywhere he found conditions that encouraged him to extend himself."[12] Andrew Jackson claimed that all that stood in the way of the hopeful and expectant many were the pampered and privileged few. Once Jackson was elected president, "the hero" was referred to simply as "the government"[13] (Figure 4.1).

Like Jefferson, Jackson held that class conflict was a permanent part of social life. Jackson believed that small producers were solid, dependable, contributing members of society. "The real people," or "the producing classes," were the planters and farmers, small merchants and businessmen, craftsmen and mechanics, that raised, made, or sold real goods, usually in the local marketplace. These virtuous citizens were simple, hardworking, frugal, honest, and self-reliant. Their wealth grew incrementally. Opposed to the producing classes were the "nonproducing classes," who lived by promotion, trade, and speculation in paper representations of real assets. These were men with soft hands and hard hearts. They were the bankers, merchants, speculators, and corporate stockjobbers who benefited by the mysteries of finance at the expense of those who grew the crops and built the machines. Amos Kendall, an influential journalist and member of President Jackson's "kitchen cabinet," warned, "Those who produce all wealth, are themselves left poor. They see principalities extending and palaces built around them, without being aware that the entire expense is a tax upon themselves."[14] President Jackson also believed that the nonproducing classes, with their command of the economic and social high ground of corporations, colleges, and churches, bent politics, law, and policy to their advantage. He declared in the famous message vetoing the recharter of the Bank of the United States that "it would be an unqualified blessing" if government "would confine itself to equal protection, and, as Heaven does its rains, shower its favors alike on the high and the low, the rich and the poor."[15] As "the government," Jackson intended that his administration be "an unqualified blessing" to America's striving multitudes.

Orestes A. Brownson, Jacksonian minister, author, and editor, summarized the major political and policy turn of the period by declaring, "We believe property should be held subordinate to man, and not man to property, and

Figure 4.1. "President's Levee, or All Creation Going to the White House," 1829, by Robert Cruikshank. Democracy is on the rise as President Andrew Jackson threw the White House open to the public during his inaugural celebration, 1829. (Library of Congress, Prints and Photographs Division, reproduction LC-USZ62-1805)

therefore that it is always lawful to make such modifications of its constitution as the good of Humanity requires."[16] But as Brownson well knew, property, the dollar, and the market had the means to defend themselves and win advantages. Brownson's image of a balance between the man and the dollar, between human rights and property rights, would be a continuous theme in partisan politics for the next century and more. The Jacksonian dream was of free white men, competing on a fair field, without artificial penalty or privilege, for the benefits held out by a boundlessly wealthy continent.

Jacksonian America's most famous visitor was Alexis de Tocqueville. Tocqueville's *Democracy in America* (1835) has long been seen as the most insightful book ever written on the American society and democracy. Alexis de Tocqueville was a young French nobleman sent by his government to study American prisons. Expanding his mandate vastly, Tocqueville pondered America in the flow of time. He and his companion, Beaumont, spent nine months, May 1831 through February 1832, covering a 7,000-mile circuit that took them throughout the east, as far west as Green Bay, and as far south as

New Orleans. Tocqueville believed that western civilization was on a providential path toward democracy. America had arrived in the democratic future first, but France and the rest of Europe would surely follow, and the path might be smooth or rocky, depending on whether the Europeans learned from the American experience. Tocqueville hoped that if Europe learned well, it might produce a fuller and richer democracy than the one he studied in America.

America was, for Tocqueville, a joint project in which God and man were crafting the future. America seemed "as if it had been kept in reserve by the Deity" for a special experiment in freedom and opportunity. He said, "I see the destiny of America embodied in the first Puritan who landed on these shores ... Their ancestors gave them the love of equality and of freedom; but God himself gave them the means of remaining equal and free, by placing them upon a boundless continent." He marveled that the "gradual and continuous progress of the European race towards the Rocky Mountains has the solemnity of a providential event; it is like a deluge of men rising unabatedly and daily driven onwards by the hand of God." Elsewhere, he noted, "Millions of men are marching at once toward the same horizon; ... Fortune has been promised to them somewhere in the West, and to the West they go to find it"[17] (Figure 4.2).

Like Crevecoeur, Tocqueville assured the immigrant that America held out promise for them too. Although Europe was settled and staid, Tocqueville declared, "America is a land of wonders, in which everything is in constant motion and every change seems an improvement. . . . No natural boundary seems to be set to the efforts of man." That millions of Americans were moving west meant that immigrants might find opportunity in the east as well as on the frontier. "The European emigrant always lands . . . in a country that is but half full, and where hands are in demand; he becomes a workman in easy circumstances, his son goes on to seek his fortune in unpeopled regions and becomes a rich landowner. The former amasses the capital which the latter invests; and the stranger as well as the native is unacquainted with want."[18]

The partnership between God and man was one in which God held the continent in trust, directed Europe's first advocates of liberty to it, and set their gaze to the west, but it was up to men to build and nurture democracy. Tocqueville was both hopeful and concerned for America. Fundamentally, he thought that freedom and opportunity had come so easily to Americans that they were by turns arrogant, desperate, and timid. The uncritical arrogance came from the widespread sense, in which Tocqueville obviously shared, that

Figure 4.2. This classic representation of the American spirit of Manifest Destiny, variously entitled "American Progress," "Westward the Course of Destiny," "Westward Ho," and "Manifest Destiny," is from an original 1872 John Gast painting. Note the pioneers leading settlement forward and pushing the Indians and buffalo before them. (Library of Congress, Prints and Photographs Division, reproduction LC-USZ62-737)

America was blessed. He complained, "For the last fifty years no pains have been spared to convince the inhabitants of the United States that they are the only religious, enlightened, and free people. . . . hence they conceive a high opinion of their superiority and are not very remote from believing themselves a distinct species of mankind."[19]

On the other hand, the majestic image of America as a land of unlimited opportunity put great pressure on individuals to succeed in visible, if not dramatic, ways. If everyone was on the move, although there was a continent to be won, those who did not move quickly might be left behind. Tocqueville marveled that "It would be difficult to describe the avidity with which the American rushes forward to secure this immense booty that fortune offers. . . . Before him lies a boundless continent, and he urges onward as if time pressed and he was afraid of finding no room for his exertions." The fear of failure,

Tocqueville thought, "may be said to haunt every one of them . . . and to be always flitting before his mind."[20] In the absence of social hierarchy, only wealth gave status, so men worked with dreary determination to acquire and maintain wealth. Tocqueville observed that "It is strange to see with what feverish ardor the Americans pursue their own welfare, and to watch the vague dread that constantly torments them lest they should not have chosen the shortest path which may lead to it." Tocqueville concluded, "In democratic times . . . man's hopes and desires are oftener blasted, the soul is more stricken and perturbed, and care itself more keen."[21]

The timidity that concerned Tocqueville arose because so many aspects of American life made each man feel as good as but no better than his fellows. Hence, when common wisdom and public opinion suggested that the majority of his fellows held to one opinion, Americans seldom had the confidence to voice a different opinion. He said, "freedom of opinion does not exist in America. . . . I know of no country in which there is so little independence of mind and real freedom of discussion as in America."[22] Despite a rigid dedication to work, wealth-getting, and the soft tyranny of public opinion, Tocqueville thought that other forces would keep America just and free. Although church and state were separate in America, Tocqueville thought the Americans were the most religious people in the world. "Thus whilst the law permits the Americans to do what they please, religion prevents them from conceiving, and forbids them to commit, what is rash or unjust." The reason that religion was so influential in America was that it comported so well with the general ethos of the nation. "Religion," Tocqueville said, "is simply another form of hope, and it is no less natural to the human heart than hope itself."[23]

Americans were nothing if not hopeful, and therefore, in Tocqueville's view, they were naturally religious. Many continued to think of America in explicitly religious terms. Herman Melville (1819–91), in *White Jacket, or The World in a Man-of-War* (1850), published the year before *Moby-Dick* (1851), echoed old John Winthrop, writing, "We Americans are the peculiar, chosen people—the Israel of our time; we bear the ark of the liberties of the world. God has predestined, mankind expects, great things from our race; and great things we feel in our souls. . . . We are the pioneers of the world; the advance guard."[24] A chosen people, brought safely to a rich and fruitful continent, could expect to thrive and prosper. But others, while retaining a religious patina to their thought and imagery, expressed themselves in equally dramatic but increasingly secular terms. Just as Paine had proclaimed two generations earlier, Ralph Waldo Emerson (1803–82) believed that American freedom and opportunity heralded a new order in the world. In "The Young American" (1841), Emerson declared, "One thing is plain for all men of common sense and common conscience, that here, here in America, is the home of man." Moreover, Emerson thought that America's role was fit and natural. He said, "It seems so easy for America to inspire and express the most expansive and humane spirit; new-born, free, healthful, strong, the land of the laborer, of the democrat, of the philanthropist, of the believer, of the saint, she should speak for the human race. America is the country of the Future . . . it is a country of beginnings, of projects, of designs, and expectations."[25]

Soon Americans would come dangerously close to worshiping work and making success a religion. Emerson, the preeminent mid-nineteenth-century literary exponent of freedom, opportunity, and wealth, believed that American individualism and self-help was underpinned by a universal appreciation of and commitment to work. In Europe, the disdain of a leisured elite made work seem an unfortunate necessity of the lower classes. In America, Emerson sang, "I hear . . . with joy . . . of the dignity and necessity of labor to every citizen. . . . Labor is everywhere welcome; always we are invited to work." He assured Americans that "the day is always his, who works in it with serenity and great aims."[26] Even pillars of the New England elite such as William Ellery Channing, for nearly 40 years pastor of the Federal Street Congregational Church in Boston, declared, "I belong rightly to the great fraternity of working men. Happily in this community we are all bred and born to work; and this honorable mark, set on us all, should bind together the various portions of the community."[27]

Like Franklin, Emerson sought to teach Americans, especially young Americans, how to succeed and prosper. Both men could communicate volumes in a sentence or a phrase. Franklin's "Poor Richard" is unsurpassed, but Emerson used a similar language and style to communicate the more muscular sense of his age. In place of Franklin's commonsense homilies came Emerson's declaration that "Genius always looks forward," "Man hopes, genius creates," "Greatness appeals to the future," "Insist on yourself; never imitate," "Every great man is a unique," and "Good luck is another name for tenacity of purpose."[28] In his essay "The American Scholar" (1837), Emerson wrote, "if the single man plant himself indomitably on his instincts, and there abide, the huge world will come round to him."[29] In "Self-Reliance" (1841), Emerson praised "the self-helping man. For him all doors are flung wide: him all tongues greet, all honors crown, all eyes follow with desire."[30] Another Emerson essay, "The Young American" (1844), suggested that markets set a fair price on human talent, saying "Trade goes to . . . bring every kind of faculty of every individual that can in any manner serve any person, *on sale.*"[31] Like Franklin, Emerson believed that "The Way to Wealth" was clearly marked and all young men of worth should hurry down that path. His essay on "Wealth" (1860) declared that "the philosophers have laid the greatness of man in making his wants few; but will a man content himself with a hut and a handful of dried pease?" Emerson answered, No! "He is born to be rich." Rather than be satisfied with a little, Emerson declared, "The manly part is to do with might and main what you can do."[32]

With buoyant optimism and confidence, young Americans were urged forward into the world. Emerson extolled "the open future expanding here before the eye of every boy to vastness."[33] The *Cincinnati Gazette* reflected the same exuberant optimism and expectation of ready success in an editorial in 1857, saying, "Of all the multitude of young men engaged in various employments of this city, there is probably not one who does not desire, and even confidently expect, to become rich, and that at an early date."[34] Yet with high expectations came keen disappointments. Emerson noted in his diary, "History gave no intimation of any society in which despondency came so readily to heart as we see it and feel it in ours. Young men, young women at thirty and even earlier seem to have lost all spring and vivacity, and if they fail in their first enterprise the rest is all rock and shallow."[35] Elsewhere, Emerson explained, although seemingly without knowing it, why failure was so keenly feared and felt in Jacksonian America. He observed, "There is always a reason, *in the man,* for his good or bad fortune, and so in making money."[36] If the price a man commanded in the marketplace were low, it obviously meant that his talents were modest. Tremendous opportunity, a continent to be tamed, a world to be built, and achievement all around left no easy place for failure.

Winners taught themselves to believe that losers experienced the fair judgment of free markets and that charity amounted to no more than coddling the weak and ineffectual. Emerson was still learning and just beginning to teach the new lessons of the market economy when he wrote "Self-Reliance" (1841). Of charity, he said, "Are they my poor? I tell thee, thou foolish philanthropist, that I grudge the dollar, the dime, the cent I give to such men as do not belong to me and to whom I do not belong." Charity was "alms to sots . . . though I confess with shame I sometimes succumb and give the dollar, which by and by I shall have the manhood to withhold." By 1860, Emerson had steeled himself. In the essay "Wealth" (1860), he simply declared that "In a free and just commonwealth, property rushes from the idle and imbecile to the industrious, brave and persevering."[37] Individualism and self-help made success a personal triumph, but they just as certainly made failure an excruciatingly personal defeat.

The farm hands and clerks that lit out for California and Colorado in the gold rushes of the 1850s added a go for broke, skies the limit, easy money, boomer element that further sharpened the edges of the American Dream. The scramble to subdue the continent, to be first to the gold in the West or the oil in the East, and the terrible, unremitting, destruction of the Civil War hardened America. Still, some men struggled to maintain their balance within the rush of national events.

Abraham Lincoln (1809–65) saw freedom and opportunity in America more broadly than any of his predecessors, most of his contemporaries, and many of ours. The Lincolns, poor farmers out of North Carolina by way of Kentucky and Indiana, arrived in Illinois in 1830. The Lincolns were not part of the first wave of explorers, hunters, and trappers, but of the second wave of small farmers, storekeepers, and traders in a still very raw frontier environment. Two years earlier, James Hall published *Letters from the West* (1828) about the Illinois of Lincoln's early manhood. In 1820 Illinois had a population of 55,000; by 1830 it was 157,000, and in 1840 it was 476,000. This tripling of population by decade, common throughout the West and exceeded in some times and places, was experienced as an avalanche of human hope and expectation. James Hall wrote that these settlers shared "the same daring soul and inventive genius; and that aptitude or capacity to take advantage of every change."[38] Although the Lincolns were overwhelmingly Jacksonian Democrats, the young Abraham Lincoln cast his first vote against Jackson and for Henry Clay in 1832. Lincoln shared with Clay the sense that it was better to throw the doors of economic growth and opportunity open than to worry that one or a few men might be getting richer than their fellows.[39] But Lincoln was unwavering in his commitment to ensure that the average man had a fair shot at success in the resulting competition.

Several prominent intellectual and cultural traditions came together in Abraham Lincoln and emerged from him transformed and energized. Jefferson and Jackson thought government was commonly a tool of the wealthy and well positioned, so they sought to keep it small and unobtrusive. Hamilton and Clay were eager to use the power of government, but mostly to expand commerce and manufacturing, leaving the little man to scramble for whatever wages the market made available. Lincoln was the first major public figure in American history to use government both to expand the economy and to ensure that "all men" could pursue the resulting benefits and opportunities. Abraham Lincoln, like Theodore Roosevelt and Franklin Delano Roosevelt after him, pursued Jeffersonian ends, the benefit of the small man, through Hamiltonian means, the aggressive use of government to expand economic opportunity.[40]

Lincoln took the mythic ideals of the Declaration of Independence as the foundation for his political career. "The principles of Jefferson are the definitions and axioms of free society," Lincoln believed, but they had never been fully applied; "The Jefferson party were formed upon its supposed superior devotion to the *personal* rights of men, holding the rights of *property* to be secondary only, and greatly inferior." Hamilton's Federalists and Clay's Whigs had made similar charges before pledging themselves to property, always forgetting that there were too few men of wealth and position to win elections. Lincoln was shrewder; he charged that Jackson's Democrats had abandoned Jefferson by concluding that the property rights of southern slaveholders completely eviscerated the human rights of slaves. Lincoln concluded by seizing the traditional Democrat claim to value the man over the dollar, declaring, "Republicans . . . are for both the *man* and the *dollar,* but in case of a conflict, the man *before* the dollar."[41]

Lincoln rarely failed to remind audiences of his own humble origins and of the self-help ideology that he shared with them. To one audience, Lincoln said, "Twenty-five years ago I was a hired laborer. The hired laborer of yesterday labors on his own account today, and will hire others to labor for him tomorrow. Advancement—improvement in condition—is the order of things in a society of equals."[42] Elsewhere, Lincoln described his social ideal as one in which "Men, with their families . . . work for themselves, on their farms, in their houses, and in their shops, taking the whole product to themselves, and asking no favors of capital on one hand nor of hired labor or slaves on the other."[43] Lincoln spoke to and for the great middling range of working Americans, and they trusted him because they knew he had risen from among them.

Lincoln believed that the embedded presence of slavery in the South had prevented the Founding generation from writing the ideals of the Declaration fully into the Constitution. The Declaration's core principal, that "all men are created equal," was compromised in the Constitution's acceptance of slavery, but the principle had not been debased or rejected. The Founders "meant simply to declare the *right,* so that the *enforcement* of it might follow as fast as the circumstances should permit. They meant to set up a standard maxim for free society which could be familiar to all, and revered by all; constantly looked to, constantly labored for, and even though never perfectly attained, constantly approximated, and thereby constantly spreading and deepening its influence, and augmenting the happiness and value of life to all people of all colors every-where."[44] The logic of Lincoln's views on race and the American Dream emerged over the course of a lifetime cut short, so they were never fully real-ized. Nonetheless, they have justly made him an icon of American history.

By the time Lincoln debated Senator Stephen A. Douglas in the Illinois sen-ate contest of 1858, he had concluded that in his "right to eat the bread, with-out leave of anybody else, which his own hand earns," the Negro "is my equal and the equal of Judge Douglas, and the equal of every living man."[45] Elsewhere, Lincoln extended the same right to labor and benefit thereby to the black female slave, saying, "In her natural right to eat the bread she earns with her own hands without asking leave of anyone else, she is my equal and the equal of all others."[46] Douglas won the election, but Lincoln won a national audience for his views. Abraham Lincoln's American Dream was of a nation in which every man, by which he came almost to mean men and women of every color, had an unobstructed chance to rise in society by dint of their own prepa-ration, sagacity, strength, and effort.

When Lincoln reached Washington as the newly elected President of the United States early in 1861, several of the southern states had already gone. He moved immediately to define the coming struggle in the broadest terms. "On the side of the Union," Lincoln declared, "it is a struggle for maintaining in the world, that form, and substance of government, whose leading object is, to elevate the condition of men—to lift artificial weights from all shoulders—to clear the path of laudable pursuit for all—to afford all, an unfettered start, and a fair chance, in the race of life."[47] Abraham Lincoln put the critical word "all" back in Thomas Jefferson's Declaration that "all men are created equal." In so doing, Lincoln opened America's "door of mercy" to persons the society previously had rejected even in their humanity and changed the debate about America's promise and meaning forever.

Abraham Lincoln was the prism through which the light of the American Dream passed to become a purer, broader beam. The American Dream of equality, opportunity, and justice was clear from first settlement, but it was narrowly conceived in the beginning. Lincoln used the Gettysburg Address (1863) to define the Civil War as the next great battle in the ongoing struggle to live up to the nation's values.[48] "Four score and seven years ago," Lincoln reminded his listeners, "our fathers brought forth on this continent, a new nation, conceived in Liberty, and dedicated to the proposition that all men are created equal." It bears noting that "four score and seven years ago"—that is, eighty-seven years before 1863—was 1776. Lincoln continued, "Now we are engaged in a great civil war, testing whether that nation, or any nation so conceived and so dedicated, can long endure." His answer, essentially, was that America would endure not by standing still, but by pressing forward. Hence, he declared, "we here highly resolve that . . . this nation, under God, shall have a new birth of freedom—and that government of the people, by the people, for the people, shall not perish from the earth."[49]

Lincoln was determined to reaffirm the promises of the Declaration of Independence and to more firmly embed them in the Constitution. Moreover, he knew that it would take more time, treasure, and blood to make the Declaration's promise good for all Americans. Hence, his second inaugural address exuded quiet determination to proceed with the work in hand beyond the war and into the nation's future. Lincoln called on his fellow citizens to persevere in the pursuit of justice: "With malice toward none; with charity for all; with firmness in the right, as God gives us to see the right, let us strive on to finish the work we are in; to bind up the nation's wounds; to care for him who shall have borne the battle, and for his widow, and his orphan—to do all which may achieve and cherish a just and lasting peace."[50] Soon, Lincoln was dead and talk of compassion, especially among congressional Republicans, was replaced by cries for vengeance, for domination, and for Reconstruction of the South.

Abraham Lincoln's broad-minded and compassionate presence masked for a time the American Dream's evolution from a vision of independence and sufficiency into a vision of continual striving, competition, consolidation, and accumulation. An honorable life of slow accumulation and frugality seemed to many to be second best to the chance to strike it rich. The line between the free-enterprising entrepreneur and the free-booting robber baron was blurring before the Civil War and was threatened with evisceration in its wake.

The Dream Embedded in Institution, Law, and Policy

Dreams of liberty, equality, and opportunity must be embedded in law and policy about property, voting rights, citizenship, and much more.

How did U.S. law and policy evolve in the era of Jackson and Lincoln? The Democratic Party of Andrew Jackson and his lieutenants, Martin Van Buren and James K. Polk, adhered to the Jeffersonian vision. Jackson harkened back to Jefferson's first inaugural address for his political philosophy, promising "A wise and frugal government, which shall restrain men from injuring one another, shall leave them otherwise free to regulate their own pursuits of industry and improvement, and shall not take from the mouth of labor the bread it has earned." He envisioned an open, competitive, entrepreneurial, environment in which white men had equal political rights and economic opportunities and government elicited no fear and offered no favor. Jackson moved systematically, much as Jefferson had three decades earlier, to kill the Bank of the United States, reduce the tariff, limit federal spending on internal improvements, and make the expanded western territory available for settlement.

Jackson's Whig opponents carried forward Hamilton's vision of a more dynamic, complex, and differentiated economy of farmers, merchants, and mechanics. At the national level, Whig leaders, including Henry Clay, Daniel Webster, and Horace Greeley, supported the traditional conservative agenda of a national bank, a protective tariff, and internal improvements to facilitate the rapid development of a vibrant commercial and manufacturing republic. They believed that government, state and national, should provide leadership, vision, and even capital to improve the commercial, transportation, and communication infrastructure of the economy. They also believed, as Hamilton had, that societies and economies are best led by a social elite of the educated, refined, and prosperous. The prominent Whig journalist and sometime presidential candidate, Horace Greeley, declared, "government . . . should exert a beneficent, paternal, fostering influence upon the Industry and Prosperity of the People."[51] Yet Whigs won the presidency only twice, once behind John Tyler (1841–45) and once behind Zachary Taylor and Millard Fillmore (1849–53). Only during the first two years of Tyler's term did Whigs also control Congress, so they were more a vocal opposition than a consistent threat during the Democratic ascendancy that shaped and molded antebellum America.

"The Democracy," as the Democratic Party of Jackson's day was known, set out to throw the doors of opportunity open to the common man. Throughout the colonial and early national periods, anyone who wished to start a business had to apply to the state legislature or to Congress for a charter. Democrats worried that elitism, with prominent legislators favoring their wealthy friends, tainted the system, while Federalists and Whigs thought that the system of legislatively chartered corporations provided order in the marketplace. Legislative charters did offer generous benefits to those who won them, especially where charter provisions granted protection against competition. But they served other purposes as well. Charters allowed for close regulation of businesses, especially those that provided a public utility or service, like passenger and freight hauling, canals, and railroads. Legislative charters often included provisions that defined the type and quality of service, set and limited fees and fares, and set maintenance, health, and safety requirements. Moreover, legislatures were understood to have the right to revise or repossess previously granted charters if the public interest seemed to demand it.[52]

Federalist concern for the rights of property, championed by Chief Justice John Marshall of the United States Supreme Court, led the court to limit the regulatory authority of state legislatures in the Dartmouth College case (1819). Marshall held in Dartmouth College that legislatively granted charters were contracts, between the state and the corporation, subject to the protection of the contracts clause of the Constitution and reposing certain legal rights in the corporation.[53] Legislatures could award corporate charters, but once awarded, the charter was a contract and could not be revised or withdrawn at the simple discretion of the legislature. Democrats argued that treating charters as contracts gave status, privilege, and property undue advantages.

By 1820 the Federalist party was in sharp decline, and although Marshall stood guard over the judiciary, the nation's commercial interests did not have a distinct partisan voice until the Whig Party coalesced in the 1830s. The Whig economic program, called "the American System," envisioned broad government support for economic growth. The Second Bank of the United States would hold government revenues and manage the nation's supplies of money and credit. The tariff would protect the nation's growing manufacturing sector and provide government funding for internal improvements, such as improving harbors and navigable rivers, building turnpikes and canals, and improving the mails. Wealthy investors and state and national governments would join forces to fund, build, and manage these important enterprises, with assurances of appropriate future returns on investment. These assurances commonly took the form of legislatively granted corporate charters awarding long-term monopolies. Unfortunately, by the time the Whigs became competitive in national elections, Marshall had passed from the scene and the judiciary was in enemy hands.

When Chief Justice Marshall died in 1835, President Andrew Jackson named his advisor and former treasury secretary, Roger B. Taney, to be chief justice. Soon Taney led a new Jacksonian majority on the court. One of the first important cases to come before the Taney court was *Charles River Bridge v. Warren Bridge* (1837), which dealt with private property, the autonomy of corporations, and the regulatory role of legislatures. An exclusive charter to operate a toll bridge across the Charles River between Boston and Cambridge had been awarded to the Charles River Bridge company in 1785. In 1828, as the region grew and bridge traffic increased, the Massachusetts legislature granted a second charter, to the Warren Bridge company, to build and operate a new bridge near the old Charles River Bridge. The charter of the Warren Bridge company allowed it to recoup expenses by charging a toll for a short period, after which use of the bridge would be free. The Charles River Bridge company sued, arguing that its charter constituted a legal monopoly that would be infringed by the competing Warren Bridge.

The Supreme Court found for the new legislature and its second bridge. The Taney court chose not to restore the discretion of legislatures to charter and thereafter regulate specific corporations. Rather, the court favored general charters of incorporation that would allow all citizens to initiate business activity on identical terms. Individuals and communities would benefit from the resulting competition, growth, and innovation. Taney reasoned that "the object and end of all government . . . is to promote the happiness and prosperity of the community by which it was established, and it can never be assumed, that the government intended to diminish its power of accomplishing the end for which it was created." Hence, the Massachusetts legislature of 1785 cannot be assumed to have intended a perpetual monopoly to the Charles River Bridge company even after the community came clearly to need a second bridge. Property, the dollar, has rights, but as Taney wrote on behalf of the court, "the community also have rights, and that the happiness and well-being of every citizen depends on their faithful preservation."[54] Jacksonian legislatures all over America sought to put competition and opportunity in the place of monopoly and privilege without threatening the sanctity of property.

General incorporation acts and free banking statutes were passed in Connecticut and New York in the late 1830s and spread through the rest of the country over the next two decades. These acts meant that any individual or business group that met certain general requirements and standards could open a business, including a canal company, a railroad corporation, or a bank, without going hat in hand to the legislature for permission. These acts generalized the business benefits of the corporate form while removing from it the stain of elite privilege and abusive monopoly power. Once privilege had been put to flight, Jacksonians were eager to use state and local governments to initiate useful projects like canals, mills, and railroads. Such initiatives, in their view, would speed economic development and provide a receptive environment in which as many new men as possible would have the opportunity to build and thrive.

In addition to clearing the way for entrepreneurs, Democrats worried about the vulnerabilities of wage workers in an increasingly monetized economy. In the 1840s, Democrats began supporting the ten-hour workday, as opposed to sunrise to sunset, which might go well over twelve hours in the summer. They also pursued workers' rights in the courts. Federalist courts held that laborers accepting employment effectively entered into a contract that left the employer with full control of the workplace. Workers joining together to seek better conditions or higher pay were declared to be engaged in unlawful conspiracies against the rights of employers and other workers. However, in the landmark case of *Commonwealth v. Hunt* (1840), in which Boston boot makers combined to force their employers to maintain a union shop, Chief Judge Lemuel Shaw affirmed the legality of unions even while limiting the means that workers might use in seeking improved conditions, wages, and benefits.

Democrats consciously used land in the West to give farmers the opportunity to labor on his own behalf, to raise the wages of eastern workers by enticing excess labor toward the frontier, and to draw immigrants to America's factories and farms. Democrats fought the deep economic depression of 1837–42 by following former President Jackson's advice to offer free land in the West "to afford every American citizen of enterprise the opportunity of securing an independent freehold."[55] During the antebellum period, immigration was restricted to whites, but essentially unrestricted for them. Fully two-thirds of all immigrants between 1820 and 1860 entered at the port of New York. Many settled, at least for a time, in the eastern cities, but many more stepped off ships and onto wagons, barges, and trains bound for the Midwest. The nation was booming, expansion was rapid, and settlers were always needed on the frontier. Democrat newspaper editor John O'Sullivan wrote that those who opposed expansion were "limiting our greatness and checking the fulfillment of our manifest destiny to overspread the continent allotted by providence for the free development of our yearly multiplying millions."[56]

The federal government set immigration and naturalization policy, but it was states that actually received the immigrants and determined what rights and privileges they would enjoy during the naturalization process. In fact, the newest states and the territories still seeking statehood were so eager for settlers that they advertised in Europe and in the cities of the East. Promises of free or cheap land and easy citizenship drew the immigrants. In 1848, Wisconsin adopted alien intent, or declarant noncitizen suffrage, allowing aliens to vote who had declared an intention to naturalize and who had lived in the United States for two years and Wisconsin for one. Michigan, Indiana, and Kansas passed similar laws during the next decade, as did the federal government in the territories of Minnesota and Oregon. During the third quarter of the nineteenth century, most southern and western states offered white, male noncitizens the right to vote.[57]

If the Jacksonians were at their best in clearing the way to equality and opportunity for white men, they were at their worst in regard to slavery. Democrats promoted both the geographic expansion of slavery and the legal expansion of slaveholder property rights. The Taney court held, in *Dred Scott v. Sandford* (1857), that southern slave owners could carry their slaves into free states and hold and use them there. The court further declared that blacks, slave or free, could not be citizens of the United States and had "no rights which the white man was bound to respect." Abraham Lincoln returned to politics, first in an unsuccessful senate bid and then in a successful presidential run, to confront slavery's expansion. Ultimately, events forced a reluctant President Lincoln to assert that black Americans did have rights that the white man was bound to respect.

Lincoln's victory in 1860 ended the broad Democratic ascendancy of the Jeffersonian and Jacksonian eras. Lincoln and the Republican Party put the full resources of the federal government, as well as the northern state and local governments, behind economic growth and individual opportunity. The scope and horror of the Civil War has masked the fact that Abraham Lincoln's first term produced one of the greatest outpourings of domestic legislation in American history. With the Democrats in Congress reduced to an inconsequential minority by the withdrawal of most southern members, the Republican majority passed its entire domestic program. Lincoln believed that economic growth fostered independence, opportunity, and self-improvement. A stable currency, adequate credit, protective tariffs, and improvements to transportation and communication infrastructure assured an expanding economy. In such an environment, Lincoln thought, securing "each laborer the whole product of his labor, or as nearly as possible, is a most worthy object of any good government."[58] Abraham Lincoln's practical brilliance was in fashioning a Republican program that made an activist national government the steward of the common man's right to rise in society.

The Republican economic program of the 1860s evinced a strong sense that individual effort had the best chance to succeed if government guaranteed a stable and efficient economic infrastructure for everyone to use. Hence, money, credit, and banking, as well as transportation and communication facilities, including turnpikes, canals, railroads, the telegraph, and the mails, were improved by government action. These improvements facilitated everyone's productivity, innovation, and entrepreneurship. President Lincoln claimed to oppose every law that would "prevent a man from getting rich" and to support every law that would give him a fair chance "to better his condition in life." The Morrill Tariff of 1861 restored Hamilton's policy of high tariffs to protect and nurture domestic manufactures. High tariffs remained the core of Republican economic policy into the 1930s. The National Banking Act of 1863 established the nation's first system of federally chartered urban banks entitled to issue national bank notes. Soon there was a national system of 1,600 banks through which the federal government could manage a national system of currency and credit.

Republican Party initiatives in transportation and communication encouraged the rapid expansion of the nation's railroad and telegraph networks. The telegraph, dominated by Western Union after 1855, often followed the railroad. In 1862 Congress passed and the president signed the Pacific Railroad Act. The act chartered the Union Pacific railroad to lay track from the Mississippi River to the California border and the Central Pacific to build out from San Francisco to meet them. The Union Pacific was given massive land grants for right of way and to sell off to help capitalize the project. Congress also authorized $60 million in government bonds and $100 million in company-issued stock as additional funding. In 1864 the government made more land and money available to the Union Pacific and chartered the Northern Pacific railroad to push west from Minneapolis to Seattle.

The Homestead Act of 1862 made vast stretches of public land in the West available, in 160-acre sections, virtually free, to those willing to settle and work the land for five years. Two and a half million acres of farmland were taken up under the Homestead Act between 1863 and 1865. In addition, the Department of Agriculture was founded to advocate for the nation's farmers and to educate them concerning the best uses of the land in light of new science and technology. And finally, the Morrill Land Grant College Act offered each state 30,000 acres of public land for each U.S. senator and representative assigned to the state. The sale of these lands was to create a fund, the interest from which would support at least one college in each state dedicated to teaching "such branches of learning as are related to agriculture and the mechanic arts."

Yet we remember Lincoln's election not for his domestic policy accomplishments, but because it signaled the start of the Civil War. Although sectional tensions had been building for decades, civil war came as a shock to most Americans. No one, least of all President Lincoln, believed that the war would drag on for four long years and cost half a million American lives. A little more than two years into the war, Lincoln set the end of slavery in train with the Emancipation Proclamation. Sadly, Abraham Lincoln's assassination on April 15, 1865, just one week after General Ulysses S. Grant accepted the surrender of General Robert E. Lee at Appomattox Courthouse, left the new peace without its wisest advocate (Figure 4.3).

Once the war was over and nearly four million slaves were free, the Republican Congress had to decide what freedom meant in real terms. Were the freedmen free in the same sense that white men were free—free to do the same things, enjoy the same privileges, exercise the same rights, and pursue the same opportunities? As Congress mulled these questions, congressman and future president James A. Garfield asked, "What is freedom? Is it the bare privilege of not being chained?"[59] Garfield and most Republicans believed that the answer had to be no, that freedom had to mean more than not being held in chains. But few white Americans could conceive that freedom meant equality. The battle over the meaning of freedom was fought out in adoption and implementation of the Thirteenth, Fourteenth, and Fifteenth Amendments to the Constitution and the Civil Rights Acts that followed. Freedom was grudgingly upheld, but equality was rejected.

The Thirteenth Amendment, which went into effect on December 18, 1865, completed emancipation; it read, "Neither slavery nor involuntary servitude, except as a punishment for crime whereof the party shall have been duly convicted, shall exist within the United States, or any place subject to their jurisdiction." Senator William Stewart, representing the new state of Nevada, warned that Congress "must see to it that the man made free by the Constitution of the United States . . . is a freeman indeed."[60] The Fourteenth Amendment sought to do precisely that. The Fourteenth Amendment declared, "All persons born or naturalized in the United States, and subject to the jurisdiction thereof, are citizens of the United States and the state wherein they reside. No state shall make or enforce any law which shall abridge the privi-

Figure 4.3. "The First Reading of the Emancipation Proclamation Before the Cabinet," 1862. This Alexander Ritchie engraving from an F. B. Carpenter painting depicts President Abraham Lincoln preparing to discuss a draft of the Emancipation Proclamation with his cabinet on July 22, 1862. (Library of Congress, Prints and Photographs Division, reproduction LC-USZ62-2070)

leges and immunities of citizens of the United States; nor shall any State deprive any person of life, liberty, or property, without due process of law; nor deny to any person within its jurisdiction the equal protection of the laws." This broad and generous language, explicitly overturning the Supreme Court's ruling in *Dred Scott,* went into effect on July 28, 1868.

Nonetheless, southern resistance to black freedom was broad and determined. Few white southerners could imagine that the recently freed slaves could ever be full and free citizens in the same sense that they were. Most freedmen had little education, no property, and few skills not immediately relevant to their former agricultural duties. Whites needed the labor of their former slaves and believed that blacks would not work unless coerced. Hence, southern legislatures quickly passed laws and regulations, generally called Black Codes, that threatened former slaves with arrest and punishment if they were not satisfactorily employed. Congress reacted by passing the Reconstruction Act of March 1867, establishing military rule in the South, and requiring that states approve the Fourteenth Amendment and adopt state constitutions treating blacks and whites equally before rejoining the union and regaining their representation in Congress. By June 1868, seven southern states had been readmitted to the union with manhood suffrage in their constitutions, and even the most recalcitrant holdouts seemed to be moving in that direction. But rights granted by the states, even if in constitutions, were insecure.

A major debate was initiated in Congress early in 1869 about how to protect voting rights and implement equality in America. Massachusetts Senator Henry Wilson took the broadest view, saying, "Let us give to all citizens equal rights, and then protect everybody in the United States in the exercise of those rights. When we attain that position we shall have carried out logically the ideas that lie at the foundation of our institutions. . . . Until we do that we are in a false position, an illogical position—a position that cannot be defended; a position that I believe is dishonorable to the nation with the lights we have before us."[61] Republican Senators Simon Cameron of Pennsylvania and Oliver Morton of Indiana also argued for a broad suffrage amendment and against excluding voters on the basis of race, ethnicity, property, religion, or education. They failed. Democrats, of course, wished to limit black voting, but many Republicans were just as determined to exclude the Democrat-leaning Irish, as well as the Chinese, American Indians, illiterates, and itinerants. Neither party envisioned female suffrage. Hence, on February 26, 1869, the Republican majority in Congress passed a narrow version of the Fifteenth Amendment, which read, "The right of citizens of the United States to vote shall not be denied or abridged by the United States or any State on account of race, color, or previous condition of servitude." Freedom had expanded in the crucible of the Civil War, but constitutional equality still glimmered in the distant future.

The Faces of Exclusion

It took a terrible Civil War to produce an end to slavery and legal equality for black men. Within a few short years, white Americans were exhausted, troubled, and doubtful. Many had become convinced that the war had carried them too far, and they yearned for the ideals of a simpler and more orderly time. The late nineteenth century was largely dedicated to retracting many of the promises made during and immediately after the war in order to recreate, as much as could be, the antebellum social order. White men in the age of Jackson had been confident that God had distinguished between the races and the sexes, giving different virtues, capacities, and roles to each, so white men could hardly be blamed for reflecting God's will in the order of society. Alexis de Tocqueville described American race relations in the 1830s in striking detail, saying, "Three races, naturally distinct, and, I might almost say, hostile to each other, are discoverable among them at the first glance. . . . Among these widely differing families of men . . . the superior in intelligence, in power, and in enjoyment, is the white, or European, the MAN, preeminently so-called; below him appear the Negro and the Indian. . . . The European . . . makes them subservient to his use, and when he cannot subdue he destroys them."[62]

Leading Americans spoke bluntly about race as well. Democratic Senator Stephen A. Douglas of Illinois challenged Abraham Lincoln directly on the issue of equality between the races in the Illinois senate campaign of 1858, which Douglas won. Douglas was unequivocal in his support for white supremacy. Douglas said in Chicago, "I am opposed to Negro equality. I repeat that this nation is a white people—a people composed of European descendants—a people that have established this government for themselves and their posterity." Two and a half months later in Jonesboro, Douglas denied Lincoln's contention that the Declaration of Independence's statement that "all men are created equal" meant "all" men. Douglas assured his listeners that the Founders "desired to express by that phrase white men of European birth and European descent, and had no reference either to the negro, the savage Indians, the Fejee, the Malay, or any other inferior and degraded race, when they spoke of the equality of men."[63]

White Americans generally held that removal was the only satisfactory solution to the presence of disorderly, or inassimilable, elements in their midst. Presidents Jackson and Van Buren carried Indian removal to cruel completion during the 1830s. Even those who thought slavery an evil, including Abraham Lincoln as late as 1862, thought that an end to slavery required removal of the freed slaves to colonies in Africa or Latin America. Nor did attitudes change quickly. Even as the Civil War drew to a bloody close, few white Americans could envision a multiracial society in which black, red, and white men and women lived side by side in anything remotely like mutual respect.

Black slavery continued to present a seemingly intractable dilemma. Between 1830 and 1860 a steady 87 percent of American blacks were slaves while the remaining 13 percent were free. Of the slaves, 97 percent were held in the South. In fact, by 1860 slavery had essentially been purged from New England; only 18 elderly slaves remained in a black population of 156,000. The still sparsely settled West had only 4,479 blacks in 1860, and only 29 were slaves. On the other hand, the North Central states had 184,239 black residents and fully 62 percent (114,948) were slaves. In the South, slavery was a massive presence. There were 4 million blacks living in the South, and 3.8 million (94 percent) were slaves. Nearly half a million free blacks lived in the United States in 1860, 260,000 in the South and another 225,000 in the North.

After the slave revolts of the 1820s, most southern states passed laws that that made it illegal to teach slaves to read and that assumed blacks to be slaves unless they could prove otherwise. Moreover, every state that entered the union after 1819 barred blacks from voting. Several states that had not formally prohibited voting by free blacks moved to do so during the Jacksonian era: Tennessee in 1834, North Carolina in 1835, and Pennsylvania in 1838. By 1860 only the New England states of Maine, New Hampshire, Vermont, Rhode Island, and Massachusetts permitted blacks to vote. New York also permitted free blacks to vote, but qualifications were higher than for whites. Less than 4 percent of American blacks lived in the six states that permitted blacks to vote.[64] Critically, the federal government also stood against the inclusion of free blacks in American life. Blacks were barred from voting in the western territories, where the federal government exercised direct control. Even more importantly, from the perspective of the American Dream, blacks were barred from taking up land in the West under the homestead statutes of the antebellum period. Four states—Indiana, Illinois, Iowa, and Oregon—barred blacks from entering their territory altogether. Finally, as already noted, the United States Supreme Court, in the *Dred Scott* case, held that blacks, whether slave or free, could not be citizens.

Despite the best efforts of most whites, northern and southern, to keep blacks at the periphery of the American society, if not in chains, protests against the South's "peculiar institution" grew. In 1852 Harriet Beecher Stowe's *Uncle Tom's Cabin* unnerved the nation with its sad conclusion that only a national commitment to "repentance, justice, and mercy" could save the nation from God's wrath. That same summer the nation's most prominent black leader, Frederick Douglass, charged white Americans as hypocrites, saying; "You boast of your love of liberty, your superior civilization, your pure Christianity, while the whole power of the nation . . . is solemnly pledged to support and perpetuate the enslavement of three millions of your countrymen."[65] White leaders hesitated. Abraham Lincoln's first public statement in opposition to slavery came in a speech on October 4, 1854. It is almost pitiful to read, but it portrays vividly the deep ambivalence of northern white Americans toward slavery and blacks. Of slavery, Lincoln said, "I hate it because of the monstrous injustice of slavery itself." He then proceeded immediately to say, "If all earthly power was given me, I should not know what to do, as to the existing institution. My first impulse would be to free all the slaves and send them to Liberia,—to their own native land." If freedom and removal proved untenable, "What next? Free them, and make them politically and socially our equals? My own feelings will not admit of this, and if mine would, we well know that those of the great mass of white people will not."[66] Nor was the idea of removing freed blacks from the country a passing fancy with Lincoln; as late as August 1862, President Lincoln met with Frederick Douglass and a delegation of black leaders to urge them to accept and advocate colonization of freed slaves to South America. Lincoln explained, "Your race suffer very greatly, many of them, by living among us, while ours suffer from your presence. . . . It is better for us both, therefore, to be separated." The President concluded by observing, "There is an unwillingness on the part of our people, harsh as it may be, for you free colored people to remain with us"[67] (Figure 4.4).

Lincoln's thinking about slavery and blacks changed little during the eleven years that he dealt with these issues publicly, even though his sense of what was required of him politically and militarily changed a great deal. In the face of unbending southern resistance, Lincoln freed the slaves as a war measure. Still, white racism remained a powerful force throughout the nation. Andrew Keyssar has pointed out that "between 1863 and 1870, proposals to enfranchise blacks were defeated in more than fifteen northern states and territories."[68] Only two such referenda, in Iowa and Minnesota, passed. Moreover, the Freedman's Bureau (1865–1872), charged to oversee the transition of slaves to freedom, was hobbled almost from its inception. The critical proposal to distribute seized and abandoned property in the South to former slaves was blocked in Congress. Without the promised "forty acres and a mule"—that is, land and the means to work it—the freed slaves were without the means to survive on their own. Within the space of a few short years, most southern blacks fell back under the control of their former owners. Vagrancy laws and the sharecropping, or the crop-lien system, tied indebted black farmers to the land only slightly less securely than had slavery. There was a century more to wait for freedom.

The rights and roles of women within American society continued to evolve

Figure 4.4. "I'm Not to Blame for Being White, Sir!," 1862. This lithograph depicts a wealthy gentleman giving alms to a poor black child and being challenged by a poor white child for what today might be called "reverse discrimination." (Library of Congress, Prints and Photographs Division, reproduction LC-USZ62-12771)

as well. The ideology of the revolutionary period, "republican motherhood," softened into the "cult of female domesticity." The "true woman" of the antebellum period was warm-hearted, kind, nurturing, emotional, passive, and cooperative.[69] Men, on the other hand, were strong, bold, self-interested, calculating, competitive, and rational, and they saw it as part of God's and nature's design that men and women, in the common phrase of the day, occupied "separate spheres." Men led their families, but they focused most of their effort outside the home, in the marketplace and the public square, on the battlefield when necessary, while women focused their effort and attention on children, hearth, and home. Poor women, to say nothing of female slaves, faced more difficult circumstances and, as always, did what was required to survive.

During the second quarter of the nineteenth century, women largely remained the wards of their fathers and husbands. Some pity was taken on hard-pressed wives as marriage laws were rewritten to make extreme cruelty, gross neglect, and habitual drunkenness legitimate grounds for divorce.[70] More positively, some educational, occupational, and associational opportunities began to open up. In 1821 Emma Willard founded the Troy Seminary, and two years later Catharine Beecher opened the Hartford Female Seminary to train women as teachers for the region's common schools. By the late 1830s fully one-fifth of native-born white women in New England spent some time teaching school, although usually only until they were married.[71] Revivalism, abolition, temperance, and moral reform also got women out of the home and into groups that fought for social change. Women's organizational skills were eminently transferable to other issues, women's issues, once these came into focus around midcentury.

The dawn of the women's movement is often traced to the Seneca Falls convention of 1848. The Seneca Falls convention marked the effective beginning of a full-blown demand for equal rights for women. The demand for equality constituted a direct challenge to several key ideas about the place of women in society. Very simply, the ideas of "republican motherhood," the "cult of female domesticity," and "separate spheres" came face to face with the idea of "equality" in Seneca Falls, New York, in the summer of 1848. The founding principles of the movement for gender equality initiated at Seneca Falls were stated in a "Declaration of Sentiments." The force and power of the Declaration of Sentiments derived from the fact that it presented the demands of the women's movement in a lightly revised version of the Declaration of Independence. The Declaration of Sentiments began with the claim that "all men and women are created equal," and "endowed by their Creator with certain inalienable rights." Government is charged to protect these rights. Like the men for whom Jefferson spoke, the women for whom Elizabeth Cady Stanton and Susan B. Anthony spoke concluded that "whenever any government becomes destructive of these ends," justice demanded change. The declaration's list of grievances built to a powerful crescendo. Men had "usurped the prerogative of Jehovah himself, claiming it as his right to assign for her a sphere of action, when that belongs to her conscience and her God." The declaration next claimed that man had "endeavored, in every way that he could, to destroy her confidence in her own powers, to lessen her self-respect, and to make her willing to lead a dependent and abject life." No more! "Now, in view of this entire disfranchisement of one-half of the people of this country, . . . we insist that they have immediate admission to all the rights and privileges which belong to them as citizens of the United States."[72] The Seneca Falls Declaration of Sentiments demanded autonomy, freedom, self-expression, and self-development for women—in fact, it demanded the whole bundle of rights, duties, and opportunities that men enjoyed.

Women made important practical gains both before and after Seneca Falls. In the late 1830s and the 1840s a number of states, including Massachusetts, Michigan, Ohio, Indiana, and New York, passed married women's property acts. These critical reforms allowed married women, previously seen in the law as *femme covert*—that is, subsumed within the legal personality of their husbands—to own, transfer, and inherit property in their own name and to retain and control earnings during marriage. These states and others soon realized that as property owners, women also had to be entitled to make contracts and to go into court to testify and bring suit in defense of their interests. Women also began to move into the wage-labor force in larger numbers. Alice Kessler-Harris reports that in the 1850s about half of adult women worked for wages before marriage. Two-thirds of women left the workforce upon marriage, leaving about one-sixth of married women in the paid workforce. The Civil War not only brought more women into the workforce, but also into a large number of voluntary and associational activities to supply clothing, food, medical supplies, money, and other necessities to the troops.

Although women made gains in the Civil War period, they also experienced major defeats. Elizabeth Cady Stanton, Susan B. Anthony, Lucretia Mott, Sojourner Truth, and many others hoped that the end of slavery would bring legal and constitutional recognition of equality for all Americans, irrespective of race or gender. But within months of the end of the war, Republican Party leaders and their male abolitionist allies, led by Wendell Phillips, began shrinking from the political challenge of confronting race and gender discrimination simultaneously. Wendell Phillips summed up the male leadership consensus in saying, "One question at a time. . . . This hour belongs to the

Negro."[73] When it became clear that male leaders, white and black, were pre-pared to award the coveted right to vote to black male former slaves while excluding women, anger became invective. At the Equal Rights Convention of 1869, Stanton objected to having "the colored man enfranchised before the women. . . . I would not trust him with all my rights; degraded, oppressed him-self, he would be more despotic . . . than ever our Saxon rulers are. . . . I desire . . . that not another man be enfranchised without the woman by his side."[74] Frederick Douglass, saddened but resolute, sought to distinguish the just claims to equality of blacks and women on grounds of immediacy and need. Douglass said, "When women, because they are women, are hunted down . . . when they are dragged from their houses and hung upon lamp-posts . . . they will have an urgency to obtain the ballot equal to our own." When Douglass was challenged from the audience with the question, "Is that not all true about black women?" he replied, "Yes, yes, yes, it is true of the black woman, but not because she is a woman but because she is black."[75] The breach between Anthony, Stanton, and Douglass would last a decade.

As always, American Indians did worse. President Jackson's Indian Removal Act, signed into law on May 28, 1830, was the first major piece of legislation requested by the new administration. The act did not require Indians to move, but it did say that if they did not, their tribal autonomy would be forfeit and they would henceforth be subject to national and state law rather than their own tribal laws. Chief Justice Marshall and the Supreme Court offered the tribes little protection. Marshall declared for the court in *Cherokee Nation v. Georgia* (1831) that while Georgia's attempt to take control of Indian lands was illegal, the Cherokee and other Indian nations were "domestic dependent nations" subject to the national government.

Most of the southern tribes, fearing the imposition of white authority and law and knowing the Jackson administration's dedication to removal, agreed to exchange their land east of the Mississippi for land in the West. During Jackson's eight years in office, more than seventy treaties were signed in which about 100 million acres of Indian land in the east was exchanged for 32 million acres of western land and about $68 million in cash, goods, and tran-sitional support. A few tribes, most prominently the Creek and the Cherokee, refused to negotiate land exchange agreements and were forcefully removed. In 1836 and 1837 almost 20,000 Creek men, women, and children, some in chains, were forcibly removed to Oklahoma Territory. At the end of the jour-ney, one old Creek chief told a white agent, "Our road has been a long one. . . . On it we have laid the bones of our men, women, and children. . . . Tell

Figure 4.5. "Trail of Tears," 1838, by Robert Lindneux. This classic painting depicts the orderly beginnings of a forced winter march (note the armed soldiers in among the Indians) from Tennessee to the Indian Territory west of the Mississippi River. (Wollaroc Museum, Bartlesville, Oklahoma)

General Jackson if the white man will let us we will live in peace and friend-ship"[76] (Figure 4.5).

President Van Buren completed Jackson's forced removal program. In 1838, 15,000 Cherokee were herded onto steamships and then cattle cars for transport west. Many completed the final leg of the journey on foot. Accounts vary, but more than 4,000 Indian men, women, and children died on the journey that became known in American history as the "Trail of Tears." Presidents from Washington to Van Buren were convinced, or allowed themselves to believe, that the only way to ensure the survival of the Indians in the face of the overwhelming white advance was to separate the races, putting the too-vulnerable Indians beyond the reach of white whiskey, greed, and guns. Hence, between 1789 and 1838, approximately 81,282 Indians, more than half of them during Jackson's eight years in office, were moved west of the Mississippi.[77]

The Mississippi River, the barrier behind which nearly 400,000 Indians were to be secure against white incursions in a permanent Indian reserve, was breached in less than a decade. The nation's march west not only continued, but picked up speed in the two decades before the Civil War. The Mexican war added Texas, the southwest, and the land between the Rockies and the Pacific to the Union. The discovery of gold in California in 1849 and then in the Rockies in 1859 drew thousands and then hundreds of thousands out into the permanent Indian reserve. The Indians again resisted, the army moved in to protect white settlers, and Jackson's solution to the Indian question crumbled. As Rogers Smith recently noted, "In 1854 alone, tribes relocated west of Missouri and Arkansas relinquished 18 million acres of the land promised to them in perpetuity."[78] By the middle of the 1850s, Indians had been removed from the American society not just physically or geographically, but civilly and psychologically as well. The attorney general held that Indians could not become naturalized U.S. citizens through the normal process because that process was open only to white foreigners. Indians were not foreigners because they were already "in our allegiance." Hence, the only path by which Indians might become U.S. citizens, even if they were living independently within the broader white community and paying taxes, was by treaty or special act of Congress.[79]

5

The Dream Threatened:

Individualism in the Age of the Robber Barons

> The law of competition . . . insures the survival of the fittest. . . . We accept and welcome, therefore, the concentration of business, . . . in the hands of a few, as being not only beneficial, but essential for the future progress of the race.
>
> —Andrew Carnegie, "Wealth"

Adding ideas drawn from Charles Darwin to the intellectual stock earlier drawn from Protestant theology, liberal individualism, and laissez-faire economics gave the social theory of the second half of the nineteenth century an unusually sharp edge. Charles Darwin (1809–82) declared in his seminal book, *The Origin of Species* (1859), that life in the plant and animal kingdoms evolved through natural selection, a process in which competition and struggle led to the survival of the fittest and the progressive improvement of the species. Darwin also held that the laws of nature that governed plant and animal life displayed the same underlying processes as those discovered by Sir Charles Lyell in geology and Thomas Malthus in population economics and social theory.[1] Strikingly, this meant that the best physical, biological, and social science of the day agreed that natural processes, working unimpeded over vast stretches of time, led inexorably to improvement in individuals, societies, and species.

Thoughtful Americans worried that the emerging Darwinian framework undermined traditional American ideals and attitudes concerning freedom, individual rights and liberties, the common good, and much more. Competition, natural selection, and survival of the fittest seemed to comport easily with American conceptions of individualism, opportunity, hard work, and personal responsibility, but they seemed just as certainly to strip away commitments to equality, fairness, and the good of one's fellow man. Familiar questions resurfaced with new intensity. Both Andrew Jackson and Abraham Lincoln argued that government, when forced to choose between property rights and human rights, between "the dollar and the man," must choose human rights and the interests of the common man. Edward G. Ryan, chief justice of Wisconsin, warned the University of Wisconsin class of 1873 that property rights were again threatening to overwhelm human rights. As the age of the robber barons dawned, Ryan warned, "For the first time really in our politics, money is taking the field as an organized power.... The questions will arise, and arise in your day, ... 'Which shall rule—wealth or man; which shall lead—money or intellect; who shall fill public stations—educated and patriotic free men, or the feudal serfs of corporate capital.'"[2] Many worried that if competition overwhelmed compassion, if property held unmediated sway over man, the American Dream would be no more.

Young Dreamers and the World Before Them

The American political tradition in the mid-nineteenth century had at its foundation the Jeffersonian vision of America as a land in which each individual, native born and immigrant, enjoyed an unparalleled opportunity to pursue life, liberty, and happiness. Yet in post–Civil War America, doubts were coming to cloud even fundamental beliefs and commitments. When the prominent Jefferson biographer James Parton in 1874 declared that "If Jefferson was wrong, America is wrong; if America is right, Jefferson was right," men did not respond immediately. Their brows furrowed; they were unsure. New ideas, hard to accept, but harder still to refute, were entering the common wisdom of the culture. Jefferson tottered on his pedestal as scholars parsed Darwin to show that inequality, not equality, was the law of nature.

Charles Darwin declared that "natural selection acts by competition" in which "the most vigorous individuals ... successfully struggled" to dominate "their conditions of life."[3] Darwin assured the reader that "the great and complex battle of life" redounded to the general good: "When we reflect on this struggle, we may console ourselves with the full belief, that the war of nature is not incessant, that no fear is felt, that death is generally prompt, and that the vigorous, the healthy, and the happy survive and multiply."[4] By the late 1860s ideas derived from Darwin had permeated the nation's corporate boardrooms and university classrooms and were generally familiar to the literate public. British sociologist Herbert Spencer and his American disciple, Yale sociologist William Graham Sumner, with Darwin's acquiescence and occasional cooperation, applied these themes to human society in a theory that came to be called social Darwinism. Social Darwinists used analogies to the natural world to suggest that social change, like biological and geological change, occurred over long stretches of time by processes too detailed, complex, and multifaceted for man to fully understand, let alone to control and direct. It was better simply to clear the social terrain of obstacles and allow competition to decide the struggle for wealth and status. In 1868 E. L. Godkin, editor of the *Nation* and one of the leading literary arbiters of the last half of the nineteenth century, declared that competition was "the law by which Providence secures the progress of the human race. . . . It is a law of human nature."[5] William Graham Sumner summarized this view in the striking declaration, "This is a world in which the rule is, 'Root, hog, or die.'"[6] During the post–Civil War boom, scramble was king, and most men did not pause to ask what kind of country they were so rapidly building.

The late nineteenth century was a period of tremendous economic growth. A nation of scattered farms and small villages was transformed into a nation of cities, corporations, factories, and wage laborers. Especially in the North, the war accelerated the expansion of transportation, communication, and mass production. 30,626 miles of track in 1860 became 258,748 miles of track in 1900. The United States surpassed Britain by about 1870 to become the world's wealthiest nation. By the end of the century the value of American manufactures was greater than that of Great Britain, France, and Germany combined.[7] The shift from an agriculturally based economy to an industrially based economy was an immensely disruptive process. In 1870 fewer than half of American workers, 47 percent, worked in commerce and industry, while by 1900, fully 62 percent did. Moreover, the share of gross domestic product produced by the nonfarm sectors rose from 62 percent in the 1870s to about 77 percent by 1900.[8] The victors in this battle for wealth and power, John D. Rockefeller, J. P. Morgan, Andrew Carnegie, Cornelius Vanderbilt, Leland Stanford, Jim Fisk, Jay Gould, Philip Armour, and their peers were known as "captains of industry," the robber barons of the Gilded Age. Immensely competitive, unrestrained by government regulation, and buttressed by the Darwinism of the age, these men and others of their class and station exercised nearly unchecked power.

American farmers suffered tremendously in the decades after the Civil War. As mechanization and improved farming methods increased production, supply often outran demand and prices fell. More importantly, national fiscal policy designed to reverse the inflation of the war years and get the country back on a hard-money footing brought a steady deflation that was particularly devastating to farmers. The wholesale price index for all farm products peaked in 1864 at 162 and then declined steadily for the next twenty years, falling through 70 in 1886 and remaining low for the remainder of the century. Similarly, wheat, which sold for about $2.50 a bushel in the late 1860s, sold above $1.75 in the early 1870s, $1.25 in the late 1870s, before it fell through $1 in 1884, bottomed out at $0.56 in 1894. Corn followed a similar trajectory, declining steadily from $0.66 a bushel in 1866 to $0.21 in 1896. Cotton fell from $0.24 a pound in 1870 to less than $0.10 a pound every year from 1891 to 1903.[9] Falling crop prices and rising costs for marketing and transportation kept the farm sector in an incipient state of rebellion throughout the last quarter of the nineteenth century.

Similar price declines affected manufacturing, but the economic results were different. The wholesale price of steel rails fell by 80 percent from 1868 to 1900, and the price of refined petroleum fell by even more. Ruthless price competition produced economic turmoil, widespread business failures, and massive consolidation. Western Union was the nation's largest company in 1865, capitalized at about $40 million. In the 1870s and 1880s, railroads became the nation's largest businesses as Jim Fisk, Jay Gould, James J. Hill, Leland Stanford, and Collis P. Huntington pulled regional roads together into great national roads with thousands of miles of track. During the 1880s and 1890s, John D. Rockefeller took control of the American oil industry and made the Standard Oil Trust the nation's most valuable business. Finally, on March 2, 1901, J. P. Morgan and Company announced the formation of U.S. Steel with a market capitalization of $1.1 billion. In just thirty-five years, the value of the nation's leading business had grown from Western Union's $40 million in 1865 to U.S. Steel's $1.1 billion in 1901. Clearly, the scope and scale of opportunity in America had changed dramatically. Just as clearly, with the stakes so high, few men could play this game, and fewer still could win.

Industrial consolidation fueled urbanization and increased immigration in post–Civil War America. The U.S. population grew rapidly, but more ominously, it began to be and to feel more diverse and unstable. Population growth averaged about 25 percent per decade, mushrooming from 40 million in 1870 to 76 million in 1900.[10] In 1870 the population was 25 percent urban and urbanization was increasing at a rate of about 5 percent per decade. Hence, by 1900, 40 percent of the population lived in cites of over 2,500 inhabitants, 38 cities had populations of over 100,000, six were over 500,000, and three, New York, Philadelphia, and Chicago, had more than 1 million inhabitants.[11] Moreover, the end of the Civil War saw the earliest beginnings of the black migration out of the rural South to the cites of the North. Between 1870 and 1900, nearly 350,000 former slaves left the South.

Yet at least as disruptive as urbanization and internal migration was increased immigration. More than 14 million immigrants entered the United States between 1860 and 1900. Immigration averaged about 2.5 million in both the 1860s and 1870s, then doubled to more than 5.2 million in the 1880s, before falling back a bit to 3.7 million during the economically depressed decade of the 1890s.[12] More importantly, the ethnic composition of the immigrant pool changed during this period. The dominant source of immigration during the first half of the nineteenth century had been northern Europe, especially England, Ireland, and Germany. Northern Europeans continued to come in large numbers, nearly 9 million between 1860 and 1900. Even here, though, Germans, Swedes, and Danes came to outnumber the English and Irish by the 1870s.

Still, it was not these Protestant northern Europeans that caused concern. Rather, a rising tide of immigrants from southern and eastern Europe, as well as Russia, began to arrive after the Civil War. At first the numbers were small, just 33,000 in the 1860s, but they increased fivefold in both the 1870s and 1880s, until they reached 1.9 million in the 1890s, outstripping the 1.6 million immigrants from Northern Europe. Italian immigration rose from less than 12,000 in the 1860s to more than 650,000 in the 1890s, while Russian immigration rose from 2,500 to more than 500,000. These new immigrants, with their unfamiliar languages, religions, and cultures, often clustered in the cities, worked for wages in the new factories, and seemed dangerously ignorant of American values. Earlier immigrants and native-born Americans, informed by social Darwinism that competition rather than natural rights determined one's legitimate place in the social order, began revising American law to control the newcomers.

Even more worrisome than the Italians, Poles, and Russians were Asians and Africans. Few Asians came to the U.S. before the 1850s. The first railroad contracts for Chinese labor brought 13,100 in 1854, an average of 5,000 a year from 1855 to 1868, 15,000 a year from 1869 to 1881, and then a surge to almost 40,000 in 1882. Western racism directed against the Chinese, especially in California, finally was salved when Congress passed the Chinese Exclusion Act of 1882. This act and others passed in its wake slowed but did not stop immigration from Asia. Immigration from Africa was miniscule; it averaged only 500 persons per decade between 1860 and 1900. Nonetheless, the mere prospect of African immigration was much on the minds of white Americans after emancipation.

Both major parties moved to limit the suffrage, check the democracy, and secure the rights of property. In post–Civil War America, of course, the Republican Party had the lead. Between 1860 and 1900, the Republicans won nine of eleven presidential elections, controlled the Senate for all but four years, and the House for all but sixteen years. Moreover, once Salmon P. Chase replaced Roger B. Taney as chief justice in 1864, Republicans enjoyed a majority on the Supreme Court for the remainder of the century. Although Democratic Party fortunes improved, especially in the South, after the formal end of Reconstruction in 1876, the last quarter of the nineteenth century was a period of conservative ascendancy in both North and South.

Social, political, and economic turmoil encouraged a general reassessment, especially among elites, of the nation's commitment to equality and democracy. Social Darwinism buttressed Democrats in their conviction that blacks, most of whom were illiterate, impoverished, and still isolated in the rural South, had no right to participate in politics and governance. Similarly, Republicans worried that the new Catholic and Jewish immigrants from southern and eastern Europe, also illiterate and impoverished, threatened property, order, and stability. In 1878 Francis Parkman, the nation's most prominent historian, announced in the nation's leading literary journal, the *North American Review*, "The Failure of Universal Suffrage."

The American Dream in the Gilded Age

During the Gilded Age, though the nation was changing rapidly, America continued to be a beacon of freedom and opportunity to the world. The iconic representation of America's role as asylum to the world became the Statute of Liberty. Lady Liberty, a gift from France to commemorate the centennial of the American Revolution, was erected on Ellis Island in New York harbor in 1886. The famous poem by Emma Lazarus, entitled "The New Colossus," that is carved into the statute's base said keep your great men, your kings and generals, and send us your working men. Holding the lamp of liberty high, Lady Liberty declared:

> Keep, ancient lands, your storied pomp! . . .
> Give me your tired, your poor,
> Your huddled masses yearning to breathe free,
> The wretched refuse of your teeming shore.
> Send these, the homeless, tempest-tost, to me,
> I lift my lamp beside the golden door![13]

To the immigrants of Europe, America was, as it had been for the followers of William Penn two hundred years earlier, a "door of mercy" opening onto a better life. Even America's intellectual elite understood the vision that continued to draw Europe's poor across the Atlantic. Henry Adams, the grandson and great-grandson of presidents, was the most prominent public intellectual of the Gilded Age. Adams' magisterial study of Jeffersonian America, entitled *History of the United States During the Administration of Thomas Jefferson* (1889), said of the common American citizen of Jefferson's day, "the American . . . dream was his whole existence."

The proud and patriotic American, exulting in his freedom and opportunity, repelled the elite of Europe but awed his poorer brothers. "'Look at my wealth!' cried the American to his foreign visitor. . . . 'See these magnificent cities scattered broadcast to the Pacific! See my cornfields rustling and waving in the summer breeze from ocean to ocean. . . . Look at this continent of mine, fairest of created worlds, . . . overflowing with milk for her hundred million children!'" Proud European aristocrats responded with scorn; snorting "Gold! Cities! cornfields! Continents! . . . I see nothing but tremendous wastes, . . . mountain-ranges a thousand miles long, with no means of getting to them, and nothing in them when you get there! . . . nor hope of better for a thousand years! Your story is a fraud, and you are a liar and a swindler!" (Figure 5.1).

Adams reported that the American patriot's response to the lords of Europe was predictable. Called a liar and a swindler, "the American, half perplexed and half defiant, retaliated. . . . For himself he cared little, but his

Figure 5.1. "The Rocky Mountains, Emigrants Crossing the Plains," 1866. This Currier & Ives lithograph depicts wagons headed west as Indians observe from the far bank. (Library of Congress, Prints and Photographs Division, reproduction LC-USZ62-22)

dream was his whole existence." The poor of Europe knew instinctively that whether these grand American assertions were literally true or not, the singular fact was that in America such promises and opportunities were addressed to them. Exultant Americans called across the sea to say, "'Come and share our limitless riches! Come and help us bring to light these unimaginable stores of wealth and power.' The poor came, and from them were seldom heard complaints of deception or delusion. Within a moment, by the mere contact of a moral atmosphere, they saw the gold and the jewels, the summer cornfields, and the glowing continent."[14] No one had to promise the poor of Europe that success in America was certain, just that it was possible.

Within America, a debate raged over how to ensure that freedom, equality, and opportunity remained healthy and vibrant in the rapidly changing society. Horatio Alger passed the traditional wisdom of Franklin and Lincoln on to new generations. For Alger, the American Dream continued to counsel that study, industry, frugality, and saving and investing for the future, leavened with sympathy and generosity toward the less fortunate, were the surest path to security and respect. But others stressed competition, striving, and struggle to the detriment, if not the exclusion, of charity, benevolence, public service, and attention to the common good. The robber barons of the age, men like Andrew Carnegie and John D. Rockefeller, believed that their tremendous economic success was evidence that the law of competition produced the survival of the fittest through a sometimes painful but always efficient process of natural selection. Increasingly, society's elites presented a description of American freedom that the common man and his representatives found difficult to argue with but that left them only the slimmest chance of winning against much more powerful actors.

Horatio Alger Jr. was so effective at presenting traditional American virtues in entertaining stories that his name practically became a synonym for the American Dream. Horatio Alger wrote a series of hugely popular novels describing the course from rags to riches. Among his most popular books was his first, *Ragged Dick, or Street Life in New York with the Boot Blacks,* initially serialized in a periodical for schoolchildren and published in book form in 1868. There followed over the next four decades a stream of popular books with titles like *Strive and Succeed, Slow and Sure, Struggling Upward,* and *Luck and Pluck.* Alger updated the American Dream for a late-nineteenth-century world that was increasingly urban and industrial, and hence fast moving, complex, and morally ambiguous. The world of Crevecoeur, Franklin, and Jefferson, the world of agriculture and small towns (even Franklin's Philadelphia was no more than ten thousand when he arrived), had been displaced by a more boisterous and threatening world in which skepticism and street smarts were needed to protect the benefits of education, hard work, and frugality.

Richard Hunter, the "Ragged Dick" in the title of the book, was orphaned early, survived on the streets of New York selling matches and fruit, and then made his living as a bootblack (shoe shine boy) into his early teens. Homeless, living in a cardboard box, possessing a single set of soiled clothes, Dick affected a carefree and blustery but tenuous self-sufficiency. He smoked, drank a little, gambled, and wasted money by going to P. T. Barnum's circus and treating his friends to chowder. Dick Hunter was honest and dependable, smarter and harder working than most, kind and generous, but he could not read or write, lacked foresight, and had no idea how to better his situation. Dick's transformation began with a chance sidewalk encounter. Dick was working the streets of New York, blacking boots enough to feed himself that day and keeping a sharp eye out for other opportunities. Outside one of the city's swank hotels, Dick overheard a distinguished gentleman, a Mr.

Whitney, explaining to his nephew Frank that he did not have time to show him the city. Dick, with dirty face and hands, ill-fitting clothes, and a more self-confident swagger than either Mr. Whitney or Frank found reassuring, offered to act as Frank's guide. After talking with Dick, cleaning him up and putting him in a spare set of Frank's much nicer and cleaner clothes, Mr. Whitney agreed and paid Dick a modest sum to guide Frank around the city.

The day that Dick spent with Frank was instructive for both. Frank, a well-educated but sheltered rural boy, was impressed by Dick's ability to avoid and even outsmart all of the urban hustlers, con men, and crooks that they encountered. Dick, on the other hand, began to glimpse the clean, comfortable, literate, middle-class life that Frank enjoyed. In his new clothes, and in Frank's good company, Dick was treated with a deference and respect that he had not known. Soon Dick confided to Frank that he would "like to be a office boy, and learn business, and grow up 'spectable."[15] Frank assured Dick that his future was in his own hands. "A good many distinguished men have once been poor boys. There's hope for you, Dick, if you'll try. . . . If you'll try to be somebody, and grow up into a respectable member of society, you will. You may not become rich—it isn't everybody that becomes rich, you know—but you can obtain a good position, and be respected." Dick promised to try and later Frank explained what it would take to succeed, telling Dick, "you must manage to get as good an education as you can. Until you do, you cannot get a position in an office or counting-room, even to run errands."[16]

Frank taught Dick by example and encouragement, but Dick's most authoritative teacher was Frank's uncle. Alger intended Mr. Whitney to conjure up images of Benjamin Franklin and the great inventor Eli Whitney. After Frank and Dick returned to the hotel and Mr. Whitney heard about their day, he thanked Dick, paid him a bonus, and they fell into conversation. "'How did you get up in the world?' asked Dick anxiously." Mr. Whitney replied, "I entered a printing-office as an apprentice . . . [shades of Franklin]. Then my eyes gave out. . . . I went into the country, and worked on a farm. After a while I was lucky enough to invent a machine, which has brought me in a great deal of money [Eli Whitney's cotton gin?]. But there was one thing I got while I was in the printing-office which I value more than money." "What was that, Sir,?" Dick asked. Whitney replied, as Franklin would have, "A taste for reading and study. During my leisure hours I improved myself by study, . . . If you ever expect to do anything in the world, you must know something of books."[17] Whitney concluded his advice to Dick Hunter by reminding him to "Save your money, my lad, buy books, and determine to be somebody, and you may yet fill an honorable position. . . . Don't forget what I have told you. Remember that your future position depends mainly upon yourself." Dick doubled his effort at boot blacking, saved his money, avoided extravagance, and before long, he rented a permanent place, learned to read and write, found a church, and planned for the future. Most importantly, Dick's hard work, frugality, and foresight led him to open a bank account to secure his small but growing fortune. He observed, "It was wonderful how much more independent he felt whenever he reflected upon the contents" of that account.[18] In Jeffersonian America, independence rested on possession of land; in Alger's increasingly urban post–Civil War America, independence rested on money in the bank.

As it always did in Alger novels, determination to improve paid off through a combination of preparation, luck, and pluck. After a year of intensive study, Dick could "read well, write a fair hand, and had studied arithmetic, . . . grammar, and geography. . . . He knew that it would take a long time to reach the goal which he had set before him, and he had patience to keep on trying. He knew that he had only himself to depend upon, and he determined to make the most of himself,—a resolution which is the secret of success in nine cases out of ten."[19] Dick had already achieved a marked improvement and laid the foundation for his future success by study, hard work, frugality, and perseverance. Dick's big break, landing a job in a counting-room, the first or apprenticeship stage in a business career, came unexpectedly as a result of both luck and pluck. One afternoon Dick determined to accompany his new roommate and tutor, Henry Fosdick, on an errand that required taking a ferry from Manhattan to Brooklyn. During the trip, a young boy of six slipped away from his father and sister and fell over the side and into the water. The father, unable to swim, cried out in anguish, "Who will save my child? A thousand— ten thousand dollars to anyone who will save him!" Dick, an excellent swimmer reacting instinctively, was in the water to save the boy even before hearing the father's promise of a reward. Although Alger does not record that the child's father, Mr. James Rockwell, actually gave Dick a reward of $10,000, he did give him a new suit of clothes and his dream job, $10 a week as a clerk in Mr. Rockwell's business.

For Dick Hunter and Henry Fosdick, as well as for other working- and middle-class boys, a "position" in a store, a business, or a counting room, a "clerkship" with the opportunity to move up, was the mid-nineteenth-century urban equivalent of Jefferson's 50-acre freehold. It was the minimum basis for security and independence and the stable foundation from which future opportunity might be sought. Dick's American Dream was a comfortable sufficiency, a place to sleep, enough to eat, an extra suit of clothes or two, some savings to fall back on, and a chance—not a guarantee, but a chance—to better himself.

P. T. Barnum, the great entrepreneur, showman, and lecturer, seconded, but also sharpened, the lessons that Horatio Alger taught young Americans of the mid-nineteenth century. Barnum was universally known for his New York museum, his traveling circus, and for the massively successful American tour that he organized for the great European singer, Jenny Lind. P. T. Barnum was among the greatest entertainers and lecturers of his age. Barnum's most popular lecture, entitled "The Art of Money Getting," first delivered in 1858 and innumerable times thereafter, reads like a condensation of the wisdom of Franklin, Emerson, and Alger. Barnum began with the assurance that "Those who really desire to attain an independence, have only to set their minds upon it, and adopt the proper means . . . and the thing is easily done." Barnum taught that one had first to recognize and avoid bad habits, like drinking, smoking, and getting into debt. Debt was particularly pernicious because it destroyed independence. Barnum said starkly, "Avoid Debt. . . . There is scarcely anything that drags a person down like debt. It is a slavish position to get in. . . . Debt robs a man of his self-respect, and makes him almost despise himself." Of course, Barnum understood that some reasons for going into debt, to buy land or start a business, were better than others, but all debt was to be viewed skeptically.[20] Barnum counseled not only that bad habits were to be avoided, but that good habits were to be cultivated. Hard work and perseverance were the keys. Barnum advised his listeners to pick the right goal, and then "Work at it, if necessary, early and late, in season and out of season, not leaving a stone unturned, and never deferring for a single hour that which can be done just as well *now.*" In words that Benjamin Franklin could very easily have uttered, Barnum reminded his listeners that "Ambition, energy, industry, perseverance, are indispensable requisites for success in business."[21] Barnum also listed a number of "Maxims" for success in money getting, one of which he attributed directly to Franklin, and all of which echoed Poor Richard and Father Abraham. Barnum advised, "the maxim of Dr. Franklin can never fail to be true—that 'honesty is the best policy.'" Barnum's other maxims included:

> Perseverance is sometimes but another word for self-reliance.
> Learn something useful.
> Let hope predominate, but be not too visionary.

Do not scatter your powers. Engage in one kind of business only. Be systematic.[22]

Clearly, Barnum looked back to the Protestant ethic of the Puritans and Franklin, but he also reflected a coarsening of that tradition that had begun in Emerson's generation and was gaining decisive momentum. The coarsening involved a new praise of "money getting" per se and a dismissive treatment of those who lost out in the race for wealth. Barnum declared, "The desire for wealth is nearly universal, and none can say it is not laudable." Responsible and humane "money-getters are the benefactors of the race." Barnum always closed his lecture on "Money Getting" with the story of a "vagabond" who claimed, "'I have discovered there is money enough in the world for all of us, if it was equally divided; this must be done, and we shall all be happy together.' 'But' was the response, 'if everybody was like you, it would be spent in two months, and what would you do then?' 'Oh! divide again; keep dividing, of course.'"[23] Audiences roared at the vagabond's suggestion that society's wealth be divided and redivided among all the citizens. They knew better because wealthy "benefactors" of the race, led by Andrew Carnegie and John D. Rockefeller, explained that society was best served when its "fittest" members controlled its wealth.

Andrew Carnegie, born to grinding Scottish poverty and an immigrant at 13, made the most famous argument for the discretion and independence of society's wealthiest members in an article entitled, simply, "Wealth." Carnegie saw the men who controlled the monopolies and trusts as winners in a Darwinian competition for dominance. He declared that while "the law of competition . . . may be sometimes hard for the individual, it is best for the race, because it insures the survival of the fittest in every department. We accept and welcome, therefore, as conditions to which we must accommodate ourselves, . . . the concentration of business, industrial and commercial, in the hands of a few, and the law of competition between these, as being not only beneficial, but essential for the future progress of the race."[24] John D. Rockefeller, perhaps the preeminent robber baron of the age, the architect of the Standard Oil Trust, and the most hated man of the half century spanning the beginning of the twentieth century, agreed with Carnegie that "the growth of a large business is merely a survival of the fittest." So too did the railroad baron James J. Hill, saying, "the fortunes of railroad companies are determined by the law of the survival of the fittest."[25] Carnegie, Rockefeller, and their fellow captains of industry assumed that Charles Elliott Perkins, president of the Chicago, Burlington, and Quincy line, was merely being rhetorical when he asked, "Are not the great benefactors of mankind the men who organize industry and help to cheapen the necessaries and conveniences of life?" Perkins admitted, "Their motives may be selfish . . . but are they not benefactors all the same?"[26]

Not only did the concentration of power and wealth reward society's fittest for their successful competitive efforts, it kept power and wealth out of the hands of the unfit. Russell Sage, a crusty entrepreneur and partner of railroad tycoon Jay Gould, expanded on Emerson's argument against charity, saying, "There are persons who ought never to have money. . . . Poverty is the only salvation of such men because in that state they can be to an extent restrained by the community."[27] Once again, Carnegie made the point in greatest detail and drew the most direct connection to the social Darwinism of the day. Carnegie simply declared, "one of the serious obstacles to the improvement of our race is indiscriminate charity. It were better for mankind that the millions of the rich were thrown into the sea than so spent as to encourage the slothful, the drunken, the unworthy. . . . Neither the individual nor the race is improved by alms-giving. . . . He is the only true reformer who is as careful and as anxious not to aid the unworthy as he is to aid the worthy."[28] Emerson had suffered the pangs of conscience when he yearned to spurn charity; Carnegie, standing on Darwin's shoulders, proudly served the race by denying the unworthy poor.

Andrew Carnegie and John D. Rockefeller were leading spokesmen for the business elite, but there were many others in the higher citadels of academe, the arts, and the church eager to support their case that the competition of social Darwinism worked in the general interest. William Torrey Harris, superintendent of the St. Louis public schools (1868–80) and U.S. commissioner of education (1889–1906), described the self-help ethic that he believed was the foundation of American education. Harris said, "We desire in our systems of education to make the citizen as independent as possible. . . . We wish him to be spontaneous,—self-active, self-governing. . . . We give the pupil the conventionalities of a perpetual self-education. With the tools to work with . . . he can unfold indefinitely his latent powers. . . . The pride of America is her self-educated men." America had always been proud of her independent, capable, self-educated men, but in the late nineteenth century, there was stick as well as carrot. Harris warned, "an edict has gone forth to the New World in our Declaration of Independence: 'Woe unto that head which cannot govern its pair of hands.' Unto the lower races who fail in this, it reads the sentence:

'If you cannot direct your own hands by your own intelligence you only encumber the ground here, and can remain by sufferance in this place only so long as land is cheap.'"[29] In other words, in this more explicitly competitive era, if you are not winning, you are losing, and if you are losing, you are just taking up space. Soon, the strong will need that space.

Another leading popularizer of this sharpened self-help ethic was Russell Conwell. Now largely lost to history, he was a major figure in his day. Conwell was a Protestant minister who built a megachurch in Philadelphia and founded Temple University there. He was also a tireless Chautauqua and Lyceum speaker, delivering a single speech, entitled "Acres of Diamonds," more than 6,000 times between 1870 and 1925. Conwell taught that the most admirable men were those that rose out of the mass by their own effort. The voice of Panglossian optimism, Conwell assured his listeners: "you ought to be rich; you have no right to be poor. . . . This is a wonderfully great life, and you ought to spend your time getting money, because of the power there is in money." Moreover, money is all the sweeter for the man who starts with little of it. Conwell declared: "It is fortunate for you that you have no capital. I am glad you have no money. I pity a rich man's son. . . . Oh! I pity a rich man's son, I do. . . . You don't need capital; you need common sense, not copper cents."[30] Conwell promised his listeners that greatness was possible. He proclaimed, "The road is open . . . between the rich and the poor. Be a man, be independent, and then shall the laboring man find the road ever open from poverty to wealth." The prospect of greatness was not compromised by obscurity, in fact, for Conwell, "greatness really consists in doing some great deed with little means, in the accomplishment of vast purposes from the private ranks of life, that is true greatness."[31]

The ideas of competition, struggle, and consolidation that Carnegie, Rockefeller, and their acolytes found so congenial, were not so much denied as reinterpreted by their opponents. Chief among their opponents were a collection of academics, journalists, and social critics that have come to be called Reform Darwinists. Both Henry George, author of *Progress and Poverty* (1880), and Edward Bellamy, author of *Looking Backward* (1888), acknowledged that a powerful trend toward consolidation defined their age, but they denied that the competition and struggle that drove evolution in the rest of nature applied to human society. Henry George asked how the tremendous increase in wealth over the course of the nineteenth century could have produced widespread poverty. "At the beginning of this marvelous era it was natural to expect, and it was expected," by men like Franklin, Jefferson, and Lincoln "that laborsaving inventions would lighten the toil and improve the condition of the laborer." Yet, as the century moved toward its close, "everywhere the greed of gain, the worship of wealth, shows the force of fear and want. The promise land flies before us like the mirage."[32] George was well aware that the presence of poverty amidst growing wealth was judged by the social Darwinists to be inevitable. He admitted, "The prevailing belief now is, that the progress of civilization is a development or evolution, in the course of which . . . the struggle for existence, just in proportion as it becomes intense, impels men to new efforts and inventions." This struggle for survival among men in the face of continually tightening resources, fuels "the tendency of the best adapted individual, or most improved individual, . . . and of the best adapted, or most improved tribe, nation, or race to survive in the struggle between social aggregates."[33] George punctured the presumption of Social Darwinism by quoting four wonderful lines from Alfred, Lord Tennyson, an eminent British poet:

> Are God and Nature then at strife
> That Nature lends such evil dreams?
> So careful of the type she seems
> So careless of the single life.[34]

Henry George's answer to the poet's question, and to the massed intellectual power of Malthus and Darwin, was that God and Nature were not at strife. In fact, God had given Nature to man for his use and support. Unlike the rest of nature, man could shape the world to his own benefit through the thoughtful and forward-looking use of science and technology. George made the point forcefully by saying, "Here is the difference between the animal and the man. Both the jayhawk and the man eat chickens, but the more jayhawks the fewer chickens, while the more men the more chickens."[35]

How, then, should society be organized to permit all of its members to address nature in ways designed to maximize their own and society's benefit? Henry George, casting back to Thomas Jefferson, thought that the solution was evident: "The laws of nature are the decrees of the Creator. . . . The equal right of all men to the use of land is as clear as their equal right to breathe the air—it is a right proclaimed by the fact of their existence." That some men claimed exclusive access to the land and other men were denied access to it was the fundamental social and economic dilemma of the age. George declared, "What I, therefore, propose, as the simple yet sovereign remedy, which will raise wages, increase the earnings of capital, extirpate pauperism, abolish poverty, give remunerative employment to whoever wishes it, afford free scope to human powers, lessen crime, elevate morals, and taste, and intelligence . . . is—To abolish all taxation save that upon land values."[36]

The tax upon land values, or the social appropriation of rent, "would be taken by the community for public uses, . . . Thus, as material progress went on, the condition of the masses would constantly improve." Even more importantly, society and government would change their whole visage and character. Society would be returned to "the ideal of Jeffersonian democracy" and government would shed its "directing and repressive power." Instead, "government would . . . become the administration of a great co-operative society."[37] From the resources made available by the land tax, government would build and maintain the economic infrastructure of the country—the railroads, telegraph, roads, and banks—that could not be safely or fairly left in private hands. In addition, the government would systematically seek to promote the development of the people themselves. Government "could establish public baths, museums, libraries, gardens, lecture rooms, music and dancing halls, theatres, universities, technical schools, . . . etc. Heat, light, and motive power, as well as water, might be conducted through our streets at public expense; our roads be lined with fruit trees; discovers and inventors rewarded, scientific investigations supported; and in a thousand ways the public revenues made to foster efforts for the public benefit." If society and government valued citizens equally and gave everyone the opportunity to thrive, "Talents now hidden, virtues unsuspected, would come forth to make human life richer, fuller, happier, nobler."[38] Henry George concluded *Progress and Poverty* with a peroration to America's most fundamental values. He identified his reform vision with the "letter and spirit of the truth enunciated in the Declaration of Independence—'That all men are created equal; that they are endowed by their Creator with certain unalienable rights, that among these are life, liberty, and the pursuit of happiness!'" In addition to summoning the shade of Thomas Jefferson, Henry George called forth the ghost of Thomas Paine, saying, "Liberty calls to us again. We must follow her further; we must trust her fully. Either we must wholly accept her or she will not stay. It is not enough that men should vote; . . . that they should be theoretically equal before the law. They must have liberty to avail themselves of the opportunities and means of life; they must stand on equal terms with reference to the bounty of nature."[39]

Though by a very different path, Edward Bellamy reached many of the same conclusions that Henry George had reached. Both thought that individualism needed to be balanced by community. Both thought that dividing men into classes, castes, and races ignored the underlying and fundamental equality of man. And both thought that humans were shaped more by nurture than by nature, by circumstances and conditions more than genes and evolution, and hence that society could change rapidly for the better as a result of thoughtful reform. Edward Bellamy's influential novel, *Looking Backward, 2000–1887* (1888), sold more than 300,000 copies in its first two years. In 1891, he founded a journal, *New Nation,* and nationalist clubs dedicated to his vision of social equality sprang up around the country. The nationalist movement was swept up in the Populist movement as the decade progressed, and Bellamy died in 1898 at the relatively young age of 48. Nonetheless, Edward Bellamy powerfully shaped the late-nineteenth-century critique of laissez-faire industrial capitalism. The literary device employed in *Looking Backward* was to transport a wealthy, well-educated Bostonian named Julian West from the Boston of 1887 to the Boston of 2000 and have him marvel at and inquire into the tremendous changes that had taken place. Julian West found himself in the year 2000 after a fire in 1887 destroyed his Boston home and reduced him to a coma in which the passage of time produced no ill physical or mental effects. Once he was discovered and awakened, attention soon turned to the differences between the Boston of 1887 and of 2000. Julian's interlocutors were Dr. Leete, a social historian of 2000 familiar with the 1880s, and the doctor's daughter, Edith.

Dr. Leete was interested to know how men of the late nineteenth century understood and accepted the poverty, class prejudice, and industrial conflict of the period, and Julian West was interested to know how those seemingly natural and inevitable social, political, and economic realities had been resolved. *Looking Backward* opened with a wonderful analogy that Julian West offered to explain late-nineteenth-century society. West described "a prodigious coach," drawn over a hilly terrain of loose and rocky soil, to which most of humanity was harnessed. Atop the coach, and never getting down no matter how sandy the soil or steep the hill, were society's elite, the wealthy, educated, and prominent. Those harnessed to the coach were very hard pressed: "the desperate straining of the team, their agonized leaping and plunging . . . , the many who fainted at the rope and were trampled in the mire, made a very distressing spectacle." Those atop the coach, by no means bereft of sympathy, "would call down encouragingly to the toilers at the rope, exhorting them to patience, and holding out hopes of possible compensation in another world for the hardness of their lot, while others contributed to buying salves and liniments for the crippled and injured. It was also agreed that it was a great pity that the coach should be so hard to pull."[40] Yet for three critical reasons, those atop the coach did no more than commiserate with their less fortunate fellows on the ropes. First, "it was firmly and sincerely believed that there was no other way in which Society could get along, except that the many pulled at the rope and the few rode." Second, it was so pleasant atop the coach and so fearsome below that the favored few held on as tight as they could. And third was a "singular hallucination which those on top of the coach generally shared, that they were not exactly like their brothers and sisters who pulled at the rope, but of finer clay, in some way belonging to a higher order of beings who might justly expect to be drawn."[41]

Dr. Leete responded that the scholarship of his day held that the basic intellectual error of the nineteenth century had been an "excessive individualism" that fueled mindless, destructive competition. The poverty, strikes, and violence had been produced by the struggle of working men against the concentration of capital. Nonetheless, while few recognized it at the time, this very process pointed the way to an unseen future, "the tendency toward monopolies, which had been so desperately and vainly resisted, was recognized at last, in its true significance, as a process which only needed to complete its logical evolution to . . . a single syndicate representing the people, to be conducted in the common interest for the common profit." Dr. Leete likened this economic evolution to the political revolution that had occurred a century earlier. He concluded, "The epoch of trusts had ended in The Great Trust. In a word, the people of the United States concluded to assume the conduct of their own business, just as a hundred-odd years before they had assumed the conduct of their own government, organizing now for industrial purposes on precisely the same grounds that they had been organized for political purposes."[42] Allowing robber barons to dominate the economy, Dr. Leete told Julian West, made no more sense than allowing the English monarchy to dominate politics had made a century earlier.

Like Henry George, Bellamy contended that changing the economic incentives to which individuals responded would reform society. Everyone would work, but the nature of the employment would be determined by choice and natural capacity and the desirability of jobs would be equalized by varying time and benefits. All citizens, irrespective of their individual capabilities of body or mind, would receive an equal share of society's wealth. Leete explained to Julian West, "the right of a man to maintenance at the nation's table depends on the fact that he is a man, and not on the amount of health or strength he may have. . . . The solidarity of the race and the brotherhood of man, which to you were but fine phrases, are, to our thinking and feeling, ties as real and as vital as physical fraternity."[43] The unquestioned right to an equal share of the social wealth removed all hunger, fear, and vulnerability among citizens and all the crime and violence that they produced.

George and Bellamy thought that life would reorganize itself completely in a society that held either land or all production in common. Yet while their visions were American dreams, they were not the American Dream. Still, it was clear to many that the American Dream of Franklin, Jefferson, and Lincoln, of independent farmers and craftsmen earning their bread by the sweat of their brow, was passing away. Frederick Jackson Turner, the prominent historian and father of the frontier thesis, famously announced to a nervous nation, in the wake of the 1890 census that "the frontier has gone, and with its going has closed the first period of American history."[44] Turner reminded Americans that land in the West had promoted widespread opportunity and political equality in the past but could not do so in the future. With the West filling up and free land becoming scarce, opportunity was sure to decline and inequality was just as sure to rise unless new foundations for aspiration and opportunity could be laid.

The Dream Embedded in Institutions, Law, and Policy

Most nineteenth-century Americans believed that society advanced most rapidly when individuals and firms competed for success and profits. Republicans, however, believed that government could advance, stimulate, and support economic growth without directing that growth or picking winners and losers. Conservative Democrats thought that government, especially at the national level, should be limited, cheap, and unobtrusive, allowing local people and their representatives to shape their communities and markets. Populists, most of whom had been and would later again be rural Democrats, worried that competition would never be fair for the little guy, unless government took control of the transportation, communication, and financial infrastructure on behalf of all the people.

The Republican Party program of the last third of the nineteenth century sought to provide and enhance opportunity over which citizens might compete, always recognizing that some would compete more effectively than others. For example, William McKinley was the leading figure in the Republican Party from the mid-1880s through the end of the century and the key architect of the party's critical tariff policy. Republican support for tariffs to protect American manufacturers from foreign competition, important to Hamilton's Federalists and Clay's Whigs earlier in the century, recognized that large businesses, even monopolies, might form behind the tariff barriers. Although the Republican Party was determined to protect American businesses from foreign competition, it had little interest in regulating business and none in taxing the wealth that business created. Business, naturally, appreciated the Republican support and reciprocated with extensive campaign contributions.

The Democratic Party stood for a modest national government, low taxes and tariffs, state and local control of internal improvements, and equal justice for white men. If William McKinley was the dominant figure in the Republican Party of the late nineteenth century, Grover Cleveland was his Democratic Party counterpart. Like his Democratic Party predecessors, Jefferson and Jackson, Cleveland stood four-square for individualism and self-help and against what he called government "paternalism." Government's only job was to provide "a fair field and no favor." Hence, when drought gripped the South in 1887 and Congress passed a bill providing $10,000 in free seed to hard-pressed Texas farmers, Cleveland vetoed the bill, saying "the lesson should be constantly enforced that, though the people support the Government, the Government should not support the people."[45] Cleveland called on state and local governments and private charities to respond to the farmers' need. Grover Cleveland was defeated for reelection in 1888 and then returned to win narrowly in 1892. Almost immediately, the nation fell into a deep recession that lasted through 1894 as a chorus of demands for help rose from the population. Cleveland was unmoved.

Major party policy left the hard-pressed farmers in dire straits throughout the 1880s and 1890s. In 1896, two decades of petition and protest culminated in a fusion of the Populist and Democratic parties behind the presidential candidacy of William Jennings Bryan. Farmers demanded that government act to address farm debt, lower the tariff, restrict alien and corporate land holding, and control the monopolists of finance and transportation. They demanded that banks, insurance companies, railroads, and grain elevators be heavily regulated or nationalized to stop these middlemen from gouging farmers and taking all of the profit out of agriculture. Republicans saw Bryan's candidacy and platform as a "vagabond" uprising against the established prerogatives of property. Equating regulation of business with theft, Republicans campaigned against Bryan behind the simple injunction, "Thou shalt not steal." God, Darwin, and William McKinley defeated Bryan in 1896 and 1900, and then the "Great Commoner" went down one more time in 1908. When the dust finally cleared, the agricultural republic of the nineteenth century had been replaced by the urban and industrial juggernaut of the American twentieth century.

Post–Civil War America was a Republican preserve occasionally interrupted by Democratic incursions. Republicans won nine of eleven presidential elections between Lincoln's first election in 1860 and McKinley's second in 1900, and they controlled Congress most of the time. The emotion that swept through the nation following Lincoln's assassination produced the Thirteenth, Fourteenth, and Fifteenth Amendments, as well as a series of civil rights acts between 1866 and 1875, promising federal protection of civil and political rights for blacks. In May 1870 Congress passed the first of a number of enforcement acts that put federal authority behind enforcement of equal rights for blacks. The Ku Klux Klan Act of 1871 authorized the president to call out troops to protect the electoral process. The Civil Rights Act of 1875 declared, "We recognize the equality of all men before the law and hold that it is the duty of government . . . to mete out equal and exact justice to all of whatever nativity, race, color, or persuasion, religious or political." The act banned discrimination in places that received the public, including restaurants, hotels, theaters, trolleys, and trains. Supporters claimed that under the terms of the Fourteenth Amendment, the Civil Rights Act of 1875 was enforceable against both governments and individuals.

Nonetheless, by the mid-1870s, both President Grant and the Congress shifted their focus from policing the South to promoting northern commerce and industry. The Supreme Court emerged as the dominant arbiter of the place of citizens, and particularly black citizens, within the American society, while Congress moved to stem undesirable immigration. Almost before the ink was dry on the Civil War amendments, the Supreme Court interpreted them in the narrowest possible terms. Soon thereafter, the Civil Rights Act of 1875 met the same fate, and by the end of the century, the Supreme Court had approved segregation of the races in virtually all public and private interactions. Together with this rapid diminution of the civil rights accorded to blacks came a stunning reassertion of the rights of property (Figure 5.2).

The Supreme Court decision that began to dismantle the hopes of the former slaves did not even involve blacks, although its implications for them

Figure 5.2. "This Is a White Man's Government," 1868. This Thomas Nast cartoon from the September 5, 1868, *Harper's Weekly* highlights rising white opposition, among the immigrant Irish, the unreconstructed South, and northern capital, to black equality. (Library of Congress, Prints and Photographs Division, reproduction LC-USZ62-121735)

were immense. The *Slaughterhouse Cases* (1873) were brought by a group of white New Orleans butchers who claimed that the creation of a slaughterhouse monopoly by the Louisiana state legislature denied them the equal protection of the laws promised by the Fourteenth Amendment. The Supreme Court rejected their plea, arguing that the Fourteenth Amendment was designed specifically to protect the citizenship rights of blacks, not to provide new legal remedies for whites against their state governments. What, then, were the rights of U.S. citizens? Justice Samuel F. Miller, writing for the majority of a court divided 5–4, held that national and state citizenships were essentially separate. National citizenship included only those rights, privileges, and immunities connected to the national government's responsibilities in interstate and international affairs. Under Justice Miller's reading, national citizenship protected a citizen while traveling abroad, engaging in interstate or foreign commerce, or engaging in activities not within the jurisdiction of a single state. All other rights belonging to Americans as citizens belonged to them as citizens of particular states. The *Slaughterhouse Cases* announced that state governments would be allowed to define the domestic rights of their citizens, including their black citizens, as narrowly as they wished and that the federal government would not interfere.

Over the next two decades, the Supreme Court moved very systematically to strike down the broadest interpretations of the Civil War amendments and the civil rights and enforcement acts until virtually nothing was left. The Court held in *U.S. v. Reese* (1876) that the Fifteenth Amendment did not confer the right to vote on anyone, white or black, but only held that the right could not be denied on account of race, color, or previous condition of servitude. This ruling declared key sections of the Enforcement Act of 1870 unconstitutional and returned control of elections to the states. The negotiated end of the disputed presidential election of 1876 soon brought the end of Reconstruction, the withdrawal of Union armies from the South, and the rapid return to dominance of the region's white majority.

The first major test of the Civil Rights Act of 1875, which made most racial discrimination illegal, whether practiced by public institutions or by private individuals, came in a set of cases known as the *Civil Rights Cases* (1883). In an 8–1 decision, Justice John Marshall Harlan I dissenting, the Supreme Court declared the Civil Rights Act of 1875 to be unconstitutional. Justice Joseph P. Bradley explained that the Fourteenth Amendment prohibited discriminatory "state action" against blacks; it did not prohibit and could not reach the private discrimination of one individual against another. In fact,

Bradley advised blacks to stop seeking "to be the special favorite of the laws" and be satisfied with "the rank of mere citizen." With this astounding admonition, the federal government withdrew from the fight against private discrimination against blacks.

Within a decade, the court would sanction state-mandated and -enforced separation of the races in public places. In 1890, the state of Louisiana passed a law requiring railroads to "provide equal but separate accommodations for the white and colored races" and requiring that "no person be permitted to occupy seats in coaches other than the ones assigned to his race." Homer Plessy, a citizen of Louisiana and one-eighth black, set out to test the law by boarding a train and occupying a seat in a car designated for white passengers. After Plessy's arrest, his lawyer argued that the Louisiana statute violated the Thirteenth and Fourteenth Amendments, and most particularly the "equal protection" clause of the Fourteenth Amendment. The court upheld the Louisiana statute and, by implication, most other segregation statutes, noting that "the action was not discriminatory since the whites were separated just as much from blacks as the blacks were separated from the whites." Justice Harlan wrote in vehement dissent, pointing first to the obvious hypocrisy of the claim that segregation by race was no "badge of inferiority" for blacks subjected to it. Justice Harlan went on to state the case for black equality that he believed to be inherent in the Thirteenth and Fourteenth Amendments. He explained that "there is in this country no superior, dominant, ruling class of citizens. . . . Our constitution is color-blind, and neither knows nor tolerates classes among citizens. In respect of civil rights all citizens are equal before the law. The humblest is the peer of the most powerful. The law regards man as man, and takes no account of his . . . color when his civil rights . . . are involved." It would be more than half a century before these powerful words would be accepted by a majority of the nation's highest court.

The outcome of the Civil War also seemed to require changes in who could become an American citizen. Congress passed a new Naturalization Act in 1870 that reflected domestic emancipation by allowing the naturalization of African immigrants, but the tide was already turning against liberal egalitarianism. The impact of Darwinian ideas on American thinking about immigration, naturalization, and citizenship was evident in a debate over declarant alien suffrage (whether to allow immigrants to vote before their naturalized U.S. citizenship was official) in the Ohio Constitutional Convention of 1873–74. A delegate named Lewis D. Campbell was concerned that shifting immigration patterns from Britain and northern Europe to southern and eastern Europe, to say nothing of Asia and Africa, made it dangerous to allow noncitizens to vote. Campbell sought to terrify his colleagues with the prospect that alien suffrage "will be granted not only to the unnaturalized foreigner who comes here from European countries, but also to the unnaturalized African who might be brought over . . . by Dr. Livingstone; a specimen of the connecting link between man and the animal, as described by the theory of Darwin, and bring him to Ohio, that link could not only claim to become a citizen of the United States, but without naturalization . . . claim to be a sovereign, a voter and an officeholder. . . . The Chinese, the Japanese, and even the Ashantees . . . could become voters."[46] Whether Campbell's concerns carried the day is unclear, but it is clear that following extensive debate the proposal to allow alien suffrage was defeated.

Congress soon began tightening immigration policy as well. The Immigration Act of 1882 barred undesirables of all races, specifically prohibiting felons, lunatics, idiots, and persons likely to become public charges. In fact, shipping companies were made responsible for the return passage of any undesirable that they might carry to American shores. Congress also bowed to western pressure by passing the Chinese Exclusion Act. The Chinese Exclusion Act of 1882 tightened the rules on Chinese immigration and declared Chinese already in the country to be "aliens ineligible for citizenship." The Geary Act of 1892 extended the Chinese Exclusion Act for another decade, and by the end of the century restrictions on immigration and naturalization included virtually all Asians.[47]

Social Darwinism convinced the nation's traditional elites, almost all Protestant Anglo-Saxons, that they were in danger of being overwhelmed by hordes of Catholics, Jews, Moslems, and Buddhists, from southern and central Europe, India, and Asia. Professor E. H. Johnson of the Crozier Theological Institute warned his readers of the danger, saying "I have stood" in the Port of New York "and seen races of far greater peril to us than the Irish. I have seen the Hungarians, and the Italians, and the Poles. I have seen these poor wretches trooping out, wretches physically, wretches mentally, wretches morally, and stood there almost trembling for my country. . . . In the name of God, what shall we do if the American race is to receive constant influx of that sort of thing."[48] Henry Cabot Lodge, representative and then senator from Massachusetts, knew what to do—halt the influx. Lodge sponsored literacy tests for immigrants, which he believed, would rest lightly on northern Europeans while excluding just those wretches that had so horrified Professor

Johnson. Senator Lodge drew on evolutionary theory to explain that what made a race of people like the Americans was "the slow growth and accumulation of centuries of toil and conflict" that created a distinctive, but vulnerable, "stock of ideas, traditions, sentiments, modes of thought," which form the "soul of a race." That very soul, "the quality of our race," was at risk, Lodge warned, when "a lower race mixes with a higher race in sufficient numbers."[49]

Social Darwinists believed that once the fundamental integrity of the society was secured the legitimate responsibilities of government were few, involving only the protection of life and property, the administration of justice, and the provision of collective goods, like national defense. If government provided an environment of peace, safety, and security, then freedom, choice, and contract could govern the rest of man's interaction with his fellows. Social Darwinists saw the right to contract as the best way for free men to make decisions about their interests and opportunities. The right to contract allowed individuals to reach agreement among themselves about how to deploy their persons and their property in the economy and the society. Populists and reform Darwinists argued that the freedom of the individual farmer to contract with the railroad to carry his grain to market was little more than a license for the railroad to rob each isolated, helpless farmer. They argued that the railroads, banks, and grain elevators, the middlemen that stood between the farmer and the consumer and drained off all the profit in agriculture, should be heavily regulated or nationalized and administered by the state for the benefit of the society.

For at least forty years after the end of the Civil War, advocates of laissez-faire worked through the nation's federal courts to weaken, limit, or strike down legislative initiatives designed to regulate and control corporations. By the middle of the 1880s, the U.S. Supreme Court had developed several lines of defense against the regulation of private property by the state and national governments. First, the Supreme Court declared, in the *Railway Commission Cases* (1886) and elsewhere, that most attempts at government regulation of private property were violations of "substantive due process"—in other words, that the mere attempt to regulate was a violation of the due process rights of property holders. Laws and regulations that limited the individual's right to make decisions about where to live, what kind of business or employment to undertake, and under what conditions and circumstances were unconstitutional limitations on free markets and free men. Second, the Supreme Court declared that the Fourteenth Amendment, initially intended to protect the rights of newly freed slaves, also protected property from government action. The Fourteenth Amendment forbade any state "to deprive any person of life, liberty, or property, without due process of law; nor deny to any person . . . the equal protection of the laws." In the case of *Santa Clara County v. Southern Pacific Railroad Company* (1886), the court held that the word *person* in the Fourteenth Amendment applied equally to corporations and to individuals. Hence, corporate and personal property enjoyed the same benefits of due process and equal protection. Third, the Supreme Court specifically limited the ability of states to regulate powerful economic actors like banks and railroads. Populists had enjoyed some success in urging state governments to assume regulatory control of institutions—like railroads, banks, and grain elevators—whose monopoly positions allowed them to threaten the security and prosperity of millions of citizens. But when Illinois sought to regulate the railroads operating within its boundaries, the Supreme Court declared in *Wabash v. Illinois* (1886) that states could not regulate railroads or other businesses that operated in interstate commerce. Once the court struck down state regulation of railroads, Congress tentatively moved to offer some relief. In 1887 Congress created the first independent regulatory agency, the Interstate Commerce Commission (ICC). The ICC was charged to set fair and equitable rates for passengers and freight, enforce its regulations, and adjudicate disputes. Against the Congress's initial determination to regulate aspects of corporate behavior in the marketplace, the court declared "the general rule of the absolute liberty of the individual to contract" in *People v. Budd* (1889).[50]

The high point of the court's battle against regulation of business and employment agreements between individuals came in the case of *Lochner v. New York* (1905). New York had sought on grounds of health and public safety to limit the hours that bakers might work to no more than sixty hours a week and ten hours a day. Evidence was presented indicating that bakers who worked longer suffered from lung and respiratory ailments that might be passed to the public. The Supreme Court rejected the rationale and the law, with Justice Peckham arguing for the court, "There is no reasonable grounds for interfering with the liberty of person or the right of free contract, by determining the hours of labor. . . . There is no contention that bakers as a class are . . . not able to . . . care for themselves without the protecting arm of the state interfering with their independence. . . . They are in no sense wards of the state." Though the New York law seeking to protect bakers from the ill effects of their work was declared unconstitutional, Justice Oliver Wendell Holmes penned a stinging dissent. Holmes reminded his colleagues that "the 14th Amendment does not enact Mr. [Herbert] Spencer's *Social Statics*. . . . A

Constitution is not intended to embody a particular economic theory, whether of paternalism . . . or of laissez-faire." Within a few short years, social Darwinism would be in a slow retreat not completed until the 1930s, if then, but between about 1875 and 1905, it came close to being the law of the land.

As the social and economic elites of the late nineteenth century cleared the terrain for competition, they did recognize that that terrain had shifted. Land and education took on different meanings than they had born at earlier stages of American history. During the last third of the nineteenth century, Americans settled more territory than they had during the previous two hundred fifty years. This period was extraordinarily tumultuous, including the building of the great western railroads, a tremendous westward migration, the opening of vast stretches of Indian territory, and the last of the major Indian wars. When the dust cleared, the continent had been claimed, if not quite settled. More than 130 million acres was given to the railroads by the federal government between 1862 and 1885. The first transcontinental railroad was completed on May 10, 1869, when the Central Pacific, pushing west from Chicago, linked up with the Union Pacific, pushing east from San Francisco, at Promontory Point, Utah. The Southern Pacific Railroad, connecting New Orleans to California, was completed in 1882 and the Northern Pacific Railroad, connecting Minneapolis to Portland, Oregon, was competed in 1883. In 1893 the Great Northern Railroad opened between St. Paul and Seattle to compete with the Northern Pacific. The land grants to the railroads totaled three times the land area of New England and included "a fifth of the land in Montana . . . and an eighth of the land in California."[51] The railroads financed their western construction by selling land to settlers. Railroad agents scoured American and European cities as far east as Russia and Poland for families that wanted to migrate to the American West. The railroads knew that they could only make money if the land along the route filled up with farms and towns so they had people and freight to carry (Figure 5.3).

In addition to the land grants to railroads, about 10 million acres were awarded under the Morrill Act for the support of land grant colleges, and nearly 100 million acres were awarded under the Homestead Act to settlers willing to occupy and improve the land. Miners and prospectors also scoured the mountain west and the Black Hills of South Dakota in search of riches. The General Mining Act of 1872 opened federal land in the West to mining at very low cost and with few restrictions on land use or environmental impact. With so much at stake for those who got there early enough to stake out the best homestead, mining site, or railroad right of way, the scramble was intense.

Figure 5.3. "The Great Race for the Western Stakes," 1870. This Currier & Ives print depicts the contest between Cornelius Vanderbilt and James Fisk for dominance of the nation's railroads. (Library of Congress, Prints and Photographs Division, reproduction LC-USZ62-1374)

Although pockets of available land lasted well into the twentieth century, the identifiable line of settlement that had pushed west for most of American history had broken up and settlements were scattered across the continent. The great Oklahoma land rush of 1889, the last great battle between the U.S. Army and the Plains Indians at Wounded Knee in 1890, and the formal declaration in the census of 1890 that there was no longer an identifiable frontier line in the West, marked the end of an era in American history.

As open land grew scarce and the American society and economy evolved from overwhelmingly rural and agrarian to increasingly urban and industrial, the importance of a well-educated population became increasingly clear. Moreover, education was seen as a prime means of Americanization, particularly after the Civil War, when the flow of immigrants became more diverse. School texts were explicitly designed to inculcate American history, culture, and values. When Catholic immigrants resisted the overwhelmingly Protestant cast of American public education by building their own schools, the

Protestant majority fought back. By the end of the century, two-thirds of the states had passed laws declaring that no public monies should be allocated to religious or parochial schools.

Business and community support for elementary education was strong because it taught the fundamental skills that students needed to read their Bible, follow the events of the day, and play a productive role in farming, commerce, and manufacturing. Public school attendance (kindergarten through eighth grade) increased from 6.8 million students in 1870 to 15 million in 1900. In addition, the proportion of all children attending public school increased from 57 percent in 1870 to 72 percent in 1900. The number of teachers working in public schools more than doubled between 1870 and 1900, from 200,515 to 423,062, while elementary school spending also grew sharply, from about $63 million to nearly $215 million. Business and community interests were much more critical of the nation's high schools. High schools taught a college-prep curriculum that focused on Greek, Latin, philosophy, European and ancient history, religion, and political economy. These subjects were seen as preparing students for a leisured literary life, so few working- and middle-class young men even considered high school. Hence, in 1870 only about 80,000 students were attending high school in the United States and only about 2 percent of 18-year-olds graduated from high school. By 1900, more than half a million students were attending high school, but the graduation rate had only climbed to 6.4 percent.[52] High school graduates went on to college where theology, law, and medicine were the main courses of study. Andrew Carnegie, ever ready with a striking opinion, declared that colleges educated young men "as if they were destined for life on some other planet. . . . The fire and energy have been stamped out of them, and how to so manage as to live a life of idleness and not a life of usefulness has become the chief question with them."[53] Yet the 300 colleges in existence by 1860 had become more than 800 by 1880 and nearly 1,000 by 1900, and their curricula were evolving.

Both agriculture and manufacturing required more scientific knowledge than had formerly been necessary and universities began to respond after midcentury. The University of Michigan established a College of Agriculture in 1857 and the Morrill Land Grant Act of 1862 encouraged the establishment of agricultural colleges throughout the nation. In 1881, the Philadelphia merchant Joseph Wharton established the Wharton School of Finance and Economy to train "educated young men with a taste for business, vigorous, active workers, of sturdy character and independent opinion."[54] Business leaders like Johns Hopkins, Leland Stanford, and John D. Rockefeller either founded or endowed universities to assist in training a new business elite.[55] Finally, in 1887, Congress passed the Hatch Act, which established a thick network of agricultural experiment stations with federal assistance, to promote "a sound and prosperous agriculture and rural life." A strong agricultural economy, the act noted, was "indispensable to the maintenance of maximum employment and national prosperity and security." As the new century dawned, national policy was steadily coming to recognize that education was an increasingly important requisite to success in America. But success was still a goal that only white American men could pursue.

The Faces of Exclusion

The violence of the American Civil War was physical, intellectual, and emotional. The intellectual and emotional violence of the war and its aftermath broke apart traditional patterns of cooperation among those working for equality and left each group standing isolated before a social consensus that rejected their arguments and demands. Before the war, blacks, women, and labor had demanded the natural rights promised to all Americans in the Declaration of Independence. After the war, natural rights claims were compromised by the contention that status and rights were determined by the laws of nature through competition and struggle leading to the survival of the fittest among individuals and peoples. Charles Darwin had been quite clear in the famous chapter on "Natural Selection" in *Origin of Species* that competition led not just to individual winners and losers, but to survival and extinction for species. In nature, including that corner of nature that is human society, "the struggle for existence" produces "a constant tendency . . . to supplant and exterminate." The tendency to "supplant and exterminate" is the inevitable result of competition and struggle, in which "One large group [read white Anglo-Saxons, or simply whites] will slowly conquer another large group [read Africans, Asians, Indians, and so on], reduce its numbers, and thus lessen its chance of further variation and improvement. . . . Small and broken groups will finally tend to disappear."

The rising sentiment among Anglo-Saxon elites was captured by the British epic poet Rudyard Kipling in his classic reference to the "white man's burden." Caleb Cushing, American commissioner to China in the 1840s and U.S. attorney general in the 1850s, articulated an especially raw version of this idea in 1870 when he declared his commitment "to the excellent white race, . . . whose power and privilege it is, wherever they may go . . . to Christianize and to civilize, to command and to be obeyed, to conquer and to reign. I admit to an equality with men, sir, the white man—my blood and race. . . . But I do not admit as my equals either the red man of America, or the yellow man of Asia, or the black man of Africa."[56] In the struggle for survival, in which the small and broken groups that competition left behind would face extinction, Caleb Cushing would stand with "the excellent white race."

One of the most powerful effects of Darwinian social theory was to undermine the ability of excluded groups to make claims on society. Scientific racism compromised Reconstruction by suggesting that although freedom and equality were formally granted to black men in the wake of the Civil War by the Thirteenth, Fourteenth, and Fifteenth Amendments to the Constitution, real freedom and equality had to be earned in the open competition of the marketplace. Success in the marketplace confirmed, indeed demonstrated, freedom and equality, while failure to thrive confirmed inability and inferiority. If the freedmen failed to thrive, as most did, the immediate conclusion was that the gift of freedom and the related assumption of equality had been ill advised.

At the end of the Civil War, blacks were freed with no land, no income, and few skills. Not surprisingly, most former slaves soon fell into a form of quasi-slavery known as the sharecropping or crop-lien system that would dominate southern agriculture into the 1930s. White landowners, oftentimes former slave masters dealing with their former slaves, would contract with black families to farm part of their land. The landowner would supply the land, seeds, tools, and food and supplies to keep the family through the winter in exchange for a portion of the next crop. The real effect of the system was to keep black sharecroppers in constant and often deepening debt to white landowners. Southern redeemer governments bound black workers in place by passing harsh vagrancy laws that required blacks to be employed and prohibited employed blacks from leaving a job until the contract period had expired. Blacks were also forbidden to leave the county in which they resided until they were debt free.

Southern state governments moved inexorably throughout the 1880s and 1890s to limit and then exclude black participation in political, legal, and civil processes. The Fifteenth Amendment promised that men would not be denied the right to vote on the basis of race, color, or previous condition of servitude. Nonetheless, state legislatures were endlessly creative in developing intricate registration processes, literacy and property requirements, poll taxes, grandfather tests, and white primaries to remove blacks from the electoral and political processes. By the end of the century, few southern blacks could cast a ballot, serve on a jury, or attend school. Outside the South, segregation was subtler, but blacks were often unwelcome and unprotected.

In addition to economic and political discrimination, blacks were socially and culturally spurned and humiliated. By 1860 about half of the states had laws against interracial sex and marriage. Emancipation led more states to pass laws and states that already had them moved to strengthen them. Mississippi made interracial marriage a felony carrying a penalty of life imprisonment. By the late nineteenth century fully 80 percent of the states outlawed marriage between blacks and whites, and about half of these outlawed interracial sex. Sexual fantasies and fears, legitimated by a thin veneer of Darwinist rhetoric, produced endless talk of mongrelization of the white race should mixing with lower races occur. The Supreme Court held that since both races, white and black, were forbidden to have sex or marry across racial lines, such laws did not violate "equal protection of the laws."

How blacks should respond to this unremittingly hostile environment was a subject of heated debate within the black community and among black leaders. Frederick Douglass, the foremost black leader in nineteenth-century America, called for the fulfillment of the egalitarian vision to which he had coaxed Abraham Lincoln. Douglass held that "All that any man has a right to expect, ask, give, or receive in this world, is fair play. When society has secured this to its members, and the humblest citizen of the republic is put into the undisturbed possession of the natural fruits of his own exertions, there is really very little left for society and government to do."[57] Douglass knew that such a day had not yet come, and to his dying day in 1897 he decried the unwillingness of a great nation to live up to its values.

Women also pushed an equal rights agenda in post–Civil War America. The nation's centennial celebration in 1876 seemed an obvious setting in which to renew these demands. Although denied space in the official Philadelphia exhibit halls, Elizabeth Cady Stanton and others prepared a "Declaration of Rights for Women" reminiscent of the 1848 Seneca Falls Declaration of Sentiments. The Declaration of Rights read, "we declare our faith in the principle of self-government; our full equality with man in natural rights; . . . We ask of our rulers, at this hour, no special favors, no special privileges, no special legislation. We ask justice, we ask equality, we ask that all the civil and political rights that belong to citizens of the United States, be guaranteed to us and our daughters forever."[58]

Once again the federal courts were at the forefront of maintaining the subservient role of women in American society. The federal courts were consistent in upholding state and federal laws that barred women from the practice of law (*Bradwell v. Illinois,* 1872), voting (*U.S. v. Anthony,* 1873 and *Minor v. Happersett,* 1875), and jury service (*Strauder v. West Virginia,* 1879). In all of these cases, the Supreme Court held that the privileges and immunities guaranteed to citizens in the Fourteenth Amendment did not cover the right to practice law, vote, or serve on juries. States could grant or withhold these privileges as they saw fit. In *Bradwell,* Justice Bradley wrote, "'nature herself,' along with 'the divine ordinance,' indicated 'the domestic sphere as that which properly belongs to the domain and functions of womanhood.'"[59] By 1876 feminist Lucy Stone was arguing in the *Woman's Journal* that "the old opposition, founded on texts of Scripture, has ceased to be urged or nearly so; ... the later form of scientific objection is now coolly affirmed"[60] (Figure 5.4).

As egalitarian feminism waned, at least for a time, a new brand of difference feminism arose which some women found ideologically comfortable and politically useful. Many who found the idea of equality between men and women unacceptable could accept the idea that although nature made men and women different, women had distinctive virtues and capabilities that deserved respect and could work a positive influence on society. Others simply saw white women as a cultural and political balance to the Slavs, Asians, Mexicans, and former slaves that threatened the dominance of traditional elites. Hence, during the last three decades of the nineteenth century, women emerged from the home to make advances in education, the workplace, and the community, even if full equality continued to elude them.

Two western territories—Wyoming in 1869 and Utah in 1870—awarded women the right to vote, and by the early 1890s, twenty states allowed women to vote in school board elections. Frances Willard, president of the Women's Christian Temperance Union from 1879 to 1899, pushed a program of limited female suffrage called the "Home Protection Ballot." The movement for a Home Protection Ballot argued that women's responsibility for the quality and character of home life made it critical that they have the political access and authority to prohibit liquor and prostitution in their neighborhoods, and to support their own educational development, as well as schools and health care for their children. The call for a "maternal commonwealth" was the call for a commonwealth that accepted and reflected the special virtues and vision—of a peaceful, sober, nurturing, and family-centered community—of the nation's women.

Woman Devotes Her Time to Gossip and Clothes Because She Has Nothing Else to Talk About.   Give Her
Broader Interests and She Will Cease to Be Vain and Frivolous.

Figure 5.4. "Woman's Sphere," undated, circa 1880s. This image from the
National American Woman Suffrage Association Collection of the Library of
Congress depicts women peering from their limited sphere of home and
children into the broader world beyond. (Library of Congress, Prints and
Photographs Division, digital ID n7140 rbnawsa)

The image of America as a maternal commonwealth did not challenge traditional gender roles directly, although it did claim that women needed to be
better informed and educated if they were to protect their homes and shape
peaceful, wholesome communities. Several women's magazines reflecting an
enhanced appreciation of domestic life were launched after the Civil War,
including *Women's Home Companion* (1873), *Women's Home Journal* (1878),
Ladies Home Journal (1883), and *Good Housekeeping* (1885). Moreover, by
1870 elementary and secondary education was almost entirely coeducational.
Vassar, Smith, Wellesley, and Radcliffe opened as women's colleges between
1860 and 1900, and more than one-quarter of the nation's colleges and universities, including most of the new state universities in the West and
Midwest, were open to both men and women. Between 1870 and 1900, the
proportion of college students who were women nearly doubled from 21 percent to 40 percent.

The job market for women was evolving as well. After 1870, clerical and sales positions for young, native-born white women expanded dramatically. The invention of the typewriter made many of the clerk positions formerly open only to men available to women, and the development of urban department stores required young, usually middle-class, women with good language and arithmetic skills. By 1890, 18 percent of women over age 14 were in the workforce. Black women were twice as likely as white women to work for wages (38 percent to 16 percent), and young, single women were about eight times more likely to work for wages than married women (37 percent to 4.5 percent). Only 3 percent of married white women worked for wages outside the home. As the nineteenth century closed, women's position in society was improving slowly.

Not so for Native Americans. As the nineteenth century neared its close, American Indians were about as good an example as one might find in the world of a human social group that was, in Darwin's terms, "scattered and broken" and awaiting its final demise. Henry George explained that the plight of the Indians was no accident, but a predictable result of the attitudes and policies of the larger and dominant group in society: the white majority. George said, much as Tocqueville had a half century earlier, that "To the Anglo-Saxon of the frontier, as a rule, the aborigine has no rights which the white man is bound to respect. . . . In America the Anglo-Saxon has exterminated, instead of civilizing, the Indian."[61]

By 1867 the federal government had established reservations, mostly in the Dakotas and Oklahoma. President Grant's "peace policy" envisioned one last attempt to educate and Christianize the Indians in anticipation of their immersion in the dominant culture. The peace policy sought to strip away the Indian culture and replace it with white, middle-class, Christian individualism so that Indians could compete for their place, high or low, in the broader American society. Most Americans believed that this sink-or-swim policy, as Darwin had suggested more generally, might be hard on the least competitive individuals, but it was best for the race, and the pain involved, after all, was inevitable.

In 1887, the peace policy gave way to the Dawes Act. Attempts at education and socialization had been made; now tribes should be rendered into individuals who should strive, struggle, and compete for their share of the American bounty. The Dawes Act, also called the General Allotment Act, offered U.S. citizenship to Indians who "adopted the habits of civilized life" and accepted a private allotment from the tribal lands. The general allotment offered individual Indians title to 80 acres. Families could get 160 acres. Although some tribal lands remained, much of the undistributed land was declared surplus and sold to non-Indians. Indian lands that stood at 138 million acres in 1887 had declined to no more than 78 million acres by 1900.[62] In the sink-or-swim world of the late nineteenth century, it seemed that assimilation was possible for some Indians, but that extermination was likely for most. Such was nature's way.

The Dream Defended: The Age of Reform from TR to FDR

Our job was to preserve the American ideal of economic as well as political democracy, against the abuse of concentration of economic power that had been insidiously growing up among us in the past fifty years.

—Franklin Roosevelt, campaign address, 1936

Modern America became recognizable in the early years of the twentieth century. The commercial application of electricity in the first decade of the century powered lights, mass transit, and round-the-clock use of factories. Soon came telephones, radio, and movies. In the second decade of the century, railroad building declined and road building increased, reflecting and promoting growth in the oil, gas, and auto industries. Through the first third of the century, consumer goods continued to displace capital goods as the leading products of American business. Advertising and marketing became increasingly important as America became a mass consumption society.

Despite rapid social and economic change, conservatives argued for adherence to the competitive individualism that they believed underlay the nation's evident growth and prosperity. Alternatively, reformers argued that these changes demanded careful thought and detailed planning to assure social order and economic efficiency. Reformers did achieve some of their most important goals. The role of government expanded under Theodore Roosevelt and Woodrow Wilson, with new independent boards and commissions created to oversee activities in areas like health, education, taxation, corrections, and natural resources. But broader reform initiatives were defeated or weakened by conservative opposition. Indeed, many saw the Republican ascendancy of the 1920s as a "return to normalcy" because it restored business priorities, market principles, and a "night watchman" view of government. Not until the Great Depression shattered the basic assumptions of nineteenth-century political economy were most Americans receptive to new ways to conceive the relationships between business, government, society, and citizens. Franklin Roosevelt argued that common people were more vulnerable in an urban, industrial society, where they worked for wages or ran small businesses, than they had been when most lived on farms and in rural villages. Roosevelt explicitly sought to redefine the American Dream for the urban and industrial America of his day and to make the national government responsible for restoring broad access to it.

Still, the long night of exclusion continued for many Americans. The dawn came first for women, even as minorities, immigrants, and American Indians continued in darkness for decades more. Urban society offered women new social and economic opportunities, and by 1920 the struggle for suffrage was won. Eventually, the New Deal brought hope to minorities and Indians that their exclusion would lessen. Yet ethnic and racial discrimination remained entrenched national policy until World War II forced the nation to acknowledge its shortcomings before a world sickened by Hitler's racism.

Young Dreamers and the World Before Them

The rapid social and economic change that occurred during the two decades on either side of 1900 left Americans frightened and uncertain. Economic entities of unprecedented size, the new monopolies and trusts, seemed beyond the control of individuals and even governments. By 1900 a generation of industrial titans, led and epitomized by John D. Rockefeller, Andrew Carnegie, and J. P. Morgan, stood astride American business. Rockefeller's strategy of combination and control left him in command of 90 percent of the domestic oil industry in 1900, and in 1901 Morgan bought out Carnegie to create U.S. Steel, the largest business enterprise of its day. Morgan sought to expand his empire to shipping and telephones, but by the early years of the twentieth century, the unrestricted right of entrepreneurs to organize and control the nation's productive capability was coming under increasing scrutiny.

No critic of the old order was more scathing than the economist Thorstein Veblen. Veblen's classic *The Theory of the Leisure Class* (1899) was followed by *The Theory of Business Enterprise* (1904) and *The Instinct of Workmanship* (1914). *The Theory of the Leisure Class* was so joyfully irreverent toward the laissez-faire philosophy of the late nineteenth century that many readers took it to be satire. Veblen argued that unregulated competition favored the destructive instincts of the few over the creative and humane workmanship of the many. Although Veblen shook up the way society thought about work, success, and consumption—he coined the famous phrase *conspicuous consumption*—he was too iconoclastic to enjoy direct political influence. Ida Tarbell, on the other hand, was both a leading reformer and a shrewd political activist. Tarbell's *History of the Standard Oil Company* (1904) laid bare the human cost, unscrupulous business practices, and political chicanery that accompanied the trust's rise to power. Herbert Croly, although a more retiring academic sort, had the good fortune to write a book that came to the animated attention of Theodore Roosevelt. Croly's influential book, *The Promise of American Life* (1909), described industrial concentration as an immediate and general threat to American public life and values. Croly argued, "The rich men and the big corporations have become too wealthy and powerful for their official standing in American life. . . . Children, as they are, of the traditional American individualistic institutions, ideas, and practices, they have turned on their parents and dealt them an ugly wound." Like Veblen, Tarbell, and many others, Croly concluded, "Either these economic monsters will destroy the system of ideas, institutions, and practices out of which they have issued or else be destroyed by them."[1]

Although economic turmoil attracted much attention, there was also great concern about the threats posed by social and cultural turmoil. A million immigrants, mostly from southern and eastern Europe, mostly poor and illiterate, and mostly Catholics and Jews, arrived every year from 1900 to 1914. The vast majority of the new immigrants came from Russia, central Europe, and Italy. Far fewer, averaging less than 100,000 each year, came from northern Europe. Both the large numbers and the unfamiliar cultures of the new immigrants concerned traditional elites. World War I and its aftermath, especially the rise of communism in Russia and the subsequent red scare in America, capped three decades of growing concern about how to control and "Americanize" these foreign hordes.

Black migrants from the southern countryside also raised concern. As late as 1914, 90 percent of blacks lived in the South, most in the rural South.

During World War I, 400,000 blacks served in the army, and nearly twice that number found work in northern industries, including the railroads, the auto and steel industries, and the textile industry, all formerly closed to them. The census of 1920 reported that the black population of New York had nearly tripled in the previous decade, Pittsburgh's black population had more than doubled, and Chicago's had almost doubled. And the exodus was just beginning. A million blacks left the South between 1920 and the outbreak of World War II, and the war itself produced an even broader migration.

This burgeoning social diversity convinced many that the nation's stability depended on reestablishing a homogeneous and cohesive social order. A. Lawrence Lowell, a Harvard government professor and future president of that institution, and Charles Francis Adams, grandson and great-grandson of presidents, proposed limiting political participation to the native born and the well prepared.[2] Others, including leading pragmatists John Dewey and William James, argued for a more inclusive ethic. They trusted public education to teach children—native born and immigrant—a broadly progressive American ethic. "The end in view," Dewey declared of the schools, "is the development of a spirit of social cooperation and community life." Dewey saw schools not as institutions for rote memory and training, but as open spaces for innovation, experimentation, and learning by doing. Dewey thought that schools should "lay hold upon the rudimentary instincts of human nature, and, by supplying a proper medium, so control their expression as . . . to facilitate and enrich the growth of the individual child."[3]

William James's most famous book, entitled *Pragmatism* (1907), espoused the same activist posture that Dewey extolled. Unlike the social Darwinists, for whom nature and natural law were irresistible forces, progressive reformers saw knowledge, intelligence, and rationality as "implements." As James explained, "We don't lie back upon them, we move forward, and, on occasion, we make nature over again by their aid."[4] Walter Lippmann, the young protégé of Croly, Dewey, and James, published a book entitled *Drift and Mastery* (1914) in which he proclaimed education, innovation, and science to be the saving forces of the new century. He identified "the scientific spirit" as "the discipline of democracy" and "the outlook of a free man." Rejecting the Darwinian complacency of the previous generation, Lippmann said, "Rightly understood science is the culture under which people can live forward in the midst of complexity, and treat life not as something given but something to be shaped."[5]

Leading politicians also concluded that the increasing diversity of American society and the continuing concentration of economic power demanded a more competent federal government. Both Theodore Roosevelt (1901–9) and Woodrow Wilson (1913–21) eschewed the passive presidency of the nineteenth century in favor of an assertive presidency intended to educate the public and shape their opinions. The "bully pulpit," as TR described the presidency, was new. The telegraph and telephone, as well as proliferation of newspapers, magazines, and books, allowed Roosevelt to reach the people with an immediacy that his predecessors had never enjoyed. Improvements in photojournalism and then film gave presidents a personality and a centrality that enhanced their impact and influence. TR's muscular presidency convinced Wilson that presidents should not only act forcefully but that they, not Congress, should lead the government. In *Constitutional Government in the United States* (1909), Wilson declared that the state "must every day act with straightforward and unquestionable power, with definite purpose and consistent force, choosing its policies and making good its authority," whatever the problems at hand. Moreover, "so far as the government itself is concerned, there is but one national voice in the country, and that is the voice of the President."[6]

World War I forced President Wilson to shelve his program to regulate economic power. Instead, he was forced to go into partnership with corporate America to win the war. In the wake of the war, pent-up demand and the need to feed and rebuild Europe produced a decade of social experimentation and unprecedented economic expansion—the Roaring Twenties. The novelist F. Scott Fitzgerald later wrote that once "The uncertainties of 1919 were over—there seemed little doubt about what was going to happen—America was going on the greatest, gaudiest spree in history. . . . The whole golden boom was in the air—its splendid generosities, its outrageous corruptions and the torturous death of the old America."[7] The "golden boom" of the 1920s seemed to produce wealth and opportunity in abundance and to make further political and economic reform unnecessary. Those least well off, as President Hoover noted, could look to private charity in difficult times. Soon, such complacency would have no place.

The stock market crash of October 1929 paralyzed the American economy, and the Great Depression of the 1930s slowly strangled prosperity for most Americans. Virtually every measure of national and individual wealth and well-being in the United States plummeted in 1929, reached its lowest point in 1932–33, and then climbed slowly and unevenly back. At the broadest level, gross national product reached $104.4 billion in 1929. By 1933 it was down

Figure 6.1. "Line at a Soup Kitchen," 1930. The gangster Al Capone ran a soup kitchen in Chicago to help the unemployed at the height of the Depression. This photo was taken on November 16, 1930. (Corbis/Bettmann, image NA002617)

nearly one-third, to $74.2 billion, and it did not recover its 1929 levels until 1939. Wholesale prices and average weekly wages fell by about one-third between 1929 and 1933, not again reaching their 1929 levels until the early 1940s.[8] Unemployment, which had averaged 4.65 percent between 1900 and 1929, averaged almost 19 percent during the 1930s and over 20 percent for four years running, 1932–35, cresting at nearly 25 percent (13 million workers) in 1933. There were still more than 10 million unemployed in 1938, and the 1929 level of 3.2 percent and 1.55 million unemployed were not again reached until World War II, 1942–43[9] (Figure 6.1).

Even the nation's most powerful corporations and businesses suffered tremendously. Between 1929 and 1933 stock values fell by 75 percent, the value of industrial and railroad stock by 80 percent, and the value of General Motors stock, one of America's top companies, fell by almost 90 percent, from a high of $72.75 in 1929 to a low of $7.63 in 1932. More than 40 percent of U.S. banks failed between 1929 and 1934; most simply closed their doors, and the unlucky depositors were left with nothing. The U.S. economy grew by only 3.7 percent between 1929 and 1939.[10] Along with opportunity and prosperity, the American Dream suffered greatly in the 1930s. Most Americans stopped dreaming altogether. Instead, they lay awake at night worrying about what new horrors tomorrow would bring. Franklin Roosevelt faced the daunting task of rebuilding, and not simply on the old foundations, American confidence as well as the American economy.

The American Dream in the Age of the Roosevelts

In the nineteenth century, the fundamental requisite to economic opportunity and the chance to rise in society was access to land. Hard work, intelligently applied, would usually make the land bloom, and that would support a man and his family. But by 1890 the frontier was no more, and for nearly two generations, intellectual and political leaders pondered how to protect both property and opportunity in the new environment. Walter Lippmann observed, "the size and intricacy which we have to deal with have done more than anything else, I imagine, to wreck the simple generalizations of our ancestors."[11] The Jeffersonian ideal of the sturdy yeoman farmer standing independent and secure on his own land had passed, but the shape and rhythms of the future were yet to emerge.

Intellectuals and political leaders struggled to think clear of social Darwinist assumptions about human nature, individual motivation, social evolution, and progress to better understand how the future might be shaped. By the first decade of the new century, an increasingly influential cluster of intellectuals, including Herbert Croly, Walter Weyl, and Walter Lippmann, argued that government action was needed to regulate the economy and shape the social environment if justice and opportunity were to flourish. Although the specific policy recommendations varied, Croly's *The Promise of American Life* (1909), Wyel's *The New Democracy* (1912), and Lippmann's *Drift and Mastery* (1914), all held that the laissez-faire environment of the nineteenth century would not suffice for the new century. Mastery, control, planning, and regulation would play larger roles, but just what roles only the politicians and the voters could say. But leading politicians, even leading progressive politicians like TR and Wilson, had come of age in the last quarter of the nineteenth century. They and many of the voters they courted retained strong commitments to ideals of competition, individualism, and self-help. The charge that expanded government threatened individual liberty still seemed axiomatic to many. Hence, Woodrow Wilson once responded to a question about the threat that government posed to liberty with exasperation, saying, "Of course, we want liberty, but what is liberty? Old words . . . consecrated throughout many generations" become tools of oppression when they lose touch with current reality. "Freedom today is something more than being let alone. The program of a government of freedom must in these days be positive, not negative merely."[12]

Both publicists and politicians struggled to accommodate the tenets of individualism to those of community in ways that honored the past, were effective for the present, and were promising for the future. Herbert Croly sought to square this circle in his classic, *The Promise of American Life* (1909), by describing an American Dream that had been in place since the Founding. Croly's "promise of American life" was J. Hector St. John de Crevecoeur's "dream." Croly said, "No more explicit expression has ever been given to the way in which the Land of Promise was first conceived by its children than in the 'Letters of an American Farmer.'" Croly believed, just as Crevecoeur had one hundred thirty years before, that "the Promise of America . . . consisted largely in the opportunity which it offered of economic independence and prosperity. . . . This conception of American life and its Promise is as much alive today as it was in 1780. . . . The Promise . . . is a promise of comfort and prosperity for an ever increasing majority of good Americans."[13]

But as the new century dawned, it was clear that America had changed; the frontier was closed, the continent was owned, and workers were flowing from the countryside to the cities to take jobs in the burgeoning factories. What would independence, autonomy, and opportunity mean for them? Croly described what they should mean—must mean—if America were to maintain its historic promise. "What the wage-earner needs, and what it is to the interest of a democratic state he should obtain, is a constantly higher standard of living. . . . The American state is dedicated to such a duty, not only by its democratic purpose, but by its national tradition . . . the American people, particularly those of alien birth and descent, have been explicitly promised economic freedom and prosperity," and that requires "a constantly higher standard of living."[14]

How would the new urban, industrial America of the early twentieth century restore the promise of American life? Croly argued that American history had been dominated by "two different and, in some respects, antagonistic groups of political ideas—the ideas which were represented by Jefferson, and the ideas which were represented by Hamilton."[15] Much as Lincoln had done a half century earlier, Croly proposed to "unite the Hamiltonian principle of national political responsibility and efficiency with a frank democratic purpose"—that is, to pursue Jeffersonian ends by Hamiltonian means. Croly believed with Hamilton that economic opportunity was best protected by authoritative national action. But he also believed that the ends toward which national power was to be directed should be distinctively Jeffersonian—the rights, opportunities, and benefits of individual people. Croly declared, "Democracies . . . have been right in assuming that a proper diffusion of effective responsibility [i.e., political equality] and substantive benefits [i.e., wealth] is the one means whereby a community can be supplied with an ultimate and sufficient bond of union."[16] Like Jefferson, Croly believed that "The real vehicle of improvement is education. It is by education that the American . . . proposes to better his democracy."[17]

Finally, Croly reached back to Abraham Lincoln's famous analogy of democratic competition as a fairly run race. Croly observed, "The democratic principle requires an equal start in the race while expecting at the same time an unequal finish." But a fair start to the race required more than legal equality. Croly argued that an economic competition that began with gross inequalities in wealth between the competitors "is as if a competitor in a Marathon cross country run were denied proper nourishment or proper training, and was obliged to toe the mark against rivals who had every benefit of food and discipline. Under such conditions . . . it would be absurd to claim that, because all the rivals toed the same mark, a man's victory or defeat depended exclusively on his own effort."[18]

Herbert Croly's book and President William Howard Taft's reversion to traditional Republican policies radicalized Theodore Roosevelt. In July 1910, former President Roosevelt wrote to Croly, saying, "I do not know when I have read a book that profited me so much. . . . I shall use your ideas freely in speeches I intend to make." Those speeches announced TR's return to national politics. Between August 23 and September 11, 1910, TR traversed the country, giving dozens of speeches and interviews in fourteen states on a program for rejuvenating the American society. *The New Nationalism,* comprised mostly of selected speeches from the tour, was published late in 1910 and served as the manifesto of TR's 1912 Bull Moose campaign to regain the presidency.

Roosevelt's "New Nationalism" still put a premium on individual effort but saw a much broader and deeper role for government than previously allowed.

TR declared in the maiden speech of his tour, "I stand for the square deal. But when I say that I am for the square deal, I mean not merely that I stand for fair play under the present rules of the game, but that I stand for having those rules changed so as to work for a more substantial equality of opportunity." Later in the trip, he advised his listeners to "shape your political action with two things in view. In the first place, try to get by legislation, national and state, a better chance for the average man, a greater equality of opportunity for that man." Again, though, he reminded his audience of the importance of individual effort and the limits to government action. "Now, the second part is this: After everything has been done which can be done by legislation, remember that the fundamental factor in any man's success in life must be that man's own character. The wisest laws and the best government will not help a man who will not work, or who cannot work well and wisely."[19] TR was always careful to assure his audiences that while he demanded the right of the average man to equal opportunity, he was not hostile to wealth or property. "We grudge no man a fortune which represents his own power and sagacity, when exercised with entire regard to the welfare of his fellows." In fact, he said, "We cordially believe in the rights of property. We think that normally and in the long run the rights of humanity, coincide with the rights of property. . . . But we feel that if in exceptional cases there is any conflict between the rights of property and the rights of man, then we must stand for the rights of man."[20]

Like Jackson and Lincoln before him, TR had come to believe that the country's future hinged on assuring the proper balance between the rights of the man and the dollar. Property rights had been secured in the nineteenth century; human rights were still vulnerable. Hence, TR went beyond Lincoln to consider the case for equality made by utopians like Bellamy and George. Roosevelt declared that "the most pressing problems that confront the present century are not concerned with the material production of wealth, but with its distribution . . . to administer to the needs of the many rather than . . . the profit of the few." Throughout the tour, TR reminded audiences, "Our republic has no justification unless it is a genuine democracy—a democracy economically as well as politically—a democracy in which there is a really sincere effort to realize the ideal of equality of opportunity for all men."[21] No single word or phrase rolled off TR's tongue more frequently than that quintessentially American word—opportunity.

Guaranteeing genuine democracy was a far broader mandate than any American president had sought before, and TR knew that he had to address the issue of government size and intrusiveness. "We who work for the New Nationalism," he declared, "believe in the hearty encouragement and reward of individual excellence, but we believe also in steadily using the power of the government to secure economic democracy as well as political democracy." TR assured his listeners that he knew that this was new ground and that many would be uneasy. He said, "This, I know, implies a policy of far more active governmental interference with social and economic conditions in this country than we have yet had, but I think we have got to face the fact that such an increase in governmental control is now necessary."[22]

TR promised that he was not proposing new ideals, just new means to secure old ideals. He declared, "the New Nationalism really means nothing but an application to new conditions of certain old and fundamental moralities." "Our ideal," he said, "is to secure . . . a reasonable approximation to equality of opportunity for all men, so that . . . each man shall have the chance to start fair in the race of life and show the stuff that is in him." This was the standard American ideal of equal opportunity and self-help. But elsewhere TR described the "ideal" of the New Nationalism more broadly and hence, for some, more disconcertingly. He said, "Our ideal should be a rate of wages sufficiently high to enable workmen to live in a manner conformable to American ideals and standards, to educate their children, and to provide for sickness and old age."[23]

Herbert Croly's analysis underpinned Theodore Roosevelt's New Nationalism in the election of 1912, but it was Woodrow Wilson's New Freedom that carried the day. TR, coming to progressivism out of the Republican Party, adopted a broad vision that reflected and built upon the earlier nationalist strains of Hamilton, Clay, Lincoln, and McKinley. Wilson, coming to progressivism out of the Democratic Party, sought to reclaim and protect equal opportunity, competitive markets, and popular democracy in the tradition of Jefferson, Jackson, and Cleveland. Not surprisingly, Wilson announced, "What this country needs above everything else is a body of laws which will look after the men who are on the make rather than the men who are already made." Americans had always bragged that their nation was uniquely open to talent and effort. Wilson was convinced that "America will insist upon recovering in practice those ideals which she has always professed."[24]

How America would be brought back in line with its highest ideals was the topic of Woodrow Wilson's first inaugural address of March 4, 1913. As Franklin Roosevelt would do after him and Thomas Jefferson and Abraham Lincoln had done before, Woodrow Wilson sought to place the present moment within the broader flow of American history. Wilson declared that the economy was "incomparably great in its material aspects, in its body of wealth, in the diversity and sweep of its energy, in the industries which have been conceived and built up by the genius of individual men and the limitless enterprise of groups of men. . . . But the evil has come with the good, with riches has come inexcusable waste." The cost of America's economic progress had been levied against both people and principles. Property rights had been allowed to rise far above the rights of men. "We have been proud of our industrial achievements, but we have not hitherto stopped thoughtfully enough to count the human cost, the cost of lives snuffed out, of energies overtaxed and broken, the fearful physical and spiritual cost to the men and women and children upon whom the dead weight and burden of it all have fallen pitilessly the years through." President Wilson closed his analysis and critique of the current state of affairs by remarking, "There has been something crude and heartless and unfeeling in our haste to succeed and be great. Our thought has been 'Let every man look out for himself; let every generation look out for itself,' while we reared giant machinery which made it impossible that any but those who stood at the levers of control should have a chance to look out for themselves." Wilson moved immediately to assure his listeners that men should look out for themselves, but that in the new industrial era they could only do so when the competition was fair and the rules applied equally to everyone in the game. Wilson promised to put government "at the service of humanity, in safeguarding the health of the nation, the health of its men and its women and its children, as well as their rights in the struggle for existence." Life was, Wilson wished to acknowledge, a struggle for existence, but it need not be a fight to the death. President Wilson concluded with the promise that "The scales of heedlessness have fallen from our eyes. We have made up our minds to square every process of our national life again with the standards we so proudly set up at the beginning and have always carried at our hearts. Our work is a work of restoration."[25]

Although politicians like TR and Wilson had to speak reassuringly of change as "restoration," intellectuals like Walter Lippmann and John Dewey sought not only to restore but to enlarge old ideals. Walter Lippmann's *Drift and Mastery* (1914) argued that industrialization had so changed the scope and scale of the American society that its traditional ideas and ideals no longer served it well. Lippmann said, "No mariner ever enters upon a more uncharted sea than does the average human being born into the twentieth century. Our ancestors thought they knew the way from birth through all eternity:

we are puzzled about the day after tomorrow." Elsewhere, he said, "We are all of us immigrants in the industrial world, and we have no authority to lean upon."[26] New ideas, not unrelated to the old ideas, but not limited to them either, were needed but not yet present.

Like Croly, Lippmann was convinced that Wilson and the Democrats held too blindly to the Jeffersonian traditions of individualism, limited government, and states' rights. The Jeffersonian vision of the sturdy yeoman farmer, standing free and independent on his own land, did not fit, and could never again be made to fit, the emerging order. Yet Lippmann argued that "the typical American reformer," including Secretary of State William Jennings Bryan and President Wilson, clung to a fading "American dream, which may be summed up . . . in the statement that the undisciplined man is the salt of the earth."[27] "I submit," Lippmann declared of the nineteenth-century American dream, "that it is an unworthy dream." But Lippmann did not intend to reject the American Dream; he merely demanded that it be made worthy of the new century. "Our business," he declared, "is not to lay aside the dream, but to make it plausible." That required adopting the "scientific spirit" of James and Dewey; it demanded that one "drag dreams out into the light of day, show their sources, compare them with fact, transform them to possibilities." Modern America, Lippmann declared, "calls for a dream that suffuses the actual with a sense of the possible."[28]

Lippmann was convinced that building a better future was more an issue of vision and will than of methods and means. "The wealth exists to pay for democracy. Our dreams are not idle. . . . And all through society there runs an increasing agitation for better cities, for more attractive countryside, for enlarged schools, for health campaigns, for a thousand elements of civilization." This agitation for an improved quality of life and enhanced social services came not from Barnum's "vagabonds," but from society's rising urban and professional middle classes. Barnum's laugh line about vagabonds dividing society's wealth had become Bellamy's utopian vision, and now, in Lippmann's view, was an agitation that ran "all through society."

Pragmatism and the scientific spirit called for planning, not for utopian speculation, so Lippmann sought to define an achievable goal for modern America to work toward: "To create a minimum standard of life below which no human being can fall is the most elementary duty of the democratic state." In words that Lyndon Johnson would echo a half century later, Lippmann declared, "modern democrats recognize that the abolition of poverty is the most immediate question before the world today, and they have imagination enough to know that the success of the war against poverty will be the conquest of new territory for civilized life."[29] Lippmann's progressivism evinced a touching confidence that would soon be gone from American public life. World War I (1914–17) brought an end to progressivism, but it left Americans uncertain about the nation's future course. Many celebrated the new energy and freedom of modern life, spectacularly including speakeasies, flappers, and ragtime, while others worried that all of this threatened traditional American values.

No one represented the Jazz Age in the public mind, then or now, better than F. Scott Fitzgerald. Fitzgerald, born in the Midwest, stylishly educated through private schools and Princeton, served as a stateside aide-de-camp during World War I before marrying his aristocratic, southern belle sweetheart and achieving national acclaim and wealth at twenty-two. Fitzgerald's wealth, fame, and marriage to Zelda Sayre were all secured by the dramatic success of his first book, *This Side of Paradise* (1920). There followed in rapid succession *The Beautiful and the Damned* (1922) and his masterpiece, *The Great Gatsby* (1925). *Gatsby* confirmed his status as a luminary in Europe and America; he was a wealthy man—or at least great wealth passed through his hands—and an exemplar and arbiter of important aspects of his times. Yet by the early 1930s, both Scott and Zelda Fitzgerald were spent, intellectually and emotionally drained, and by 1940 Scott Fitzgerald was dead at 44.

The Great Gatsby, Fitzgerald's most lasting creation, is the story of a young man from the American Midwest, James Gatz, who created a glamorous life out of whole cloth and saw it collapse tragically around him. At seventeen Jim Gatz changed his name to Jay Gatsby and was taken into service by Dan Cody, a millionaire world traveler. A five-year tour of Europe added a veneer of knowledge and sophistication to Gatsby's native wit and charm. Cody's death and the outbreak of World War I led Gatsby into the army. While training as a young officer at Camp Taylor, near Louisville, he met, courted, and fell deeply in love with Daisy, the pampered daughter of one of the city's leading families. Although they pledged themselves to each other, family pressure and Gatsby's absence in Europe led to Daisy's wedding to Tom Buchanan, from a prominent and wealthy Chicago family. Gatsby's memory of Daisy, refined and elaborated through five years of singular obsession, became the center of an existence dedicated to reclaiming her. After leaving the army, Gatsby achieved wealth through shady means, bought a mansion near Daisy and Tom Buchanan's estate, and prepared for the past to unfold anew.

Gatsby's marvelous mansion, modeled on a French chateau, was appointed

with fine furniture; English suits and shirts filled the closets; and lavish parties attended by dozens of anonymous guests ran late into summer nights.
Long Island society crackled with wild rumors about Gatsby's origins, character, and wealth. When Gatsby's hope that Daisy would be drawn to one of
his famous parties was unfulfilled, he launched a scheme through neighbors
and acquaintances to lure Daisy to his house. He assumed, reasonably
enough within the confines of the story, that Daisy would be drawn to his
wealth and glamour and choose to complete their life together as he had long
envisioned it.

The Great Gatsby is commonly seen as a derisive commentary on, and perhaps even a profound critique of, the American Dream. Jay Gatsby had everything—looks, money, and reputation; his name was on everyone's lips. But is
a mock French chateau, animated by endless, aimless, parties, the American
Dream? It seems simpler and more reasonable to say that Gatsby reminds us
that not every American dreams the American Dream. From Crevecoeur and
Jefferson to Croly and Roosevelt, the American Dream was the patrimony of
the man who rose by the dint of his own effort, improved his talents, and succeeded by their application. Gatsby dreamed, to be sure, but his dream lacked
reality, substance, and worth. Moreover, Gatsby pursued his dream through
deception, deceit, and theft. Unlike the classic dream of land in the woods, or
a business of one's own, both of which are eminently concrete if not yet real
for the dreamer, Gatsby's dream of capturing lost love and purity was vapid,
shallow, and naive. Hence, Nick Carraway, Gatsby's young neighbor and the
book's narrator, said of Gatsby that while "there was something gorgeous
about him, some heightened sensitivity to the promise of life, . . . an extraordinary gift for hope," some "foul dust floated in the wake of his dreams."[30]
Gatsby simply dreamed of the unreal and the impossible—of a woman that
had never been, of a time gone by, of another man's wife. The collision
between ill-conceived ends and illegitimate means was bound to conclude
badly, and it did.

Gatsby's life story, as well as his personality and its projection into the
world, was more a hologram than a human life grounded in effort and reality.
Hence, its power rested in his confidence that others would accept it, believe
it, and willingly act on it. Doubt, to say nothing of outright rejection, destroyed
its power. When his dream seemed to coming alive, as when he saw Daisy
again and she seemed to respond to the old memories they shared, "he literally glowed; without a word or gesture of exaltation a new well-being radiated
from him." But Gatsby's glow was dependent both on Daisy's continued belief

in him and his own confidence in it. As Gatsby showed Daisy his magnificent mansion, her attention drifted, and Nick saw an "expression of bewilderment . . . come back into Gatsby's face, as though a faint doubt had occurred to him as to the quality of his present happiness."[31] Outright rejection killed the dream and brought Gatsby's complete collapse. In the direct personal confrontation between Gatsby and Tom Buchanan over Daisy, Tom went straight for Gatsby's constructed self. Gatsby had claimed roots in a prominent and wealthy midwestern family; Tom connected him to Jewish underworld figures, saying, "Who are you, anyhow? . . . You're one of that bunch that hangs around with Meyer Wolfsheim—that much I know. . . . I picked him for a bootlegger the first time I saw him." Tom was more right than he knew; Gatsby's money came from bootlegging, securities fraud, and more. And when Nick later asked Wolfsheim whether he had given Gatsby his start, Wolfsheim responds, "Start him—I made him."[32]

Gatsby, of course, knew and feared all of this, so when Tom challenged him, Gatsby "began to talk excitedly to Daisy, denying everything, defending his name against accusations that had not been made. . . . 'Jay Gatsby' had broken up like glass against Tom's hard malice."[33] The dream was punctured—both Gatsby and Daisy knew it—and all that remained was reality. Daisy had to choose between the vaporous gangster that she had once loved and her hard, cruel, but predictable millionaire husband. It was no choice. Nick Carraway concluded that "Gatsby . . . paid a high price for living too long with a single dream."[34] Perhaps, but a more reasonable conclusion would be that Gatsby paid a high price for living too long with the wrong dream. The dream of adolescent fame, wealth, and romance proved an insufficient basis for later stages of adult life and accomplishment. In all of Fitzgerald's stories, and certainly in *The Great Gatsby,* wealth either exists as the story opens or is attained quickly and mysteriously. It is never earned by the steady application of admirable talents and virtues. In fact, there are no paths to success, no means by which wealth and security are created, no virtues maintained and used to good and growing effect over time. Hence, *Gatsby* is a cautionary tale that reminds us of the importance of holding the traditional means and the ends of American life in a healthy and proper relationship to each other.

Another midwestern boy, Herbert Hoover, also confronted early poverty and insecurity in his life. Unlike the fictional Jim Gatz, who looked East, to New York, Europe, and the gambling resorts of the Mediterranean, from which he took a thin veneer of culture and the nefarious skills to accumulate an illegitimate fortune, young Hoover set his face to the West. An Iowa native orphaned at nine, Hoover was raised by an uncle in Oregon, worked his way through the new Stanford University, and then became an internationally famous and wealthy civil engineer and construction executive, before, like Franklin, turning to public service in his 40s. Herbert Hoover, again like Franklin, was an American icon, an exemplar of the American Dream throughout the 1920s.

Hoover became a tireless spokesman for the Republican Party's vision of American life. In 1922 Hoover wrote *American Individualism: The Challenge to Liberty* to defend American individualism from collectivist urges that he saw rising in Europe and at home. Hoover assured Americans that "while we build our society upon the attainment of the individual, we shall safeguard to every individual an equality of opportunity to take that position in the community to which his intelligence, character, ability, and ambition entitle him; . . . while he in turn must stand up to the emery wheel of competition."[35] Hoover's view was that within the broad confines of the rule of law and protection of private property, initiative and competition produced individual fairness and social justice. The emery wheel of competition exposed unmerited claims and scraped away artificial advantages to leave the energetic and talented in possession of society's top spots and best rewards. Hoover approached his campaign for the Republican presidential nomination in 1928 convinced that "The most the individual can expect from government is 'liberty, justice, intellectual welfare, equality of opportunity, and stimulation.'"[36]

Hoover gave a series of speeches late in the campaign that laid out his sense of the majestic stability of the American Dream even in light of the tremendous changes that had taken place during his lifetime. The most famous of these speeches was given at his boyhood home near West Branch, Iowa. Hoover remembered a bucolic boyhood on a nearly self-sufficient family farm. He recalled to the assembled crowd of West Branch residents and touring newspapermen, "We ground our wheat and corn on toll at the mill; we slaughtered our hogs for meat; we wove at least part of our own clothing; we repaired our own machinery; we got our fuel from the woods; we erected our own buildings; we made our own soap; we preserved our own fruit and grew our own vegetables."

In the intervening half century, Hoover informed the crowd, both rural and urban life had improved dramatically. In the countryside, "We have improved seed and live-stock; we have added a long list of mechanical inventions for saving labor; we have increased the productivity of the land." Although rural life had improved and become more efficient, electricity, telephones, automobiles, radio, and movies had transformed urban life. These discoveries and inventions enhanced productivity and expanded plant capacity and profits, permitting increased wages and a better life for most Americans. Moreover, free citizens exercising personal initiative within a political order of limited government had achieved all of this. This "self-reliant," "rugged" individualism imparted "a genius to American institutions" that was "the real basis of American democracy."[37]

Hoover's August 11, 1928, address accepting the Republican nomination for president again made the case that individualism and equal opportunity produced American growth and prosperity. Hoover noted that an increasingly productive economy brought rising individual aspirations. Yet even these new demands and needs were best met not through government action, but through individual effort in a fair contest. Hoover declared, "Equality of opportunity is the right of every American—rich or poor, foreign or native-born, irrespective of faith or color. It is the right of every individual to attain that position in life to which his ability and character entitle him. . . . Only from confidence that this right will be upheld can flow that unbounded courage and hope which stimulate each individual man and woman to endeavor and to achievement." Hoover then turned to Lincoln's comparison of equal opportunity to a fairly run foot race to help communicate his vision. Hoover wanted both to bathe in Lincoln's sense that fair competition made unequal outcomes legitimate and to reject Croly's criticism that economic inequality rigged the race in favor of the privileged to the detriment of new men seeking to move up. Hoover posited, "The ideal of individualism based upon equal opportunity to every citizen is . . . as if we set a race. We, through free and universal education, provide the training of the runners; we give to them an equal start; we provide in the government the umpire of fairness in the race. The winner is he who shows the most conscientious training, the greatest ability, and the greatest character." Hoover's unblinking belief in the fundamental fairness and openness of the American economy was deeply felt and unshakable. Hence, Hoover concluded, "Equality of opportunity is a fundamental principle of our nation. With it we must test all our policies. The success or failure of this principle is the test of our government."[38] Hoover entered onto his term as president in March 1929 convinced that he and his party represented the great American political tradition of individualism, enterprise, limited government, laissez-faire, progress, and prosperity. Herbert Hoover was perfectly equipped by experience and temperament to govern in a period of Republican growth, but ill equipped to govern in, or even understand, its collapse.

Franklin Delano Roosevelt ran for president in 1932 against a discredited and demoralized incumbent President Herbert Hoover. Hence, while the proximate goal of the Roosevelt campaign was to win the election, its ultimate goal was to reassure the American people that recovery was possible. FDR rightly declared, "all our great Presidents were leaders of thought at times when certain historic ideas in the life of the nation had to be clarified." Times of crisis and uncertainty provide a "superb opportunity for reapplying, applying in new conditions, the simple rules of human conduct to which we always go back."[39] Franklin Roosevelt redefined the American Dream for an urban industrial society in which most men, and increasingly women, worked for wages and old ideas of rural autonomy and independence seemed remote. A steady job for good pay was the foundation for economic success for most Americans. Economic stability and a healthy job market were the context within which new workers could start small, learn, work, save, and seek to move up over time. Economic instability, then, was the equivalent of the natural disasters of the nineteenth century—the floods, tornadoes, and prairie fires that swept hope and opportunity away. A healthy and growing economy was necessary if work and saving were to produce security and success in the twentieth century.

In the fall of 1932, before the Commonwealth Club of San Francisco, FDR gave what would become the most memorable speech of the campaign. The Commonwealth Club speech began with a broad description of American political development from the Founding period, through the tremendous economic expansion of the nineteenth century, to the Progressive reforms of the early twentieth century, and the Republican heyday of the 1920s that ended in the collapse of 1929. FDR rejected Hamilton's focus on the needs of an economic elite in favor of Jefferson's focus on the needs and interests of the common man. FDR traced the American commitment to individualism and the broad outlines of the traditional American Dream to Jefferson's triumph in "the great election of 1800." Jefferson was committed to the autonomy and independence of the yeoman farmer. "So began," Roosevelt declared, "the day in which individualism was made the great watchword of American life. The happiest of economic conditions," a growing population in a rich and fertile continent, "made that day long and splendid. On the western frontier, land was substantially free. No one, who did not shirk the task of earning a living, was entirely without opportunity to do so." Ideas and reality, the traditional American Dream of hard work applied to extensive opportunity, reflected each other perfectly.

But as the course of national development moved forward, railroads, industries, and cities spread across the landscape. Roosevelt told his audience, "It was in the middle of the nineteenth century that a new force was released and a new dream created. The force was what is called the industrial revolution. . . . The dream was the dream of an economic machine, able to raise the standard of living for everyone; to bring luxury within the reach of the humblest." Government and citizens wanted this new economic machine and the wealth that it promised to arise as quickly as possible. "There was, however, a shadow over the dream. To be made real, it required the use of the talents of men of tremendous will and tremendous ambition." These men built great corporations and produced great wealth, but the costs imposed on common men and on the society were greater than had been anticipated. "In retrospect," FDR declared, "we can now see that the turn of the tide came with the turn of the century. We were reaching our last frontier; there was no more free land and our industrial combinations had become great uncontrolled and irresponsible units of power within the State." The builders of the great industrial enterprises of the nation had become threats more than benefactors. Hence, just as TR and Wilson had before him, Franklin Roosevelt argued, "Our task now is not . . . producing more goods. It is the soberer, less dramatic business of administering resources and plants already in hand, . . . of adapting existing economic organizations to the service of the people. The day of enlightened administration has come."

But what ends, what goals, what values were enlightened administrators to pursue? As from the nation's earliest days, the values that would guide it through the darkness of the Depression were the natural rights, the human rights, set forth in the Declaration of Independence. As it had been for Jackson, Lincoln, TR, Wilson, and now for FDR, "The task of statesmanship has always been the redefinition of these rights in terms of a changing and growing social order." The terms of the American social contract, FDR declared, "are as old as the Republic, and as new as the new economic order." Life was the first human right for both Locke and Jefferson. In the new day, Roosevelt declared, "Every man has a right to life; and this means he has also a right to make a comfortable living. He may by sloth or crime decline to exercise that right; but it may not be denied him. . . . Our Government formal and informal, political and economic, owes to everyone an avenue to possess himself of a portion of that plenty sufficient for his needs, through his own work."

Roosevelt defined property not so much as land and buildings, but savings and economic security. "Every man has a right to his own property; which means a right to be assured . . . in the safety of his savings. . . . In all thought of property, this right is paramount," and if to secure economic safety and security, "we must restrict the operations of the speculator, the manipulator, even the financier, I believe we must accept the restriction as needful, not to hamper individualism but to protect it." As Roosevelt knew, most men worked for wages; they did not own businesses or live on the land. Their property, their security in time of economic difficulty, illness, or old age, depended on the safety of their savings. "The final term of the high contract," Roosevelt explained, "was for liberty and the pursuit of happiness." The old liberty of being left alone, of drift as Lippmann called it, was no longer sufficient. "We have learned a great deal . . . in the past century. We know that individual liberty and individual happiness mean nothing unless both are ordered in the sense that one man's meat is not another man's poison. . . . We know that liberty to do anything which deprives others . . . is outside the protection of any compact; and that Government in this regard is the maintenance of a balance, within which every individual may have a place if he will take it; in which every individual may find safety if he wishes it." Roosevelt concluded the Commonwealth Club speech with the solemn promise that "we recognize the new terms of the old social contract. We shall fulfill them."[40]

Roosevelt knew that the American people expected action, government action, but he also knew that old commitments to individualism and self-help, while shaken, were alive. Throughout his presidency, but particularly in the early days, he groped for the right balance, in rhetoric and policy, between government activism and personal responsibility. In the second of his famous Fireside Chats, delivered on September 30, 1934, FDR assured the American people that his New Deal rested on the firm middle ground between "the theory that business should and must be taken over into an all-embracing Government. . . . [and] the equally untenable theory that it is an interference with liberty to offer reasonable help when private enterprise is in need of help." He declared that the New Deal was "in complete accord with the underlying principles of orderly popular government. . . . We count, in the future as in the past, on the driving power of individual initiative and the incentive of fair private profit, strengthened with the acceptance of those obligations to the public interest which rest upon us all." FDR assured his listeners that traditional American values were being respected even as the New Deal looked beyond unconstrained individualism and unregulated laissez-faire to a "broader definition of Liberty under which we are moving forward to greater freedom, to greater security for the average man than he has ever known before in the history of America."[41]

By the spring of 1936, as the Depression dragged on, President Roosevelt became increasingly determined to state the case for a strong and consistent government presence in American social and economic life. He personally drafted the Democratic Party platform of 1936. FDR again drew on the powerful image of Jefferson's Declaration of Independence, declaring on behalf of the Democratic Party: "We hold these truths to be self-evident—that government in a modern civilization has certain inescapable obligations to its citizens, among which are: (1) Protection of the family and the home; (2) Establishment of a democracy of opportunity for all people; (3) Aid to those overtaken by disaster." In a powerful speech accepting the Democratic nomination for president on June 27, 1936, Roosevelt continued his project of refining America's core values. Before a crowd of 100,000 in Philadelphia's Franklin Field stadium, he explored the meaning of liberty in America, declaring, "Liberty requires opportunity to make a living—a living decent according to the standard of the time, a living that gives man not only enough to live by, but something to live for." Without the opportunity to make a living, "life was no longer free; liberty no longer real; men could no longer follow the pursuit of happiness."

Franklin Roosevelt fought the Depression to a draw throughout the 1930s. Although he won the election of 1936 overwhelmingly, and won again in 1940, war in Europe demanded that he broaden his vision and sense of purpose. He responded by declaring that traditional American rights were, in fact, human rights. FDR's 1941 State of the Union address, known as his Four Freedoms speech, declared, "Since the beginning of our American history, we have been engaged in change—in a perpetual peaceful revolution—a revolution which goes on steadily, quietly adjusting itself to changing conditions." The new conditions, an increasingly interdependent world threatened by tyranny, required new ideals and new means to attain them. Roosevelt urged America to look "forward to a world founded upon four essential human freedoms: (1) freedom of speech and expression, (2) freedom of every person to worship God in his own way, (3) freedom from want, (4) freedom from fear." He closed his address by declaring, "Freedom means the supremacy of human rights everywhere"[42] (Figure 6.2).

As World War II slowly turned in the allies' favor, FDR's thoughts returned to the long-term goals of his beloved New Deal. In his 1944 State of the Union address, President Roosevelt called for a "second Bill of Rights," this time an

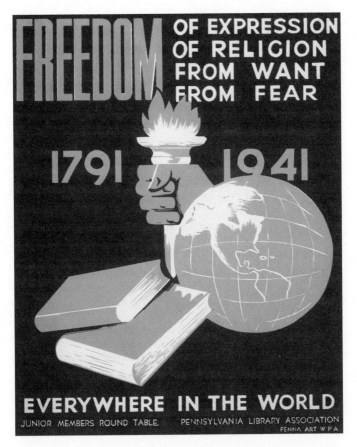

Figure 6.2. "Four Freedoms" Poster, 1941. President Roosevelt declares that freedom of expression and religion, as well as freedom from want and fear, should exist throughout the world. (Library of Congress, Prints and Photographs Division, reproduction LC-USZC2-5436)

economic bill of rights. He declared, "It is our duty now to begin to lay the plans and determine the strategy for the winning of a lasting peace and the establishment of an American standard of living higher than ever before known. We cannot be content, no matter how high the general standard of living may be, if some fraction of our people . . . is ill-fed, ill-clothed, ill-housed and insecure. . . . In our day these economic truths have been accepted as self-evident. We have accepted, so to speak, a second Bill of Rights under which a new basis of security and prosperity can be established for all—regardless of station, race, or creed."[43] FDR believed that the restoration of the American Dream in the wake of a decade and a half of depression and war required that government be responsible for shaping the social climate and economic context within which individuals could strive and compete for security and success.

The Dream Embedded in Institutions, Law, and Policy

American politics, parties, law, and policy were recast in the age of reform. The Republican Party, dominant in the North and East, entered the twentieth century as a business-oriented coalition that supported high tariffs, corporate subsidies, light regulation, and low taxes on individuals and corporations. The Democrats, dominant in the South and West and in some of the nation's major cities, supported local control, states' rights, some regulation of public utilities and transport, and low taxes, including reduction or elimination of tariffs. Progressive elements in both parties demanded that government actively seek to balance conflicting group interests in a search for the broader public interest. Progressives thought that modern society, in all of its variety and complexity, had to be guided by intelligence and expertise and those who possessed them. They sought to move the initiative in government from the courts, parties, and Congress to the presidency and the experts resident in the executive branch. Theodore Roosevelt's presidency initiated an important shift in public and official opinion from a nonintrusive "night watchman" view to a sense that the national government simply had to regulate and tame corporate and monopoly economic power. Although the strength and exuberance of TR's personality drew attention and influence to the presidency, it was Woodrow Wilson who consolidated and institutionalized his regulatory initiatives and put the power of the national government behind a broad agenda of social and political reform.

The federal government's initial forays into corporate regulation came with the Interstate Commerce Commission (ICC) in 1887 and the Sherman Anti-Trust Act in 1890. The ICC was created to ensure that interstate railroads, operating across many state jurisdictions, were effectively monitored. The Sherman Anti-Trust Act was intended to broaden federal regulatory authority to punish the nation's largest corporations for driving their competitors out of business to ensure their own monopoly control of the market. Both the ICC and the Sherman Act were seriously weakened by the Supreme Court's finding in *E. C. Knight* (1895) that regulation of corporate structure and activity fell under the jurisdiction of the chartering state rather than the federal government. With national regulatory authority in question, most state governments formed independent regulatory commissions after 1900 to manage natural monopolies like water, power, and telephone companies, but entities like the railroad, steel, copper, sugar, and tobacco trusts were simply beyond the ability of individual states to manage. President Theodore Roosevelt viewed trusts as dangerous concentrations of economic power that political power simply had to master in the national interest. He initiated several high profile antitrust cases, including the famous Northern Securities Case (1904) against the holding company of the Great Northern and the Northern Pacific railroads. The court agreed that the railroads, controlled by financiers James Hill and J. P. Morgan, were colluding to create a monopoly in the northern tier of states and that the government could intervene under the Sherman Anti-Trust Act. In 1906, Congress passed and TR signed the Hepburn Act expanding the ICC's authority beyond regulatory oversight to setting the rates and fares for railroads involved in interstate commerce.

The Wilson administration knew that if the federal government was going to do more, it needed the resources to fund its actions. In 1913 Congress passed and the states approved the Sixteenth Amendment to the Constitution, declaring, "The Congress shall have power to lay and collect taxes on incomes, from whatever source derived, . . . without regard to any census of enumeration." Wilson immediately slashed the Republican's cherished tariff to its lowest levels since the Civil War and proposed a tax on incomes. The income tax touched relatively few people in 1913, taking only 1 percent of the first $20,000 of taxable income. Exemptions for single persons on the first $3,000 of income and the first $4,000 for married couples left 98 percent of Americans with no tax bill at all. Yet with an income tax in place, it was relatively easy to increase rates and limit exemptions as the nation prepared for World War I.

The new Democratic administration moved to take a more aggressive regulatory posture toward the national economy and to define the places of business, labor, and agriculture in it. In 1913 the Federal Reserve Act created a central bank to monitor the nation's financial and credit systems and to ensure that they supported the smooth functioning of the economy. President Wilson responded to labor's complaints that its interests were generally lost in the

Department of Commerce and Labor by creating separate departments for Commerce and Labor. In 1914 he moved to strengthen the regulatory authority of the federal government by chartering the Federal Trade Commission (FTC) and passing the Clayton Anti-Trust Act. The FTC, an independent regulatory commission modeled on the ICC, was to oversee and police business practices and the Clayton Act, hailed as the Magna Carta of labor, declared that strikes, pickets, and boycotts did not constitute illegal restraints of trade. The Federal Farm Loan Act put the federal government in the business of supplying the flexible credit that farmers had sought for more than a century. In 1916 President Wilson signed the Adamson Act giving railroad employees an eight-hour day, and in 1917, as a war measure, he brought all of the railroads under federal control. In May 1917 Congress passed the Overman Act, creating the National War Industries Board, placing virtually all industry under national direction.

The Wilson administration also moved to clean up politics, cleanse the electorate, and produce a more stable, homogenous society. Progressive political reforms began with the Australian, or secret, ballot in the late 1880s. The Australian ballot was prepared by the state, not the parties, and listed the candidates of all parties on a single ballot. Voters then could study the candidates and the issues and cast an informed vote for the best candidate, irrespective of party. After the Australian ballot came personal registration, the direct primary, campaign finance reform, initiative, referendum, and recall. The Seventeenth Amendment to the Constitution approved direct election of U.S. senators in 1913. Many progressives sought to go even further and remove politics from local government by adopting nonpartisan elections, city manager and commission forms of local government, and independent regulatory and investigatory commissions where technical issues seemed to require them.

The Prohibition and Women's Suffrage Amendments, added to the Constitution in 1919 and 1920, respectively, continued the progressive attempt to cleanse American politics. The Eighteenth Amendment, prohibiting "the manufacture, sale, or transportation of intoxicating liquors" within the United States, was intended to improve male behavior. The Nineteenth Amendment, declaring that "the right of citizens of the United States to vote shall not be denied or abridged by the United States or by any state on account of sex," was intended to encourage the cleansing effects of female sobriety, morality, and religiosity throughout American politics. Protective laws for female workers, to set maximum hours, minimum wages, and safe and healthy working conditions, were generally enacted on the argument that women were physi-

WOMAN'S SPHERE
IS ~~THE HOME~~
WHEREVER
SHE MAKES
GOOD —

THE HOME
THE LAW
INDUSTRY
THE SCHOOL
THE STAGE
BUSINESS
THE ARTS

REVISED

Figure 6.3. Woman's Sphere Revisited, 1917. This
cartoon, from the magazine *Puck,* April 14, 1917,
suggests that the definition of Woman's Sphere is about
to be broadly revised. (Library of Congress, Prints and
Photographs Division, reproduction LC-USZC2-1199)

cally weaker and emotionally more vulnerable than men. Women of childbearing age were often protected, even against their will, from working around
potentially harmful chemicals and products, lifting too much weight, or working at night. Although women's protective legislation did improve some wages
and conditions, it also limited women's opportunity to make some choices and
decisions that men were free to make[44] (Figure 6.3).

The tumult of domestic reform and foreign war left Americans yearning for stability. Republican Presidents Harding (1921–23) and Coolidge (1923–29) moved decisively to restore social stability and economic growth. Continuing concern for the coherence and order of the American society led to historic changes in immigration and naturalization policy. The Immigration Act of 1921 and the National Origins Quota Act of 1924 drastically reduced the number of southern and eastern Europeans eligible to immigrate to the United States and reduced overall immigration to levels not seen in nearly a century. The Immigration Act of 1921 sought to limit immigration to 3 percent of each white nationality group recorded in the 1910 census (nonwhites were excluded from the calculation completely). The goal was to produce an immigrant pool of about 350,000, a majority of whom would come from northern and western Europe. The National Origins Quota Act of 1924 further limited total immigration to 170,000 in 1925 and 150,000 by 1927. In addition, the base census year was moved back from 1910 to 1890 to further limit the pool of future immigrants to northern and western Europe (again, nonwhites were excluded). The national quota regime held into the 1940s.

To guide Republican economic policy, Presidents Harding and Coolidge both named financier Andrew Mellon, one of America's richest men, to Hamilton's old post at the treasury. Tariffs were adjusted upward and income taxes were adjusted downward. President Coolidge famously reminded his exuberant countrymen, "The business of America is business," and then he used his 1924 State of the Union message to make the then-novel argument that steep tax cuts would both spur economic growth and increase government revenues. Coolidge argued, "the larger incomes of the country would actually yield more revenue to the Government if the basis of taxation were scientifically revised downward."[45] Secretary Mellon explained, "high rates tend to destroy individual initiative and enterprise and seriously impede the development of productive business."[46] The Mellon Plan reduced top income tax rates from 77 percent to 25 percent, cut the inheritance tax in half, and abolished the gift tax. The booming economy of the 1920s seemed full validation of the Republican program of low taxes, deregulation, and individual initiative. Yet the devastating stock market collapse of October 1929 and Hoover's ineffective response to it steadily undermined confidence in the Republican economic model.

When Franklin Roosevelt assumed the presidency in March 1933, the nation was mired in a depression nearly four years old. FDR was determined to move immediately and decisively on a number of fronts, all intended to rebalance, reorganize, and rejuvenate the American economy. To rebalance the economy, he sought to increase the power of labor, reduce the power of business, and make government the arbiter and manager of their future relationship. Even before Franklin Roosevelt assumed the presidency, new Democratic majorities in the House and Senate adopted the Norris-LaGuardia Anti-Injunction Act of 1932. The Norris-LaGuardia Act limited the right of courts to intervene in labor disputes, further legitimated strike activities, and enhanced the rights of labor in relation to management. FDR pushed the rights of labor much further. The National Industrial Recovery Act of 1933 and the National Labor Relations Act of 1935, commonly called the Wagner Act after New York Senator Robert Wagner, gave legal recognition to labor's right to unionize and to bargain collectively on issues like wages, hours, and working conditions. The Wagner Act also established the National Labor Relations Board to oversee and regulate labor-management relations; it worked systematically to disband company-dominated unions and to facilitate the establishment of independent unions. The craft unions of the American Federation of Labor were soon supplemented by the much larger and more aggressive mass labor unions of the Congress of Industrial Organizations. The Fair Labor Standards Act of 1938 further strengthened labor rights.

Roosevelt moved to enhance the regulatory authority of government over corporate and financial power in America. The Securities Act of 1933 established the Securities and Exchange Commission, with authority to regulate the issuance of stocks to the public and monitor the stock exchanges. The Glass-Steagall Banking Acts of 1933 and 1935 fundamentally reorganized American banking. Glass-Steagall gave the federal government greater regulatory and oversight powers, forced banks to choose between commercial and investment banking functions, required them to divest insurance and brokerage functions, and created a system of deposit insurance. The forced separation of commercial and investment banks, and banks from insurance and brokerage services, was intended to clarify financial roles and remove potential conflicts of interest from the nation's financial system. On the consumer side, the Federal Deposit Insurance Corporation was chartered to insure bank deposits so that citizens would not lose their savings if a bank failed. FDR next moved to ensure that revenues would be sufficient to the federal government's new and expanded responsibilities. In June 1935 the president asked Congress to restore the inheritance and gifts taxes that President Coolidge and Secretary Mellon had dismantled. He also asked that progressive tax rates on "very great individual incomes" be restored, including a tax on dividends, and that a graduated tax on corporate incomes be established. The Democratic Congress happily restored progressivity to the tax code.

Perhaps most shockingly of all, given the sharp break with past policy, Franklin Roosevelt strengthened government regulation and management of agriculture. Roosevelt's first New Deal for farmers was the Agricultural Adjustment Act (AAA) of 1933. The AAA sought to raise prices by limiting production. When the Supreme Court struck down the AAA in early 1936, the administration hurriedly passed a soil conservation bill designed to limit production while avoiding another veto. Congress also undertook a multipronged assault on rural poverty. The Bankhead-Jones Farm Tenancy Act of 1937 created the Farm Security Administration (FSA) to oversee programs designed to assist farmers in buying their own land and working it efficiently. The FSA was authorized to make loans at 3 percent over 40 years to allow tenants to buy family-sized farms. The FSA also made loans to farmers willing to become "clients" of the agency. Client farmers committed to undertake training, develop plans for the development of their farms, and to accept guidance and supervision from the FSA. Finally, in 1941 the Bankhead Commodity Loan Act was passed, with amendments in 1942, putting commodity farm price supports at 90 percent of parity.[47] Once-independent American farmers were by the mid-twentieth century among the most highly regulated and dependent sector of the American economy.

World War II again brought direct government control of American industry. In the wake of Pearl Harbor, Congress created the National Resources Planning Board (NRPB) to manage the wartime economy. The NRPB ordered a halt to production for civilian use of most automobiles, planes, and durable consumer goods to focus the nation's productive capability on military vehicles and equipment. Moreover, as early as 1943, the NRPB was planning for the postwar peace "based on full employment, a greatly expanded welfare state, and widely shared 'American Standard of Living.'"[48] Government was, for the first time in American history, declaring its intention to manage the American economy, not just in wartime, but in the peace that would follow.

Depression and war also changed the way Americans thought about social policy. So overwhelming were the social consequences of the Great Depression that ideas and policies that seemed right and natural during the nineteenth century cracked under the pressure of events. Into these cracks were pressed new ideas and policies that could both cement the pieces back together and serve as bridges between the old and the new. For example, in the winter of 1933–34, the Civil Works Administration took 4.2 million men and women from the relief rolls and put them on the federal payroll at $15 a week building and maintaining streets, sewers, schools, playgrounds, and airports. Roosevelt let the Civil Works Administration lapse in the spring of 1934 because he was concerned that government support, even though it required work and was not charity, would sap the independence and spirit of working men and women. By early 1935 the persistence of the Depression convinced FDR that work relief programs were simply unavoidable. The Civilian Conservation Corp employed 2.5 million young people in the outdoor work of land conservation, reforestation, and improvements to parks. The Works Progress Administration (WPA) employed millions more, often skilled workers, engineers, and artists, on larger public projects like roads, bridges, water and sewer systems, schools, libraries, courthouses, and other public projects all over the nation. The largest such project, the Tennessee Valley Authority, was designed to bring flood control, electricity, and economic development to one of the nation's poorest sections. The Federal Arts Project of the WPA created thousands of public murals, statues, paintings, poems, and songs.[49]

The New Deal also moved to protect hard-pressed homeowners from default and loss of their homes. In 1933 Congress chartered the Home Owners' Loan Corporation to underwrite existing home loans by lending money to families struggling to meet mortgage payments. By late 1935 the Home Owners' Loan Corporation had made more than one million loans totaling more than $3 billion. In 1934 Congress chartered the Federal Housing Administration to encourage private lenders to provide home loans backed by government guarantees against default by the borrower. These and related programs made it federal government policy to expand home ownership for the working and middle classes.

FDR also laid the foundations for a permanent American welfare state. He sought not just to alleviate the immediate fear and need caused by the Depression, but also to build an economic floor under working- and middle-class Americans. The Social Security Act of 1935 created two kinds of income security programs—social insurance programs and means-tested programs—that still comprise the core of American social welfare programming. Social Security, like other forms of insurance, link premiums paid, in this case taxes paid during work, to benefits paid to retirees. The Social Security Act also provided benefits to three explicit categories of persons who were not in a position to take care of themselves through work: the elderly poor, the blind, and widows with dependent children. Unemployment compensation was a program jointly administered by the federal and state governments to provide transitional support to unemployed workers while they searched for new employment. Americans were still urged to look to state and local government, churches, charities, and family, but this initial version of the American welfare state was intended to acknowledge that a civilized nation must provide basic income security to working families and the deserving poor.

Education also became a focus of government policy and planning in the twentieth century. Herbert Croly opened the concluding chapter of *The Promise of American Life* (1909) by declaring, "The American national Promise can be fulfilled only by education."[50] America agreed. High school and college attendance grew steadily throughout the first half of the twentieth century. Urbanization and industrialization made education both more convenient and more important. High school attendance surpassed 500,000 in 1900, 2 million by 1920, and 4.4 million by 1930. The Depression and World War II actually spurred high school attendance. With no jobs available, students had little choice but to stay in school. Attendance jumped from 4.4 million in 1930 to 6.6 million in 1940. Between 1900 and 1940, the proportion of 17-year-olds graduating from high school increased from 6 percent to 51 percent.

College attendance soared from 238,000 (4 percent of 18- to 21-year-olds) in 1900, to 598,000 (8 percent) in 1920, and 1.1 million (12 percent) by 1930. Again, the Depression fueled increases in college attendance, reaching 1.5 million (16 percent) by 1940. The post–World War II GI Bill increased college attendance from 1.7 million in 1946 to 2.7 million in 1948. Moreover, the number of bachelors degrees tripled between 1940 and 1950, while the numbers of masters and doctorates both doubled.[51] Although education remained the preserve of state and local government through the first half of the twentieth century, Americans increasingly saw a high school education as the ticket to economic security and college as the ticket to economic and social leadership.

Shadows on the Dream

The first half of the twentieth century was the hazy predawn of the American Dream's expansion. The sun, still below the horizon, cast a promising glow, but the chill of discrimination was still in the air. Women saw slow advances during the early decades of the new century, the dramatic burst of suffrage success around 1920, and then the ebb and flow of economic inclusion and exclusion through the Depression and war years. Minorities and Indians saw their situations deteriorate through the first three decades of the century, improve relatively in the 1930s only because everyone was suffering, and then begin to improve more steadily during and after World War II.

Victorian standards for women's behavior gave way to a more public, active, sexualized view of women during the progressive era. Recreational opportunities expanded women's public presence in movie theaters, amusement parks, speakeasies, and dance halls. Economic change opened jobs for women in fields such as clerical work and sales; even medicine, law, and the professions began to open. Soon, the image of the young, independent working girl by day and flapper by night became pervasive in the emerging consumer culture of the new century. The legitimacy of female sexuality and pleasure, as well as a more egalitarian view of love and marriage, were new and only partially understood. Ideas were changing faster than reality, and women had to make sure they did not mistake the one for the other. Both men and women realized that, in the end, male success was determined in the workplace and female success was determined in marriage and the home.

Politicized women continued to differ, as they had since the 1850s, about how to describe the role they envisioned for themselves as citizens. Prominent women like Lucy Stone, Frances Willard, and Jane Addams thought that the universalist claim to equal rights ran against a strong progressive tide in favor of electoral reform, educated voters, and government by experts. If universality meant votes for blacks and illiterate immigrants, as well as women, women would likely find themselves rebuffed again. Jane Addams wrote "Why Women Should Vote" (1910) to explain that women's traditional responsibility for the sanctity of the home and the education of children were compromised by the drunkenness, prostitution, and pornography that urban families found just outside their doors. Hence, Addams argued, society would benefit if women could use their votes to confront dangers that threatened the comfort, safety, and morality of their homes. Other women, like Rheta Childe Dorr of the generation that came of age in the progressive era, "wanted all the freedom, all the opportunity, all the equality there was in the world. I wanted to belong to the human race, not to a ladies' aid society, to the human race."[52] Fighting for the ballot, especially in the decade leading up to adoption of the Nineteenth Amendment in 1920, was the glue that held the women's movement together. Once the ballot was secured, the glue loosened and the movement lost much of its coherence and energy. Although an Equal Rights

Amendment was put forward almost immediately, it went nowhere, and only modest gains were made on the broader women's agenda during the 1920s.

The continued movement of women into the economy during the first half of the twentieth century provided the pressure that forced the system slowly to open up. In 1900, about 20 percent of the workforce was female, but most working women were young and employed temporarily while awaiting marriage. Most women who worked for wages held semiskilled jobs in areas like housekeeping and the garment industry. As the economy continued to evolve in the first two decades of the century, new jobs opened in secretarial and sales work, as well as in education, health care, and social services. These jobs quickly became defined as female and hence low-paid. As late as 1920, more than 80 percent of women voluntarily left the paid workforce when they married. These patterns were severely disrupted by the Great Depression.

The Great Depression put virtually all American families under some psychological and economic pressure. Most men measured themselves by the prestige of their occupations and the size of their paychecks, so they were shaken to their foundations by the loss of their jobs and their inability to find new work. Many employed women found a heightened sense of self-worth as their incomes became more critical to their families. Many others, however, especially married women, came under pressure to give up their jobs so that unemployed men, the traditional breadwinners of American families, could fill them. In fact, women lost ground even in jobs, including teaching and nursing, that men had traditionally spurned.

Nonetheless, for the first time in American history, women had friends in high places. Franklin and Eleanor Roosevelt were the first occupants of the White House to think seriously about women. FDR was the first president to name a woman, Frances Perkins, to his cabinet as secretary of labor, and the first to name a woman, Florence Allen, to the Circuit Court of Appeals. Molly Dewson headed the first women's division of the Democratic National Committee. Other women served throughout the Roosevelt administration and assured a more receptive climate for women and women's issues than had ever existed in government before. As a result, by the late 1930s, women were making significant gains in the political and legal realms. Most states had laws that allowed women to retain their own wages, inherit and hold property in their own names, sign contracts, appear in court, serve on juries, and retain the children in the event of divorce[53] (Figure 6.4).

In the first half of the 1940s, with men once again off to war, government

Figure 6.4. "Women in the War," 1942. This poster from the
War Manpower Commission declares of women war
workers, "We Can't Win Without Them." (Library of
Congress, Prints and Photographs Division, reproduction
LC-LSZ62-111835)

and society declared it women's patriotic duty to join the workforce. Rosie the
Riveter, attractive but competent and strong, was the universal image of
America's working women during war. Six million women who had never
worked for wages before entered the workforce, and millions more who had
worked in low-paying clerical and service jobs moved up to higher-paying,
more prestigious jobs during the war. As white women filled the better factory
jobs, black women moved into the clerical and sales jobs from which they had

previously been barred. Female union membership expanded more than tenfold, from fewer than 300,000 in 1930 to 3 million in 1944. As with all previous wars, when the emergency passed and the men returned, women were expected to make way for them in the workplace and return to their more traditional duties in the home. But women were energized and enlivened by the additional responsibilities that fell to them in wartime and by the evident fact that they had fulfilled these responsibilities admirably. With less to do at home, many women sought to remain in their jobs after the war. In the new postwar consumer economy of the 1950s, two incomes, even if one was clearly supplemental, meant access to more of the good things that society had to offer.

The progressive era saw an increasingly thorough program of Jim Crow segregation of the races fastened upon the South. A somewhat less overt, but still pervasive and frequently intense, pattern of racial discrimination covered the rest of the nation. Progressive leaders, including scientists and social scientists, justified segregation as necessary to bring a healthy order and efficiency to American society and politics. Eugenicists purported to demonstrate the intellectual inferiority of blacks and social scientists concluded that democracy would be protected and improved by grandfather clauses, literacy tests, and poll taxes. Politicians eagerly enacted laws to segregate the races and award exclusive political control to the white majority. In fact, Presidents Theodore Roosevelt and Woodrow Wilson were both convinced of the intellectual superiority of Anglo-Saxons. Roosevelt thought blacks "wholly unfit for the suffrage," and Wilson segregated the federal workforce.[54] Whites enforced their dominance with a ferocity unknown in American history outside of war, and blacks attempted, sometimes violently, to protect their rights. Approximately four thousand blacks were lynched between 1890 and 1950. Some of the worst race riots in the nation's history occurred during the early twentieth century in New York City (1900), Atlanta (1906), Springfield, Illinois (1908), and Tulsa (1921) (Figure 6.5).

In 1937, a poem by Abel Meeropol, entitled "Strange Fruit," a version of which was later recorded by Billie Holliday, captured the sadness and the rage of black America. Part of Meeropol's poem read:

> Southern trees bear a strange
> Fruit,
> Blood on the leaves and blood at
> the root,

Figure 6.5. "Two African-American Men, Lynched," 1930. This photograph from the National Association for the Advancement of Colored People's archives depicts a lynching near Marion, Indiana, in 1930. (Library of Congress, Prints and Photographs Division, reproduction LC-USZ62-35347)

> Black body swinging in the
> Southern breeze,
> Strange fruit hanging from the
> Poplar trees.[55]

The Depression and FDR's response to it began a process of rapid change in black America. From the end of slavery to the early 1930s blacks had voted Republican when they were allowed to vote. In 1932 a majority of blacks dutifully voted for Hoover, but FDR initiated a Negro Division within the Democratic National Committee and made significant black appointments in most of the New Deal agencies. By 1936 black leaders were urging black voters to "turn Lincoln's picture to the wall" and vote for the Democrat, Franklin Roosevelt. Although FDR did win a majority of the black vote in 1936, he remained deeply aware that the Democratic majority nationally rested on a base of conservative white votes in the "solid South." As late as 1938, FDR refused to confront southern Democrats in Congress as they successfully moved to scuttle an antilynching bill that had been before the Congress since 1933.

Southern Democrats in Congress made sure that the New Deal generally passed blacks by. For example, the centerpiece of the New Deal and of the welfare state that subsequently developed was the Social Security Act of 1935. The social insurance components of the program, principally social security and unemployment compensation, excluded workers in agriculture, domestic service, and low-paying jobs, which meant that most blacks remained outside the system. The federal government and the states administered the welfare components of the system jointly. The states of the South, where most blacks lived, declined to fund the programs or funded them at very low rates.

As late as 1940, three-quarters of black men lived in the South, two-thirds had not gone beyond the seventh grade, most worked in agriculture, service roles, or menial blue-collar jobs, and black men made only 40 percent of what white men made.[56] However, as war loomed and Roosevelt struggled to prepare the nation to fight, threatened demonstrations by blacks protesting discrimination in the government and in war industries led Roosevelt to issue Executive Order 8802 on June 25, 1941. Executive Order 8802 barred government agencies and contractors from discriminating on the basis of "race, creed, color, or national origin." Black employment in government and in the war industries tripled between 1942 and 1945. The door to opportunity was open more than a crack, but desegregation, swinging the door wide open, was still decades in the future.

The social Darwinism of the late nineteenth century suggested a particularly foreboding future for Indians. Submersion or extinction seemed to be their only choice. By 1930 Indian political and cultural traditions had nearly been destroyed, yet few Indians had entered the mainstream society and economy. As the Depression took hold, fully half of Indians had income of less than $200 a year, while the average American family enjoyed an annual income more than five times that amount. President Franklin Roosevelt was determined to make major changes in the way the federal government related to Indians. First, he charged Harold Ickes as secretary of the interior and John Collier as director of the Bureau of Indian Affairs to revise American Indian policy. Collier headed the Bureau of Indian Affairs for twelve years, 1933 to 1945, and was a tireless advocate of Indian political and cultural integrity and autonomy. Lawrence Kelly, a leading student of Native American history, wrote, "Collier fought to realize a dream in which Indian tribal societies were rebuilt, Indian lands rehabilitated and enlarged, Indian governments reconstituted or created anew, and Indian culture not only preserved but actively promoted."[57]

Although western economic and political interests and their representatives in Congress resisted, President Roosevelt signed the Indian Reorganization Act, aptly referred to as the Indian New Deal, into law on June 18, 1934. The Indian New Deal reversed more than half a century of harshly assimilationist policies in favor of policies intended to promote Indian self-determination and to develop Indian economic resources.[58] The Indian Reorganization Act repealed the allotment laws, restored excess reservation lands to tribal ownership, and created a fund to purchase additional land for tribal use. Governance rights were lodged in tribal councils. Between 1936 and 1938 more than eighty tribes adopted constitutions, and most adopted business charters to take more direct control of their political and economic resources. Funds were allocated and loans made available to develop education and training programs that would supplement and support Indian traditions and culture.

Depression and war eventually diverted the Roosevelt administration's attention. By 1940 western business interests and their political allies had cut funding to Indian programs and reasserted the values of assimilation. By March 1945 the Bureau of Indian Affairs budget had been trimmed to 1935 levels and John Collier was forced to resign. Postwar America, supremely confident of its virtue and its strength, expected conquered peoples, whether Indians at home or Germans and Japanese abroad, to test the benefits of free markets and democratic politics. Separate paths, cultural integrity, economic self-determination, and tribal sovereignty seemed a willful rejection of mainstream American ideals and institutions.

The Dream at High Tide:
Opportunity to Entitlement
from Truman to LBJ

I say to you, my friends, . . . I still have a dream. It is a dream deeply
rooted in the American Dream, that one day this nation will rise up
and live out the true meaning of its creed,—we hold this truth to be
self-evident that all men are created equal.
—Martin Luther King Jr., "I have a dream," 1963

From the late nineteenth century forward, intellectual and political leaders, including Henry George and Herbert Croly, Theodore Roosevelt,
Woodrow Wilson, Franklin Roosevelt, and many others declared that enough
wealth and power were at hand to do justice in America. In the wake of World
War II, most Democrats and liberals claimed that if justice could be done and
was not, only evil intent could explain the inaction. Most Republicans and conservatives replied scornfully that the vagabonds were simply calling yet again
for an equal share of wealth that others had earned. Most moderates, both
Democrats and Republicans, admitted that more justice demanded to be done,
but they warned that equality, absent the striving and competition that had
always characterized American life, might be an attractive dream, but it was
not "the" American Dream.

The U.S. emerged from World War II as the dominant cultural, political,
military, and economic power in the world. In 1946, an exuberant young Texas
congressman named Lyndon Baines Johnson spoke for many in saying, "We
in America are the fortunate children of fate. From almost any viewpoint ours

is the greatest nation; the greatest in material wealth, in goods and produce, in abundance of the things that make life easier and more pleasant. . . . nearly every other people are prostrate and helpless. . . . If we have excuse for being, that excuse is that through our efforts the world will be better when we depart than when we entered."[1]

Congressman Johnson was right: the United States of America was the wealthiest and most powerful society the world had ever known. Most Americans were comfortable and confident about using that power and wealth to support freedom in the world. Most were even comfortable with opening rights and opportunities to Americans that previously had been excluded. But as the number of claims expanded and the groups with claims proliferated, promise outran performance, and violence flared. White Americans, seeing rage where they had expected gratitude, withdrew into a sullen determination to defend their possessions and privileges.

Young Dreamers and the World Before Them

The Depression and World War II changed the way Americans thought about individuals, communities, and society. Hoover failed to recognize, but FDR was instinctively aware, that the Depression had laid bare the great changes that industrialization and urbanization had produced in the American society. The transition from rural to urban life, the diversification of the economy, and the increasing importance of education, science, and technology—and the decreasing importance of strong backs and the rising importance of strong minds—had changed the meanings of freedom, equality, and opportunity.

World War II not only returned the economy to full employment, but wartime demands spurred plant expansion, productivity, and innovation. The U.S. gross national product (GNP) grew by 50 percent during the war, whereas the Europeans, Soviets, and Japanese lost a quarter or more of their economies. In 1945, at the end of the war, the United States accounted for more than half of the value of goods and services produced in the world and more than 60 percent of the value of manufactured goods produced in the world, and the United States dominated virtually all of the leading-edge technologies of the midcentury. Not only did the American economy dwarf other national economies, so too did the largest American corporations. In 1955 the value of the goods produced by General Motors, the world's largest corporation, was equal to 60 percent of the GNP of Japan and equal to the GNP of Italy.

The American economy had several advantages as it emerged from World War II. First, the decade-long depression of the 1930s left many ideas, inventions, and innovations still to be implemented, and the war itself produced countless new developments in aeronautics, electronics, and petrochemicals. Second, the Depression actually raised education levels in the United States; with no jobs, people stayed in school longer, and World War II created a stable, well-trained workforce. Third, strong domestic and foreign demand fueled the transition to a peacetime consumer economy. Family income in the United States had risen by one-third between 1939 and 1946, while wartime taxes and rationing had limited consumption and foreign economies needed American products to rebuild. Average annual family income then doubled in the quarter century following the end of World War II. Most of this new wealth, and much more, was expended on personal consumption. Between 1946 and 1960 consumer debt expanded nearly tenfold as the number of private automobiles increased by 33 million and the number of owner-occupied homes increased from 17 million to 33 million.

The postwar years were an extraordinarily robust period for the American economy. Nearly everyone benefited as incomes rose across income categories. The middle decades of the twentieth century saw a great migration of American blacks from the rural South to the urban North. From the colonial period to World War I, more than 90 percent of blacks lived in the South, first as slaves and then generally as impoverished farm laborers. Although a million and a half blacks left the South for the North during the 1920s and 1930s, the 1940s and 1950s saw more than 3 million blacks migrate north. The push that fueled black migration was the mechanization of southern agriculture. The pull was the opportunity to work in the northern war industries and then to seek some role in the postwar boom that ran through the late 1960s. By 1970, half of American blacks lived outside the South, and 80 percent lived in urban settings.[2]

However, as always, benefits were not evenly distributed, and dynamics were at work that over time would separate the winners and losers. As new groups, including minorities and women, moved to take better places in the American economy, the economy continued to evolve, oftentimes seeming to recede before its pursuers. Most dramatically, just as the black exodus out of the rural South into the northern cities reached its crest, an interregional movement of industry out of the urban North to the South and West got underway. Even those businesses that did not move interregionally often followed their traditional workforces to the suburbs, where land prices were lower and services and amenities greater. Hence, as black migration to the cities continued, the central cities where most blacks lived lost much of their old employment base.

On the other hand, as the economy continued to evolve from manufacturing to services and to relocate from the cities to the suburbs, many of the new jobs were in areas traditionally open to women, including teaching, office and retail work, health care, and finance. In postwar America, women married younger, had fewer children, and lived longer; hence, they literally had decades of active life remaining once their children were in school. Moreover, the postwar home was easier to maintain, leaving more time to spend on leisure, community activity, and volunteer work, or, increasingly, on paid employment to supplement the family income. By 1960 more women, nearly 40 percent, were in the paid workforce than had been at the height of World War II.

The political parties, of course, competed to claim credit for the newfound prosperity and to nurture or block social change. Franklin Roosevelt's death in April 1945 brought his new vice president, former Missouri Senator Harry S. Truman, to the presidency. Truman's political strategy was to defend and, where possible, build upon FDR's New Deal legacy. Truman's "Fair Deal" sought to extend Democratic Party domestic policy into greater federal aid to education, health care for the elderly, urban renewal, and civil rights, but he was checked at nearly every turn by a coalition of conservative southern Democrats and Republicans. The Republicans swept the congressional elections of 1946 by campaigning for smaller government and against a Democratic Party economic policy that they claimed threatened prosperity. Republicans picked up fifty-six seats in House and thirteen in the Senate to take control of Congress for the first time since 1930. Truman's prospects of being elected president in his own right in 1948 looked bleak. As the election neared, Republicans nominated New York Governor Thomas E. Dewey, and he campaigned confidently. Nonetheless, Truman's attack on the "do nothing Republican Congress" produced a narrow victory that brought the Democrats back into control of Congress (Figure 7.1).

The voters did replace the Democrats in 1952 when they elected World War II hero Dwight David Eisenhower president and gave the Republicans narrow majorities in both houses of Congress. Eisenhower, a moderate, did

Figure 7.1. Truman Wins, 1948. Truman's come-from-behind win in 1948 caught many, including the *Chicago Tribune,* by surprise. (Library of Congress, Prints and Photographs Division, reproduction LC-USZ62-115068)

not seek to dismantle the New Deal, as many in the old Hoover wing of the party had hoped he would, but neither did he extend it. He focused on bringing more efficiency to government and buttressing national security through diverse programs, including science training and a national defense highway system. Although the voters loved Ike, they returned control of both houses of Congress to the Democrats in 1954. Eisenhower easily won reelection in 1956, but he had virtually no coattails. Then in 1958 a restive electorate rejected Republican quiescence by returning big Democratic majorities in Congress, 283 to 154 in the House and 64 to 34 in the Senate.

In 1960 the Republicans nominated Eisenhower's vice president, Richard M. Nixon, and the Democrats nominated a young Massachusetts senator named John F. Kennedy. The first televised presidential debate in American history allowed Kennedy to address concerns about his religion and his foreign policy expertise. During the campaign Kennedy warned that Nixon would threaten the New Deal legacy, and he reached out to Martin Luther King Jr., thereby speeding the movement of blacks from the Republican to the Democratic Party. Kennedy defeated Nixon by fewer than 115,000 votes out of nearly 70 million cast while the Democrats maintained comfortable control of both houses of Congress.

Kennedy campaigned on the promise to "get the country moving again," but his narrow win left him at the disposal of the conservative Democratic barons of the House and Senate. Kennedy had served in both the House and the Senate, but he had never been in the leadership or even intimate with the leaders. Vice President Lyndon Johnson had been an intimate of Sam Rayburn in the House and had himself been an extremely effective majority leader of the Senate. But Johnson was uncomfortable with and distrusted by the Harvard-trained eastern elites that surrounded John and Bobby Kennedy. Hence, while Kennedy's stirring first inaugural speech called for courage and sacrifice in the national interest, the agenda he placed before Congress was timid.

John Kennedy's tragic assassination in Dallas, Texas, in November 1963 unleashed an emotional reassessment of the nation's meaning and purpose. The direct result was that Lyndon Johnson was empowered to push a massive expansion of federal government responsibility for poverty, education, housing, health care, and civil rights. Moreover, the presidential campaign of 1964 saw an exuberant Lyndon Johnson sweep away an ill-fated Republican challenge by Barry Goldwater. LBJ won 61 percent of the popular vote, surpassing even FDR's tremendous victory of 1936, while adding to the Democrat's already hefty margins in the House and Senate.

Johnson worked feverishly during the spring and summer of 1965 to secure as much of his "Great Society" agenda as he possibly could. LBJ, the master legislator, knew that presidential mandates following landslide elections, while real, were short-lived. His did not outlive the summer. Just days after the seminal Voting Rights Act of 1965 passed the Congress, the impoverished Watts district of Los Angeles erupted in racial rioting and violence that went on for five days. During the four summers from 1965 to 1968, two hundred fifty American cities experienced rioting, violence, arson, and theft, much of it televised. White Americans, even many who had supported the early stages of the civil rights movement and of LBJ's Great Society, withdrew support from Johnson, the Democratic Party, and the movement culture that seemed to threaten the nation.

The GOP approached the congressional elections of 1966 with a promise of "law and order." Republicans picked up forty-seven House seats, three Senate seats, and eight governorships and seemed well positioned for the 1968 presidential election. Every summer brought racial violence, the campuses erupted with antiwar demonstrations, and demands for change seemed to conservatives to be spinning out of control. Republicans promised to slow the change while many Democrats, including Minnesota's Senator Eugene McCarthy, thought to push through the turmoil to a "New Politics" of social justice. Just months before "Clean Gene" McCarthy stepped forward to challenge LBJ for the Democratic presidential nomination in 1968, he described the turmoil wracking the nation as "a special kind of insurrection . . . by the poor and the exploited—those who have been denied their part in the American Dream."[3]

The civil rights movement supplied the template for two related but distinct sets of movements in the late 1960s and 1970s. The first set of movements, directly related to the civil rights movement and using many of the same arguments, organizational structures, and strategies, were the Chicano movement, the women's movement, the Native American movement, and the gay rights movement. In each case, distinct racial, ethnic, gender, and sexual preference groups organized to demand improved access and opportunity. In fact, by the late 1960s, demands moved beyond equality of opportunity to affirmative action to equalize outcomes across previously limited or excluded groups. The second set of movements, using the same organizational techniques and strategies as the civil rights movement but claiming to represent the public interest, were the antiwar movement, the environmental movement, and the consumer movement. These movements produced a flowering of public interest groups, including the Consumer Federation, Common Cause, Environmental Action, Friends of the Earth, and the Natural Resources Council. Openness in government and participatory democracy were key demands of the new social movements. The cacophony of new groups, interests, and demands, posed a threat to, and were perceived as a threat by, traditional white elites and their middle-class supporters.

The splintering of the New Deal coalition after 1965 opened the door to a conservative populism eventually harnessed by the Republican Party. As the social movements of the 1960s pushed the rights revolution beyond opportunity to outcomes, the rhetoric of freedom, individualism, and responsibility was ceded to the Republicans. Democrats became identified with a panoply of rights claims that seemed to require intrusive regulation, high taxes, and expansive bureaucracy. Moreover, Democrats seemed to reject traditional requirements for hard work, frugality, self-help, and personal responsibility as unfair, demeaning, and probably racist. A resurgent Republican Party glee-fully scooped up the abandoned pieces of America's traditional values and claimed them as their own. The prominent black conservative, Shelby Steele, complained after the 1960s, "And to this day the liberal looks at black diffi-culties—high crime rates, weak academic performance, illegitimacy rates, and so on—and presumes them to be the result of victimizing forces beyond the control of blacks." Standards to which others are held, based on "prin-ciples of merit, excellence, hard work, delayed gratification, individual achieve-ment, personal responsibility, and so on—principles without which blacks can never achieve true equality," are not to be expected of victims.[4] Many conser-vatives, including the Hispanic author and activist Richard Rodriquez, argue that once liberal elites admitted that America had been unfaithful to its val-ues—had discriminated against blacks, women, and others—they lacked the courage and conviction to reclaim and restore them.[5] Rather, they wandered off into a morass of apology, double standards, affirmative action, and prefer-ences that further weakened traditional American values. Liberals countered that that they were not lost; they simply believed that wrongs had to be made right before traditional values would again have real meaning.

The American Dream in an Age of Affluence

As Depression memories faded, the American Dream came to focus on a high-consumption, leisure-oriented, and pleasure-filled private life. For the white middle and working classes, this meant securing and enjoying private homes, cars, televisions, washing machines, refrigerators, and lawn mowers. Modern amenities such as indoor water and plumbing, electricity, central heat, and later air conditioning became standard or at least common in American homes. Men provided the principal income, and women, even when they supplemented family income, managed the private domain of peace, plenty, and pleasure. But much had changed; most workers toiled within large organizations. The blue-collar worker gave long, hard hours on an assembly

Figure 7.2. World's Highest Standard of Living, 1950s. This billboard was part of a National Association of Manufacturers' celebration of the "American Way." (Library of Congress, Prints and Photographs Division, reproduction LC-USF34-016211-C)

line without ever feeling the autonomy, security, and personal pride of the master craftsman. The white-collar worker climbed the career ladder, taking on more responsibility and gaining more income and prestige, but rarely achieving the independence and control that goes with ownership. Many women, eyeing both a job market evolving from industrial production to services and a consumer goods market advertising many things their family might need or just enjoy, chose to work either part time or full time. Women's incomes often brought working-class families into the middle class and taught middle-class families that they might aspire to a bigger house, a second car, and college for the children. Nonetheless, as women moved into the workforce, tensions grew over gender roles, home life, and family authority. Prosperity and the choices it made available forced changes in ideas about work, domesticity, gender, class, and opportunity (Figure 7.2).

Scholars were deeply concerned about the changes that modern society encouraged in American character, virtues, and aspirations. David Riesman's classic *The Lonely Crowd* (1950) argued that other-directed conformist bureaucrats were displacing the inner-directed entrepreneurs of the Protestant ethic. The Marxist social critic C. Wright Mills described the decline of independent entrepreneurialism before bureaucratic management in a prominent book, entitled *White Collar: The American Middle Classes* (1951). Mills continued his analysis with an extraordinarily influential book, entitled *The Power Elite* (1956), describing a new interlocking set of governing elites that were closing off the paths that generations of entrepreneurs had traveled to opportunity, success, and status in America. William Whyte's *Organization Man* (1956) worried that "belongingness," the safety and predictability of the large corporation, threatened the individuality and creativity of the white-collar worker.

While intellectuals struggled to understand and describe the changes taking place in the American society, politicians struggled to articulate a vision of America's present and future prospects. Throughout the 1950s the dominant Republican voice was that of Dwight Eisenhower, and the dominant Democratic voice was that of Adlai Stevenson. That Eisenhower defeated Stevenson in the presidential elections of 1952 and 1956 indicates that his voice rang through most clearly. Eisenhower and Stevenson both sensed that the balance between the material and the spiritual in American life was shifting. Eisenhower complimented Americans on what they had achieved, while Stevenson challenged them to do more. Voters accepted the compliment, but not yet the challenge.

Late in the 1952 campaign, Eisenhower promised that if he were elected, "The world will again recognize the United States of America as the spiritual and material realization of the dreams that men have dreamt since the dawn of history."[6] Just four months later, in his first inaugural address, Eisenhower reminded his listeners that America could only be an example to others if it was true to its own best values, "this truth must be clear before us: whatever America hopes to bring to pass in the world must first come to pass in the heart of America. The peace we seek, then, is nothing less than the practice and fulfillment of our whole faith among ourselves and in our dealings with others." The new president called upon his fellow citizens to "proclaim anew our faith. This faith is the abiding creed of our fathers. . . . It establishes, beyond debate, those gifts of the Creator that are man's inalienable rights, and that make all men equal in His sight. In the light of this equality, we know that the virtues most cherished by free people—love of truth, pride of work, devotion to country—all are treasures equally precious in the lives of the most humble and of the most exalted." Moreover, Eisenhower was at pains to say that these treasured rights belonged to all men. The American faith "warns that any man who seeks to deny equality among all his brothers betrays the spirit of the free and invites the mockery of the tyrant." Elsewhere in the speech, Eisenhower declared, "we hold all continents and peoples in equal regard and honor. We reject any insinuation that one race or another, one people or another, is in any sense inferior or expendable."[7]

Although foreign policy and national security, including the cold war in Europe and the hot war in Korea, demanded most of President Eisenhower's attention, domestic economic and social issues reasserted themselves during the campaign of 1956. Eisenhower easily won reelection, and in his second inaugural address, as in the campaign, he celebrated the nation's power and wealth even in a dangerous world. He said, "We live in a land of plenty. . . . In our nation work and wealth abound. Our population grows. Commerce crowds our rivers and rails, our skies, harbors, and highways. Our soil is fertile, our agriculture productive. The air rings with the sound of our industry—rolling mills and blast furnaces, dynamos, dams, and assembly lines—the chorus of America the bountiful."[8] Eisenhower celebrated America's material success. Adlai Stevenson, although defeated a second time, called upon Americans to look beyond work and even wealth. Stevenson declared, "I believe with all my heart that, under democracy, this country is going forward to an uplifting of all its citizens, not just in terms of new goods and gadgets, but even more in terms of a broadening and deepening of the mind and heart of the nation."[9] But the Depression and war were just a decade in the past, and many were still settling into the middle class. Although Adlai Stevenson would not be called to lead the nation forward, John Kennedy offered a refurbished "city on a hill" called Camelot.

Camelot was utopia, a realm in which the good King Arthur, having warred for decades to defeat evil, promised peace, justice, and beauty to his grateful subjects. When John Kennedy was elected president in 1960, there were still battles to be fought, powerful forces of evil still ruled over large parts of the globe, and stubborn injustice was visible at home, but the wealth and power to suppress both seemed to be at hand. Reaching back beyond his Massachusetts forebear, the Puritan Governor John Winthrop, to Pericles, the fountainhead of the western democratic tradition, President-elect Kennedy promised to pursue freedom and justice, at home and abroad, with energy and verve. John Kennedy used a speech to a joint session of the Massachusetts legislature on January 9, 1961, and his inaugural address on January 20, 1961, to rally the nation to a renewal of its fundamental principles. To an appreciative Massachusetts audience, Kennedy declared that "what Pericles said to the Athenians has long been true of this commonwealth: 'We do not imitate—for we are a model to others.'" Kennedy reminded his listeners, just as Winthrop had reminded his listeners on the deck of the *Arabella* more than three centuries before, "We must always consider that we shall be as a city upon a hill—the eyes of all people are upon us." Kennedy warned his sober colleagues, "we are setting out upon a voyage in 1961 no less hazardous than that undertaken by the *Arabella* in 1630. We are committing ourselves to tasks of state craft no less awesome than that of governing the Massachusetts Bay Colony, beset as it was then by terror without and disorder within."[10] John Kennedy developed these themes in his famous inaugural address. Kennedy began by reminding his listeners that America stood guard over "beliefs for which our forebears fought. . . . We dare not forget today that we are the heirs of that first revolution." Then he intoned the famous declaration, "Let the word go forth from this time and place, to friend and foe alike, that the torch has been passed to a new generation of Americans—. . . proud of our ancient heritage—and unwilling to witness or permit the slow undoing of those human rights to which this nation has always been committed. . . . Let every nation know, whether it wishes us well or ill, that we shall pay any price, bear any burden, meet any hardship, support any friend, oppose any foe to insure the survival and success of liberty." Like Pericles, Kennedy warned his countrymen that a free people must defend its liberties. Freedom grown too comfortable becomes lazy, and lassitude invites loss of liberty. "In your hands, my fellow citizens, more than mine, will rest the final success or failure of our course. Since this country was founded, each generation of Americans has been summoned to give testimony to its national loyalty. . . . Now the trumpet summons us again." Kennedy closed his charge to the American people by promising that "The energy, the faith, the devotion which we bring to this endeavor will light our country and all who serve it—and the glow from that fire can truly light the world. . . . And so, my fellow Americans: ask not what your country can do for you—ask what you can do for your country."[11]

As John Kennedy assumed the presidency, the two gravest problems facing America were international communism and racial discrimination. Each posed a serious threat to human freedom and dignity. There was broad bipartisan commitment to oppose communism with every element of national power. No such consensus existed in regard to civil rights. President Kennedy was painfully aware that the Democratic Party, with its electoral dependence on southern votes and the legislative sway of powerful southern committee chairs in Congress, was an unlikely vehicle for confronting racism. Events forced Kennedy to move forward, despite the difficulties.

Kennedy made two major speeches to the nation about civil rights. The first was on September 30, 1962, in response to James Meredith's struggles to be admitted to the University of Mississippi, and the second was on June 11, 1963, when the National Guard was called out to help manage the desegregation of the University of Alabama. The Mississippi speech was a cool and almost dispassionate lecture on judicial process and the importance of the rule of law. The president closed with echoes of Winthrop and Lincoln by reminding Mississippians, "The eyes of the Nation and of all the world are upon you and upon all of us, and the honor of your University and State are in the balance. . . . Let us preserve both the law and the peace and then healing those wounds that are within we can turn to the greater crises that are without and stand united as one people in our pledge to man's freedom."[12]

Mississippi and the South chose to resist, tensions grew, and the Freedom Summer of 1963 brought violence and death as the nation and the world watched. Kennedy responded with a powerful call, the first presidential call in nearly a century, that the nation live up to its founding values. Kennedy opened his national radio and television address on the evening of June 11, 1963, by reminding his countrymen, "This Nation was founded . . . on the principle that all men are created equal, and that the rights of every man are diminished when the rights of one man are threatened. . . . It ought to be possible," the president said, "for every American to enjoy the privileges of being American without regard to his race or color. . . . But this is not the case." Other presidents, including FDR, Truman, and Eisenhower, had acknowledged and even criticized racism, but they had seen the social and political resistance to equality as too great to overcome. Kennedy posed the issue differently, saying, "This is not a sectional issue. . . . Nor is this a partisan issue. . . . This is not even a legal or a legislative issue alone. . . . We are confronted primarily with a moral issue. It is as old as the scriptures and is as clear as the American Constitution." The president said that racism impugned the integrity of every American and of the nation itself. No president since Lincoln had said quite as much; none had said that America simply cannot be like this. "One hundred years of delay have passed since President Lincoln freed the slaves, yet their heirs . . . are not fully free. . . . And this Nation," Kennedy continued, "for all its hopes and all its boasts, will not be fully free until all its citizens are free."

John Kennedy, initially quite timid on civil rights, called America's bluff by declaring from the White House that the nation had not lived up to its most cherished principles, that its rhetoric was hollow so long as the reality of black lives remained so bleak. Hence, Kennedy declared, "Now the time has come for this Nation to fulfill its promise. . . . A great change is at hand, and our task, our obligation, is to make that revolution, that change, peaceful and constructive for all. . . . Next week," Kennedy announced, "I shall ask the Congress of the United States to act, to make a commitment it has not fully made in this century to the proposition that race has no place in American life or law."[13] The president then outlined a bill to provide equality of access to public accommodation and services, desegregation of schools, and voting rights.

Just two and a half months after John Kennedy defined civil rights as a moral challenge to the nation's integrity, Martin Luther King Jr. delivered his famous "I have a dream" speech to a quarter million people assembled before the Lincoln Memorial and to tens of millions more in the nation beyond. The Kennedy administration had bargained with King and others to forestall the march, and when that proved impossible, to control the rhetoric and moderate the tone of those who addressed the crowd. The Kennedy administration did not want the speakers to scare away support from the proposed civil rights bill (Figure 7.3).

Martin Luther King's "I have a dream" speech hewed not only to Kennedy administration wishes, but like the call-and-refrain work songs of slavery times, King and Kennedy passed themes back and forth from the civil rights movement's standing demands, to the president's June 11 speech, to King's speech. Standing in the shadow of the Great Emancipator's memorial, King echoed back Kennedy's observation that one hundred years after the Emancipation Proclamation, "the Negro is still not free." King also echoed Kennedy's observation that the promise of the American founding had still not been fulfilled for blacks. King said, "In a sense we have come to our nation's capital to cash a check. . . . a promissory note. . . . This note was a promise that all men would be guaranteed the inalienable rights of life, liberty, and the pursuit of happiness." King also joined Kennedy in calling for redress of public discrimination against blacks. Kennedy had called for equal access to public accommodations and for voting rights; King declared, "We can never be satisfied as long as our bodies, heavy with the fatigue of travel, cannot gain lodging in the motels of the highways and the hotels of the cities. . . . We can never be satisfied as long as the Negro in Mississippi cannot vote and the Negro in New York believes he has nothing for which to vote." King said that black Americans "will not be satisfied until justice rolls down like waters and righteousness like a mighty

Figure 7.3. Martin Luther King at the March on Washington, 1963. Martin Luther King Jr., with the Washington Memorial in the background, delivered his famous "I have a dream" speech on August 28, 1963. (Corbis/Hulton-Deutsch Collection, image HUO52225)

stream." King closed by tying black demands firmly, but reverentially, not just to the promises of the Declaration of Independence and the Emancipation Proclamation, but to the broader American Dream. In a closing that built to a powerful crescendo, King said, "I say to you today, my friends, that in spite of the difficulties and frustrations of the moment, I still have a dream. It is a dream deeply rooted in the American dream. I have a dream that one day this nation will rise up and live out the true meaning of its creed: 'We hold these truths to be self-evident; that all men are created equal.'" Only when the dream has been made reality will all of America's citizens, "black men and white men . . . be able to join hands and sing in the words of the old Negro spiritual, 'Free at last! Free at last! Thank God Almighty, we are free at last!'"[14]

Just ten weeks after Martin Luther King spoke in the shadow of the Lincoln Memorial about the unrequited dreams of black Americans a century after emancipation, John Kennedy, like Abraham Lincoln, was shot and killed by an assassin. Kennedy was assassinated in Dallas on November 22, 1963. Just five days later, on November 27, President Lyndon Johnson addressed a joint session of the Congress about the slain president's dreams and about his intention to fulfill them. Johnson sought to mythologize the fallen president in order to fuel passage of an agenda larger than Kennedy had ever thought plausible to pursue. Johnson told a grieving Congress and country, "the ideas and the ideals which he so nobly represented must and will be translated into effective action. . . . We have talked long enough in this country about equal rights. . . . It is time now to write the next chapter, and to write it in the books of law."[15] But Johnson had more than civil rights in view.

On May 22, 1964, Lyndon Johnson famously urged students at the University of Michigan to join him in making America a "Great Society." Like TR, Wilson, and FDR, LBJ tried to place his vision of a Great Society within the broader sweep of American history. America, he began, was founded to protect and foster the life, liberty, and property of its people. "For a century we labored to settle and subdue a continent. For half a century we called upon unbounded invention and untiring industry to create an order of plenty for all of our people. The challenge of the next half century," Johnson declared, "is whether we have the wisdom to use that wealth to enrich and elevate our national life, and to advance the quality of our American civilization." Unbridled growth, Johnson told his audience, was not the solution. "The Great Society rests on abundance. . . . But that is just the beginning. The Great Society . . . serves not only the needs of the body and the demands of commerce but the desire for beauty and the hunger for community. . . . It is a place where men are more concerned with the quality of their goals than the quantity of their goods." Johnson closed his address by calling the next generation of Americans to the great task of their forebears. The president declared, "Those who came to this land sought to build more than just a new country. They sought a new world. So I have come here today . . . to say that you can make their vision our reality. . . . You can help build a society where the demands of morality, and the needs of the spirit, can be realized in the life of the Nation. . . . Will you join in the battle to build the Great Society, to prove that our material progress is only the foundation on which we will build a richer life of mind and spirit?"[16]

Johnson's aspirations continued to soar through the winter of 1965. LBJ's remarkable State of the Union address, delivered to a joint session of Congress and a national radio and television audience on January 4, 1965, laid out a broad domestic program to take Americans beyond the material to the moral. As the 1960s boom buried memories of the Depression, LBJ advised Congress and the American people to "turn increased attention to the character of American life." Wealth was not the problem, it was present in abundance, so the pressing issue was how best to use it in the interest of the country and its people. "The Great Society asks not how much, but how good; not only how to create wealth but how to use it; not only how fast we are going, but where we are headed." Fascinatingly, Johnson suggested to the Congress and the country that these questions, at first glimpse perhaps disconcertingly broad, had standing answers in America. Johnson assured the Congress and the nation that "A President does not shape a new and personal vision of America. . . . It existed when the first settlers saw the coast of the new world, and when the first pioneers moved westward. It has guided us every step of the way. . . . There was a dream—a dream of a place where a free man could build for himself, and raise his children to a better life—a dream of a continent to be conquered, a world to be won, a nation to be made." This dream, Johnson reminded his listeners, "sustains every President. But it is also your inheritance," he reminded each congressman and woman, "and it belongs equally to all the people that we all serve."

Johnson closed by reminding his colleagues and country, just as FDR had more than three decades earlier, that the American Dream was a heritage to be cherished and nurtured. The American Dream "must be interpreted anew by each generation for its own needs; as I have tried, in part, to do tonight. . . . This, then, is the state of the Union: Free and restless, growing and full of hope. So it was in the beginning. So it shall always be, while God is willing, and we are strong enough to keep the faith."[17] Two weeks later, Johnson again addressed a joint session of Congress in his inaugural address. Again, he closed with a call to Congress and to the American people to join him in fulfilling the nation's promise, saying, "I will lead and I will do the best I can. But you, you must look within your own hearts to the old promises and to the old dream. They will lead you best of all."[18]

Johnson continued through the spring and summer of 1965 to focus the nation's attention on civil rights and to place civil rights within the context of American political development and the fuller realization of the American Dream. On March 15, 1965, the president addressed another joint session of Congress; this time his message was titled "The American Promise," and it announced that he was sending them a bill assuring voting rights to blacks. Speaking of blacks seeking not just the right to vote, but a full share in the American Dream, Johnson said, "Their cause must be our cause too. Because it is not just Negroes, but really it is all of us, who must overcome the crippling legacy of bigotry and injustice. And we shall overcome."[19] Drawing from the famous civil rights movement promise, "We shall overcome," Johnson told Congress that the next stage of the nation's moral development would be judged by whether blacks were allowed full access to American life.

Johnson extended his promise of black inclusion beyond equality of opportunity to equality of results in a June 4, 1965, commencement speech at Howard University. Johnson drew on Lincoln's century-old justification for the fairness of open competition—the justice of the fairly run race. He began by saying, "Freedom is the right to share, share fully and equally, in American society—to vote, to hold a job, to enter a public place, to go to school. It is the right to be treated in every part of our national life as a person equal in dignity and promise to all others. But freedom is not enough," Johnson continued. "You do not wipe away the scars of centuries by saying: Now you are free to go where you want, and to do as you desire. . . . You do not take a person who, for years, has been hobbled by chains and liberate him, bring him up to the starting line of a race and then say, 'you are free to compete with all the others,' and still justly believe that you have been completely fair." The president declared that America had reached "the next and more profound stage of the battle for civil rights. We seek not just freedom but opportunity. We seek not just legal equity but human ability, not just equality as a right and a theory but equality as a fact and equality as a result." Johnson closed his Howard University speech by reiterating the basic right of blacks to a full share in the American Dream. "From the first," Johnson said, "this has been a land of towering expectations. . . . It was a rich land, glowing with more abundant promise than man had ever seen. Here, unlike any place yet known, all were to share the harvest. . . . Each could become whatever his qualities of mind and spirit would permit—to strive, to seek, and, if he could, to find his happiness." Again, Johnson sought to summon the next generation to the work of extending the American dream, saying, "So, it is the glorious opportunity of this generation to end the one huge wrong of the American Nation, and, in so doing, to find America for ourselves, with the same immense thrill of discovery who gripped those who first began to realize that here, at last, was a home for freedom."[20]

But Johnson's dreams were about to be dashed as black hope and aspiration became disappointment and rage. In the summer of 1965, in the midst of the Great Society's most impressive legislative triumphs, Watts erupted in rioting. One of the Johnson administration's top black officials, Roger Wilkins, explained, "In earlier decades, the overwhelming majority of Negroes retained a profound faith in America, her institutions, her ideals.... Now, however, there is a growing and seriously held view . . . that white people have embedded their own personal flaws so deeply in the institutions that those institutions are beyond redemption."[21] The Muslim leader, Malcolm X, was, of course, more blunt, saying, I am "one of 22 million black people who are victims of Americanism. . . . I don't see any American dream; I see an American nightmare."[22] Although Malcolm X was assassinated in February 1965, his sense that America was, despite the pervasive rhetoric of the mainstream of the civil rights movement and of the Johnson administration, simply incapable of encompassing blacks spread through the northern ghettoes.

President Johnson's focus on civil rights, and the escalating demands of blacks and other minorities, left many whites concerned that their interests and ideals were being challenged directly. Until well into the twentieth century, the American Dream required hard work, steadily applied, in a climate where success was possible, even common, but still uncertain. For Jefferson, Jackson, Lincoln, Hoover, and any number of others, although one might begin as hired labor, hard work eventually led to ownership of land or a business that produced something real and tangible like crops or goods for sale. Although the Dream culminated in autonomy, success, and security, it was the uncertainty that produced the hard and steady work. During the 1960s and 1970s the American Dream of equal opportunity in an environment of plenty threatened to evolve into a demand that society guarantee success, and if success could not be fully guaranteed, that failure be well cushioned.

Just as some Americans seemed to reject the traditional expectation of hard work, others seemed to reject the traditional view of success as wealth and status. By the latter half of the twentieth century, many Americans worked in large corporate entities where they faced a career ladder that never ended in ownership, autonomy, or control. Moreover, many workers produced and sold intangibles like advertising, public relations, entertainment, and travel. As work became more abstract, fulfillment and satisfaction became things one sought in one's free time to achieve a balanced life in which work did not overwhelm family, leisure, and pleasure. Could the "vague dread" that Tocqueville and Emerson noted more than a century before actually be banished from American life? And if so, would an American Dream that stretched beyond the material to the psychological and philosophical, that promised Americans a certain quality of life beyond abundance, still be the American Dream?

Many were uncertain. Penn's vision of a balance between the inner and outer plantations and Jefferson's vision of a widespread agrarian sufficiency had long since given way before the materialism of the gold rush, the Gilded Age, and the Roaring Twenties. Work, creativity, and competition had made the United States a very wealthy society. But how society might grant more opportunity to the formerly excluded, encourage a more wholesome balance between work and private life for the comfortable classes, and maintain the characteristic American commitments to hard work, determination, and productivity was unclear. Once change sparked instability, conservatives had little difficulty in convincing the comfortable that a firm defense of work and wealth was the only way to keep the vagabonds at bay.

The Dream Embedded in Institutions, Law, and Policy

Dreams often float well out ahead of reality, but opportunity has to be grounded in law and policy. How to assure opportunity in post–World War II America was a matter of deep concern. Many Americans feared that reduced government spending might tip the economy back into recession or even depression. A growing number of economists and government planners, on the other hand, had become convinced that new ideas and policy prescriptions associated with the British economist, John Maynard Keynes, allowed governments to manage economic growth and stability. Keynes argued that governments could manage economic performance through social, fiscal, and monetary policy while leaving decisions about production and consumption mostly in private hands. Officials in the late Roosevelt and early Truman administrations moved aggressively and across a broad front to prepare the nation for peace and prosperity. Hence, major new initiatives were undertaken in education, economic management, and civil rights.

Americans always realized that they needed education to succeed in the world. In the nineteenth century, a rough literacy sufficed for most Americans, permitting them to read, write, and calculate enough to get along in a world of barter, occasional purchase, newspapers, and the Bible. As the economy evolved over the course of the twentieth century, the need for more education became clear. Although historically the federal government had been little involved in education, Franklin Delano Roosevelt signed the GI Bill of Rights on June 22, 1944. The GI Bill was intended to reward soldiers for their service in World War II and to provide assistance for their transition to a peacetime economy, especially if that economy was plagued by unemployment. The GI Bill also included support for agricultural training, vocational training, on-the-job training, elementary and secondary education, and college and university education. In the ten years after the end of World War II, more than 15 million GIs took advantage of one or more of these programs.

The higher education title of the GI Bill provided that each soldier was eligible for one year of college support plus additional support equal to the time spent on active duty. Hence, a soldier that had spent two years on active duty was eligible for three years of college support; three years of active duty earned four years of support. In addition, soldiers received support for tuition, books, and supplies up to a maximum of $500 per year and a monthly living stipend of $50 for singles and $75 for married veterans. In December 1945 and April 1948 Congress extended and improved both the educational benefits and the financial supports in the GI Bill. When colleges and universities opened for the fall semester of 1946, more than a million servicemen were enrolled, and in the peak year of 1947, half of all students in the nation's colleges and universities were veterans. Over the next ten years a total of 2,232,000 vets, including nearly 65,000 women, attended college under the GI Bill. Similar, although somewhat scaled down, GI Bills were provided after the Korean and Viet Nam wars. The GI Bills made higher education available to a generation of working and middle-class young men and women who would not have thought it possible otherwise.

The first major debate to focus directly on postwar economic policy swirled around the Truman administration's Full Employment Act. The Full Employment Act proposed to make it national policy that any American able and willing to work should have access to a job. As the fear of depression faded in the postwar prosperity, debate turned to a more moderate proposal that eventually became the Employment Act of 1946. The Employment Act of 1946 formalized Washington's responsibility for maintaining the health of the American economy. This act stated, "it is the continuing policy and responsibility of the Federal Government to . . . promote free competitive enterprise . . . and useful employment, for those able, willing, and seeking to work, and to promote maximum employment, production, and purchasing power." The Employment Act also gave the president and Congress tools to use in managing toward full employment in a free market economy. The act established the Council of Economic Advisers in the executive office of the president to recommend policies that would promote economic growth, price stability, and full employment. It also made the president responsible for submitting an economic report on the state of the union to the Congress every year and established the Joint Economic Committee in Congress to evaluate and recommend responses to that report.

The largest private actors in the economy, including major corporations and unions, also moved to plan and coordinate their economic relationships. In the peace and prosperity of 1948, the General Motors Corporation offered the United Auto Workers a contract that included both an annual cost-of-living adjustment (COLA) and an annual 2 percent wage increase in anticipation of future productivity increases. By the early 1960s the COLA principle spread to most union contracts, and by the early 1970s it was a part of Social Security, certain welfare and income support programs, and many government employee and nonunion contracts. COLA provisions represented a new economic amendment to the traditional social contract in which American business and government agreed to guarantee their workers' income against inflation.

Civil rights policy also evolved rapidly in postwar America. As the 1948 election approached, Truman decided that the only way to break the conservative stranglehold on Congress was to confront the southern wing of his own party. On February 2, 1948, President Truman presented a ten-point civil rights program to the Congress, calling for an antilynching bill, voting rights, and integration of the armed forces. Congress balked, but Truman upped the ante by insisting that a strong civil rights plank be inserted into the Democratic platform for the 1948 campaign. The platform read: "The Democratic Party commits itself . . . to support our President in guaranteeing these basic and fundamental American principles: (1) the right of full and equal political participation; (2) the right to equal opportunity of employment; (3) the right of security of persons; (4) and the right of equal treatment in the service and defense of our nation."[23] The Dixiecrats, led by South Carolina Governor Strom Thurmond, bolted the convention. Within days, Truman issued Executive Order 9981, declaring, "there shall be equality of treatment and opportunity in the Armed Services without regard to race, color, religion, or national origin." Over the next fifteen years, desegregation of the U.S. military, especially the army, was one of the early success stories of the civil rights movement.

While Truman was making small gains against strong opposition in Congress, the courts were pursuing a piecemeal review of the doctrine that "separate but equal" public schools for blacks and whites were constitutional. The states of the deep South and most of the border states ran dual, or segregated, school systems from kindergarten through college. Two landmark cases from 1950 raised the question of how equal separate facilities had to be. The precedents established in *Sweatt v. Painter* and *McLaurin v. Oklahoma* made the point that if educational facilities are to be separate, they must truly be equal. The appointment in 1953 of Earl Warren as chief justice of the Supreme Court moved the reconsideration of racial segregation to the top of the court's agenda. Warren was a shrewd political leader and former governor of California rather than a judicial scholar. He moved the court from the New Deal posture of judicial restraint and deference to the political branches of the government to the posture of an assertive, even demanding, advocate of individual rights and liberties. The Warren court made a long series of dramatic rulings expanding individual rights in such diverse areas as racial and gender equality, voting and political participation, the rights of the accused, and freedom of expression and conscience. While Congress and the president moved to assure that the economy provided ample opportunity, the court moved to assure that civil and human rights were protected and expanded.

In the landmark case of *Brown v. Board of Education of Topeka, Kansas* (1954), Chief Justice Earl Warren urged the Supreme Court to confront directly the constitutionality of segregation in public education. The court asked: Can separate be equal, or is separate inherently unequal and therefore discriminatory within the meaning of the Fourteenth Amendment? Writing on behalf of a unanimous court, Warren reasoned that education "is a principal instrument in awakening the child to cultural values in preparing him for later professional training. . . . In these days it is doubtful that any child may reasonably be expected to succeed in life if he is denied the opportunity of an education." Moreover, "Segregation of white and colored children in public schools has a detrimental effect upon the colored children." Therefore, Warren concluded, "in the field of public education the doctrine of separate but equal has no place. Separate educational facilities are inherently unequal. . . . The plaintiffs . . . have been deprived of the equal protection of the laws guaranteed by the Fourteenth Amendment." When the decision in *Brown* was released to the public on May 17, 1954, seventeen states and the District of Columbia mandated segregation in their elementary and secondary schools. Although the District of Columbia and most of the border states complied with the instruction to desegregate their schools, the states of the deep South dug in for a decade-long contest called "massive resistance." At the national level, President Eisenhower repeatedly refused to endorse *Brown,* and the conservative coalition in Congress actively obstructed enforcement of the court's ruling.

Nonetheless, the Eisenhower administration did move major policy initiatives in both education and civil rights in its second term. Congress responded in 1958 to the shock of Russian success in orbiting *Sputnik,* the first man-made satellite to circle the earth, by establishing the National Aeronautics and Space Administration and passing the National Defense Education Act (NDEA). The NDEA provided $280 million to match state funds directed toward improving elementary and secondary instruction in science and foreign languages. The NDEA represented the first major infusion of federal funds into elementary and secondary education. Additional funds were provided for fellowships for graduate students planning to go into college teaching of sciences and languages. The Eisenhower administration responded to the civil rights movement by passing, with a strong assist from Lyndon Johnson, the Democratic majority leader of the Senate, the Civil Rights Act of 1957. That bill, the first major piece of civil rights legislation since Reconstruction, had established the U.S. Civil Rights Commission and enhanced the Civil Rights Division of the Justice Department. While able to respond to citizen complaints, the Civil Rights Commission and the Civil Rights Division did not have the authority to drive the civil rights agenda nationally.

As late as 1960 not a single black student attended a public school or university with whites in Alabama, Georgia, Louisiana, Mississippi, or South Carolina. Moreover, when John Kennedy took the oath of office as president of the United States early in 1961, less than 4 percent of voting-age blacks in Mississippi were registered to vote. The Kennedy administration had to be pushed to move on civil rights, but it moved with confidence on economic policy. The Kennedy economic program sought both to guide and to grow the American economy. In 1962 Kennedy followed traditional Democratic economic doctrine by dramatically reducing tariffs and opening the economy to international trade. Then in 1963 he moved to reduce income taxes. Even from a Democratic Party perspective, the tax rates required to fund World War II and the Korean War were prohibitively high in peacetime. Tax rates started at 20 percent on small incomes and went all the way to 91 percent on the largest incomes. Kennedy cut tax rates between 17 and 30 percent, depending on the bracket, to spur additional economy activity. Throughout the 1960s and 1970s governments sought to shape monetary and fiscal policies to deliver economic growth and rising personal incomes.

John Kennedy's assassination made Lyndon Johnson president and unleashed an electoral landslide and legislative flood that came to be known as the Great Society. Johnson quickly appointed seventeen task forces to develop

Figure 7.4. President Lyndon Baines Johnson Signing the Civil Rights Act, 1964. Dignitaries, including Martin Luther King, Walter Fountroy, Congressman Peter Rodino (D-NJ), and AFL-CIO President George Meany, look on. (LBJ Library photograph)

program proposals across the full range of domestic policy. Joseph Califano, Johnson confidant and secretary of the Department of Health, Education, and Welfare, recalled that Johnson submitted and Congress approved more than 100 major programs in both the 89th (1965–66) and 90th (1967–68) Congresses. These major programs accounted for more than five hundred separate social programs, including "such important policy departures as Medicare, Medicaid, the Voting Rights Act of 1965, the Elementary and Secondary Education Act, the War on Poverty, the Air Pollution Control Act, and legislation to establish the Department of Transportation and the Department of Housing and Urban Development."[24] LBJ did what Truman had been unable to do: move beyond FDR's "economic bill of rights" to provide education, health care, housing, legal aid, and much more to the nation's poor (Figure 7.4).

In the wake of President Kennedy's assassination, President Lyndon Johnson dramatically strengthened Kennedy's civil rights bill. The new bill was passed into law as the Civil Rights Act of 1964. Its critical Title VI held that "No person in the United States shall, on the ground of race, color, or national origin, be excluded from participation in, be denied the benefit of, or be sub-jected to discrimination under any program or activity receiving Federal finan-cial assistance." Title VII of the act prohibited discrimination by employers and labor unions in businesses with one hundred or more employees; pro-hibited segregation or denial of service in any public accommodation, includ-ing motels, restaurants, movie theaters, or sports facilities; and permitted the U.S. attorney general to represent citizens attempting to desegregate state facilities including public schools. A prohibition against discrimination on account of sex was added to the Civil Rights Act of 1964 as a weakening amendment that some thought might actually kill the bill. Elements of Title VII forbade gender discrimination in hiring, firing, pay, and other conditions of employment. This important legislation made it illegal to pay men and women differently for the same work merely on account of sex. The Great Society initiatives, expanded and formalized by President Richard Nixon in uneasy cooperation with overwhelmingly Democratic Congresses, demanded "affirmative action" to assure that minorities participated fully in the American economy and society.

Although the Kennedy tax cuts fueled the rapid economic growth of the early 1960s, Johnson's Economic Opportunity Act (EOA) of 1964 was in-tended to ensure that as many Americans as possible got a share of the pros-perity. The EOA sought to open pathways to economic success to those who lacked access and skills. The Job Corps offered training to mostly inner-city teens, and the Community Action Program offered counseling, training, and support for the economic and social development of underprivileged commu-nities. There were also rural development funds, small business loans, and work programs for welfare recipients. The point of the EOA was to give people that increment of education or training that would allow them to effectively engage the booming economy.

The landmark education legislation of the 1960s was the Elementary and Secondary Education Act (ESEA) of 1965. Although the name does not sug-gest it, it was also a powerful civil rights bill. The ESEA provided federal edu-cation funds to school districts with large numbers of low-income students. These funds could be denied or discontinued if schools were found to be dis-criminating. The provision of federal money to support state and local pro-grams—and the threat that it could be withdrawn—was instrumental in breaking the back of segregation. The most striking result of the movement of the Congress and the executive branch into the fray over desegregation was that the percentage of black schoolchildren attending school with whites in the South rose from 1.2 percent in 1964 to 91.3 percent in 1972.[25] Moreover, the ESEA's higher education provisions provided additional support through scholarships, grants, and work study to assist all Americans with the requisite talent to go to college. The results of America's investments in education were stunning. The proportion of young Americans completing high doubled from 38 percent in 1940 to 75 percent in 1970, while the proportion completing college almost tripled from 5.9 percent in 1940 to 16.4 percent in 1970. Most astoundingly, the number of degrees awarded by American colleges and universities increased fivefold, from 217,000 in 1940 to 1,073,000 in 1970, with almost two-thirds of that increase coming between 1960 and 1970. Like land in the nineteenth century, education by the mid-twentieth century had become the foundation for individual aspiration and the pathway to the American Dream.

The Voting Rights Act of 1965 permitted blacks increasingly unfettered access to political influence in their communities. A complicated array of rules and practices, including literacy tests, poll taxes, white primaries, and grandfather clauses kept blacks, other minorities, and the poor generally from registering and voting in elections. Specifically, the Voting Rights Act of 1965 prohibited literacy tests and other practices deemed to have a discriminatory impact. It directed the U.S. Department of Justice to initiate legal action to challenge the constitutionality of poll taxes in state and local elections. And it sent federal marshals into southern states to assure that local election officials permitted all citizens to register and vote in elections.[26] By 1970, 10 million new black voters were on the rolls. Finally, in the wonderfully titled case *Loving v. Virginia* (1967), the United States Supreme Court confronted the issue of interracial marriage. Into the mid-twentieth century, most states had and enforced legal prohibitions against interracial marriage. Sixteen states still had such laws in 1967 when the Supreme Court used the *Loving* case to declare them void.[27]

The Kennedy and Johnson administrations also saw immigration reform in relation both to U.S. foreign policy and the domestic civil rights movement. LBJ passed immigration reform as part of his Great Society program. The Immigration Reform Act of 1965, also known as the Hart-Celler Act, set aside the national origins quota system in favor of family reunification, protection of refugees, and preferences for skilled workers. Johnson signed the bill in the shadow of the Statute of Liberty, saying the old "system violates the basic principle of American democracy—the principle that values and rewards each man on the basis of his merit as a man. It has been un-American in the highest sense, because it has been untrue to the faith that brought thousands to these shores even before we were a country."[28] The Hart-Celler reforms set off an immigration boom and shifted the focus of immigration from Europe to Mexico, the rest of Latin America, the Caribbean, and Asia. Immigration from Europe nearly doubled in the next decade, but to the surprise of many, immigration from Central America grew fivefold, from Mexico grew sevenfold, from South America and the Caribbean tenfold, and from Asia twelvefold. America was about to emerge from a biracial era into a multiracial era and not everyone was ready.

Another centerpiece of Johnson's Great Society program was the War on Poverty. In Johnson's view, the New Deal had secured the position of the white working class within the American society and economy. What remained was to focus intently on the poor, the bottom 20 percent, and develop programs designed to prepare them for successful inclusion in American life. The War on Poverty sought to remove blocks to success through education and training, health care, food and nutrition programs, adequate housing, child care, family planning, legal aid, and community organization. LBJ expanded eligibility to social security and enhanced benefits. More importantly, he added to social security a health care benefit that FDR, Truman, and Kennedy had all been denied. Medicare and Medicaid, both passed in 1965, made the retired elderly and the nonworking poor eligible for medical care. Medicare, designed as a part of the Social Security system, was a social insurance program in which working people paid premiums so that they were eligible for benefits upon retirement. Medicaid was a means-tested poverty or welfare program to provide health care to the nonworking poor. Community health centers focused on preventive medicine and on health and nutritional education. Food stamp and school lunch programs sought to assure adequate nutrition for the poor.

Even after civil unrest and the Vietnam War had drained the emotional and financial supports of the Great Society, federal attention to the quality of American life remained high. Landmark health and safely legislation included the Federal Hazardous Substances Act (1960), the Food and Drug Amendments (1962), and the Fair Packaging and Labeling Act (1966). Key environmental legislation included the Clean Air Acts of 1963, 1967, 1970, 1974, and 1977; the Clean Water Acts of 1965, 1970, and 1972; the Solid Waste Disposal Act of 1965; the Motor Vehicle Pollution Control Act of 1965; and the Wild and Scenic Rivers Act of 1968. The Endangered Species Acts of 1966, 1969, and 1973 and the Marine Mammal Protection Act of 1972 made the federal government responsible for the protection of all species. Ultimately, Johnson held that a Great Society not only assures that everyone has enough to eat and a roof over their head, it also assures that the society pleases, energizes, and uplifts them.

Remarkably, the regulatory surge of the late 1960s and early 1970s reached its crest after Richard Nixon became president in 1969. To monitor and enforce the new regulatory requirements, Nixon and the Democrats in Congress created the Environmental Protection Agency (1970), the Occupational Health and Safety Administration (1970), and the Consumer Products Safety Commission (1970).[29] Economic opportunity had always been a responsibility of government in America, but FDR's New Deal made economic security a government responsibility, and LBJ's Great Society went even further, making the quality of life in America a government responsibility too.

Finally, much as 1964 and 1965 were the peak years for civil rights legislation, 1972 and 1973 were the peak years for rulings and legislation regarding women and women's rights. A series of 1972 amendments to the Elementary and Secondary Education Act of 1965, especially the now-famous Title IX, forbade discrimination based on gender in any education program receiving federal funds. Title IX had its greatest impact by advancing equality in the funding of college sports programs. Nonetheless, women quickly moved toward equality with men in college and university admissions and made steady progress in admission to and completion of prestigious professional and graduate programs.

In 1972 the House (354–24) and Senate (84–8) also passed the Equal Rights Amendment (ERA) and sent it to the states for ratification. The proposed amendment read: "Equality of rights under the law shall not be denied or abridged by the United States or by any State on account of sex." Ratification seemed imminent. Twenty-two of the thirty-two state legislatures that convened during 1972 passed the ERA, many by large margins. Soon, however, opposition began to build and enthusiasm began to wane. By 1978 thirty-five states had approved, although by now, three had sought to withdraw their votes, and little more positive movement seemed likely. Although Congress extended the deadline for three more years, to June 30, 1982, no more states ratified, and the amendment failed. In the end, citizens and legislators worried that too much social change would result from its adoption defeated the ERA.[30]

In 1973 the justices of the U.S. Supreme Court declared that the Constitution guaranteed a "right to privacy" that included a woman's right to choose abortion. In *Roe v. Wade,* Justice Harry Blackmun, writing for a court divided 7–2, described a broad right to privacy residing in the Ninth Amendment (which declared that there are rights beyond those specifically listed in the Constitution and the Bill of Rights) and in the due process clause of the Fourteenth Amendment that include a woman's right to choose abortion. Although Blackmun did not deny that the states have a legitimate interest in regulating some aspects of the provision of abortion services, the decision in *Roe v. Wade* invalidated, in whole or in part, the abortion laws of forty-six states and the District of Columbia.

The Supreme Court also used the equal protection clause of the Fourteenth Amendment to require that substantial and reasonable grounds exist for treating women and men differently in most public settings. Laws and judicial rulings held that women and men must be treated equally on the job, and by banks, credit agencies, and landlords. Moreover, during the 1970s legislatures and courts revamped family law, easing divorce laws and changing the assumptions regarding child custody and alimony. No-fault divorce and limited alimony both presumed to view men and women more as equals in marriage, society, and the economy.

Shadows on the Dream

Tremendous strides were made by minorities, women, and others in the three decades following the end of World War II; yet to many white Americans, especially white men, those changes felt like dangerous turmoil. The civil rights movement slowly picked up momentum through the 1940s and 1950s, achieved spectacular successes in the mid-1960s, and then flamed out in the urban riots of the late 1960s. Nonetheless, the causes and contests of the 1960s began a process of rethinking and reassessment that changed the nation. The demand for rights, inclusion, and respect by the formerly marginalized and exploited, brought a slow and grudging, but broad and thoroughgoing, change in the tone of the American society. Over time, one heard far fewer racial epithets, ethnic slurs, and demeaning characterizations of women. Although action did not always follow thought, thought was clearly changing. For many of those caught in the nightmare of exclusion from the American dream, dawn seemed to be at hand.

Blacks made great progress between 1940 and 1970, but they started from a position of deep and fundamental discrimination. In 1940, at the tail end of the Depression and before the United States had fully begun to gear up for World War II, black workers who could find full-time, year-round work made just 45 percent of what white full-time workers made. Many, of course, could not find full-time work, and when one considers all workers, full and part time, black men made only 41 percent of what their white counterparts made. Half of all black men still worked in the rural South, and only one-third (compared to three-fourths for whites) had completed the seventh grade. Millions of blacks left the South during World War II to find jobs in the defense plants of the North. With labor in high demand, incomes rose, so that by 1950 black men working full-time made an average of 61 percent of what whites made.[31] During the stolid 1950s, black income as a ratio of white income drifted downward into the mid-1950s, and by 1960 recouped a bit to 58 percent. The 1960s boom benefited blacks greatly because it kept unemployment low and wages high. By the end of the decade, the percentage of the U.S. population living below the poverty line had fallen from 22 percent to 12 percent, and black income had risen to 67 percent of white income.[32] Against this background of slow economic progress out of deep deprivation for black workers, the civil rights movement gained traction and won a series of victories.

Throughout the civil rights struggle, even in the mid-1960s, when success seemed to come in waves, policy makers wondered whether nondiscrimination would suffice or whether some more aggressive stance would be required to achieve black equality. The Kennedy administration was the first to use the phrase "affirmative action" in Executive Order 10925 ordering federal contractors to take "positive steps" to ensure a diverse workforce.[33] Nonetheless, Kennedy and Johnson administration officials were deeply aware that the nature and pace of civil rights reform was a volatile issue that needed to be managed with great care. In April 1964 Daniel Patrick Moynihan told Secretary of Labor Willard Wirtz that the attitude of policy makers toward affirmative action was "one of bewilderment and confusion at a wholly unfamiliar proposition. . . . But we cannot avoid it. The Negroes are asking for unequal treatment. More seriously, it may be that without unequal treatment in the immediate future there is no way for them to achieve anything like equal status in the long run." Moynihan was deeply concerned about "the major and sometimes wrenching changes in our way of doing things that will be required if we are going to bring [blacks] in as full-fledged members of the larger community."[34] President Johnson also was keenly aware both that something beyond nondiscrimination would be required to make equality meaningful for black Americans and that it would be extraordinarily controversial. Johnson hoped that the conservative white votes lost as a result of civil rights initiatives would be replaced by a rising tide of white liberal and black votes. It was not to be.

Much was accomplished—the Civil Rights Acts of 1964 and 1965, the Elementary and Secondary Act of 1965, and the Voting Rights Act of 1965— but the dream remained beyond the reach of too many. The middle-class southern ministers Martin Luther King, Roy Abernathy, Roy Wilkins, and Whitney Young, who had pressed change on Kennedy and Johnson, were unable to speak for the northern ghettoes. The civil rights movement fractionalized as street-corner incendiaries grasped the initiative. Kenneth Clark noted in 1967, "The masses of Negroes are now starkly aware of the fact that recent civil rights victories benefited a very small percentage of middle class Negroes while their predicament remained the same or worsened."[35]

Women experienced great change as well, but for them, it was a challenge of balancing new opportunities and old responsibilities. In the welcome peace and prosperity of the post–World War II middle-class home, women were not just mothers and homemakers; they were self-conscious consumers and household managers as well. The extra time produced by labor-saving conveniences, like vacuum cleaners, washers and dryers, and automobiles for marketing and errands, went to volunteer work, community service, and increasingly, to paid employment outside the home. About 80 percent of single white women between 20 and 40 were employed, but only about a quarter of married women of the same age worked for wages. White women who did work full time made a median wage about two-thirds that of white men. Black women, on the other hand, always worked in much higher proportions, kept working after marriage, and tended to make about half of what white women made and one-third of what white men made.[36] Over the course of the 1950s both the labor market and women's attitude toward it continued to change. Many women came to see work, at least part-time work to supplement the family budget and provide access to attractive goods beyond the necessities, as no great infringement on their domestic responsibilities or their sense of femininity. Moreover, more traditionally female jobs became available in education, health care, social services, and clerical work. Seasonal and part-time work in retail, restaurants, and hotels also increased. The extra income proved addictive to wives and to initially skeptical husbands.

Nonetheless, most women who entered the paid workforce neither really left the domestic realm nor fully entered the paid workforce. Virtually all working women, except the very few that could afford paid help at home, still bore the bulk of household responsibility. Moreover, women were frequently in and out of the workforce, in low-paying jobs, usually with limited benefits and no retirement program. Although the 1960s were a time of great dynamism and change, most women were caught midway between the stultifying safety of the home and the exciting uncertainly of the marketplace. Then a truly formative event occurred—in 1960 the U.S. Food and Drug Administration approved the first birth control pill. "The pill" gave women direct and personal control over the decision to bear children and, just as importantly, over the timing and spacing of pregnancy and childbearing. The pill made it possible to separate sex and childbearing, thereby helping to give women control over one major problem, but it only made the question of how to use that control more pressing. What goals should women pursue in their lives?

As women groped to understand and articulate their place in the American society, Betty Friedan's *The Feminine Mystique* (1963) emerged as definitive. Friedan's famous first chapter, entitled "The Problem that Has No Name," described a malaise that millions of women recognized in their lives. Sara Evans described Friedan's "problem with no name" as a "passive and infantilizing domesticity." Millions of talented and educated middle-class suburban women were trapped in increasingly comfortable, electrified, user-friendly homes without important outside work and responsibility to give their lives independent meaning. The culture advised femininity and domesticity while the abilities, inner needs, and objective interests of women advised education, preparation, and accomplishment.

Both the opportunities and constraints that women felt were highlighted in a particularly striking way where the civil rights and women's rights movements came together. In a famous 1964 exchange during a meeting of the Student Non-Violent Coordinating Committee (SNCC), Stokely Carmichael hooted down a presentation on "The Position of Women in SNCC," saying, "the only position for women in SNCC is prone."[37] Although women were often rejected as full participants, their involvement in the movements of the 1960s provided them with experience, training, and organizational skills that would be put to excellent use in the rejuvenated women's movement of the late 1960s and 1970s. The National Organization for Women (NOW) was founded in 1966 to rally women and to prod government to fulfill its legal responsibility to protect the equal rights of women. NOW's organizers were convinced that the civil rights of women would be taken less seriously than those of blacks unless they could focus particular attention on them. NOW's statement of purpose is clear: "To take action to bring women into full participation in the mainstream of American society now, exercising all the privileges and responsibilities thereof in truly equal partnership with men."[38]

While minorities and women demanded full involvement in the American mainstream, full involvement in the American mainstream was demanded of Native Americans. "Termination," as the policy of the late 1940s and 1950s came to be called, aimed to terminate the status of Indians as wards of the federal government. In August 1946 President Truman, with bipartisan support in Congress and broad support among Native American leaders, signed a bill that created the Indian Claims Commission. The legislation gave Indians five years to file tribal and individual claims to land, money and income, or rights and privileges due them under earlier treaties but denied or infringed. The president and Congress hoped that the Indian Claims Commission could work through any claims that might be brought forward, resolve them, and thereby free Indians to leave the reservations in search of opportunity in the broader society and economy. Unfortunately, the commission defined its task narrowly, moved slowly, and paid only five claims before Truman left office in early 1953.

In August 1953, Congress and the Eisenhower administration reasserted its intention to end the status of Indians as wards of the national government and make them freestanding American citizens. Congress passed Public Law 280, which authorized all states, at their discretion, to assume civil and criminal jurisdiction over Indians within state boundaries. California, Minnesota, Nebraska, Oregon, and Wisconsin assumed jurisdiction immediately, while promising to respect tribal water, hunting and fishing, and treaty rights.[39] Many Indians expected to benefit from state control of law enforcement, health care, and education, but many others were deeply concerned that termination of federal authority would mean loss of tax and treaty advantages, tribal sovereignty, and cultural integrity. Indian resistance stymied termination by the late 1950s. Native Americans, on the other hand, continued to search for an elusive balance between tribal sovereignty and federal protection and support.

Both national political parties supported Indian self-determination and cultural identity in their 1960 party platforms. President Kennedy appointed a task force to study Indian issues, and President Johnson made Indian reservations a particular focus of his War on Poverty. The myriad poverty, health care, education, and job training programs that comprised the War on Poverty channeled unprecedented amounts of federal money to the reservations and their tribal governments. In 1970, President Nixon declared, "We must assure the Indian that he can assume control of his own life without being separated involuntarily from the tribal group. . . . [or] being cut off from Federal concern and Federal support."[40] By 1973, early in Nixon's second term, Congress actually began restoring federal recognition to tribes whose federal ties had been terminated two decades earlier. Indian reservations remained among the poorest and most dismal places in America.

8

The Dream at Ebb Tide: Entitlement to Responsibility from Reagan to Clinton

In this present crisis, government is not the solution to our problem, government is the problem. . . . It is no coincidence that our present troubles parallel and are proportionate to the intervention and intrusion in our lives that result from unnecessary and excessive growth of government.
—Ronald Reagan, first inaugural address, January 20, 1981

Today we can declare: Government is not the problem. . . . As times change, so government must change. We need a new government for a new century. . . . The preeminent mission of our new government is to give all Americans an opportunity—not a guarantee, but a real opportunity—to build better lives.
—Bill Clinton, second inaugural address, January 20, 1997

Ronald Wilson Reagan and William Jefferson Clinton defined themselves as defenders of the American Dream. They spoke of the sanctity of the American Dream early, often, and in the most prominent public settings, including the four inaugural addresses that they delivered between them. Nonetheless, as the quotations above show clearly, they had vastly different senses of how government should relate to the society and economy to ensure that the American Dream would be there for this and future generations. Although both oversaw extended periods of economic growth, neither succeeded in restoring confidence and opportunity broadly throughout the society and economy; neither reestablished the American Dream.

Lyndon Johnson's vision of a Great Society reflected the tremendous prosperity of post–World War II America. Growth in median family income grew by 38 percent during the 1950s and 37 percent during the 1960s. LBJ promised a Great Society in which permanent prosperity would pave the way to self-fulfillment. Others worried that permanent prosperity might make Americans too comfortable to work, strive, and compete as hard as had previous generations. Among the keenest analysts of post-1960s America was the sociologist Daniel Bell, author of *The Coming of Post-Industrial Society* (1973) and *The Cultural Contradictions of Capitalism* (1976). Bell explained that the nation's economy was evolving from an industrial configuration in which manual labor had produced goods to a postpostindustrial configuration in which mental labor would produce services like information and entertainment. Bell warned that the transformation of work from labor to thought and creativity might leave the least creative behind and divert the most creative from the traditional virtues of the Protestant ethic to leisure, pleasure, and self-fulfillment.

New and threatening dynamics emerged within the American economy just as Bell issued his warnings. Economic growth slowed and income inequality rose as the economy distinguished between winners and losers, the successful and the unsuccessful, ever more starkly. Growth in median family income slowed to 7 percent in the 1970s and 6 percent in the 1980s. The poor languished while the rich got richer, and the very rich got much richer. Between 1970 and 1990, the poorest one-fifth of families saw their income increase just 3 percent, while the richest one-fifth saw their incomes grow by 31 percent, or by more than ten times as much.[1] These dramatic changes in the growth and distribution of family income reflected equally dramatic changes in the growth and distribution of opportunity within the American economy.

In 1980 Ronald Reagan won the presidency of a nation that was uncertain whether its best days were still ahead of it or already behind it. Over the two decades between 1980 and 2000 Presidents Reagan, Bush, and Clinton presided over economic recovery and the nation's return to unquestioned global supremacy. Nonetheless, the booming economy of the 1980s and 1990s seemed to distribute its benefits in dangerously narrow ways. Many asked what the American Dream meant in an era in which only a select few seemed to harvest most of prosperity's benefits. How should young Americans prepare for an uncertain future? Were immigrants still welcome, still needed, or were they a threat to hard-pressed workers already here? Finally, what was government's appropriate role, first in promoting prosperity, and then in promoting a healthy distribution of that prosperity? Republicans and Democrats, Reagan and Clinton, had vastly different responses, if not exactly answers, to these questions.

Young Dreamers and the World Before Them

The transformation of the American economy in the last three decades of the twentieth century, from a goods-producing to a knowledge-driven service economy, was a case study in the "creative destruction" of modern capitalism. Unrelenting economic change produced political instability and tumult. Several major changes worked their way through the American economy in the closing decades of the twentieth century. Each had its effect steadily and incrementally; none hit like a thunderclap, but by the 1970s it seemed that the driving dynamics of the American economy were weakening. Four of the most important changes were the continued movement of women into the labor force, increased educational attainment, especially among minorities and women, the decline of organized labor, and the steep increase in immigration. Each of these reflected a more general evolution of the economy from the industrial colossus of midcentury to the service economy of the late twentieth century.

The gender composition of the American workforce changed dramatically in the second half of the twentieth century, especially after 1970. In 1950, 79 percent of adult men and 29 percent of adult women were in the paid workforce. By 1970, men had held essentially steady at 80 percent while workforce participation had risen to 43 percent for women. By 1980, men were at 77.4 percent and women had climbed to 51.5 percent, including more than 60 percent of women with school-age children and 45 percent of women with children under 6. By 2000, men's workforce participation had dropped to 74.7 percent while women's had risen to 60.2 percent, including 77 percent of women with school-age children and 63 percent with children under 6. In 2000 women accounted for 47 percent of the workforce, and analysts were speculating that within a decade they would be a majority.[2]

Educational attainment, for everyone, but especially for women and minorities, improved in the second half of the twentieth century. In 1950, less than one-third (32.5 percent) of adults had completed high school and only 6 percent had completed college. By 2000, the high school graduation rate had more than doubled to 84.1 percent and the college graduation rate had quadrupled to 26 percent. Among blacks the progress was much greater because they started further back. In 1950, only 13 percent of blacks had graduated from high school and only 2 percent had graduated from college. By 2000, 78.5 percent of blacks had graduated from high school and 16.5 percent had graduated from college.

Over approximately the same time frame, the proportion of the nonagricultural workforce represented by unions declined by nearly two-thirds, from 31.9 percent in 1950 (it had crested at 35.8 percent in 1945 and reached 35.1 as late as 1954) to just 13.5 percent in 2000. This decline in the unionized workforce was part of a much broader and more thoroughgoing change in the structure of the American economy. Manufacturing employment actually fell by more than 2 million jobs between 1980 and 2000 as the percentage of the labor force involved in manufacturing declined from more than 22 percent to just 14 percent. Remarkably, employment in all goods-producing industries held almost perfectly steady at 25.6 million between 1980 and 2000, while employment in service-producing industries increased from 64.7 million to 105.7 million.

America again threw open its doors to immigrants in the last third of the twentieth century. A total of 3.3 million came in the 1960s, 4.5 million in the 1970s, 7.3 million in the 1980s, and 9.1 million, the greatest ten-year total in American history, came in the 1990s. Of the more than 16 million immigrants that came to the United States in the 1980s and 1990s, only 13 percent were from Europe, and after the fall of the wall in the early 1990s, nearly one-third of those were from the former Soviet Union. Fully 35 percent of immigrants between 1980 and 2000 were from Asia, with the largest numbers coming from China and India. Mexico alone contributed 25 percent. The Caribbean, together with Central and South America, contributed another 24 percent. Africa contributed only 3 percent.

Not surprisingly, the transition from a native white male-dominated goods-producing economy to a much more diverse service-producing economy was choppy. As more persons, women, minorities, and immigrants, traditionally paid low wages, moved into the economic mainstream, real median income for both families and households peaked in 1973, at $40,059 and $34,943 respectively, and then stagnated for more than two decades. Frank Levy has reported, "In the eight years following Nixon's first term (1973 through 1980), the average family's annual income did not grow at all. From Ronald Reagan's first term in office through most of Bill Clinton's first term (1981 through 1996), it grew by a total of 9 percent."[3] Real median incomes of families and households in 1996 stood at $43,945 and $36,872 respectively. As American workers suffered, manufacturing workers suffered most. Their incomes, adjusted for inflation, did not rise at all between 1965 and 1995.

Moreover, many of the workers in the disappearing manufacturing jobs did not have the skills required by the new jobs being created in the service sector, and those they were fitted for paid less than their old jobs. The new jobs in computer sciences, communication technologies, engineering, and health sciences often required college degrees. At the end of the twentieth century, fully 40 percent of the jobs created by the American economy were in the information and life sciences. The information industries, including finance, business services, computing and communications, education, and entertainment, make up one-quarter of the economy, whereas the life sciences, including biotechnology, energy, and pharmaceuticals, make up another 15 percent.[4] Inevitably, a major shift in the income distribution occurred in favor of the highly educated. Between 1978 and 1998 the wages of high school graduates working in manufacturing and service jobs dropped by 20 percent in real terms. At the same time, the average income of college graduates was rising so that what had been a wage gap of 39 percent between high school and college grads in 1978 became 86 percent by 1998. Holders of advanced and professional degrees made more than twice as much as high school graduates.[5]

The evolution from a goods-producing to an information-producing economy placed tremendous pressure on the American political system. Neither party seemed able to explain what was happening or to design policies to ease the pain that many Americans felt. Confidence in government fell precipitously and voter turnout followed in its wake. Rarely did the electorate trust either party with complete control of the government. Republicans were never given complete control of the government, and on those few occasions when the Democrats were—the Carter years of 1976–80 and the first two years of Clinton's first term, 1992–94—they proved unable to formulate and implement a coherent program. Voters regularly awarded control of the White House to one party, most frequently the Republicans, and control of one or both houses of the Congress to the other, most frequently the Democrats.

The rise of Ronald Reagan reenergized American conservatism after nearly a half century of post-Depression doldrums. In a three-way race for the presidency in 1980, against incumbent President Jimmy Carter and independent candidate John Anderson, Reagan won a broad national victory. In addition, the Republicans picked up twelve Senate seats, the second greatest Republican pickup in the twentieth century, to take control of the Senate for the first time since 1952. The thirty-four-seat pickup in the House, the third biggest turnover in sixty years, still left the House in Democratic hands. Although Reagan won an overwhelming victory in 1984, carrying forty-nine of the fifty states, Democrats built a hundred-seat majority in the House and retook the Senate in 1986.

The centerpieces of Reagan's presidency were the Economic Recovery Act of 1981, which featured a three-year program of tax cuts designed to lower individual income tax rates by 25 percent, and the 1986 reductions that took the top marginal tax rate on income to a fifty-year low of 31 percent. Reagan cut taxes to reduce the size and scope of government and to free up individualism, choice, and opportunity. Similarly, he argued that an undue focus on rights claims by individuals and groups had undercut personal responsibility and weakened traditional American values of work and family. Welfare, affirmative action, and reproductive rights came under pressure as the minority and women's rights movements of the 1960s and 1970s seemed to stall and then to begin giving up ground.[6] Although Reagan lost momentum in his second term, as almost all presidents lucky enough to win a second term do, he changed the tone of American politics.

Ronald Reagan did not just lead the Republican Party to series of victories over the Democrats in the 1980s, he made the Democrats' leading ideas—liberalism, the welfare state, and big government—anathema to most Americans. This lesson was driven home with great force when Reagan's vice president, George H. W. Bush, forgot the master's teaching and paid a heavy price. After campaigning successfully on a pledge of "no new taxes," President Bush compromised with congressional Democrats to raise taxes and cut spending to close large and persistent budget deficits. Conservatives pilloried Bush for breaking his antitax pledge. A sharp economic downturn in 1991 sealed his fate, and despite success in the Gulf War, he was defeated for reelection by former Arkansas Governor Bill Clinton in 1992.

Bill Clinton was elected president in 1992 and 1996 to become the first two-term Democratic president since Franklin Roosevelt, though he never won a majority of the popular vote. Bill Clinton made his decision to run for president in 1991 when then-incumbent President George Bush was at the height of his post–Gulf War popularity. Many top Democrats shied away from the race, but Clinton believed that a stagnant domestic economy made Bush vulnerable. Texas billionaire Ross Perot agreed, initiating a highly effective independent campaign that focused on the fiscal irresponsibility of the national government. Perot led in national polls as late as July 1992 before withdrawing from the race, reentering, and fading late in the contest. Still, Perot polled 19 percent of the national vote, the best showing by an independent since Teddy Roosevelt in 1912. Bill Clinton got 43 percent of the national vote to President George Bush's 37 percent.

The Clinton campaign in 1992 kept itself focused by posting a famous injunction on the wall of the campaign's "war room"—"It's the economy, stupid." Clinton recognized, as Reagan had and perhaps Bush had not, that economic prosperity was the background requirement for individual initiative, opportunity, and achievement in the modern American economy. Absent prosperity, Americans could not prepare, compete, and achieve, and without the believable promise of prosperity, political campaigns could not succeed and politicians could not govern. Hence, like Reagan, Clinton grounded his administration on an economic program. Unlike Reagan, Clinton promised that a combination of spending cuts and tax increases would reduce the deficit, bring down interest rates, and spur growth.

Despite Clinton's victories, congressional Democrats took a terrible beating in the mid-1990s, from which they are still struggling to recover. Even as Bill Clinton was winning the presidency in 1992, the Democrats lost nine seats in the House while picking up only one in the Senate. Then came 1994, a once-every-century political earthquake, spawned by Democratic fecklessness and a well-coordinated Republican counterattack promising smaller, less intrusive government. The Democrats lost fifty-three seats in the House and eight in the Senate while no Republican incumbent was defeated for reelection to the House, Senate, or governorship.[7] Republicans won majority control both of the House and the Senate for the first time since 1952. In 1996, with the economy improved and budget deficits coming under control, President Clinton won reelection easily, but Democrats failed in both 1996 and 1998 to regain their traditional majorities in Congress.

Clinton finished his second term as president to decidedly mixed reviews. Although the public held his political and policy skills in high regard, reaction to the scandals that swirled around him cut deeply into the public's assessment of the president as a person. On the policy side, inflation and unemployment fell to post–World War II lows, and a thirty-five year series of budget deficits melted away by 1998. On the personal side, a long series of minor scandals, including Whitewater, Paula Jones, and Travelgate culminated in Bill Clinton's 1998 sexual dalliance with a White House intern named Monica Lewinsky. Republicans, feigning shock and outrage, impeached the president, and Democrats, feigning their own shock and outrage, argued that private mistakes should not impugn public accomplishments. The impeachment failed at trial in the Senate. With the 2000 elections approaching, voters were left to wonder whether they might have a little integrity with their prosperity; before long, they were wondering where all the prosperity had gone.

Refocusing the American Dream

For most of American history, the Dream promised a fair chance to compete for the good things that the society had to offer. Success required hard work, perseverance, frugality, and dedication in a competitive environment where failure, due to insufficient attention and effort or to simple bad luck, was an ever-present possibility. Running scared was just part of working hard and exercising reasonable foresight in the open, competitive, volatile environment of democratic capitalism. Postwar prosperity seemed to drain some of the danger, some of the energy and direction, out of the American Dream. Incomes more than doubled in the quarter century between 1945 and 1970, and LBJ declared that a nation as wealthy as ours was bound to expand equality of opportunity to encompass equality of results. Moreover, the Great Society promised a nation in which people were not just well-fed and safe, but in which they were allowed and encouraged to nurture and develop their intellectual and artistic abilities and talents as well. Others worried, as they had since the nation's earliest days, that prosperity might compromise and weaken traditional American values. Would people really continue to work hard, save, and plan for the future in the presence of plenty? Would prosperity and ease unwind the tight springs of faith, responsibility, and virtue?

As the broadly shared income gains of the 1950s and 1960s began to give way to a widening gap between high and low wage earners in the early 1970s, new concerns emerged. Academics and journalists began to warn that the American Dream was slipping beyond the grasp of many. In 1980 Ronald Reagan promised to restore both the old opportunity and its accompanying discipline by lowering taxes and reducing government regulation, thus freeing the economy to reward education, experience, talent, hard work, dedication, imagination, and creativity. Reagan reminded Americans that good character leads to success, bad character leads to failure, and that is as it should be. Yet Reagan remained a puzzle to many.

Among the great American presidents, several were considered by their contemporaries and by historians to have been second-rate intellects. This was certainly true of Ronald Wilson Reagan, but it was also true of George Washington, Andrew Jackson, and Franklin Roosevelt. Only two great presidents—Thomas Jefferson and Ronald Reagan—were uninterruptible both to their contemporaries and later historians. Merrill Peterson, the foremost Jefferson scholar of the twentieth century, said, "Of all his great contemporaries Jefferson is perhaps the least self-revealing and the hardest to sound to his depths." Peterson made the "mortifying confession" that Jefferson "remains for me, finally, an impenetrable man."[8] With Jefferson, the biographer was flummoxed by the multiplicity of the man and the fact that his elements and aspects, each one brilliant and intriguing, never formed a full and rounded picture.

With Reagan, it was the opacity, the lack of interior dimension, the fixed and unchanging character of the man that defied description and analysis. Edmund Morris, the Pulitzer Prize–winning biographer of Theodore Roosevelt, broke his lance on Ronald Reagan. Morris was Reagan's authorized biographer, given full access to the president, senior officials, and all of their papers. Although he ultimately produced a biography entitled *Dutch: A Memoir of Ronald Reagan,* some sixteen years after the project was first broached, the book was subject to more ridicule than praise. Along the way, as Morris labored for nearly a decade beyond his initial deadline, he declared, "Ronald Reagan is a man of benign remoteness and no psychological curiosity, about himself or others." Elsewhere, Morris declared, "Reagan has been primarily a phenomenon of the American imagination—a mythical apotheosis of the best and the worst in us."[9]

Only recently have scholars and analysts, led by Hugh Heclo, begun to reconsider Reagan's impact on American politics and the means by which that impact was achieved. No one claims new ideas for Reagan, but some do claim that he put force and energy back into America's oldest ideas—its founding principles. Heclo argued, "The important point is not that Reagan ever said anything fundamentally new, but that in the new context created by the Sixties Reagan continued to uphold something old."[10] Ronald Reagan refocused the American Dream on individual responsibility, work, and striving in a way that it had not been since the early 1960s, perhaps since the 1920s. He believed that government should ensure that the rules are clear and the game is fair; but who wins the game and what they do with their winnings is none of the government's business. Those who lose should be encouraged to try again and to depend on their church, neighbors, and family in the meanwhile.

Reagan saw much of government from the New Deal to the Great Society as a mistaken and unnecessary burden on the openness, dynamism, and richness of the American society and economy. When Reagan spoke of an "economic bill of rights" on Independence Day 1987, echoing FDR's phrase of almost half a century earlier, Reagan did not mean FDR's government supports and guarantees. Reagan's four freedoms were "The freedom to work. The freedom to enjoy the fruits of one's labors. The freedom to own and control one's property. The freedom to participate in a free market."[11] Ronald Reagan's economic bill of rights was a set of guarantees that persons would be let alone to make their way in the free market. Calvin Coolidge or Herbert Hoover could easily have made these commitments, and both Reagan and his opponents knew it.

What made Ronald Reagan so frustrating for both his political opponents and for later academics, analysts, and biographers was that he seemed so immobile, so unchanging—in fact, so out of touch—that besting or belittling him should have been easy. It was not. Reagan's great strength was that he believed in the American Dream with every fiber of his being. Others thought the world complicated. America was now an advanced industrial nation, a superpower; surely that required adjusting old ideas, if only to make them relevant to the new age. Reagan thought the old ideas were relevant just as they were, and in fact, earlier attempts to adjust them were mistakes best undone. Ronald Reagan believed that the pattern of American history had been well set in the beginning; hence, staying on course was the goal; changing course was decay, disorder, and declension.

Ronald Reagan's entrance onto the national political stage came on October 27, 1964, when he addressed the nation on behalf of Republican presidential candidate Barry Goldwater. Reagan aligned himself with Goldwater's vision of a strong national defense and limited domestic program and against LBJ's vision of a Great Society in which the national government would assure that all had their rightful place. Reagan argued that fundamental American values were being perverted. An overly powerful central government threatened to make the "natural unalienable rights" of citizens appear to be a "dispensation of government." He called for less government and lower taxes as "a start toward restoring for our children the American Dream that wealth is denied to no one, that each individual has the right to fly as high as his strength and ability will take him."[12]

When Goldwater was roundly defeated by LBJ in the presidential election of 1964, Reagan became the focus of the conservative movement. After serving two successful terms as governor of California, Reagan challenged incumbent, but unelected, Republican President Gerald Ford for their party's nomination in 1976. Ford used the powers of his office to hold off the challenge, but Reagan was allowed to address the convention in the hope that he would call for party unity in the fall. Instead, Reagan's endorsement of Ford was tepid. He saved his real passion for a clarion call to conservatives to keep the faith. Even in defeat Reagan rallied his followers to their shared vision, saying to his delegates and the nation, "Don't give up your ideals. . . . Recognize that there are millions and millions of Americans out there who want what you want. . . . a shining city on a hill."[13]

Throughout his mature political life, Reagan taught that free men should look to themselves and not to government for their liberties, hopes, goals, and aspirations. Reagan's first inaugural address (1981) was the first in more than half a century to warn against a bigger and more active national government. Reaching back beyond LBJ and even FDR, Reagan warned, "In this present crisis, government is not the solution to our problem; government is the problem. From time to time we've been tempted to believe," by previous Democratic presidents, Reagan might have said, "that society has become too complex to be managed by self-rule, that government by an elite group is superior to government for, by, and of the people. Well," Reagan asked, "if no one among us is capable of governing himself, then who among us has the capacity to govern someone else?"[14]

A renewed commitment to freedom at home and abroad was America's best defense in a dangerous world. Ronald Reagan's most dramatic attempt to apply his vision of freedom to foreign policy and international affairs came in a speech delivered on March 8, 1983, to the National Association of Evangelicals. This speech, famous for its use of the phrase "evil empire" to describe the Soviet Union, announced a confrontation between freedom and tyranny that freedom was destined to win. Reagan told the gathered faithful that freedom was a gift of God, saying "I believe . . . the source of our strength in the quest for human freedom is not material, but spiritual. And because it knows no limitation, it must terrify and ultimately triumph over those who would enslave their fellow man. For in the words of Isaiah," the president reminded his listeners, "'they that wait upon the Lord shall renew their strength; they shall mount up with wings as eagles; they shall run, and be not weary.'"[15]

By the 1984 reelection campaign, Reagan was prepared to declare victory at home and to redouble the effort on behalf of freedom in the world. The Republican national convention film that reviewed Reagan's first term reminded delegates that during the Carter years, "People were losing faith in the American Dream," but that the dream was now restored. Campaign ads declared that it was "morning in America" once again: "Today, the dream lives again. Today, jobs are coming back. The economy is coming back. And America is coming back, standing tall in the world again." The ads closed with the simple declaration: "President Reagan, rebuilding the American dream."[16] Reagan won the 1984 election in a landslide and used his 1985 State of the Union address to lay out the broader meaning of America's role in the world. President Reagan announced, "The time has come to proceed toward a great new challenge—a second American Revolution of hope and opportunity; a revolution. . . . that taps the soul of America, enabling us to summon greater strength than we've ever known; and a revolution that carries beyond our shores the golden promise of human freedom in a world of peace."[17] Ronald Reagan dedicated his last days in the presidency to clarifying his vision of the American Dream, reminding Americans of the breadth of its historic significance and of the need to foster and protect it for the future.

George Washington used his farewell address to warn against entangling alliances abroad. Dwight Eisenhower used his to warn against a "military-industrial complex" at home. Much of Ronald Reagan's farewell address was dedicated to "warning of an eradication of the American memory that could result, ultimately, in an erosion of the American spirit." Reagan asked, "Are we doing a good enough job teaching our children what America is and what she represents in the long history of the World?" He worried that we were not and thought that clarifying what he meant when he talked about freedom and America's distinctive role in the world might begin to change that. Reagan sought to restore old ideas, not to offer new ones. He said, "I know we always have [stood for freedom], but in the past few years the world again—and in a way, we ourselves—rediscovered it. . . . They call it the Reagan revolution. Well, I'll accept that, but for me it always seemed more like the great rediscovery, a rediscovery of our values and our common sense."[18] Reagan reminded his listeners that the phrase, the "shining city upon a hill . . . comes from John Winthrop, who wrote it to describe the America he imagined . . .

like the other pilgrims, he was looking for a home that would be free." Reagan went on to say, "I've spoken of the shining city all my political life, but I don't know if I ever quite communicated what I saw when I said it. But in my mind it was a tall, proud city built on rocks stronger than oceans, wind-swept, God-blessed, and teeming with people of all kinds living in harmony and peace; a city with free ports that hummed with commerce and creativity. And if there had to be city walls, the walls had doors and the doors were open to anyone with the will and the heart to get here. That's how I saw it, and see it still." Reagan closed, as he so often did, with striking imagery, this time of the "shining city" still playing its historic role of beacon and promise to men everywhere who would be free. "After 200 years, two centuries, she still stands strong and true on the granite ridge, . . . And she's still a beacon, still a magnet for all who must have freedom, for all the pilgrims from all the lost places who are hurtling through the darkness, toward home."[19]

Ronald Reagan spoke less in public after leaving the presidency and much less in the 1990s until he announced in 1994 that the onset of Alzheimer's disease was dimming his powers. When he did speak in the early 1990s, it was frequently to continue his conversation with the American people, and in a real sense, the people of the globe, about the special mission of the United States in the world. The most memorable occasion occurred on July 15, 1991, when an expansive Ronald Reagan addressed the Captive Nations Week conference nearly two years after the fall of the Berlin Wall, saying, "We who are privileged to be Americans have had a rendezvous with destiny since that moment in 1630 when John Winthrop, standing on the deck of the tiny *Arabella* off the coast of Massachusetts, told the little band of Pilgrims, 'We shall be as a city upon a hill. The eyes of all people are upon us.' . . . I have long believed," Reagan continued, "that the guiding hand of Providence did not create this new nation of America for ourselves alone, but for a higher cause: the preservation and extension of the sacred fire of human liberty. The Declaration of Independence and the Constitution of these United States are covenants we have made not only with ourselves, but with all of mankind"[20] (Figure 8.1).

Ronald Reagan was nothing if not steadfast in his beliefs. What made Reagan so confident was that he thought that these beliefs were both divinely inspired and widely shared among his fellow Americans. In one of his earliest speeches, during the 1952 campaign (while still a Democrat, he would vote for Eisenhower), Reagan said, "I . . . have thought of America as a place in the divine scheme of things that was set aside as a promised land. . . . I believe

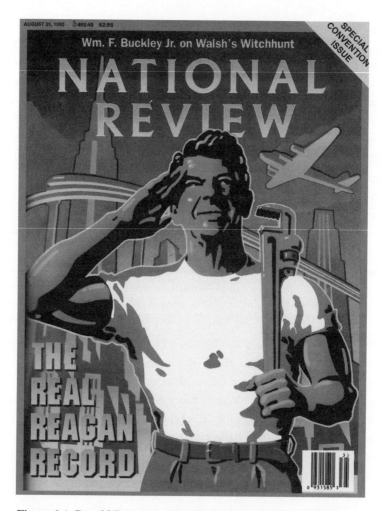

Figure 8.1. Ronald Reagan on the *National Review* Cover, 1992.
This iconic image appeared on August 31, 1992. Reagan was
widely credited by conservatives with restoring the American
economy and defeating communism. (Reprinted by permission,
National Review, Inc., 215 Lexington Avenue, New York, NY
10016)

that God . . . kept an eye on our land and guided it as a promised land for those
people . . . with the courage . . . to strive for freedom."[21] Almost five decades
later, in his last radio address as president, Reagan returned to his sense of
the peculiar mission of America and its people, saying, "Whether we seek it or
not, whether we like it or not, we Americans are keepers of the miracles. We

are asked to be guardians of a place to come to, a place to start again, a place to live in the dignity God meant for his children. May it ever be so."[22]

Reagan harkened back to the original vision of the American Dream, the city on the hill, as envisioned and described by conservatives from John Winthrop to Calvin Coolidge and Herbert Hoover. Heclo noted, "More than any other politician in the last half of the twentieth century, Reagan continued to speak the vision boldly and with deep personal conviction."[23] Ronald Reagan never doubted, never reconsidered, never even imagined that the American Dream might need to be updated for the new era. He believed that the American Dream had always been in place, all one had to do was aspire to it, strive for it, reach out and grasp it. It was the natural right of all Americans.

Ronald Reagan taught, or retaught, Democrats the powerful rhetoric of American exceptionalism. Democrats had never lost touch with these historic themes, Kennedy spoke of America as a city on a hill, and LBJ promised to make the race for opportunity fair for all competitors, but it seemed to many that Democratic promises drifted beyond opportunity to guarantees of security, if not success. The American Dream's traditional invitation to compete with a good chance of success, but no guarantee, lost its ability to motivate when failure became an unacceptable outcome, perhaps even evidence of invidious discrimination. Republicans stood smugly on the fairness and efficiency of free markets in rewarding talent and effort, while Democrats mumbled that it could not be so or the differences in success by race and gender would be less stark.

By the late 1980s Democrats were actively seeking an articulation of traditional American values—the American Dream—that balanced social and personal responsibility. Michael Dukakis, the Democratic nominee for president in 1988, assured voters that Democrats "believe with all our hearts in a dream, a uniquely American dream, a unifying dream, a dream of opportunity for each and every citizen in this land, no matter who they are or where they came from or what the color of their skin. . . . The best America doesn't leave anybody behind; we bring everybody along."[24] Voters listened for, but did not hear, a call for personal responsibility. Even as the Dukakis campaign fell before aggressive Republican charges that it was soft on defense, patriotism, crime, and taxes, Arkansas Governor Bill Clinton offered the voters of his state a New Covenant that tied opportunity to responsibility and community. In 1991, as he prepared to announce his candidacy for president, Clinton declared before a Democratic Leadership Conference, "Our burden is to give the people a new choice rooted in old values. A new choice that is simple, that offers opportunity, demands responsibility, gives citizens more say, provides them responsive government."[25]

Like Ronald Reagan, Bill Clinton had an ear wonderfully tuned to the rhythms and tones of American politics. Also like Reagan, Clinton used stories and examples highlighting individual people to bring the American Dream alive. Reagan's stories tended to be about people, soldiers or immigrants, who defied obscurity, poverty, and danger to perform nobly. Clinton's heroes needed help, always a hand up, not a handout, but he did not expect people to make it on their own. When Governor Bill Clinton stepped out onto the front portico of the Old State House in Little Rock, Arkansas, to announce his candidacy for the presidency, he declared his campaign to be "a commitment to . . . preserving the American dream, restoring the hopes of the forgotten middle class, reclaiming the future of our children." Like most Americans, he declared, "I was raised to believe in the American dream, in family values, in individual responsibility, and in the obligation of government to help people who were doing the best they could." Bill Clinton ran for president in 1992 on a promise to even the playing field and ensure that a greater share of the society's benefits went to those who showed up, worked hard, and played by the rules.

For Ronald Reagan, government was a burden that slowed Americans' pursuit of their dreams; for Clinton, government created, or failed to create, the climate within which the economy grew, wealth was created, and people prospered. Only if government fulfilled its responsibility by fostering a robust economy was it reasonable to hold individuals responsible for working hard and striving to do their best. Clinton believed that Republicans under Reagan and Bush had fostered an "every man for himself" environment in which a few had done spectacularly well while most had struggled just to stay even. Bill Clinton declared, "We need a new covenant to rebuild America. . . . Government's responsibility is to create more opportunity. The people's responsibility is to make the most of it." In accepting his party's nomination for president in 1992, Bill Clinton returned, as he would again and again during the general election contest and through eight years as president, to the theme of the positive role of government in people's lives. Clinton promised, "a New Covenant—a solemn agreement between the people and their government—based . . . on old values. We offer opportunity. We demand responsibility. We will build an American community again."[26]

The pivotal speech in Bill Clinton's 1992 campaign was delivered at his alma mater, Georgetown University. He sought to restore in the public mind the sense that government could be an effective and efficient servant and partner. Clinton declared, "Today we need to forge a New Covenant that will repair the damaged bond between the people and their government and restore our basic values—the notion that our country has a responsibility to help people get ahead. . . . people have lost faith in the ability of government to change their lives for the better."[27] But Bill Clinton well understood that the American people were ambivalent about government; they wanted it to be both limited and good at what it did. He used his victory speech on election night to promise "a government that offers a hand up, not a handout."[28]

Throughout his first term as president, Bill Clinton defined the purpose of his New Covenant as the restoration of the American Dream. But unlike Ronald Reagan, for whom restoration meant returning to fixed principles, Bill Clinton believed that restoration required adapting to new realities. Reagan spoke of continuity, Clinton of change. Like earlier presidents facing turbulent times, Clinton used his first inaugural address to place his administration and its program within the broader sweep of American history. Clinton reached back to the first Democratic president, Thomas Jefferson, to support his sense that change was necessary to growth and progress, saying, "Thomas Jefferson believed that to preserve the very foundations of our nation, we would need dramatic change from time to time. Well, my fellow citizens, this is our time. Let us embrace it."[29]

Bill Clinton's goal was to link opportunity to responsibility so that Americans would be comfortable thinking about inclusion, community, and interdependence. In his 1994 State of the Union address, he asked Americans to return "again to the principle that if we simply give ordinary people equal opportunity, quality education, and a fair shot at the American dream, they will do extraordinary things." In his 1995 State of the Union address, he said, "We all gain when we give, and we reap what we sow. That's at the heart of this New Covenant. Responsibility, Opportunity, Citizenship. They're still the virtues by which we can fulfill ourselves . . . the eternal promise of this country, the enduring dream from that first and most sacred covenant," the Declaration of Independence and its promise of life, liberty, and the pursuit of happiness for all.[30]

Almost every time, Clinton followed the promise of a New Covenant with an explicit commitment to universalism—the dream must belong to absolutely everyone who did not, him- or herself, turn away. In his 1994 State of the Union address, he said, "I want the American dream to be alive for every single man and woman and boy and girl who is willing to work for it, no matter what their race, their background, their income, their gender, their condition of disability." Clinton pointed with particular pride to his AmeriCorps program as proof that "the American idea is a universal idea; that the notion of personal responsibility, the notion of opportunity for everybody, the notion that we're all better and stronger when we work together than when we are divided. . . . That's what these young people in AmeriCorps prove day-in and day-out."

Bill Clinton organized his 1996 reelection campaign as a referendum on the party's respective visions of the American Dream—at least as he wished to characterize them. Clinton knew that Americans were hopeful but anxious. Surveys conducted by the Hudson Institute during the first Clinton adminis-tration (1994) found that four-fifths of Americans were confident about their own futures, two-thirds were confident about the nation's future, and three-fourths agreed that "In America, if you work hard, you can be anything you want to be." Nonetheless, all was not well. A 1995 poll that asked whether "The American dream of equal opportunity, personal freedom, and social mobility has been easier or harder to achieve in the past ten years." Two-thirds responded that it had become harder, while slightly less than a third said it had become easier.[31]

In preparation for the 1996 campaign, Clinton offered a book-length state-ment of his values and his intentions for a second term, entitled *Between Hope and History.* He reminded voters that he had always been and remained com-mitted to a reasonable and balanced view of America's traditional values. He said, "The promise embedded in our founding documents is clear: America promises liberty, but demands civic responsibility. America promises the opportunity to pursue happiness, but does not guarantee it. . . . Nearly four years ago, I took the oath of office. . . . I wanted an America where the American Dream is alive and attainable for every single American willing to work for it."[32] Republicans offered a different view, Clinton warned. "Here, at the edge of a new century, we must decide between two visions of America. One vision," the Republican vision, "foresees an 'every man for himself,' 'you're on your own' America. . . . Our administration and the new Democratic party take a different view. We say the era of big government is over, but we must not go back to an era of 'every man for himself.'" The best summary of the difference that Clinton saw between his own vision and the one that had governed the Republican party since Reagan, and in a sense for much longer, was his declaration that "America is not just about independence, but also about *interdependence.*"[33]

However, Clinton was, as always, careful to describe a role for government that helped people but did not dictate to them. Clinton had learned from Reagan that the American people loathed big government and overweening bureaucracy. But Clinton knew far better than the Republicans of the 1990s that people also expected a great deal from government. Clinton framed his 1996 campaign by declaring, "America needs a government that is both smaller and more responsive. One that both works better and costs less. One that shifts authority from the federal level to the states and localities as much as possible. One that relies upon entrepreneurs in the private sector when the private sector can do the job best. One that has fewer regulations and more incentives. One, in short, that has more common sense and seeks more common ground."[34] With a foot on every base, it was nearly impossible for Clinton to be called out. In fact, as the Dole challenge stalled, Clinton reiterated his vision, saying "the America I want in the year 2000—[is] an America in which all responsible citizens have a chance to live their dreams, an America growing together, an America leading the world to greater peace, freedom, and prosperity."[35] None of this, Clinton reminded his listeners, was likely to happen in an "every man for himself" scramble for personal advantage. Not surprisingly, the blunt message of Bill Clinton's second inaugural address was, "The preeminent mission of our new Government is to give all Americans an opportunity, not a guarantee but a real opportunity, to build better lives."[36]

Campaign speeches and inaugural addresses are occasions for high rhetoric, and references to the American dream of freedom, equality, and opportunity abound. Governing, on the other hand, requires choices, allocating money to this rather than that, to affect people's lives for the better. What choices characterized and defined our politics in the 1980s and 1990s?

The Dream Embedded in Institutions, Law, and Policy

Ronald Reagan blamed the economic malaise of the late 1970s on an overly large, costly, and intrusive government. Reagan ran in 1980 on the promise that limiting the role of government, removing regulations, and depending on free markets to reward work and productivity would expand the economy and benefit every American. He used his first inaugural address to announce his "intention to curb the size and influence of the federal establishment." He reminded listeners, "we are too great a nation to limit ourselves to small dreams," or to be satisfied with the safety and comfort of government handouts: "We have every right to dream heroic dreams."[37] During President Reagan's first three days in office, he ordered a freeze on federal government hiring, directed reductions in travel and spending, and appointed a presidential Task Force on Regulatory Relief with Vice President Bush as chair.

The Reagan Revolution, like FDR's New Deal and LBJ's Great Society, marked a fundamental turning point in the relationship of government to the economy and society. In response to the Great Depression, Franklin Roosevelt promised the American people that an activist government would monitor and manage economic performance with an eye toward demanding fairness of the wealthy, ensuring the security of the middle class, and fighting poverty and spreading opportunity among the poor. Democratic presidents after FDR sought to expand and improve the social safety net provided by the modern welfare state, while Republican presidents sought only to slow its growth without challenging its basic premises.

Reagan challenged the premises of post–New Deal American politics. Where for half a century the role of government in managing and directing the economy and society had grown, Reagan declared the determination to reduce the role of government and return freedom, opportunity, and choice to the individual citizen. The key to individual freedom, Reagan thought, was to cut taxes and regulations and thereby limit the size and intrusiveness of government. He was convinced that if his program was adopted, private initiative would flourish, businesses would grow, profits would rise, new jobs would be created, and the poor could compete for jobs rather than wait by the mailbox for government checks and benefits (Figure 8.2).

The Reagan economic program envisioned sharp cuts in individual income taxes, especially on the highest incomes, cuts in business taxes, and regulatory relief to spur business expansion and economic growth. Heavy spending on defense, offset by deep cuts in domestic spending, was expected to aggravate deficits in the short term, but the supply-side model suggested that growth spurred by the tax cuts would soon produce more revenue than the old system, thereby closing the revenue gap and leaving a healthy, growing economy, and a balanced budget. The Economic Recovery Tax Act (ERTA) of 1981, the landmark legislation of Reagan's first term, included a 25 percent reduction in personal income taxes over three years, a reduction in the top marginal rate from 70 percent to 50 percent, a cut in the capital gains tax rate from 28 percent to 20 percent, as well as important tax and regulatory relief to business. Ronald Reagan's 1981 tax cuts were the largest since the multi-

Figure 8.2. Reagan and the Spirit of America, 1984. President Reagan's staff were careful to place him against backdrops that highlighted his confidence in the American entrepreneurial spirit. (Corbis/Bettmann, photographer Larry Rubenstein, January 26, 1984, image U2133751)

year program of tax cuts initiated by Treasury Secretary Andrew Mellon in the 1920s. Although Congress joined enthusiastically with President Reagan in reducing the tax burden on their constituents, Congress, again with a wary eye on their constituents, declined to join Reagan in cutting programs and spending. Reagan, reluctant to take all the blame, did not fight energetically for his proposed spending cuts. The combination of large tax cuts, big increases in defense spending, and smaller-than-planned cuts in domestic spending produced unprecedented annual budget deficits and a quadrupling of the national debt over the course of Reagan's two terms. From President Reagan's perspective, however, the rising deficits had the desirable effect of putting a tight lid on Democratic hopes for new programs and increased spending.

Tax simplification and fairness were the themes of President Reagan's Tax Reform Act of 1986. The 1986 act removed or limited tax preferences for particular kinds of economic activity, like real estate development, and collapsed income tax rates into three broad bands of 15, 25, and 31 percent. Reagan argued that no American, no matter what their income, should pay more than one-third of that income in taxes. To attract Democratic support for steep cuts in the top rate, Reagan agreed to remove nearly 6 million low-income taxpayers from the income tax rolls altogether. The Reagan economic program sought to shift income from the less productive, the welfare class, to the more productive, the entrepreneurial class, and to limit opportunities for government to interfere with competition and innovation among the more productive. Economic growth was restored through a program of tax cuts, deregulation, privatization, and enterprise zones. The result, however, was a prosperity enjoyed predominantly by the affluent. Thomas and Mary Edsall concluded that the Reagan years "produced one of the most dramatic redistributions of income in the nation's history. . . . The income of families in the bottom decile fell by 10.4 percent . . . while the income of those in the top one percent rose by 87.1 percent."[38]

Reagan's determination to reduce the size of the federal government, limit its regulatory role, and free up markets and individuals also guided him on social policy. Nowhere was this determination more clear than in his crusade against welfare. Reagan hoped to restore the role of individualism, work, and personal responsibility as well-trod pathways to the American Dream. Through most of American history, welfare meant charity and was a matter both of private shame and public concern. Even when the federal government undertook expanded welfare programs during the depression, FDR warned against the "dole" as a threat to traditional American independence, autonomy, and self-respect. Only in LBJ's Great Society did welfare payments approach being seen as a right, and then only briefly. Reagan well understood that most Americans saw welfare as a favor granted by a charitable public for short-term support of well-intending persons between jobs, not a permanent right, and certainly not a lifestyle.

The Welfare Reform Bill of 1988 was intended to wean people from welfare by promoting individual independence and economic security. Daniel Patrick Moynihan (D-NY) sponsored the bill. During congressional hearings on the bill, Governor Bill Clinton (D-AR), testifying on behalf of the National Governor's Conference, argued that the bill advanced a new covenant of mutual responsibility between government and welfare recipients. President Reagan endorsed the bill and large bipartisan majorities, 317 to 53 in the House and 96 to 1 in the Senate, approved it. Reagan signed the bill on October 13, 1988, saying that it would lead to "lasting emancipation from welfare dependency."[39] The bill required that welfare recipients be enrolled in education or job training to maintain eligibility for benefits.

Immigration policy also became a major social and economic issue during the 1980s and 1990s. Strikingly, more immigrants entered the United States between 1980 and 2000, more than 16 million, than came between 1920 and 1980. Some welcomed the new immigrants in all of their numbers, while others worried that they were too many to be accommodated, that they took jobs from needy citizens, that they were a burden on social welfare programs, and that they shielded millions more illegals. The Immigration Reform and Control Act of 1986 was purportedly designed to control illegal immigration by levying sanctions on employers that hired illegals. Although the Immigration and Naturalization Service received additional funding for enforcement, there was no efficient way to distinguish legal from illegal employees. Moreover, the Reagan administration's sensitivity to business interests and its commitment to deregulation meant that employer sanctions were not aggressively pursued. In fact, to assure that no abuse occurred during implementation of the act's provisions, Democrats required antidiscrimination provisions and a broad amnesty program that permitted 3 million illegal aliens already in the country to gain permanent resident status. Although intended to staunch the flow of illegals into the United States, the effect of the 1986 reform was to regularize the status of illegal aliens already here. Even more extensive reform was undertaken in the Immigration Act of 1990. A general willingness to allow increased immigration became a free-for-all in which each interest sought to secure their preferences by agreeing not to oppose the policy goals of others. In general, Democrats sought to protect the interest in family unification of new Latin American and Asian immigrants, while Republicans sought to protect the interest of business in more immigrants with special skills and advanced education. They settled on more of each, and the Bush administration supported the bill as advancing both its family values and economic growth agendas.

Ronald Reagan's policies restored economic growth and recharged the American spirit, but by the early 1990s many concluded that the society had become less open and fair and that budget deficits had become threateningly large. Although the Reagan economic program did produce rising federal revenues throughout the 1980s, spending rose faster. During President Bush's term, annual deficits approached $300 billion and the national debt, about $1 trillion when Reagan took office, had quadrupled to $4 trillion. The Clinton campaign in 1992 promised to cut the annual budget deficits in half during the first term, deliver a middle-class tax cut, and undertake a big investment program in health care, education, and job training.[40]

President Bill Clinton promised a third-way, or New Democrat, agenda that charged government to ensure that the benefits of economic growth were spread more evenly across all Americans. Clinton favored moderate Democratic positions, especially on social, fiscal, and military and defense policy, where the Reagan Republican party seemed to have gained decisive advantage. On controversial social issues, Clinton put distance between himself and the liberal wing of his party by supporting tough criminal penalties, including the death penalty, and moderate positions on school prayer, gun control, and welfare reform. The economic program that Clinton submitted to Congress in February 1993 highlighted deficit reduction, higher taxes on the wealthy and on corporations, reduced military spending, and tax relief for the working poor. Federal Reserve Board Chairman Alan Greenspan, as well as key Clinton administration officials, led by Treasury Secretary Lloyd Bentson and Chairman Robert Rubin of the National Economic Council, agreed that deficit reduction would lower long-term interest rates and fuel economic growth.

In fundamental ways, the Clinton economic program sought to shift, if not repeal, the assumptions and incentives of the Reagan economic program. Congress approved deficit reduction totaling $500 billion over five years, raised taxes on the top earners to 36 percent on incomes over $115,000 and 39.6 percent on incomes over $250,000, increased the top corporate tax rate by 1 percent, and approved a 4.3 cent a gallon hike in the gas tax. At the lower end of the income spectrum, Congress approved an Earned Income Tax Credit to reward poor workers with children for staying in the workforce.[41] In the wake of the economic plan's passage, Clinton declared, "After 12 long years, we can say to the American people tonight we have laid the foundation for the renewal of the American dream. . . . After a long season of denial and drift and decline, we are seizing control of our economic destiny."[42] Clinton passed his economic program with virtually no Republican votes. His other major economic initiatives, passage of the North American Free Trade Agreement (NAFTA) and the General Agreement on Tariffs and Trade (GATT), were passed with Republican votes and over stringent Democratic objections.

Bill Clinton's social program got off to a less auspicious start. He knew instinctively that while voters wanted effort and responsibility from the recipients of government aid, they expected government to help citizens cope successfully with the major opportunities and difficulties of life. Hence, less than a week after assuming the presidency, Bill Clinton appointed First Lady Hillary Clinton to head a task force to reform the American health care system. Key goals were to stem rising costs and expand coverage to the unin-

Figure 8.3. Clinton's Commitment to Better Health Care, 2000. President Bill Clinton made health care reform a centerpiece of his domestic policy program. (AFP/Corbis, photographer Stephen Jaffe, March 13, 2000, image FT0030940)

sured. The hugely complex and expensive national health care program brought forth by Hillary Clinton's task force was wildly unpopular. Health care reform was never brought to a vote in either house of Congress, although both the House and Senate had comfortable Democratic majorities. Worse, this early social policy debacle seemed to confirm the Democratic Party's penchant for big, expensive, bureaucratic government (Figure 8.3).

Bill Clinton was forced to settle for a series of small, but ideologically important, social policy victories in the first year in office. The first bill that Clinton signed, on February 4, 1993, was the Family Leave Act. The family leave bill, twice vetoed by President Bush, provided workers up to three months of unpaid leave each year to respond to medical emergencies like the illness of a family member or the birth of a child. In November 1993 Congress passed and Clinton signed the Brady Bill, named for James Brady, the Reagan spokesman shot during the 1983 assassination attempt on the president. The Brady Bill provided for a five-day waiting period for anyone wishing to purchase a handgun.

The pain inflicted by Clinton's economic program, the dismay of labor and environmentalists with NAFTA and GATT, and the 1993–94 debacle of the Clinton health care reform effort led to sweeping Republican gains in the 1994 midterm elections. Clinton and the Democrats were immobilized by shock and disbelief as the now-dominant Republicans, led by Newt Gingrich (R-GA), the new speaker of the House, pushed an agenda that featured deep tax and budget cuts. At the core of the Republican budget proposal of 1995 was a Medicare cut of $270 billion over seven years and a tax cut, directed mainly to the upper class, totaling $245 billion over the same time period. Democrats framed the fight as a Republican attempt to cut Medicare in order to give big tax breaks to the wealthy. Clinton vetoed the Republican budget on December 6, 1995, and the Republicans retaliated by shutting down the government. With the federal government closed between December 15, 1995, and January 5, 1996, public opinion turned on Gingrich, and the Republicans and Bill Clinton began a long, slow climb back into the public's good graces.

Clinton was at his most effective when he sought to steal the wind from the Republican's sails by coopting their most popular positions while defending the Democrat's most popular positions. For example, Clinton used his 1996 State of the Union address to declare that "the era of Big Government is over" and to call for a balanced budget and welfare reform. On the other hand, he pledged to defend Social Security, Medicare, education, and the environment against Republican "extremists."[43] Although Bill Clinton effectively tagged the Republicans as extremists for their assault on Medicare and other social programs and easily won reelection in 1996, congressional Republicans forced him to reduce spending and move toward a balanced budget more quickly and with more determination than he preferred.

The sometimes creative tension that existed between Bill Clinton and the Republican majorities in Congress after 1994 was evident in the debate over welfare reform. Although Clinton promised during the 1992 campaign to reform welfare, it took the Republican takeover of Congress in 1994 to spur action. Although Clinton twice vetoed Republican welfare reform bills and many congressional Democrats continued to oppose vehemently, the president agreed in July 1996 to sign the Personal Responsibility and Work Opportunity Act. This act ended welfare as a federal right and replaced it with limited state programs requiring work for benefits. States had great discretion to organize and design their own welfare programs. Moreover, there was a five-year limit on payments, and adults had to find work within two years. The 1996 welfare reforms also made legal immigrants ineligible for Supplementary Security

Income and food stamps until they achieved naturalized citizen status or paid into Social Security for 40 eligible quarters. Broader immigration reform in 1996 enhanced border security, tightened asylum criteria, required immigrants to have financial sponsors, and made immigrants subject to expedited deportation for much less serious crimes than had previously been required.

Through most of Clinton's second term, with the economy booming, federal revenues pouring in, and the president distracted by scandals, Republicans pushed for additional tax cuts and for market-based approaches to education, health care, and retirement security issues. Clinton and the Democrats in Congress opposed these Republican initiatives and called for additional funding for education, prescription drugs, preventive health care, Medicare, Social Security, and environmental protection. Through the late 1990s, as both parties tried to position themselves for the 2000 election, deadlock prevented either partisan agenda from making more than incremental gains. Nonetheless, at the end of the 1998 fiscal year, Bill Clinton announced that the federal government had its first budget surplus in almost thirty years and largest in American history at $70 billion. By the time Clinton left office two years later, surpluses were running at more than $150 billion annually and it seemed reasonable to talk about paying off the national debt within the first decade of the new century. Clinton could also point to a strong economy with more than 20 million new jobs, more than had been created during the Reagan years, no meaningful inflation, low unemployment, excellent productivity growth, and rising incomes for the middle class and working poor as well as the wealthy.

Although Bill Clinton was able to stem the conservative tide, he was unable to turn it back. He revised Reagan's economic and fiscal policies but was forced to adopt modified versions of Reagan's social policies while a powerful conservative undertow pulled at him from the courts. Chief Justice William H. Rehnquist and Associate Justice Antonin Scalia were the acknowledged leaders of the conservative majority on the nation's highest court. Both were staunch advocates of states' rights, limited government, and federalism. Rehnquist was named to the Supreme Court by President Nixon in 1971 and was nominated by President Reagan to be Chief Justice in 1986. Scalia was nominated by Reagan, also in 1986, to replace Rehnquist as associate justice. Through the late 1980s and early 1990s, the court loosened the constraints on police conduct, limited affirmative action, upheld state regulation of abortion counseling and services, and strengthened the protection of private property. Still, the law is slow to change, and Rehnquist and Scalia often had trouble bringing their moderate colleagues, Kennedy, O'Connor, and Souter, along for the full distance that they wanted to go.

A classic example of the late-twentieth-century struggle to define the constitutional limits of government's responsibility to shape and manage the society involved civil rights and affirmative action. The civil rights agenda of the 1950s and 1960s demanded equality of opportunity and nondiscrimination. These ideas were embedded as promises and guarantees in the civil rights and voting rights acts of the mid-1960s. Affirmative action, on the other hand, envisioned making up for the effects of past discrimination suffered by specific racial and gender groups by giving their members preference today in admission to training and education programs and in decisions concerning hiring, promotion, and firing on the job. From the famous *Bakke Case* (1978) through *Johnson v. Transportation Agency, Santa Clara County* (1987) the Supreme Court held that employers, including public sector or government employers, could make employment decisions intended to bring the workforce into line with the local labor market.[44]

Conservatives claimed that affirmative action was "reverse discrimination" and patently illegal. Ronald Reagan charged that social programs initially intended to provide equal access to educational and job opportunities for minorities and women had been extended to provide these groups with special privileges. Appeals to traditional American values like equality, fairness, and work made it relatively easy to discredit affirmative action as just one more form of noxious discrimination—affirmative action for minorities and women was reverse discrimination against white men—equal opportunity, to be sure, but then results should be based on energy and talent well applied. The court has slowly moved to agree. During the early 1990s, the Supreme Court executed a general retreat from affirmative action. In 1995 the Supreme Court invalidated a University of Maryland program that set aside a certain number of scholarships exclusively for minorities, a federal program that gave minority highway construction contractors an advantage in competing for work, and congressional district lines drawn for the specific purpose of creating majority minority districts.

The 1997 case of *Piscataway Board of Education v. Taxman* again raised the issue of how far a public employer can go to achieve and maintain racial diversity in the workforce. The Piscataway School Board needed to reduce its workforce by one math teacher. Two teachers, one black, one white, equally qualified and with equal seniority, were on the bubble. The school board took the view that maintaining racial diversity was an important goal and fired the white teacher, Sharon Taxman. Taxman sued under Article VII of the 1964 Civil Rights Act, which forbids racial discrimination in employment. After two lower courts ruled that the school board had violated Sharon Taxman's civil rights, several civil rights organizations financed a private settlement of the suit so that the Supreme Court could not use it to severely limit affirmative action. Many public institutions struggled mightily to act affirmatively toward those previously discriminated against while the courts were increasingly firm in saying no more discrimination, even in what some might take to be a good cause.

The Rehnquist court also moved to define reproductive rights and limit access to abortion services. The right to choose abortion has been among the most intensely debated issues in our society. Women's groups, led by the National Organization for Women (NOW) and the National Abortion and Reproductive Rights Action League (NARAL), have argued that free persons have a right to control their own bodies and that control of reproductive decisions are central to women's ability to act independently within the American society. Conservative women's groups have argued that no person has the right to end a life and that decisions about child-bearing and child-rearing are best made by families. Not surprisingly, state and federal politicians who favor a woman's right to choose abortion often want that choice to be free and want public support for poor women to decide as they see fit. Politicians who wish to limit or deny access to abortions have consistently sought to enlarge the state interest in regulating abortion. In the case of *Webster v. Reproductive Health Services* (1989), the court upheld a Missouri law regulating abortion clinics and preventing public money and facilities from being used to perform abortions. Struggles continued throughout the 1990s over whether government could mandate waiting periods, counseling, or parental notification, before the decision for abortion could be made. Generally, the Supreme Court has permitted states to regulate abortion while stopping short of overturning *Roe v. Wade*.

Finally, the Supreme Court has moved systematically over more than a decade to reverse the twentieth-century flow of political power and initiative from the states to the federal government. In a series of 5–4 decisions, beginning with *U.S. v. Lopez* (1995) and extending through *U.S. v. Morrison* (2000), the Supreme Court limited the ability of the president and Congress to use the commerce clause of the U.S. Constitution to push states in directions that they did not wish to go. In *Lopez* the court decided that the national government's prohibition on guns near schools was too loosely connected to regulating commerce to be justified. Similarly, in *Morrison* the court held that the 1994 Violence Against Women Act was unconstitutional because its impact on commerce was too remote to displace the rights of the states to legislate as they saw fit in this area. Another line of cases decided since 1995 strengthened the "sovereign immunity" of states against being sued against their will in their own courts or the federal courts by state government employees or citizens. The U.S. Supreme Court has sought to protect state sovereignty by limiting the ability of the president and Congress to make laws binding on state governments. So far, federal laws concerning worker rights, federal regulatory authority, and age discrimination have been struck down when state government employees sought to use them against state governments.

Fundamentally, Ronald Reagan changed the rhetoric and the substance of American politics in the 1980s by shifting debate and policy to the right. He reasserted both the nobility of the individual and the threat that government posed to individuals and their dreams. He asserted the goodness of individual Americans, the isolated occurrence of discrimination, and the need for each individual to compete for his or her place in the sun. Bill Clinton spent most of the 1990s searching for a third way between the liberalism of the post–World War II Democratic Party and the conservatism of Reagan's Republican Party. Clinton's tremendous political skills, undermined by his personal flaws, checked the Reagan Revolution for a time, but only for a time.

Shadows on the Dream

The United States has made great but uneven strides in providing equal access to the American Dream to all of its citizens. Some now argue that recent economic gains by minorities and women prove that opportunity is broadly available and that future progress is simply a matter of individual career choices and hard work. Others argue that progress has been painfully slow, that women and minorities remain far behind white men in annual income and total wealth, and that momentum will be lost if societal efforts on behalf of equality are not maintained and even enhanced. Moreover, the progress toward social justice made in the latter half of the twentieth century has divided minority and women's groups internally and separated them from each other. Legal and social theorist Bruce Ackerman, among others, claims, "At no time since the 1920s has the movement for social justice in America been as fractionated as today. Rather than bonding with one another, the labor movement and the peace movement, blacks and ethnics, feminists and environmentalists look upon each other with anxiety and suspicion."[45] In fact, political theorist Jennifer Hochschild has presented evidence that among white and black men and women, each group feels that the others benefit by special treatment but that they do not. "Men think women and minorities benefit unfairly; women think men and minorities benefit unfairly; blacks think whites and perhaps women benefit unfairly."[46]

Optimists suspect that fairness and equality probably reign when all sides claim that others are being treated better than they. Pessimists suspect that the recent embrace of nondiscrimination by traditional elites masks fear of more change and a preference for the status quo. Realists wonder whether individual choices, the unequal burdens of family responsibility, and the constant pressure of long-standing cultural norms and expectations, will always produce differences in economic results and social roles between American men and women. It seems likely that differences will always exist in society, but are we comfortable with the particular differences in economic results and social roles that persist by race and gender in America today?

Although there is no doubt that conditions confronting blacks have improved over the past four decades, broad sectors of the black community have been left behind, and the entire black community remains ambivalent about its place within the American society. A number of polls from the mid-1990s show that two-thirds of blacks still believe in the American Dream and that three-quarters are satisfied with their jobs, housing, current standard of living, and the way things are going in their personal lives. On the other hand, the most successful, the well-educated middle and upper-middle class blacks, are more likely to be dissatisfied and to say they regularly experience discrimination.[47]

Educational gains among blacks have been substantial since the end of segregation. The proportion of blacks over 25 with a high school diploma in 1980 was 51 percent and by 1999 the number had risen to 77 percent. Although the proportion of whites that had graduated from high school in 1999 was higher, at 84 percent, the dropout rate for blacks and whites was essentially the same.[48] Blacks tend to perform almost equally with whites in the tax-supported public schools. In fact, where income is held constant, blacks do as well or better than whites on some measures. But in the real world, income is not held constant; it varies systematically by race. When tuition barriers kick in, as at the college level, blacks attend at lower rates, struggle more, and drop out at higher rates. In 1997, 14 percent of blacks between the ages of 35 and 44 had bachelor's degrees, while just over twice as many, 29 percent, of whites did. The disparity was even greater at the level of professional and advanced degrees.

Still, education gains have been reflected in income gains among blacks. Both black men and black women saw economic gains between 1967 and 1995, but black married couples did best. In 1967 the median income of black families headed by a married couple was 68 percent of comparable white families. Three decades later, in 1995, the black married couple made $41,307, or 87 percent of the income of comparable white families. In fact, for the first time in American history, one category of black women, black women with bachelor's degrees, made more money than did white women of similar educational attainment.[49]

Nonetheless, black men and women are relatively rare in the most prestigious and lucrative occupations while they are concentrated in less prestigious and lower-paying occupations. The presence of black men is only one-quarter that of white men in engineering and the natural sciences, one-third among doctors, dentists, lawyers, judges, and college professors, and one-half among executives, managers, and sales people. On the other hand, black men are about even with whites as a proportion of social workers, are overrepresented among machine operators, truck drivers, public safety workers, and are more than twice as common in proportion to their presence in the population among laborers, food service, and personal service workers. Similar patterns hold for black women.[50]

Moreover, blacks are less secure in their communities than are whites. Home ownership has been one of the main pillars of family security in America. Blacks have always been less likely than whites to own their own homes. Black home ownership actually declined slightly in the 1980s before surging from 1993 through 1999. In 1993, 42 percent of blacks owned their own home; by 1999 that number had risen to 47 percent, while 73 percent of whites owned their homes by 1999. Much of the difference between white and black home ownership rates is explained by the differences in education and income, but some is the result of continuing discrimination. During the 1990s, the Clinton administration prodded banks and other lenders, as well as government regulators, to prohibit redlining and to make more loans and better rates available to middle- and lower-income home buyers. Nonetheless, recent studies suggest that blacks are twice as likely to be denied conventional 30-year loans than whites with similar incomes and credit histories and are regularly quoted higher interest rates.[51]

Family structure limits prospects for home ownership and family security and stability with the black community. Increasing numbers of black children start life in female-headed households struggling near the poverty line. In 1960, 25 percent of black children were born to single mothers, by 1980 the proportion was 45 percent, and by 2000 it was 65 percent. The driving dynamic behind these sad and destructive numbers is that poor people marry later and less frequently than do the more secure. Hence, only 42 percent of black adults were married in 2001 while 62 percent of whites were married.[52] Children born to black married couples enjoy more security and more financial support, and hence more opportunity. In our advanced postindustrial society, where education is the acknowledged key to success, most black children are in poverty and at risk.

Crime statistics within the black community are staggering. Although blacks make up about 12 percent of the U.S. population, they comprise about 45 percent of those serving time in local, state, and federal jails and prisons. Black inmates now outnumber whites, with more than three-quarters of a million black men and boys behind bars and many more just a parole violation away from returning to jail. In fact, one in every five black men will spend some time in jail in his lifetime, and in many urban communities one-third to one-half of all young black men are in jail, on parole, or under arrest.[53] Not surprisingly, middle-class blacks often despair of being treated on their own merits by a suspicious and fearful white community. Jennifer Hochschild quoted a young man named Anthony Walton, saying, "I see that I am often treated the same as a thug, that no amount of conformity, willing or unwilling, will make me the fabled American individual."[54]

Most whites understand, if only vaguely, that at least through the mid-1960s, blacks experienced discrimination that barred them from most good social, educational, and economic opportunities. However, most whites believe that the removal of these limitations on black access and opportunity in the 1960s and 1970s gave blacks an equal opportunity to compete and succeed in the American society. Whites have long been convinced that blacks are making rapid economic progress and that a broad equality exists for blacks and whites in jobs, education, housing, and the criminal justice system. Most blacks disagree.[55] Gains have been made; the dream is still alive, but equality remains maddeningly elusive.

The role of American women also remains in flux. The Equal Rights Amendment debate of the 1970s and early 1980s highlighted fundamental disagreements concerning the proper place of women within the American society and how that place could be secured and enhanced. Liberal feminists demanded that the full panoply of choices and opportunities within the American society be available to women. More conservative women stressed the importance of family and child-rearing for the health and development of individuals and of society in general. They argued that society was better off if it made policy that supported, rather than denigrated, the traditional female roles of wife, mother, and homemaker. Black and Hispanic women often found this battle between white men and women over gender roles and between liberal and conservative white women over the best way to organize their lives and choices to be quite beside the point. Black women frequently resented white women claiming that their oppression was similar to racial discrimination, and Hispanic women often balked at the centrality of abortion rights to the NOW and NARAL agendas. The relative virtues of stay-at-home motherhood versus a career seemed less important to minority women than assurances that they would be fairly treated in the job market and the workplace. Because minority women felt more vulnerable, they supported affirmative action while white women often did not.

Women continued to make economic gains during the last decades of the twentieth century, but these gains remained uneven. During the 1980s and 1990s the wage gap between men and women narrowed for two reasons. First, while men's wages fell during the 1980s, women's fell less rapidly, and, in the case of the well-educated women, actually rose throughout the decade and into the 1990s. Second, women continued their educational gains. As late as 1980, men still received more than half of the bachelor's and master's degrees awarded in the United States. Men received more than twice as many doctoral degrees and more than three times as many professional degrees than women. By 1997, however, women had surpassed men at both the BA and MA levels and were claiming about 70 percent of the doctoral and professional degrees being claimed by men.

Women's educational gains prepared the way for more women to move into better-paid, traditionally male occupations. Between 1979 and 1996 women doubled their presence in executive, management, engineering, science, medical, and legal positions. By 1996 women were about one-quarter of all doctors and lawyers and nearly one-half of all college teachers. On the other end of the job scale, women's presence in lower-paid, blue-collar and service jobs declined. For example, in 1979 nearly one-third of working women were secretaries. By 1996 less than one-quarter of working women held these positions. Similarly, female machine operators declined from near 9 percent of all working women in 1979 to just over 4 percent in 1996. Still, while gains have been made, the top corporate jobs are still almost all held by white men. Only eleven of the Fortune 1000 companies were led by women.

Native Americans have largely passed from the national consciousness. In the late 1990s, most of the 2.4 million Indians, less than 1 percent of the U.S. population, lived on the nation's 550 reservations. Although casinos have enlivened and enriched some reservations and their inhabitants, Indians are still among the poorest Americans. With proportionately few registered voters and little tradition of political involvement or participation, Indians have little political leverage. So lax has been federal attention to Indian issues and interests that a class-action suit was filed in 1996 on behalf of 300,000 Indians charging that Interior Department inattention had squandered at least $10 billion in land-use royalties that should have gone to Indian Trust system accounts. The Pine Ridge Reservation, near Rapid City, South Dakota, suggests the depth of the problems faced by many reservations. On the Pine Ridge Reservation, up to 80 percent of adults are alcoholics, unemployment approaches 85 percent, and the per capita income of $3,100 makes it among the poorest areas in the nation.[56] President Bill Clinton's visit to the Pine Ridge Indian Reservation in July 1999, late in his second term, was the first visit by an American president to an Indian reservation since FDR briefly visited the Cherokee reservation in North Carolina in 1936.[57]

Indian poverty is reflected in the low performance of Indian children and young people in school. Indian children score in the bottom fifth of most national exams, and they have the highest dropout rate of any racial or ethnic group. From one-half to two-thirds of Indians drop out of high school, only about 17 percent of high school graduates go on to college, and most of them fail to earn college degrees. After decades of neglect, the Clinton administration increased spending on preservation of Indian culture and language and, most importantly, on Indian education. Indian-related educational spending increased from $8.2 billion in 2000 to $9.4 billion in 2001, the largest increase ever. Moreover, the Education Department recently created an Indian Teacher Corps to train one thousand new teachers.[58] Darwin still haunts the scene.

9

The American Dream in the Twenty-First Century

Dreams are the touchstones of our character.

—Henry David Thoreau, *A Week on the Concord and Merrimac Rivers* (1849)

Henry David Thoreau's juxtaposition of "character" with "dreams" offers a penetrating insight into the basic premise of the American Dream. Thoreau understood that dreaming well, dreaming about the right things in the right way, required and reflected character; in fact, dreaming well is the measure of character both for persons and peoples. This critical insight is missed or ignored by those who trivially imagine that there are as many American dreams as there are Americans dreaming. When we dream, whether individually or collectively, of security, prosperity, and respect, but without foresight, work, and honesty, we are not dreaming the American Dream. Dreams without ballast, with no obvious connection between the thing envisioned or desired and the means of achieving it, simply float off into the ether.

The American Dream has always involved a clear sense of the goals to be pursued and means by which they are to be achieved. The American Dream has clear expectations both for the individual and the nation. At the individual level, as Penn, Franklin, Alger, and so many others knew, the Dream demanded character—preparation in school and shop, honesty, hard work, frugality, and persistence. At the national level, the Dream demanded that society stand for opportunity and provide an open, fair, competitive, entrepreneurial environment in which individual merit could find its place.

Americans have always had a sense that the world was watching, that God had a special role for them to play in the world, and that their insights and experiences should inform mankind. After narrower beginnings, a peculiarly attractive and balanced understanding of the American promise emerged over the course of the eighteenth century. Benjamin Franklin, Thomas Paine, J. Hector St. John de Crevecoeur, Benjamin Rush, Ezra Stiles, and others described America as a place in which a human flowering was about to occur. They foresaw a society characterized by peace and plenty, by political and economic freedom and opportunity, and by accomplishments in religion, morality, and art. They envisioned harmony between the outer plantation of the world and the inner plantation of the human heart and soul. Yet they knew from history and experience that such societies did not exist in nature. They had to be artfully created and carefully sustained against the ravages of time.[1]

The Founders well understood that a free, stable, and prosperous society required constitutional rules of the game that were carefully crafted. Individuals were responsible for their own character and preparation. They were expected to foster good habits and avoid bad habits; to be honest, fair, and truthful; and to avoid lying, drinking, and swearing. They were also to prepare themselves, through education and preparation for a job or career, to be useful members of their society. Then they were expected to work hard, save, invest, persevere, and with a little luck, to succeed and perhaps to prosper. But no matter how well they prepared, how hard they were willing to work, society and the economy had to be well organized and vibrant enough to provide the opportunities over which they might compete. As John Schwarz has correctly argued, "The founders believed that the federal government had a crucial role to play in fostering the level of economic opportunity necessary to enable Americans to attain independence and a decent livelihood."[2]

Through most of the nineteenth century, the American Dream of land in the woods or independent craftsmanship remained open to each new generation and to a constantly increasing flow of immigrants. Yet over the course of the nineteenth century, the balance of the Founders' dream eroded, the limits slipped away, and the American heart hardened. The push west, with its steady annihilation of the Indians, the frantic scramble for wealth in the California gold fields, the seemingly endless horror of the Civil War, and breakneck industrialization, stripped the American character of much of its sense of propriety, balance, and scale. Individualism and competition displaced community and cooperation as men fought to tame the continent, seize its wealth, and control the course of its development. As the nineteenth century neared its close, thoughtful men were well aware that the dynamics of the old century would not be those of the new. The rough equality and competition allowed by a seemingly limitless western frontier had given way to a harsh competition in which the robber barons of the age threatened to deny hope and opportunity to everyone else. At this dangerous juncture, leading progressive intellectuals and political leaders struggled to describe the distinctive bases of American freedom, equality, and opportunity—of the American Dream—before they slipped away. Citizens were worried, even frightened, so they listened intently for an explanation of how the country was changing and what the implications would be for them. Every leading president of the twentieth century used his first inaugural address to answer two questions: How did we get to this place in our history, and how do we ensure that the fundamental dynamics of the nation's early history live into the future? Theodore Roosevelt, Woodrow Wilson, Herbert Hoover, Franklin Roosevelt, Lyndon Johnson, Ronald Reagan, Bill Clinton, and George W. Bush all asked how to secure the American Dream in their time.

Three images—the city on a hill and its golden doors, the balance between the dollar and the man, and the fairly run footrace—have been used throughout the nation's history to sharpen and clarify the fundamental meaning of the American Dream. First, from Winthrop to Reagan, America has been described as a city on a hill. But this city was not a fortress, powerful, austere, and unapproachable; there were doors, golden doors, which gave access to the security and prosperity within. The shining city on a hill was both an example to the world and a destination for all who would be free. The city belonged not just to her defenders within, but to kindred spirits without who would stand with them against the darkness of tyranny, poverty, and injustice in the world.

Second, within the city, care was taken, through culture, constitutions, law, and policy, to ensure that openness and opportunity continued to characterize the society through time. As Andrew Jackson, Theodore Roosevelt, and many others well knew and clearly said, freedom and opportunity demand that a balance be maintained between the dollar and the man, between property rights and human rights. If property and the dollar become too powerful, too concentrated, they foreclose opportunity to the man on the make, the little man just starting out, and to the next generation. Just as certainly, the stark demand for equality limits liberty and forecloses the possibility to rise above the mean.

Third, the image of the fairly run race was used by Abraham Lincoln,

Lyndon Johnson, and many others to humanize and soften thinking about the American Dream. It provided particular insight into the competition between the traditionally advantaged and the historically disadvantaged. A fairly run race does not demand that each runner be equally likely to win; some may be stronger, some may be better trained and prepared, but putting the demonstrably ill prepared, the injured, sick, and crippled, in a race against the strong and swift offends the common sense of justice. To be fair, the strong must forebear while the society nourishes and strengthens the weak before the results of any race in which they are to compete can be given credence.

These images remain powerfully resonant today because each generation of Americans must relate the nation's Founding ideals to the developments and dangers of a new age. The American Creed, based in the Declaration of Independence and all of the documents and demands that have flowed from it, promised a nation committed to liberty, equality, individualism, populism, laissez-faire, and the rule of law under a constitution. But a healthy balance must continually be sought between freedom and equality, between individualism and the rule of law, and between populism and constitutionalism. The American Dream is a constant reminder that America's true nature and distinctive grandeur is in promising the common man, the man on the make, a better chance to succeed here than common men enjoy anywhere else on earth.

As we enter the twenty-first century, we are at one of those points in American history, not unlike the early years of the previous century, when many Americans feel ill at ease, vulnerable, and worried that the society provides fewer opportunities and less mobility than it once did.[3] Recent surveys uniformly find Americans less sanguine about their own prospects and about those of the next generation, their children, than at any point in the last half century. Even at the height of the 1990s boom, a CBS News/*New York Times* survey found that 55 percent of respondents believed the American Dream would be more difficult to realize in the next generation, compared to only 9 percent that thought it would be easier and 34 percent who thought it would be about the same.[4]

Hence, like every previous generation of Americans, we must ask what the nation can do to ensure that the American Dream thrives for this and future generations. Public opinion, parties, and politics will ultimately determine the path that we take, but there is a direction that will lead to a strong and vibrant American Dream for the twenty-first century. Americans have long held the view that individual initiative and markets are the most efficient distributors of opportunities and benefits in a free society. They have also recognized that while markets produce fantastic wealth, they sometimes distribute that wealth so unevenly that democracy is threatened. For the past quarter century, we have been involved in a national debate in which the Republican party has advocated smaller government, lower taxes, deregulation, and self-reliance, while the Democratic party has stood for larger, more energetic, government designed both to assure and promote equality. In an historical moment like this nearly a century ago, Herbert Croly's *The Promise of American Life* (1909) counseled the pursuit of Jeffersonian ends of democratic individualism and opportunity by Hamiltonian means of authoritative government.

The challenges of the terrorist attack on September 11, 2001 (9/11), shifted this debate somewhat, privileging a larger and more powerful national government but setting off a fierce battle over civil liberties and domestic policy priorities. All Americans recognize that the shining city on the hill has to be secure if it is to cast the light of freedom into the dark corners of the world. Yet some worry that we might forget what made the city shine, what made it an example to the world, and what precisely it is about this homeland that made it worth defending. The answer, of course, is the social order within— the freedom, opportunity, and security to pursue one's dreams. As always, we must keep our eye on the goal; the American Dream envisions certain kinds of people in certain kinds of settings. It envisions secure, well-rounded, responsible individuals competing on an even playing field for the good things, material and intellectual, the fruits of the outer plantation of the world and of the inner plantation of the human mind, heart, and soul, which make life rich and full.

To secure the American Dream in this new century, we must address several key issues. First, we ask how Americans balance the worlds of work and family. American men and women have always worked hard, but in recent decades, as women have entered the paid workforce in increasing numbers, dangerous pressures have built around family life, and women have felt these pressures most keenly. Second, we examine the closely related roles of income and education in strengthening families and ensuring that children are prepared to succeed in the modern world. Finally, we consider how race and immigration should be treated to assure inclusion and opportunity for those who have been excluded in the past and those who would seek to be included in America's future.

The Politics of Work, Family, and Community

Americans have never been very good at balancing work and leisure, factory and family, the outer plantation and the inner. American individualism and its focus on the importance of work as the pathway to security and status has energized a nation and created great wealth and power, but it has always had a darker side. In 1684 William Penn warned his Quaker brethren to protect their inner resources, their hearts, minds, and souls, against the harsh external world of politics and work. With a continent to win, Penn's counsel faded from memory, and in 1835 Alexis de Tocqueville noted the "strange melancholy" and pervasive fear of failure that prevailed among Americans even "in the midst of abundance." Ralph Waldo Emerson noted that Americans were driven to unending labor by a fear that others might surpass them or that what they had might be lost. No amount of wealth ever seemed to be enough.

Even before the twentieth century dawned, social critics like Henry George and Edward Bellamy argued that the Industrial Revolution had produced more than enough wealth for everyone to live comfortably. Progressive social theorists, including Herbert Croly, William James, and Walter Lippmann, as well as progressivists Presidents Theodore Roosevelt and Woodrow Wilson, argued that administration and distribution, not production, were the main problems facing society in the new century. Nonetheless, although criticism of endless money-grubbing was prominent throughout the twentieth century, Americans still work longer and harder than people in any other wealthy nation.

In fact, a major study conducted by the International Labor Organization, entitled "Key Indicators of the Labor Market," compared 240 countries on eighteen indicators of work and productivity for the years 1980 through 2000. Americans worked more than workers in any other advanced, industrial country. While Americans worked an average of 1,979 hours per year, workers in Japan worked 1,842 hours, while those in Canada, Britain, and Norway clocked 1,767, 1,719, and 1,375, respectively. Moreover, despite strong economic growth and tremendous wealth creation in the 1980s and 1990s, Americans worked 5 percent more in 2000 (the 1,979 hours per year noted above) than they had in 1980 (1,883 hours per year).[5]

Another study, this one by the liberal Economic Policy Institute, found that the average hours per year worked by middle-class families, husband and wife, rose from 3,000 hours in 1980 to 3,335 in 1997.[6] Seen another way, the average hours worked per year by husbands increased substantially over the last two decades (about 100 hours, or two and a half weeks per year), while paid work by wives increased even more (about 233 hours, or six additional weeks per year). That additional 8 weeks of work per year comes out of family and leisure time. With longer workdays come benefits, of course, including rising incomes, investments, and home values. But there were problems as well; many Americans resented the increasing pressure of work and looked to both the public and private sectors for relief.

Responses to the pressures faced by families have come in both the public and the private sectors. The key public sector response, the Family and Medical Leave Act of 1993, required businesses with more than 50 employees to offer up to 12 weeks of unpaid leave each year to allow employees to respond to the birth, illness, or death of a family member or loved one. In the private sector, some corporations, including Ford, IBM, and J. C. Penney, now offer expanded day and after-school care. The most extensive program belongs to Ford and includes several dozen family service and learning centers providing day care, after-school tutoring and enrichment programs, study groups, and field trips. Although welcome, these initiatives fall far short of the need. Few workers can afford to take unpaid leave, unless forced to do so by truly dire circumstances, and the private sector programs are available to only the narrowest slice of working America. American social policy must focus more intently on the quality of personal, family, and community life in the twenty-first century. The Nobel Prize–winning economist Robert Fogel has predicted, "In the era that is unfolding, fair access to spiritual resources will be as much a touchstone of egalitarianism as access to material resources in the past."[7] Although tight labor markets may encourage businesses to respond to the needs of some workers, such responses will be partial and uneven. "Government," John Schwarz has noted, "is the mechanism by which the community as a body is represented and acts collectively. No other such mechanism exists."[8]

Although prosperity is the proximate goal of work, an inner sense of peace and security, demands time off the treadmill, time with family and children, even time alone. American workers should be entitled, where reasonable, to flexible schedules, the right to limit or decline overtime, and more paid vacation. Only about 30 percent of American workers have the option of flexible schedules, and most of these are well-paid professionals. Some jobs do not permit flexible schedules, but most do, and the option should be provided where possible. Moreover, workers should know that law and policy protect their right to be paid for overtime worked and to decline overtime when it conflicts with other goals and interests. Finally, the Bureau of Labor Statistics (BLS) reports that full-time workers in medium and large businesses receive an average of 10 days' vacation in the first year of employment, 14 days at five years, 17 days at ten years, and 20 days at twenty years. The BLS also reports that the average job tenure of wage and salary workers in 2002 was 3.7 years, so not many workers get even three weeks of paid vacation each year. Workers in smaller businesses get even less, with 14 percent of U.S. workers getting no paid vacation at all. European workers, on the other hand, average four to six weeks of vacation each year.

Moreover, American public policy should seek to buttress workers' confidence that they can, when necessary, turn away from the workplace to attend to the critical moments of private life. The Family and Medical Leave Act should be expanded to cover all full-time employees. It should be revised to provide one week of paid leave to both men and women at the death of a family member, two weeks when one marries, four weeks for fathers at the birth of a child, and eight weeks off with pay for mothers at the birth of a child. These are rare but seminal events that people deserve to give their full attention. Most occur only one or a few times in a person's life. Finally, an additional week of paid vacation each year would lighten the load on American workers while still falling a week or two short of European standards. Such reforms would, of course, drive new costs into American business, but if applied universally and implemented over the course of a decade, they would not cause undue disruption. These reforms would help to rebalance work and family life in America.

Gender and the American Dream

Although families need help, women need particular help. Women now comprise 47 percent of the U.S. labor force and make about 75 percent of what men make.[9] Although single women have participated in the labor force at approximately the same rate as men for several decades, married women moved toward parity only in the late twentieth century. Claudia Goldin, an economic historian at Harvard, reported that almost two-thirds (65.7 percent) of the nation's married women were employed or actively seeking work in 2000. Slightly more women with children under 18 (73.1 percent) were in the labor force, and more than 80 percent of adult women with college degrees were employed in 2000.[10] These figures make clear that most women work and most families depend on women's wages, even when they are not the primary wage earner. Women's wages often provide the difference between working-class and middle- or upper-middle class status for families.

Women's wages, however, are more vulnerable than men's. Ann Crittenden pointed out, in a book entitled *The Price of Motherhood,* that young women make more than 90 percent of what young men make until they have a child, and then they fall back to about 75 percent of what men of similar age and credentials make.[11] Moreover—and this is critical—the lost momentum and economic clout is permanent. Knowing this, many women return to the workforce sooner than they would like to minimize the damage to their careers and incomes. Moreover, women in their late 20s and 30s feel tremendous pressure to maintain a career and start a family or to choose one over the other. Many women attempting to do both well have felt compromised, overburdened, and unfulfilled at work and at home.

The pressures that women face in the workplace are perhaps most evident among professional women. Professional women have made notable progress in scaling the corporate ladder. In 1996 women held just 10 percent of Fortune 500 corporate board seats. By 2002 that number had climbed to 16 percent, and six women led Fortune 500 companies (up from two in 2000). Although these numbers are still quite modest, they do represent progress over the recent past. But progress often comes at a cost. One singular fact that may represent part of the cost has been evident for more than a century. Sara Evans reported that just over half of college-educated women married in the late nineteenth century.[12] In 2002 *BusinessWeek* carried a review by Catharine Arnst entitled "The Loneliness of the High-Powered Woman," which reported that 43 percent of high-achieving women over 40 in corporate jobs were unmarried, compared with 17 percent of similarly situated men. A total of 49 percent of these women were childless at 40, compared to 19 percent of men.[13] The more promising the woman's career, the more intense the pressure to choose between career and family.

Men do not face the forced choice between work and family in the same way women do. The pressure to manage work and family is simply much more direct on women. Some men wish they had more time for family, but only women can have children, and then they usually have the leading role in child care and family management. Hence, after rising inexorably for nearly three decades, the proportion of women in the workforce with children under 3 began dropping in the late 1990s from almost 61 percent to 57.5 percent in 2001. Sharon Hoffman, director of the MBA program at Stanford, observed, "Women are realizing it's impossible for a human being to have it all . . . You can have it sequentially, but not concurrently."[14] Perhaps so, at least under the current set of social and economic rules.

But are the current social and economic rules appropriate to the new century? The United States provides very little support or protection to women who leave the workforce to have a child and virtually none to women who leave for a more extended period to care for and raise a child. Other nations do much more. Sweden, for example, allows women to request a six-hour day until a child is 8 and assures women a year off with pay reflecting past earnings. Although we are unlikely to take our policy lead from Sweden, we might profitably ask what path we might follow to a similar goal—becoming a society that values a woman's natural roles in the family and the economy.

America must support women as they both nurture children and build a career that will provide affirmation and remuneration for life. First, as noted above, two months of paid maternity leave surrounding the birth of a child is necessary. Second, women should have the right to return to their jobs within one year of the birth of a child with no loss in pay or responsibility. Third, businesses should be encouraged, through tax and regulatory policy, to compete for talented employees with benefits and services designed to ease family life. Finally, as outlined in greater detail below, state and federal governments should assist poor women with day care, transportation, and health care.

Income, Wealth, and Poverty in America

American entrepreneurialism, creativity, and hard work have produced tremendous wealth. Yet too many American families are struggling against very long odds. The United States has the greatest concentration of wealth, the greatest income inequality, and the highest poverty rates in the advanced industrial world. Moreover, the gaps between the rich and poor have been increasing for more than two decades. In 1980, the average family in the top 5 percent of the income distribution made about 10 times as much as the average family in the bottom 20 percent of the income distribution. By 2000, the average family in the top 5 percent made almost 20 times as much as the family in the bottom 20 percent.[15] Similarly, in 1980, the top 1 percent of wealth holders controlled about 20 percent of total wealth, while in 2000, that same top 1 percent controlled about 40 percent of total wealth.

As wealth concentrated near the top of the American income and wealth distributions, poverty festered near the bottom. Even at the height of the 1990s boom, with income rising for the bottom 20 percent of wage earners for the first time in two decades and black and Hispanic unemployment at all-time lows, "economist Stephen J. Rose released data showing that about 20 million workers living in low-income families earn $15,000 a year or less. That is about a seventh of the total labor force working hard without very much to show for it. And the vast majority of these workers are the principal breadwinners in their families."[16] About half of these workers, Rose explained, would never move into higher wage brackets, leaving fully 10 million low-wage workers and their families mired in long-term poverty. More broadly, cross-national studies show that the U.S. poverty rate, which stands persistently above 12 percent, is not only the highest poverty rate of any advanced industrial nation, but is more than twice the average for that group.

Experts on poverty in contemporary America point to four major areas of concern: easing the stress on the working poor, moving nonworking adults from welfare to work, making affordable health care available to poor families, and giving special attention to the impact of poverty on children. Republicans note that the bottom 35 percent of wage earners pay no income tax, and they point with pride to the 2001 tax cuts that lowered the bottom bracket from 15 percent to 10 percent. Democrats propose to assist the working poor through an enhanced Earned Income Tax Credit, increased minimum wage, training programs for those currently working in low-paying jobs, improved access to quality child care, enhanced child health care programs, and expanded eligibility for children and parents under the State Child Health Insurance Program (S-CHIP).

The transition from welfare to work was the central focus of the dramatic welfare reform effort of 1996. Welfare recipients are required to be preparing for or looking for work to maintain eligibility, and they are subject to a five-year lifetime limit on federal assistance. Welfare reform and the booming job market of the late 1990s trimmed welfare rolls by nearly half, from more than 10 million persons to 5.4 million by 2002. As Congress debated the second phase of welfare reform in 2002 and 2003, Republicans and some Democrats called for increased work requirements while most Democrats and a few Republicans called for enhanced training and education, as well as expanded support for child care and transportation.

Ensuring adequate health care has always been a major problem for the poor and is increasingly difficult for middle- and upper-middle-class families. At the height of the 1990–1992 recession, the number of uninsured persons passed 35 million, but then continued to rise even during the boom years of the late 1990s. Today, nearly 44 million Americans lack health insurance, and a 2003 report by the Congressional Budget Office suggested that fully 60 million lack health insurance during part of every year. The principal reason for the increase in uninsured persons even during good economic times was that spiraling health care costs made insurance prohibitive for many small businesses. Although small businesses create most of the new jobs in America, almost half of them no longer offer health insurance to their employees. Persons who do have employer-sponsored health insurance pay premiums averaging about one-quarter of the annual cost of about $12,000. Those who do not have health insurance at work must pay the whole cost themselves. Increasingly, even middle- and upper-middle-class wage earners buckle under the weight of health insurance costs. Both political parties recognize the need to provide greater access to health care for the poor and to provide price relief to families and small businesses. Most Republicans favor tax credits to help individuals and businesses buy health insurance in the private market. Most Democrats favor mandates and tax incentives for businesses or extensive public sector programs, including expanding access to Medicaid or opening the popular S-CHIP to the parents of eligible children.

Finally, the poverty rate for children in America is nearly twice that for the elderly. Sixteen percent of American children live in poverty, and among minority children, the numbers run to nearly 40 percent. Moreover, studies report that many children experience poverty throughout childhood. Professors Peter Gottschalk and Sheldon Danziger measured the upward economic mobility of children between 1970 and 1990. They divided children into five groups (quintiles) based on their family income. They found that about 60 percent of the children in the lowest group—the poorest 20 percent—were still in the bottom income group ten years later. Almost 90 percent of children in the bottom group remained in the bottom two income groups ten years later.[17] Moreover, young children, the most vulnerable children, experience higher poverty rates than do older children. Tremendous benefits come to children when families are strengthened and made more secure.

The American Dream demands, as Jackson, Lincoln, and the Roosevelts knew, that policy aid the "man on the make," now the "man or woman on the make," without dissuading from further effort the man or woman who is already made. As always, if opportunity is to bubble through the American society, it has to bubble from the bottom. Hence, American tax policy must be progressive without being punitive. It must provide adequate revenue to government from those in the best position to pay, without stunting innovation and entrepreneurship. Further, democracy demands that tax policy exert a steady downward pressure on the accumulation and transmission of extraordinary wealth.

Tax rates can be punitive. In fact, U.S. tax rates have fluctuated tremendously over the past half century or so. The top tax rate on large incomes from World War II into the early 1960s was 90 percent. Kennedy cut the top rate to 70 percent and spurred the economic boom of the 1960s. Ronald Reagan slashed the top income tax rate to 50 percent and then to 31 percent and produced both economic growth and a string of deficits. Bill Clinton raised the top rate to 38.5 percent and produced both continued economic growth and shrinking deficits that turned into surpluses by the late 1990s. Over the course of the 1990s, the proportion of income taxes paid by the top 5 percent of income earners rose from about 45 percent to 55 percent, while the proportion paid by the bottom 50 percent declined from about 6 percent to 4 percent. The Clinton administration also passed the Earned Income Tax Credit, which gave tax rebates to the lowest income earners.

The Bush tax cuts of 2001 removed millions more of the poor from the income tax rolls. By 2002, a family of four, with two children under 17, making $18,100, taking standard deductions and exemptions, received a net tax refund of $3,200. In fact, the family of four had to earn $32,000 before it incurred an income tax obligation (about $23). Still, a family of four living on $32,000, although that was twice the poverty rate for 2002, was on a tight budget. In addition, the tax cuts that President Bush won in 2001 and 2003 lowered the top tax rate to 33 percent, removed the marriage penalty, increased the standard deduction and child tax credit, and phased out the inheritance tax. These tax cuts, along with 9/11 and the slow economy of 2001 to 2003, produced some of the largest deficits in recent American history. Federal revenues must be maintained at levels that allow us to address the most serious needs of our society. A top tax rate of 35 to 37 percent will provide adequate revenues.

Finally, an inheritance tax, set above the level that would impact the vast majority of farms and small businesses, must be seen as an important element of our tax system. In 2002 the estate tax was levied against less than 2 percent of estates; those worth more than $1 million, $2 million for married couples. Still, some express concern that family businesses or farms might have to be sold at the death of the founder to pay the estate tax. Senator Kent Conrad (D-ND) proposed raising the estate limit to $3.5 million ($7 million for couples), which would strike only one in seven hundred estates. Others have proposed a $5 million ($10 million for couples), which would strike only one in one thousand estates. An estate tax set at $5 million would still bring to the treasury about $15 billion annually, as opposed to the $30 billion it produced in 2000. The level at which the tax is set is less important than that an estate tax be maintained. Democracy suffers from the effects of extraordinary and unconstrained differences in intergenerational family wealth.

Education as Preparation for Work and Leisure

Most Americans, from top political leaders to average citizens, believe that quality education, and particularly access to higher education, is the key to economic success and personal fulfillment in the modern world. During the 2000 presidential campaign, one of George W. Bush's favorite stump speech lines was, "Reading is the new civil right because if you can't read, you can't access the American Dream."[18] At the same time, President Bill Clinton used his 2000 State of the Union message to declare, "To make the American dream achievable for all, we must make college affordable for all."[19] In addition, a study completed in 2000 by the National Center for Public Policy and Higher Education found that fully 87 percent of adult Americans believed that a college education was as important today as a high school education had been in the past. Still, 70 percent of parents thought that college was more difficult to afford than it had been a decade ago and, not surprisingly, poor parents were most concerned about the cost of college.

Income and education are intertwined well before the cost of college comes into play. Fundamentally, one's experience in the educational system has a very great deal to do with how one enters and moves through the job market and occupational structure. The fortunate student, emerging from a secure and prosperous family into good schools and then good colleges, will enter the upper half of the occupational hierarchy and will, with some hard work and good fortune, advance from there. The unfortunate student, emerging from a broken, insecure, or impoverished family into poor schools and an unforgiving job market will find it difficult to do more than just get by. The amount and quality of educational preparation determines how well Americans do economically, and class determines what educational opportunities are available.

The close relationship between income and educational opportunity is impossible to evade. High school juniors and seniors from families with less than $10,000 annual income taking the Scholastic Aptitude Test (SAT) for college admission score a combined 871 points on the verbal and math sections of the exam. SAT scores increase inexorably with every additional increment of family income. Children from families making between $10,000 and $20,000 average 907 on the SAT (+36), between $20,000 and $30,000 they score 954 (+47), between $30,000 and $40,000 they score 986 (+32), and between $40,000 and $50,000 they score 1011 (+25). Thereafter, although scores continue to rise with income, they rise at less than half the rate they did at lower income levels. Between $50,000 and $80,000 they rise at a rate of about 15 points per $10,000 increase in income, while above $80,000 they rise at a decreasing rate of less than 10 points per $10,000 increase in income. Students from families with incomes over $100,000 a year score 1130 on the exam. On the one hand, it may not be surprising that rich kids do better than poor kids on college admission exams. On the other hand, it clearly suggests that equal opportunity would be well served by focusing on the education of poor children.

Inadequate early education often simply forecloses the opportunity to go to college. As Bruce Ackerman and Anne Alstott noted in their 1999 *The Stakeholder Society,* "At the end of the day, 51 percent of students from the top quarter of the economic hierarchy earn bachelor's degrees, compared to 22 percent of the middle status students and only 7.2 percent in the lowest socioeconomic quartile." Moreover, they noted, "These numbers become especially poignant when one recognizes that poor children, once they have graduated from a four-year college, earn, on average, as much as those from wealthier backgrounds."[20] Clearly, adequate funding for elementary and secondary schools and broad access to college must be central components of America's egalitarian ethic in the twenty-first century.

At the level of elementary and secondary education, some progress has been made in the last two decades. In 1983, the federal Department of Education issued a report, entitled "A Nation at Risk," declaring that the nation's public schools were gravely deficient, especially in math and science. In 2000, the Department of Education issued a report, entitled "The Condition of Education," claiming that the proportion of students taking advanced math classes had risen from 26 percent in 1982 to 41 percent in 1998, while those taking advanced science classes had increased from 31 percent to 60 percent. In 2000 American public schools averaged about one computer for every four students, and fully 75 percent of classrooms were connected to the Internet. Still, U.S. students continue to score well below students in other advanced industrial nations on math and science.

President Bush made educational reform a focus of the 2000 campaign, and his No Child Left Behind initiative became law in January 2002. This initiative increased federal spending on education in exchange for annual testing and assessment of students in grades 3 through 8. Additional funds were provided to enhance early reading programs. Schools were required to assure that teachers were properly trained in the subjects they taught, and parents were given the right to move students from perennially poor schools to better schools. Nonetheless, the 2004 federal budget proposed only three-quarters of the funds authorized for the program (a little more than $21 billion of the $29 billion authorized).

Funding America's colleges and universities has proven to be an even more difficult problem. In the mid-1970s federal and state higher education policy was designed to maximize access. State governments subsidized public universities to keep tuition low, and the federal government offered Pell grants to cover most of the costs. In 1981 Pell grants, which students do not have to repay, covered up to 98 percent of tuition at a public four-year college. However, in the past two decades, tuition charges have increased far faster than Pell grant authorizations. Today, the annual maximum Pell grant covers only about half of tuition at public four-year colleges. The college-funding gap has been covered by loan programs, which place a heavy burden on the poor, and by politically popular tuition tax rebate programs for which the poor may not qualify.

Two major studies released in 2002, one from the National Center for Public Policy and Higher Education, entitled "Losing Ground," and another from Congress, entitled "Slamming Shut the Doors of College," decry the increasing burden of college on poor families. Advocates of greater college access call for many reforms, including tuition remission programs for good students, increased funding of Pell grants, and tax credits that are reimbursable to the poor like the Earned Income Tax Credit. Successful completion of college is no guarantee of success, but it is a tremendous advantage. In the soft job market of 2002, the unemployment rate for college graduates was 2.9 percent, while that for high school graduates was exactly three times higher, at 8.7 percent.

If education is the modern equivalent of open land in the West, then it must be as widely available, at reasonable levels of quality, so that every American child has a realistic chance of fulfilling his or her dreams. At the elementary and secondary levels, the key goals must be to get to students as early as possible and to concentrate on the children of the poor. Getting them young means full funding for Head Start and a concentration on reading in the early grades. In 2002, Head Start served 908,000 four-year-olds. More than three-fourths of these children were from families making less than $15,000 per year. Although Head Start is a terribly important and well-proven program, fewer than half of eligible children are enrolled in Head Start or any other early educational enhancement program. Steady movement toward full enrollment is decidedly in the nation's interest.

Full funding of the No Child Left Behind Act of 2002 would provide critical support to early reading programs, science and math programs, and educational enrichment and tutoring programs for students in danger of falling behind. An early focus on reading provides a solid foundation for later educational attainment. It is also important to continue the focus on math and science, with increasing numbers of students taking advanced courses and truly excellent training available to the best students. A reasonable goal for the coming decade would be to have two-thirds of high school students enrolled in advanced science and math. The United States should seek, over the course of a decade, to move from the lower ranks into at least the middle ranks of advanced industrial nations on test scores in math and science.

Fortunately, the United States has the best system of higher education in the world. At the pinnacle of that system are exclusive private and prestige public universities. Below them are many fine public and private universities and colleges, and below those are a diverse set of community colleges and trade schools. Equal opportunity does not require that every student have access to the very best schools in this system, but it does require that every student have access to all of education that he or she needs to realize their potential. First, the president and Congress must increase Pell grants in the coming decade until they again cover at least 90 percent of the cost of tuition at midlevel state universities. The average cost of tuition, fees, and room and board at a four-year college or university in 2003–4 was between $10,000 and

$15,000. Increasing Pell grants by $400 per year (from the current maximum of $4,050 annually) over the next decade, even in light of the tuition increases that will occur over that period, would accomplish this important goal.

Second, many states also have programs that help young people afford college. Georgia's HOPE Scholarship program, initiated in 1993, allows any high school graduate in the state who has maintained a grade point average of 3.0 or better on an approved curriculum to attend college without having to pay tuition. Moreover, Georgia's HOPE-eligible curriculum has been strengthened since its introduction. The promise of free college tuition pulls students into more rigorous high school classes, and they arrive in college better prepared. Other states have started with limited programs, providing partial funding or funding just the freshman year, but popular reception of these programs has been predictably enthusiastic. These are tremendous programs and should be widely replicated.

Race in the American Future

Scholars, analysts, and pundits remained fixated on the problem of race in America. Within months of each other, early in 2000, two well-known syndicated columnists, Clarence Page of the *Chicago Tribune* and Michael Barone of *U.S. News and World Report,* assessed the state of race relations in America. Page, who is black, entitled his column "Colorblind Society Remains Elusive at Century's Turn," while Barone, who is white, entitled his column "American Dreamers: Blacks, Latinos, and Asians Follow a Well-Trod Path to Success."[21] As these column titles suggest, some believe that race is still a major problem in America, while others believe that race, while once a serious problem, is in the process of naturally passing away.

Page opened his column by quoting W. E. B. DuBois, the prominent black sociologist and social activist of a century ago. In 1902, at the dawn of the twentieth century, with the yoke of Jim Crow segregation firmly fixed on the nation's neck, DuBois declared, "the problem of the 20th century is the problem of the color line: the question is how far racial differences . . . will be made the basis of denying . . . people the right of sharing to their utmost ability the opportunities and privileges of modern civilization." Barone did not deny the evils of slavery and Jim Crow; he simply declared, "blacks, Latinos, and Asians are already moving on the paths the Irish, Italians, and Jews followed."

Will the same processes work for racial minorities as worked for white ethnic and religious minorities in the past? The answer is yes, to some extent, but there is more going on and more that may need to be addressed directly. First-generation white ethnics were easily identified and therefore discriminated against because their language, dress, and manners made them stand out. But this was less true of the second generation and untrue of the third and later generations. Differences of race and gender are both obvious and permanent and therefore can be the basis for more resistant and hardy forms of discrimination.

Opportunity comes harder to minorities than it does to white men. A few facts will help to make the case. Minorities experience poverty at more than twice the rate that whites do. Poverty afflicts 15.5 percent of white children up to 18 years old, while 39.5 and 39.9 percent of black and Hispanic children are impoverished. Whites over 65 are impoverished at a rate of 9.4 percent, while 25.3 percent and 24.4 percent of black and Hispanic elderly live in poverty. Minorities are twice as likely to be laid off during an economic downturn. In 2002, 15 percent of whites said they had been laid off during the year, while 30 percent of Hispanics and 32 percent of blacks said that they had been laid off. Finally, a fascinating experiment in which resumes of candidates with race-typed names (including Kristen, Carrie, and Laurie for whites and Ebony, Latonya, and Kenya for blacks) and otherwise identical qualifications were offered in response to job ads. "Applicants with white-sounding names were 50 percent more likely to be called for interviews than were those with black-sounding names."[22]

The long history of discrimination in America has led some to suggest radical remedies. The "reparations" movement demands compensation for the injustice and lingering effects of slavery, segregation, and Jim Crow. Representative John Conyers (D-Michigan) is an advocate, introducing a bill in Congress each year, as are Randall Robinson, president of the lobby group TransAfrica, Charles Ogletree of the Harvard Law School, and Louis Henry Gates Jr. of the Harvard Afro-American Studies Department. The rationale for reparations is simple: white Americans stole the value of the labor performed by blacks during more than three centuries of slavery and Jim Crow. White families benefited through the generations from the enjoyment and investment of income and wealth that rightly should have gone to black families.

Reparations are a fascinating idea, although unlikely to be adopted and implemented. There is no doubt that value—money, capital, and opportunity—was stolen by whites from blacks. But the grossest perpetrators and the most pitiable victims are all long dead, and most white Americans are simply unwilling to assume personal responsibility for injustices committed from two to ten generations ago. Moreover, white skepticism is growing. Young whites, raised well after segregation, let alone slavery, believe that equality reigns and that it is reverse discrimination to ask them to forego educational or job opportunities to give more opportunity to blacks.

Nonetheless, the idea of reparations also underpins Native American claims against the government and society. In the century after the Revolution, the federal government seized, negotiated, and cajoled most of the continent from its original inhabitants. By the time the Grant administration declared an end to treaty-making with the Indians, 371 treaties had established hundreds of reservations covering 140 million acres. Over the next century, federal policy from the Dawes General Allotment initiative of the 1870s to the Eisenhower administration's termination program of the 1950s sought to integrate Indians into the broader society and end their dependence on federal support. In the process, Indian land holdings declined to about 50 million acres. The Kennedy and Johnson administrations were friendlier to Native Americans, but by the late 1980s the Reagan administration struck on a new way to make Indians financially independent of the federal government with the Indian Gaming Regulatory Act of 1988. The results have been decidedly mixed.

In 2001, nearly three hundred Indian casinos in twenty-eight states took in almost $13 billion and retained more than $5 billion in profit. Although much of that money ended up far from the reservations and in non-Indian hands, the money retained on the reservations has helped to change the balance of power between Indians and whites in communities all over the country. Bets are being placed in the courts as well as the casinos. Indians are engaged in a series of lawsuits designed to hold the federal government to earlier treaty commitments, to win back control of tribal lands and resources, and in some cases to use gambling and other revenues to buy back lost tribal lands. One measure of the Indian's odds on winning can be seen in the results of the 2000 census. The 2000 census identified 4.1 million persons as all or part Indian, whereas the 1990 census had identified only 2 million. The increase reflected rising hope more than rising fertility.

Not surprisingly, white officialdom vehemently opposes reparations. One of the most vociferous opponents of the Indian's legal efforts has been former Senator Slade Gorton (R-WA). Senator Gorton has been quoted saying, "Making a case out of what happened to your grandfather is not the best way to decide public policy."[23] Although it is undoubtedly easier for a Mexican

American in the southwest, a Japanese American on the West Coast, or black and Native Americans across the nation to believe that what happened to their grandfathers is relevant to policy making today, it behooves white Americans to pause over the idea at least momentarily. One does not have to endorse reparations to recognize that past injustices have present implications that both justice and good public policy demand be addressed.

Reparations, whether for wrongs done to American Indians or African Americans, are unworkable. It is not simply that full reparations would be too expensive, although returning large chunks of the continent to its original inhabitants or recompensing centuries of unpaid or underpaid labor would be immensely disruptive. Rather, it is that the past cannot be undone, and therefore one is compelled to look with a clear eye to the future and seek justice there. Despite the evident injustices that stain our national history, Americans created the most open, vibrant, and successful society in the world. Justice requires that we make a conscious national commitment to open opportunity to all Americans, and particularly to those we know to have been systematically disadvantaged at earlier stages in our history. Unfortunately, it is not at all clear that we will do even that.

Democrats recognize that the American state and people perpetrated tremendous wrongs against minorities until well into the twentieth century. They often contend that past injustices must be made good before a fair competition can begin. Republicans argue that equality is the law and has been for more than a generation, so no recognition of race, negative or positive, is permissible. In late 2002, Senator Trent Lott (R-Mississippi) became enmeshed in this debate. His seemingly fond remembrances of Strom Thurmond's segregationist campaign for the presidency in 1948 concerned many Republicans because they suggested that current opposition to affirmative action might simply mask a continuing animus toward blacks. Yet even in the wake of the Republican Party's trauma over Senator Lott's comments, President Bush assured reporters on New Year's Day 2003 that the "Republican Party cares deeply about each individual, regardless of the color of their skin or their religion. And I will continue to promote policies that enable the American individual to achieve his or her dreams."[24] President Bush's focus on "the American individual" pretty clearly precluded race-conscious policies like affirmative action, let alone reparations.

Nonetheless, President Bush has called for some race-conscious policies, including public-private initiatives to "close the homeownership gap." On June 15, 2002, President Bush noted in his weekly radio address that while three-quarters of whites owned their own homes, less than half of blacks and Hispanics owned their own homes. He committed his administration to "begin to close this homeownership gap by dismantling the barriers that prevent minorities from owning a piece of the American dream." President Bush proposed a ten-year joint public-private initiative, including an "American Dream Downpayment Fund" and $2.4 billion in builder incentives for low-cost housing to assist first-time home buyers.

Various analysts, white and black, but mostly black, argue that "merely creating equal opportunities in housing, securities, and credit markets will not do enough to rectify the racial imbalance because parental asset levels (which were presumably fixed in the past) engender advantages and disadvantages that are very important for the next generation.... merely eliminating remaining discrimination—be it individual or institutional—will do little to alleviate the wealth gap."[25] President Bush's minority home ownership initiative recognized, perhaps just tacitly, that simple nondiscrimination might not be enough to address the glaring presence of group inequality in America.

Affirmative action, not just in regard to home ownership, but in regard to education and work as well, should be an ongoing American commitment. As President Bush said in his speech on minority home ownership, "The strength of America lies in the honor and the character and goodwill of its people. When we tap into that strength, we discover there is no problem that cannot be solved in this wonderful land of liberty." This is an important insight and more broadly applicable than President Bush has yet acknowledged.

Immigration and the American Dream

Even as we struggle to assure equality to every American, others hopefully approach the golden doors. For its first three centuries, America was avowedly an immigrant nation. Although each new wave of immigrants was viewed with initial suspicion, labor was always in short supply, there was land in the West, naturalization was readily available, and children born in the United States were citizens. When the immigrants kept coming even after the frontier was declared closed at the end of the nineteenth century, many Americans, and particularly the secure and prosperous, became more skeptical of the newcomers. Tight restrictions, generally limiting entry to western European whites, were imposed in 1924 and remained in place into the mid-1960s.

Lyndon Johnson's immigration reforms removed racial and national origin restrictions, opened the nation to political and religious refugees, made family unification a key component of immigration policy, and responded to the needs of business and agriculture with extensive guest worker programs. Immigration levels built slowly at first, until the 1990s saw the largest immigration surge in the nation's history—13.3 million immigrants arrived in the United States in the 1990s. Most came legally, but many came illegally. The Immigration and Naturalization Service estimated that more than 7 million illegal aliens live in the United States, with at least 350,000 more arriving annually. The Census Bureau put the numbers somewhat higher, estimating illegals at 8 million and new arrivals at 450,000 annually.

Before 9/11, the immigration debate in the United States was about how many people, with what mix of characteristics and claims, should be admitted each year. These are still important questions. We will look at these old questions first and then look at the new concerns added by 9/11. A recent set of population and demographic projections by the U.S. Census Bureau highlight the numbers driving the immigration debate. In January 2000 the Census Bureau projected that the U.S. population would grow by almost half, from 275 million to 404 million, by 2050. Most of those population gains were projected to result from continued high levels of immigration and from higher fertility rates and family sizes among minorities.

The white population is projected to grow by about 8 percent, from 196.7 million to 213 million, between 2000 and 2050. The proportion of the total U.S. population that is white will drop over this period from a little more than 71 percent to a little under 53 percent. The black population will increase by 60 percent, from about 33.5 million to about 53.5 million, although its presence in the total population will only rise from its current 12 percent to a little more than 13 percent. The Hispanic population in the United States will increase by more than 300 percent between 2000 and 2050, from 32.5 million to 98.2 million. In percentage terms, the Hispanic presence in the total population will more than double, from 12 percent to more than 24 percent. Asians numbers will increase even faster, by 337 percent, although from a smaller base. In 2000, 10.6 million Asians made up nearly 4 percent of the total U.S. population. By 2050, 35.8 million Asians will make up almost 9 percent of the population. Hence, the minority populations in the United States are projected to grow rapidly and to outstrip the traditional white majority by 2059.

Politicians are, of course, intensely aware of the nation's changing demographics because they must address them both in terms of public policy and electoral politics. One-time Republican and independent candidate for president Patrick J. Buchanan wrote a book entitled *The Death of the West: How Dying Populations and Immigrant Invasions Imperil Our Country and Civilization.* As the title boldly announced, Buchanan called for severely limiting the number of new immigrants. Mainstream politicians are much more circumspect because they recall that California's Republican Governor Pete Wilson attempted in the mid-1990s to limit the number and rights of immigrants in his state, and his party paid a terrible price. Hence, when George W. Bush addressed the National Hispanic Women's Conference during his 2000 California campaign, he proclaimed in English and Spanish, "I want the American dream, el sueño Americano, to belong to all Americans."

Nonetheless, all American politicians insist that immigration be legal and that the United States maintain control over how many come and what they bring to the table. Critics of the U.S. system, including Harvard Professor George J. Borjas, in a book entitled *Heaven's Door: Immigration Policy and the American Economy,* point out that although recent immigrants have contributed to economic expansion, they have also imposed costs on the economy and the society. Borjas and others contend that recent immigrants, two-thirds of whom come from Latin America and Asia, have two years' less schooling and earn 20 percent less than the average native-born American worker. A total of 40 percent of recent immigrants founder in the bottom one-fifth of the income distribution, and fully one-quarter draw on federal assistance such as food stamps and Medicaid. Critics also contend that the large influx of low-wage immigrants compete unduly with native-born minorities for entry-level jobs.

During the 1990s, United States policy makers approached these concerns on two dimensions. First, the Republican-sponsored reforms of 1996, highlighted by the Illegal Immigration Reform and Immigrant Responsibility Act, were intended to stem the flow of illegal immigrants and to restrict the social, legal, and economic rights not just of illegals, but also of legal immigrants, including permanent resident aliens. These reforms allowed illegal aliens to be held, adjudicated, and deported more efficiently. It limited access of legal immigrants to social services, and it made both legal immigrants and permanent resident aliens vulnerable to deportation for crimes and other violations of their immigrant status. Although some rights have been restored to permanent residents and legal immigrants, many of the restrictive reforms enacted in 1996 remain in place.

Meanwhile, at the upper end of the economy, the Republican Congress and

President Clinton responded to business' call for more skilled workers by expanding the H-1B visa program. The H-1B program was enacted in 1990 to allow foreigners with advanced degrees and special skills to be admitted to the country on a special, renewable three-year term to work for employers who petitioned on their behalf. Hi-tech companies were particularly eager to hire talented workers, at modest wages, from India, China, and around the world. The initial H-1B allocation of 65,000 per year was increased to 115,000 in 1998 and 200,000 in 2000. Although H-1B entries are not technically immigrants, experts contend that most will seek to stay. In addition, North American Free Trade Agreement permits up to 75,000 professional (Trade NAFTA or TN) workers from Mexico and an unlimited number from Canada each year. Although the hi-tech crash of the early 2000s temporarily reduced the number of visas requested, many in Congress and in the private sector would like to see the limits removed entirely so that the market could determine how many specially trained workers were admitted. Before 9/11 the Bush administration was poised to offer a broad amnesty to illegals working in the United States and to ease economic migration within NAFTA.

The terrorist attacks of 9/11 highlighted issues of border control and made them a fundamental component of national security. News that most of the hijackers had been in the country legally, living, taking flying lessons, and moving freely about, led to a full-scale review of U.S. immigration policy. Officials responsible for national security wanted to know much more about who was entering the country, with what purposes, and how they could be tracked and located once inside the country. Many immigrants were rounded up, questioned, detained, and in some cases deported. New laws and rulings limited the rights of immigrants and, to a lesser degree, citizens in the name of public safety and national security. Though deep concern focused on the presumed trade-off between individual rights and national security, the courts generally upheld the government's initiatives.

Especially in the wake of 9/11, U.S. immigration policy must work to balance the needs of potential immigrants and of the nation to which they wish to come. U.S. immigration policy must allow those who wish to come legally a reasonable chance to do so while ensuring that their presence is beneficial to the nation. This can be accomplished within a legal immigration flow of 750,000 to 1 million persons each year in all categories, including H-1B. A number of reforms will be necessary. First, the United States must cooperate with the other nations of the world to ensure that victims of conscience have an asylum. Second, the United States should give greater weight to competitive attributes, such as education, technical skills, and capital, while not ignoring refugee and family status. Third, the United States should develop an amnesty program for illegals in the country more than five years, focusing first on those with good work histories, no felony convictions, and children born in the United States. Fourth, the U.S. should strengthen defenses against illegal immigration, including improved border patrols, streamlined expulsion proceedings, and employer sanctions. The broad goal of these reforms should be to control immigration and to ensure that its impact on the domestic opportunity structure is distributed from top to bottom and perhaps even relieved at the bottom.

Finally, the United States should enhance its technological capability to identify known terrorists and their associates and to detect dangerous substances being brought into or moved within the country. Illegal aliens should be treated with authority and dispatch, but treated for what they are: illegal. Legal visitors, immigrants, and permanent residents must be accorded the full legal equality and rights to due process that they have traditionally enjoyed within the American society. Violations of American law, including immigration law, may be grounds for detention and expulsion, but legal immigrants should enjoy the full constellation of rights, opportunities, and services enjoyed by American citizens. We should invite only the number of immigrants we wish to accord full legal status.

Looking Forward

Few nations have a dream, "the promise of American life" in Herbert Croly's wonderful phrase, as well worth protecting and nurturing as do we Americans. It may be that we were simply fortunate that our Founding occurred in a time and place where men could afford to be generous. With a continent stretching westward beyond the imagination, and too few men and women to take advantage of it, the poor could command good wages and a better future, and the newly arrived were valued, if not always welcomed. But in our haste to control and benefit from nature's bounty, breathtaking injustices were committed in the names of civilization and progress. Today, America is the wealthiest and most powerful nation that the world has ever known. Americans exceed every other people in work and productivity and hence in the creation of wealth. We spend more on national security than all of the other nations in the world combined. Yet other great nations, spectacularly wealthy and powerful in their day too, fell from their high places. Perhaps this is precisely the right time, while at the height of our power, to ask how America can maintain and build upon its unprecedented wealth and strength.

The answer, almost certainly, is by being ever truer to our initial values and aspirations—to make "life, liberty, and the pursuit of happiness"—the right and real possession of every American. In the twenty-first century, this means educating all children to their natural capacities and encouraging all adults to tend the inner plantation of the heart, mind, and soul as well as the outer plantation of creativity, productivity, and work. If all of our children are well cared for and well educated, and every American adult—irrespective of gender or color—has the opportunity to compete for and enjoy the riches of this society, we will secure and extend our primacy among the nations of the world. No nation has ever harvested the full potential and creativity of all of its citizens. If we were to do so, we would truly be "a shining city on a hill" and a light unto the nations.

Still, we know that our society as it is currently ordered does not meet this high standard. Even today, both black men and white women make only 75 percent of what white men make. Black women and Hispanic men and women make even less. Glass ceilings keep all but a very few men of color and women of all colors out of the executive suite. Breaking these barriers, releasing these talents, is the great social and moral task of the twenty-first century. The special responsibility of social and political leaders is to work toward a future in which all can find an honorable place. This is asking a very great deal; but really it is simply asking that we continue to work toward Mr. Jefferson's self-evident truths, "that all men are created equal, that they are endowed by their Creator with certain unalienable Rights, that among these are Life, Liberty, and the pursuit of Happiness." We will have redeemed Jefferson's promise when the American Dream of liberty, equality, and opportunity are the patrimony—the living inheritance—of every American.

Notes

1. The American Dream and Its Role in American History

1. Louis Hartz, *Founding of New Societies*.
2. This quote appears in Pauline Maier, *American Scripture*, xvii.
3. G. K. Chesterton, *What I Saw in America*, 7.
4. Gunnar Myrdal, *American Dilemma*, 1:4, 8.
5. Samuel P. Huntington, *American Politics*, 14–15.
6. Seymour Martin Lipset, *American Exceptionalism*, 19.
7. Quoted in John E. Schwarz and Thomas J. Volgy, *Forgotten Americans*, 8.
8. Quoted in Jennifer L. Hochschild, *Facing Up to the American Dream*, 21.
9. J. Hector St. John de Crevecoeur, *Letters from an American Farmer*, 57. See letter 2, entitled "What Is an American," 35–81. Henry Adams, *History of the United States*, 1:173–74.
10. Walter Lippmann, *Drift and Mastery*, 103.
11. James Truslow Adams, *Epic of America*, 404.
12. Hochschild, *Facing Up to the American Dream*, 4.
13. John E. Schwarz, *Illusions of Opportunity*, 16–18.
14. Both Bruce Springsteen and Bill Clinton are quoted in Hochschild, *Facing Up to the American Dream*, 16, 18.
15. Dan Rather, *American Dream*, xxi.
16. Jane Flax, *American Dream in Black and White*, 2.
17. Hochschild, *Facing Up to the American Dream*, 26.
18. Rogers M. Smith, *Civic Ideals*, 2.
19. Derrick Bell, *Faces at the Bottom of the Well*, x.
20. Andrew Hacker, *Two Nations*, 9; see also Lipset, *American Exceptionalism*, 157–61.
21. Vernon Parrington, *Main Currents of American Thought*, 3:285.
22. Rather, *American Dream*, xxi.
23. Louis Hartz, *Liberal Tradition*, 48.
24. Huntington, *American Politics*, 11–12.
25. Paul Berman, *Tale of Two Utopias*, 186.
26. Maier, *American Scripture*, 214.
27. Robert William Fogel, *Fourth Great Awakening*, 8–9.
28. W. Michael Cox and Richard Alm, *Myths of Rich and Poor*, 141.
29. Robert Max Jackson, *Destined for Equality*, 4, 69.
30. Ibid., 130.

2. American Dreams

1. Andrew Burstein, *Sentimental Democracy,* 258. See also Joseph J. Ellis, *Founding Brothers,* 109.

2. Edmund S. Morgan, *Puritan Political Ideas,* 91–92.

3. Ibid., 168–69.

4. Karabell, *Visionary Nation,* 19.

5. Perry Miller, *The New England Mind: The Seventeenth Century,* 3–34.

6. Kenneth A. Lockridge, *New England Town,* 4, 12.

7. Frederick B. Tolles, *Meeting House and Counting House,* 56.

8. T. H. Breen, *Puritans and Adventurers,* 109.

9. Ibid., 151–53.

10. Ibid., 126.

11. Morgan, *Puritan Political Ideas,* 90.

12. Ibid., 112.

13. Ibid., 169.

14. Perry Miller, *Errand into the Wilderness,* 142; see also Kevin Phillips, *Cousins' Wars,* xxii.

15. See the Avalon Project, available at http://www.yale.edu/lawweb/avalon/states/pa04.htm.

16. Breen, *Puritans and Adventurers,* 114–15.

17. Population numbers vary somewhat by source. See *Historical Statistics of the United States,* series Z 1–19, 756; Edwin J. Perkins, *Economy of Colonial America,* 1–2; John J. McCusker and Russell R. Menard, *Economy of British America,* 54.

18. Breen, *Puritans and Adventurers,* 173.

19. Quote appears in Breen, *Puritans and Adventurers,* 72.

20. Andrew Delbanco, *Real American Dream,* 16.

21. Morgan, *Puritan Political Ideas,* 93.

22. Both Tillam quotes appear in Karabell, *Visionary Nation,* 18–19.

23. Miller, *Errand into the Wilderness,* 143.

24. Morgan, *Puritan Political Ideas,* 77, 90–92.

25. Miller, *Errand into the Wilderness,* 143.

26. Tolles, *Meeting House and Counting House,* 3; original at *An Epistle to All Planters, and Such Who Are Transporting Themselves into Foreign Plantations in America, &c* (1682), in *The Works of George Fox,* 8:218.

27. Tolles, *Meeting House and Counting House,* 54.

28. Ibid., 33–34.

29. Ibid., 63.

30. Ibid., 42; original at Friends Historical Society, *Journals* 6 (1909), 174.

31. Tolles, *Meeting House and Counting House,* 45; original in William Penn, *Collection,* 1:908–9, 898.

32. Alan K. Simpson, *Puritanism in Old and New England,* 32.

33. Perry Miller, *The New England Mind: From Colony to Province,* 49–51.

34. Tolles, *Meeting House and Counting House,* viii.

35. Ibid., 82.

36. Adams, *Epic of America,* 38.

37. Benjamin Franklin, *Papers,* 1:30.

38. Benjamin Franklin, *Autobiography,* 49, 71.

39. Ibid., 25, 37, 44–45, 63, 105.

40. Ibid., 82–85.

41. Ibid., 121.

42. Ibid., 91–92.

43. Simpson, *Puritanism in Old and New England,* 32.

44. Tolles, *Meeting House and Counting House,* 142.

45. Ibid., 123–24.

46. Morgan, *Puritan Political Ideas,* 138–39.

47. John Wise, *Vindication.* Quoted material taken from Morgan, *Puritan Political Ideas,* 252–53.

48. Smith, *Civic Ideals,* 54–55.

49. Marilyn C. Baseler, *Asylum for Mankind,* 4–6, 56.

50. McCusker and Menard, *Economy of British America,* 96, 333.

51. Burstein, *Sentimental Democracy,* 26.

52. Ibid., 33.

53. Miller, *Errand into the Wilderness,* 143–44.

54. Baseler, *Asylum for Mankind,* 58–73.

55. Sara M. Evans, *Born for Liberty,* 22.

56. Smith, *Civic Ideals,* 67.

57. Evans, *Born for Liberty,* 32.

58. Nancy F. Cott, *Public Vows,* 11–12.

59. Evan, *Born for Liberty,* 21, 30.

60. Burstein, *Sentimental Democracy,* 46.

3. The Dream Defined

1. Seymour Martin Lipset, *First New Nation.*

2. Gordon S. Wood, *Radicalism of the American Revolution.*

3. John Adams, *Works,* 4:283–98.

4. George Washington, *George Washington: Writings,* 517.

5. John Adams, *Works,* 4:193–200. See also Russell L. Hanson, *Democratic Imagination,* 90.

6. David Hume, "Idea of a Perfect Commonwealth," 384–85.

7. Richard Hofstadter, *American Political Tradition,* 11.

8. Both quotes appear in Bernard Bailyn, *Voyagers to the West,* 42.

9. Bailyn, *Voyagers to the West,* 33.

10. Alexander Hamilton, "The Federal Farmer," February 1775, in *Papers,* 1:93–94.

11. Both quotes appear in Baseler, *Asylum for Mankind,* 157, 159.

12. Glenn Porter and Harold C. Livesay, *Merchants and Manufactures,* 82.

13. Benjamin Rush, "An Address to the Inhabitants of the British Settlements," 254.

14. Thomas Paine, *Common Sense* (1776), in *Major Writings,* 3:30–31.

15. Ezra Stiles, *The United States Elevated to Glory and Honour* (Worcester, MA, 1785 [1783]), 9, 59. Quoted in Burstein, *Sentimental Democracy,* 130.

16. Benjamin Rush to Charles Nisbet, December 5, 1783, in *Letters of Benjamin Rush,* 1:315–16. Quoted in Burstein, *Sentimental Democracy,* 131.

17. *New Hampshire Magazine,* June 1793, quoted in Burstein, *Sentimental Democracy,* 200.

18. Burstein, *Sentimental Democracy,* 202.

19. Crevecoeur, *Letters from an American Farmer,* 38–39.

20. Ibid., 52, 20–21.

21. Ibid., 56–57, 53.

22. Ibid., 55, 57.

23. Ibid., 63–64.

24. Hofstadter, *American Political Tradition,* 55.

25. Joseph J. Ellis, *American Sphinx,* 54.

26. Jefferson to William Green Munford, June 18, 1799, in *Writings,* 1064.

27. Maier, *American Scripture,* 150.

28. Burstein, *Sentimental Democracy,* 110.

29. Ibid., 161–62.

30. Hofstadter, *American Political Tradition,* 27.

31. Drew R. McCoy, *Elusive Republic,* 14–15, 46.

32. Jefferson to Abbe Arnoux, July 19, 1789, in *Papers of Thomas Jefferson,* 15:282.

33. Jefferson to James Madison, December 20, 1787, in *Papers of Thomas Jefferson,* 12:442.

34. Quoted in Wendell Berry, *Unsettling of American Culture and Agriculture,* 144.

35. Thomas Jefferson, *Works,* 11:193–200.

36. Bernard A. Weisberger, *America Afire,* 21.

37. Hamilton, speech to the Federal Convention, June 22, 1787, in *Papers,* 4:216.

38. Hamilton, speech to the Federal Convention, June 18, 1787, Robert Yates's notes, in *Papers,* 4:200.

39. Hamilton, in *Reports,* 121, 132.

40. Ibid., 53, 59.

41. Tully, No. 3, *American Daily Advertiser* (Philadelphia), August 24, 1794, in Hamilton, *Papers,* 4:160.

42. Richard Brookhiser, *Alexander Hamilton,* 91.

43. Ibid., 172; see also 8.

44. Weisberger, *America Afire,* 114.

45. Eric Foner, *Story of American Freedom*, 18; Alexander Keyssar, *Right to Vote*, 16.

46. Hofstadter, *American Political Tradition*, 27; Foner, *Story of American Freedom*, 21.

47. Alexander Hamilton, John Jay, and James Madison, *Federalist*, 336–37.

48. James Madison, *Letters*, 1:328.

49. Michael Lienesch, *New Order of the Ages*. See also David J. Siemers, *Ratifying the Republic*.

50. Rather, *American Dream*, 4, 39.

51. Weisberger, *America Afire*, 58; see also Smith, *Civic Ideals*, 140–41.

52. Hamilton, *Reports*, 2, 5.

53. Ibid., 50–51.

54. Ibid., 54, 66, 73.

55. Ibid., 141.

56. Hofstadter, *American Political Tradition*, 35.

57. Fisher Ames, *Works*, 2:129.

58. Jefferson to Benjamin Austin, January 9, 1816, in *Thomas Jefferson: Writings*, 10:10.

59. Lawrence H. Fuchs, *American Kaleidoscope*, 13.

60. Baseler, *Asylum for Mankind*, 249–50.

61. James Truslow Adams, *Jeffersonian Principles*, 170.

62. Thomas Jefferson, first annual message to Congress, December 8, 1801, in *Works*, 9:340–41.

63. Rush, "Address to the Inhabitants of the British Settlements," 248, 253.

64. Thomas Jefferson, *Notes*, 138–39, 162–63.

65. Thomas Jefferson, *Autobiography*, in *Works*, 1:77.

66. Jefferson, *Notes*, 138.

67. Smith, *Civic Ideals*, 175–79; Foner, *Story of American Freedom*, 74; Keyssar, *Right to Vote*, 54–55.

68. Quoted in Linda K. Kerber, *Women of the Republic*, 78. Also in Evans, *Born for Liberty*, 48.

69. Alice Rossi, ed., *Feminist Papers*, 10–11, 13.

70. Jefferson to Anne Willing Bingham, May 11, 1788, in *Papers of Thomas Jefferson*, 13:151–52.

71. Mary P. Ryan, *Womanhood in America*, 105.

72. Robert V. Remini, *Andrew Jackson and His Indian Wars*, 16.

73. Sinopoli, ed., *From Many, One*, 70.

74. Remini, *Andrew Jackson and His Indian Wars*, 7.

4. The Dream Expanded

1. Andrew Burstein, *America's Jubilee*.

2. Daniel Webster, "Adams and Jefferson," August 2, 1826, in *Papers of Daniel Webster*, 1:269–71.

3. Jefferson to Francis Adrian Van De Kemp, January 11, 1825, in *Thomas Jefferson: Writings,* 10:377.

4. Alexis de Tocqueville, *Democracy in America,* 1:3, 2:100.

5. Ibid., 2:104–5.

6. Ralph Waldo Emerson, "The American Scholar," speech delivered August 31, 1837, before the Phi Beta Kappa Society at Harvard University, in *Works,* 1:112.

7. William Ellery Channing, *Self-Culture,* 43. "Self-Culture" was originally delivered as a speech in Boston in September 1838 and was reprinted.

8. The demographic data in this section can be found in *Historical Statistics of the United States,* series A 17, A 46, A 99–100, 106–7, 113–14, 120–21.

9. Sarah H. Gordon, *Passage to Union,* 35–36.

10. Quoted in James Truslow Adams, *Epic of America,* 186–87.

11. George Dangerfield, *Awakening of American Nationalism,* 270.

12. Hofstadter, *American Political Tradition,* 57.

13. David Crockett, *Narrative,* 7, 101, 171.

14. Quoted in Arthur M. Schlesinger Jr., *Age of Jackson,* 306.

15. Quoted in Hofstadter, *American Political Tradition,* 79.

16. Quoted in Schlesinger, *Age of Jackson,* 312.

17. Tocqueville, *Democracy in America,* 1:301–2, 414, 303.

18. Ibid., 1:443, 303.

19. Ibid., 1:410.

20. Ibid., 1:305, 2:78.

21. Ibid., 2:144, 147.

22. Ibid., 1:275, 273, 277.

23. Ibid., 1:316, 321.

24. Herman Melville, *White Jacket,* 150.

25. Emerson, "The Young American," speech delivered before the Mercantile Library Association of Boston, February 7, 1844, in *Works,* 1:369, 350–51.

26. Emerson, "American Scholar," *Works,* 1:100, 105.

27. Channing, *Self-Culture,* 6.

28. Emerson, "American Scholar," *Works,* 1:91; "Self-Reliance," *Works,* 2:60, 81; "Wealth," *Works,* 6:99.

29. Emerson, "American Scholar," *Works,* 1:114.

30. Emerson, "Self-Reliance," *Works,* 2:77.

31. Emerson, "Young American," *Works,* 1:357.

32. Emerson, "Wealth," *Works,* 6:88, 91.

33. Emerson, "Young American," *Works,* 1:343.

34. Quoted in Eric Foner, *Free Soil,* 14.

35. Joel Porte, ed., *Emerson in His Journals,* 197.

36. Emerson, "Wealth," *Works,* 6:99.

37. Ibid., 6:104.

38. Quoted in Burstein, *Sentimental Democracy,* 284.

39. Gabor S. Boritt, *Lincoln and the Economics of the American Dream,* 22.

40. Merrill D. Peterson, *Jeffersonian Image*, 220.

41. Roy P. Basler, *Abraham Lincoln*, 488–89.

42. Quoted in Hofstadter, *American Political Tradition*, 135.

43. Quoted in A. James Reichley, *Life of the Parties*, 105.

44. Basler, *Abraham Lincoln*, 361.

45. Abraham Lincoln, *Collected Works*, 3:16, 4:24–25, 2:222, 266, 405, 3:145–46, 204, 222, 226.

46. Ibid., 2:405, 520.

47. Ibid., 4:438.

48. John Patrick Diggins, *On Hallowed Ground*, 23.

49. Abraham Lincoln, *Abraham Lincoln*, 734.

50. Ibid., 793.

51. Quoted in Boritt, *Lincoln and the Economics of the American Dream*, 124.

52. Gordon, *Passage to Union*, 17–18.

53. Bernard Schwartz, *History of the Supreme Court*, 50.

54. Schlesinger, *Age of Jackson*, 325–26.

55. William B. Scott, *In Pursuit of Happiness*, 59.

56. Karabell, *Visionary Nation*, 70.

57. John J. Miller, *Unmaking of Americans*, 36–37. See also Keyssar, *Right to Vote*, 33.

58. Quoted in Boritt, *Lincoln and the Economics of the American Dream*, 113.

59. James A. Garfield, *Works*, 1:86.

60. Foner, *Story of American Freedom*, 104.

61. Keyssar, *Right to Vote*, 96.

62. Tocqueville, *Democracy in America*, 344.

63. Robert W. Johannsen, ed., *Lincoln Douglas Debates*, 34, 46, 128.

64. Smith, *Civic Ideals*, 215; Keyssar, *Right to Vote*, 55.

65. Smith, *Civic Ideals*, 243.

66. Lincoln, *Abraham Lincoln*, October 16, 1854, 291.

67. Lincoln, *Complete Works*, 8:2–4.

68. Keyssar, *Right to Vote*, 89.

69. Evans, *Born for Liberty*, 94–95.

70. Cott, *Public Vows*, 50.

71. Evans, *Born for Liberty*, 70.

72. Sinopoli, ed., *From Many, One*, 119–20.

73. Keyssar, *Right to Vote*, 177.

74. Jane V. Matthews, *Women's Struggle for Equality*, 126. See also Keyssar, *Right to Vote*, 178.

75. Frederick Douglass, *Frederick Douglass Papers*, 4:216–17.

76. Remini, *Andrew Jackson and His Indian Wars*, 273.

77. Ibid., 277–78.

78. Smith, *Civic Ideals*, 237.

79. Keyssar, *Right to Vote*, 60.

5. The Dream Threatened

1. Charles Darwin, *Origin of Species,* 63, 95.
2. James Truslow Adams, *Epic of America,* 297–98.
3. Darwin, *Origin of Species,* 472, 468.
4. Ibid., 79.
5. E. L. Godkin, "Cooperation," 173.
6. Sumner took this wonderful phrase from the famous frontiersman, Davy Crockett. See Crockett, *Narrative,* 118.
7. See Foner, *Story of American Freedom,* 116; Robert J. Samuelson, *The Good Life and Its Discontents,* 135.
8. *Historical Statistics of the United States,* Series D, 36–45, p. 72, Series F, 44–48, p. 141.
9. *Historical Statistics of the United States,* Series E, 101, p. 123. See also Grant McConnell, *Decline of Agrarian Democracy,* 10.
10. *Historical Statistics of the United States,* Series A-20, p. 8.
11. Ibid., Series A, 195–209, p. 14.
12. Ibid., Series C, 88–114, pp. 56–59.
13. Emma Lazarus, "New Collosus," 1886.
14. Henry Adams, *History of the United States,* 1:172–74.
15. Horatio Alger Jr., *Ragged Dick,* 40.
16. Ibid., 42–43.
17. Ibid., 77.
18. Ibid., 78–79, 99.
19. Ibid., 137–38.
20. P. T. Barnum, *Life of P. T. Barnum.* Chapter 31 is "The Art of Money-Getting," 169, 175.
21. Barnum, "The Art of Money Getting," 177.
22. Ibid., 188, 177, 182.
23. Ibid., 177–78, 188.
24. Andrew Carnegie, "Wealth," 655.
25. Quoted in Hofstadter, *American Political Tradition,* 218.
26. Quoted in Edward Chase Kirkland, *Dream and Thought,* 164.
27. Lendol Calder, *Financing the American Dream,* 124.
28. Carnegie, "Wealth," 662–63.
29. Quoted in Kirkland, *Dream and Thought,* 61.
30. Russell H. Conwell, "Acres of Diamonds" (1870), 4–7. Available at http://www.temple.edu/documentation/heritage/speech.html.
31. Conwell, "Acres of Diamonds," 8, 14.
32. Henry George, *Progress and Poverty,* 3, 8.
33. Ibid., 96, 478–79.
34. Ibid., 90.
35. Ibid., 131.
36. Ibid., 336, 338, 405–6.

37. Ibid., 442, 455–56.

38. Ibid., 456, 471.

39. Ibid., 545, 548.

40. Edward Bellamy, *Looking Backward,* 12.

41. Ibid., 12–13.

42. Ibid., 43.

43. Ibid., 94–95.

44. Frederick Jackson Turner, "Significance of the Frontier," 90–91.

45. "Veto Message—Distribution of Seeds," *Congressional Record,* 49th Congress, 2nd session, vol. 28, pt. 2, p. 1875.

46. Quoted in Keyssar, *Right to Vote,* 137.

47. Miller, *Unmaking of Americans,* 38.

48. Quoted in Roger Daniels, *Not Like Us,* 19.

49. Quoted in Smith, *Civic Ideals,* 364–65.

50. Schwartz, *History of the Supreme Court,* 180.

51. Karabell, *Visionary Nation,* 71.

52. *Historical Statistics of the United States,* Series H, 223–38, pp. 207–11.

53. Andrew Carnegie, *Empire of Business,* 80–81.

54. Kirkland, *Dream and Thought,* 96.

55. Fogel, *Fourth Great Awakening,* 72.

56. Claude M. Fuess, *Life of Caleb Cushing,* 2:230, 231.

57. Douglass, *Frederick Douglass: Life and Writings,* 4:272.

58. Matthews, *Women's Struggle for Equality,* 185.

59. Smith, *Civic Ideals,* 340.

60. Matthews, *Women's Struggle for Equality,* 174.

61. George, *Progress and Poverty,* 501.

62. Daniels, *Not Like Us,* 30–31; Smith, *Civic Ideals,* 393; Keyssar, *Right to Vote,* 165.

6. The Dream Defended

1. Herbert Croly, *Promise of American Life,* 116–17.

2. Smith, *Civic Ideals,* 434.

3. John Dewey, *School and Society,* chap. 2, p. 8.

4. William James, *Pragmatism,* 46, 59.

5. Walter Lippmann, *Drift and Mastery.*

6. Woodrow Wilson, *Constitutional Government,* 199, 202.

7. F. Scott Fitzgerald, *Crack-up,* 87.

8. *Historical Statistics of the United States,* Series F 3, p. 139; F 13, p. 116; D 628, p. 92.

9. Ibid., Series D 46, p. 73.

10. Ibid., Series X 351–53, p. 657. See also Samuelson, *The Good Life and Its Discontents,* 20–22, 93–94.

11. Lippmann, *Drift and Mastery,* 39.

12. Foner, *Story of American Freedom,* 159; Yehoshua Arieli, *Individualism and Nationalism,* 341.

13. Croly, *Promise of American Life,* 9–10.

14. Ibid., 206.

15. Ibid., 28.

16. Ibid., 194.

17. Ibid., 400.

18. Ibid., 181.

19. Theodore Roosevelt, *New Nationalism,* 11, 119–21.

20. Ibid., 17, 241.

21. Ibid., 126, 178.

22. Ibid., 238–40, 18.

23. Ibid., 231, 240, 143.

24. Hofstadter, *American Political Tradition,* 332.

25. Woodrow Wilson, *Papers,* 27:149–50.

26. Lippmann, *Drift and Mastery,* 112, 118.

27. Ibid., 103.

28. Ibid., 85, 172.

29. Ibid., 76, 68, 141, 143.

30. F. Scott Fitzgerald, *Great Gatsby,* 2.

31. Ibid., 90, 97.

32. Ibid., 134, 172.

33. Ibid., 135, 148.

34. Ibid., 162.

35. Herbert Hoover, *American Individualism,* 9.

36. Hofstadter, *American Political Tradition,* 387.

37. Abbott, *Exemplary Presidency,* 40–42.

38. John Gerring, *Party Ideologies in America,* 130–31.

39. James MacGregor Burns, *Roosevelt,* 151. Originally appeared in the *New York Times,* November 13, 1932, section 8, 1.

40. Franklin D. Roosevelt, *Public Papers and Addresses,* 1:742–56.

41. Fireside Chat, September 30, 1934. Available at http://www.mhrcc.org/fdr/chat6.html.

42. Roosevelt, *Public Papers and Addresses,* 9:663–72.

43. Ibid., 13:32–44.

44. Evans, *Born for Liberty,* 192–93.

45. Lawrence Lindsey, *Growth Experiment,* 23.

46. Stanley Greenberg, *Middle Class Dreams,* 77.

47. McConnell, *Decline of Agrarian Democracy,* 139.

48. Foner, *Story of American Freedom,* 233.

49. Louis Galambos and Joseph Pratt, *Rise of the Corporate Commonwealth,* 112–13; Abbott, *Exemplary Presidency,* 80–81.

50. Croly, *Promise of American Life,* 403.

51. *Historical Statistics of the United States,* Series H, 225–33, 236, 321–22, 330–36.

52. Evans, *Born for Liberty,* 167. Evans cites Rheta Childe Dorr, *Woman of Fifty,* 101.

53. Cott, *Public Vows,* 166–68.

54. Thomas G. Dyer, *Theodore Roosevelt and the Idea of Race,* 16–19, 70–80, 100–9. See also Morton Keller, *Regulating a New Society,* 255.

55. Abel Meeropol. Originally published as "Bitter Fruit" in the January 1937 issue of the *New Yorker.* In 1938 Billie Holliday recorded the poem set to song and universally known as "Strange Fruit." Billie Holliday's original rendition can be heard online at http://www.authentichistory.com/audio/1930s/Strange_Fruit.html.

56. Frank Levy, *New Dollars and Dreams,* 92–93.

57. Lawrence C. Kelly, "Indian Reorganization Act," 291–312.

58. Graham D. Taylor, *New Deal and American Indian Tribalism.*

7. The Dream at High Tide

1. Quoted in Doris Kearns Goodwin, *Lyndon Johnson and the American Dream,* 96. See *Congressional Record,* June 4, 1946, A3170.

2. William Julius Wilson, *Declining Significance of Race,* 65–71.

3. Quoted in Gareth Davies, *From Opportunity to Entitlement,* 194. See *Congressional Record,* August 8, 1967, 21782.

4. Shelby Steele, *Dream Deferred,* 13, 20.

5. Richard Rodriquez, *Brown,* 91.

6. Gerring, *Party Ideologies in America,* 152.

7. Eisenhower, *Public Papers,* 1–7.

8. Ibid., 61.

9. Adlai E. Stevenson, *Papers,* 6:244.

10. John F. Kennedy Library and Museum. Address of President-Elect John F. Kennedy delivered to a joint convention of the general court of the Commonwealth of Massachusetts, State House, Boston, January 9, 1961. Available at http://www.cs.umb.edu/jfklibrary/j010961.htm.

11. John F. Kennedy, *Public Papers, 1961,* 1–3.

12. Kennedy, *Public Papers, 1962,* 728.

13. Kennedy, *Public Papers, 1963,* 468–69.

14. Martin Luther King, "I have a dream," delivered at the Lincoln Memorial on August 28, 1963. Available at http://www.extension.umn.edu/units/diversity/mlk/mlk.html.

15. Lyndon B. Johnson, *Public Papers, 1963–64,* vol. 1, entry 11, pp. 8–10.

16. Johnson, *Public Papers, 1963–64,* vol. 1, entry 357, pp. 704–7.

17. Johnson, *Public Papers, 1965,* vol. 1, entry 2, pp. 1–9.

18. Ibid., vol. 1, entry 27, pp. 71–74.

19. Ibid., vol. 1, entry 107, pp. 281–87.

20. Ibid., vol. 2, entry 301, pp. 635–40.

21. Quoted in Davies, *From Opportunity to Entitlement*, 81.

22. Malcolm X, "The Ballot or the Bullet," April 3, 1964, in *Malcolm X Speaks*, 26.

23. Arthur M. Schlesinger, *History of American Presidential Elections*, 4:3154.

24. Joseph A. Califano Jr., "What Was Really Great," 13; Goodwin, *Lyndon Johnson and the American Dream*, 217, 287; Sidney M. Milkis, *The President and the Parties*, 184.

25. Gerald N. Rosenberg, *Hollow Hope*, 52, esp. fig. 2.1.

26. Keyssar, *Right to Vote*, 263.

27. Cott, *Public Vows*, 4, 198.

28. Johnson, *Public Papers, 1965*, vol. 2, entry 546, pp. 1037–40.

29. David Vogel, "The 'New' Social Regulation in Historical and Comparative Perspective," 161–62.

30. Jane J. Mansbridge, *Why We Lost the ERA*, 1–3.

31. *Historical Statistics of the United States*, Series G, 169–70, p. 169.

32. Levy, *New Dollars and Dreams*, 15, 34, 95.

33. Hacker, *Two Nations*, 123–24; Dalton Conley, *Being Black*, 136.

34. Quoted in Davies, *From Opportunity to Entitlement*, 66–67.

35. William Julius Wilson, *Truly Disadvantaged*, 125.

36. Levy, *New Dollars and Dreams*, 16–17.

37. Quoted in Hanson, *Democratic Imagination*, 310; Evans, *Born for Liberty*, 282.

38. The National Organization for Women's 1966 Statement of Purpose. Available at http://www.now.org/history/purpos66.html.

39. Kenneth R. Philp, *Termination Revisited*, 151.

40. William T. Hagan, "Tribalism Revisited," 5–14.

8. The Dream at Ebb Tide

1. Samuelson, *The Good Life and Its Discontents*, 70–71.

2. *Historical Statistics of the United States*, Series D 20, p. 71; Evans, *Born for Liberty*, 301; Paul Ryscavage, *Income Inequality in America*, 84, 88.

3. Levy, *New Dollars and Dreams*, 38.

4. Jeremy Rifkin, *Age of Access*, 5, 52–53.

5. Levy, *New Dollars and Dreams*, 62; David Brooks, *Bobos in Paradise*, 36.

6. Evans, *Born for Liberty*, 309.

7. Greenberg, *Middle Class Dreams*, 260–82.

8. Merrill D. Peterson, *Thomas Jefferson and the New Nation*, viii.

9. Edmund Morris, *Dutch*, vi–vii.

10. Hugh Heclo, "Ronald Reagan," 6.

11. Ronald Reagan, *Public Papers, 1987*, 1:744.

12. Ronald Reagan, "A Time for Choosing, aka The Speech, 1964." Delivered

October 27, 1964. Available at http://odur.let.rug.nl/~usa/P/rr40/speeches/ the_speech.htm.

13. Quoted in Morris, *Dutch,* 401. Speech to the 1976 Republican National Convention.

14. Reagan, *Public Papers, 1981,* p. 1.

15. Reagan, *Public Papers, 1983,* 1:364.

16. Greenberg, *Middle Class Dreams,* 135.

17. Reagan, *Public Papers, 1985,* 1:130.

18. Reagan, *Public Papers, 1989,* 2:1722.

19. Reagan, *Public Papers, 1989,* 2:1722.

20. Reagan, "The Expanding Frontiers of World Freedom," address to Captive Nations Week Convention, July 15, 1991. Available from the Ronald Reagan Library, 40 Presidential Drive, Simi Valley, CA 93065.

21. Heclo, "Ronald Reagan," 3.

22. Reagan, *Public Papers, 1989,* 2:1736.

23. Heclo, "Ronald Reagan," 6–7.

24. Quoted in Gerring, *Party Ideologies in America,* 247.

25. Keynote address of Governor Bill Clinton, to the Democratic Leadership Council's Cleveland Convention, May 6, 1991. Available at http://www.ndol.org/.

26. Clinton announcing for the presidency on October 3, 1991. William Clinton, *Preface to the Presidency,* 82, 85, 219.

27. Clinton's "A New Covenant: Responsibility and Rebuilding the American Community," delivered at Georgetown University, October 23, 1991; in *Preface to the Presidency,* 89.

28. Clinton's Old State House victory speech, Little Rock, November 3, 1992; in *Preface to the Presidency,* 419.

29. William J. Clinton, *Public Papers,* 1:1–3.

30. Ibid., 1:126, 1:86.

31. Alan Wolfe, *One Nation, After All,* 8.

32. Clinton, *Between Hope and History,* 18, 6.

33. Ibid., 118.

34. Ibid., 91–92.

35. Ibid., 172.

36. Clinton, *Public Papers,* 1:44.

37. Reagan, *Public Papers, 1981,* p. 2

38. Thomas B. Edsall and Mary D. Edsall, *Chain Reaction,* 23.

39. Reagan, *Public Papers, 1988–1989,* 2:1329–30.

40. Bob Woodward, *Agenda,* 11.

41. William C. Berman, *From the Center to the Edge,* 25–26; Woodward, *Agenda,* 127.

42. Clinton, *Public Papers,* 2:1346–47.

43. Berman, *From the Center to the Edge,* 59–60.

44. Abraham, *Freedom and the Court,* 440.

45. Ackerman, *We the People,* 318.

46. Hochschild, *Facing Up to the American Dream,* 147.

47. Ibid., 60–73; see also Wolfe, *One Nation, After All,* 211.

48. Lipset, *American Exceptionalism,* 135–36; Conley, *Being Black,* 56–57.

49. Orlando Patterson, *Ordeal of Integration,* 27.

50. Levy, *New Dollars and Dreams,* 100, 109.

51. Bill Dedman, "Segregation Persists Despite Fair Housing Act," *New York Times,* February 13, 1999, A15; Ronald Brownstein, "Success Story: Homeownership Rises Among African-Americans and Hispanics," *Dallas Morning News,* June 6, 1999, 5J; Peter Kilborn, "Bias Worsens for Minorities Buying Homes," *New York Times,* September 16, 1999, A15.

52. "Charting Parenthood: A Statistical Portrait of Fathers and Mothers in America." Available at http://fatherhood.hhs.gov/charting02.

53. Hacker, *Two Nations,* 187–213.

54. Hochschild, *Facing Up to the American Dream,* 120.

55. Patterson, *Ordeal of Integration,* 172, 55.

56. Eric Slater, "Unexplained Drownings Fuel Indians' Suspicions," *Dallas Morning News,* June 30, 2000, 41A.

57. Chaka Ferguson, "American Indians Overlooked by Presidential Candidates, Parties," Associated Press, January 13, 2000.

58. Pam Belluck, "Indian Schools, Long Failing, Press for Money and Quality," *New York Times,* May 18, 2000, A1.

9. The American Dream in the Twenty-First Century

1. J. G. A. Pocock, *Politics, Language, and Time,* 233–72.

2. Schwarz, *Illusions of Opportunity,* 124.

3. Kevin Phillips, *Wealth and Poverty.*

4. CBS News/New York Times Survey, January 24–25, 1998; Jacob Weisberg, "Whatever Happened to Politics: United Shareholders of America," *New York Times,* January 25, 1998, section 6, p. 29.

5. Lawrence Jeff Johnson et al., *Key Indicators.*

6. Steven Greenhouse, "Running on Empty: So Much Work, So Little Time," *New York Times,* September 5, 1999, section 4, Week in Review, 1.

7. Fogel, *Fourth Great Awakening,* 178.

8. Schwarz, *Illusions of Opportunity,* 135.

9. U.S. Department of Labor, Bureau of Labor Statistics, "Highlights of Women's Earnings in 2001," Report 960, May 2002. Available at http://stats.bls.gov/cps/cpswom2001.pdf.

10. Louis Uchitelle, "Job Track or 'Mommy Track'? Some Do Both in Phases," *New York Times,* July 5, 2002, B5.

11. Catharine Arnst, "Being a Mother Just Doesn't Pay," review of Ann Crittenden, *The Price of Motherhood,* in *BusinessWeek,* March 12, 2001, 22.

12. Evans, *Born for Liberty,* 147.

13. Catharine Arnst, "The Loneliness of the High-Powered Woman," review of Sylvia Ann Hewlett, *Creating a Life*, 23, in *BusinessWeek*, April 29, 2002, 23

14. Michelle Conlin, with Jennifer Merritt and Linda Himelstein, "Working Life: Mommy Is Really Home from Work," *BusinessWeek*, November 25, 2002, 101–4.

15. Alexander Stille, "Grounded by an Income Gap," *New York Times*, December 15, 2001, A15, A17.

16. Ronald Brownstein, "Still Struggling: Millions of Americans Working Without Much to Show for It," *Dallas Morning News*, June 5, 2000, 11A.

17. Peter Gottschalk and Sheldon Danziger, "Income Mobility and Exits from Poverty of American Children, 1970–1992," prepared in August 1999 for UNICEF, International Child Development Center, Florence, Italy. Available at http://www.jcpr.org/wpfiles/gottschalk-danziger.pdf.

18. Rather, *American Dream*, 166.

19. Clinton, *Public Papers*, 1:131.

20. Ackerman and Alstott, *Stakeholder Society*, 27, 52.

21. Clarence Page, "Colorblind Society Remains Elusive at Century's Turn," *Dallas Morning News*, January 2, 2000, 5J; Michael Barone, "American Dreamers: Blacks, Latinos, and Asians are Following a Well-Trod Path to Success," *U.S. News and World Report*, April 3, 2000, 27.

22. Mark Miringoff and Marque-Luisa Miringoff, *Social Health of the Nation*, 62, 82; Diane Solis, "For Many Latinos, U.S. Stands for Hope," *Dallas Morning News*, October 18, 2002, 1A, 7A; Alan B. Kruegar, "The Name Can Make a Job Harder to Find," *New York Times*, December 12, 2002, C2.

23. Timothy Egan, "Mending a Trail of Broken Treaties," *New York Times*, June 25, 2000, Wk3.

24. David Jackson, "Bush More Optimistic About North Korea than Iraq," *Dallas Morning News*, January 1, 2003, A1, A20.

25. Conley, *Being Black*, 53.

Bibliography

Abbott, Philip. *The Exemplary Presidency: Franklin D. Roosevelt and the American Political Tradition.* Amherst: University of Massachusetts Press, 1990.

Abraham, Henry. *Freedom and the Court: Civil Rights and Liberties in the United States.* 7th ed. New York: Oxford University Press, 1998.

Ackerman, Bruce. *We the People: Foundations.* Cambridge, MA: Harvard University Press, 1991.

Ackerman, Bruce, and Anne Alstott. *The Stakeholder Society.* New Haven, CT: Yale University Press, 1999.

Adams, Henry. *History of the United States During the Administration of Thomas Jefferson.* New York: Charles Scribner's Sons, 1889.

Adams, James Truslow. *The Epic of America.* Garden City, NY: Blue Ribbon Books, 1931.

———. *Jeffersonian Principles and Hamiltonian Principles.* New York: Little, Brown, 1932.

Adams, John. *The Works of John Adams.* Edited by Charles Francis Adams. 10 vols. Boston: Little, Brown, 1850–1856.

Alger, Horatio, Jr. *Ragged Dick, or Street Life in New York with the Boot Blacks.* 1868. New York: Signet, 1990.

Ames, Fisher. *The Works of Fisher Ames.* Edited by Seth Ames. 2 vols. Boston: Little, Brown, 1854.

Arieli, Yehoshua. *Individualism and Nationalism in American Ideology.* Cambridge, MA: Harvard University Press, 1964.

Bailyn, Bernard. *Voyagers to the West: A Passage in the Peopling of America on the Eve of the Revolution.* New York: Knopf, 1986.

Barnum, P. T. (Phineas Taylor). *Life of P. T. Barnum.* Buffalo, NY: Courier, 1888.

Baseler, Marilyn C. *"Asylum for Mankind": America 1607–1800.* Ithaca, NY: Cornell University Press, 1998.

Bell, Derrick. *Faces at the Bottom of the Well: The Permanence of Racism.* New York: Basic Books, 1992.

Bellamy, Edward. *Looking Backward, 2000–1887.* Garden City, NY: Dolphin Books, Doubleday, 1888.

Berman, Paul. *A Tale of Two Utopias: The Political Journey of the Generation of 1968.* New York: Norton, 1996.

Berman, William C. *From the Center to the Edge: The Politics and Policies of the Clinton Administration.* New York: Rowman and Littlefield, 2001.

Berry, Wendell. *The Unsettling of American Culture and Agriculture.* New York: Avon Books, 1977.

Boritt, Gabor S. *Lincoln and the Economics of the American Dream.* 1978. Urbana: University of Illinois Press, 1994.

Breen, T. H. *Puritans and Adventurers: Change and Persistence in Early America.* New York: Oxford University Press, 1980.

Brookhiser, Richard. *Alexander Hamilton: American.* New York: Free Press, 1999.

Brooks, David. *Bobos in Paradise: The New Upper Class and How They Got There.* New York: Simon & Schuster, 2000.

Burns, James MacGregor. *Roosevelt: The Lion and the Fox.* New York: Harcourt, Brace and World, 1956.

Burstein, Andrew. *America's Jubilee: How in 1826 a Generation Remembered Fifty Years of Independence.* New York: Knopf, 2001.

―――. *Sentimental Democracy: The Evolution of America's Romantic Self-Image.* New York: Hill and Wang, 1999.

Calder, Lendol. *Financing the American Dream: A Cultural History of Consumer Credit.* Princeton, NJ: Princeton University Press, 1999.

Califano, Joseph A., Jr. "What Was Really Great About the Great Society." *Washington Monthly* 31, no. 10 (October 1999): 13–19.

Carnegie, Andrew. *The Empire of Business.* New York: Doubleday, 1902.

―――. "Wealth." *North American Review* 148 (June 1889): 653–64.

Channing, William Ellery. *Self-Culture.* 1838. New York: Arno Press and New York Times, 1969.

Chesterton, G. K. (Gilbert Keith). *What I Saw in America.* New York: Dodd, Mead, 1922.

Clinton, William J. *Between Hope and History: Meeting America's Challenges for the 21st Century.* New York: Random House, 1996.

―――. *Preface to the Presidency: Selected Speeches of Bill Clinton, 1974–1992.* Edited by Stephen A. Smith. Fayetteville: University of Arkansas Press, 1996.

―――. *Public Papers of the Presidents of the United States: William J. Clinton.* 17 vols. Washington, DC: Government Printing Office, 1994–2002.

Conley, Dalton. *Being Black, Living in the Red: Race, Wealth, and Social Policy in America.* Berkeley: University of California Press, 1999.

Cott, Nancy F. *Public Vows: A History of Marriage and the Nation.* Cambridge, MA: Harvard University Press, 2000.

Cox, W. Michael, and Richard Alm. *Myths of Rich and Poor: Why We're Better Off than We Think.* New York: Basic Books, 1999.

Crevecoeur, J. Hector St. John de. *Letters from an American Farmer.* 1782. New York: Dutton, 1957.

Crockett, David. *Narrative of the Life of David Crockett of the State of Tennessee.* Baltimore: E. L. Carey and A. Hart, 1834.

Croly, Herbert. *The Promise of American Life.* 1909. New York: Dutton, 1963.

Cullen, Jim. *The American Dream: A Short History of an Idea that Shaped a Nation.* Oxford: Oxford University Press, 2003.

Dangerfield, George. *The Awakening of American Nationalism: 1815–1828*. New York: Harper and Row, 1965.

Daniels, Roger. *Not Like Us: Immigrants and Minorities in America, 1890–1924*. Chicago: Ivan R. Dee, 1997.

Darwin, Charles. *On the Origin of Species by Means of Natural Selection, or Preservation of Favoured Races in the Struggle for Life*. London: John Murray, 1859.

Davies, Gareth. *From Opportunity to Entitlement: The Transformation and Decline of Great Society Liberalism*. Lawrence: University Press of Kansas, 1996.

Delbanco, Andrew. *The Real American Dream: A Meditation of Hope*. Cambridge, MA: Harvard University Press, 1999.

Dewey, John. *The School and Society*. Rev. ed. Chicago: University of Chicago Press, 1915.

Diggins, John Patrick. *On Hallowed Ground: Abraham Lincoln and the Foundations of American History*. New Haven, CT: Yale University Press, 2000.

Dorr, Rheta Childe. *A Woman of Fifty*. 2nd ed. New York: Funk and Wagnalls, 1924.

Douglass, Frederick. *Frederick Douglass: Life and Writings*. Edited by Philip S. Foner. 4 vols. New York: International Publishers, 1975.

———. *The Frederick Douglass Papers: Series One; Speeches, Debates, and Interviews*. Edited by John W. Blassingame and John R. McKivigan. 5 vols. New Haven, CT: Yale University Press, 1991.

Dyer, Thomas G. *Theodore Roosevelt and the Idea of Race*. Baton Rouge: Louisiana State University Press, 1980.

Edsall, Thomas B., and Mary D. Edsall. *Chain Reaction: The Impact of Race, Rights, and Taxes on American Politics*. New York: Norton, 1992.

Eisenhower, Dwight David. *Public Papers of the Presidents of the United States: Dwight David Eisenhower*. 8 vols. Washington, DC: Government Printing Office, 1954–1960.

Ellis, Joseph J. *American Sphinx: The Character of Thomas Jefferson*. New York: Vintage Books, 1996.

———. *Founding Brothers: The Revolutionary Generation*. New York: Knopf, 2001.

Emerson, Ralph Waldo. *The Works of Ralph Waldo Emerson*. 14 vols. Boston: Houghton Mifflin, 1855–1893.

Evans, Sara M. *Born for Liberty: A History of Women in America*. New York: Free Press, 1997.

Fitzgerald, F. Scott. *Crack-up*. Edited by Edmund Wilson. New York: New Directions, 1941.

———. *The Great Gatsby*. New York: Charles Scribner's Sons, 1925.

Flax, Jane. *The American Dream in Black and White: The Clarence Thomas Hearings*. Ithaca, NY: Cornell University Press, 1998.

Fogel, Robert William. *The Fourth Great Awakening and the Future of Egalitarianism*. Chicago: University of Chicago Press, 2000.

Foner, Eric. *Free Soil, Free Labor, Free Men: The Ideology of the Republican Party Before the Civil War*. New York: Oxford University Press, 1970.

———. *The Story of American Freedom*. New York: Norton, 1998.

Franklin, Benjamin. *The Autobiography of Benjamin Franklin.* New York: Macmillan, 1997.

———. *The Papers of Benjamin Franklin.* Edited by Leonard W. Larabee. New Haven, CT: Yale University Press, 1959–1999.

Fuchs, Lawrence H. *The American Kaleidoscope: Race, Ethnicity, and the Civic Culture.* Hanover, NH: Wesleyan University Press, 1990.

Fuess, Claude M. *Life of Caleb Cushing.* 2 vols. New York: Harcourt, Brace, 1923.

Galambos, Louis, and Joseph Pratt. *The Rise of the Corporate Commonwealth: United States Business and Public Policy in the 20th Century.* New York: Basic Books, 1988.

Garfield, James A. *The Works of James A. Garfield.* Edited by Burke Hinsdale. 2 vols. Boston: J. R. Osgood, 1882–1883.

George, Henry. *Progress and Poverty.* 1880. New York: Robert Schalkenbach Foundation, 1966.

Gerring, John. *Party Ideologies in America, 1828–1996.* New York: Cambridge University Press, 1998.

Godkin, E. L. (Edwin). "Cooperation." *North American Review* 106 (January 1868): 150–76.

Goodwin, Doris Kearns. *Lyndon Johnson and the American Dream.* 1976. New York: St. Martin's Press, 1991.

Gordon, Sarah H. *Passage to Union: How the Railroads Transformed American Life, 1829–1929.* Chicago: Ivan R. Dee, 1997.

Greenberg, Stanley. *Middle Class Dreams.* Rev. ed. New Haven, CT: Yale University Press, 1996.

Hacker, Andrew. *Two Nations: Black and White, Separate, Hostile, Unequal.* New York: Ballantine Books, 1995.

Hagan, William T. "Tribalism Revisited: The Native American Since the End of Termination." *Western Historical Quarterly* 12, no. 1 (January 1981): 5–16.

Hamilton, Alexander. *The Papers of Alexander Hamilton.* Edited by Harold C. Syrett. 27 vols. New York: Columbia University Press, 1961–1987.

———. *The Reports of Alexander Hamilton.* Edited by Jacob Cooke. New York: Harper Torchbook, 1964.

Hamilton, Alexander, John Jay, and James Madison. *The Federalist.* Edited by Edward Mead Earle. New York: Modern Library, 1937.

Hanson, Russell L. *The Democratic Imagination in America: Conversations with Our Past.* Princeton, NJ: Princeton University Press, 1985.

Hartz, Louis. *The Founding of New Societies.* New York: Harcourt, Brace & World, 1964.

———. *The Liberal Tradition in America.* New York: Harcourt, Brace & World, 1955.

Heclo, Hugh. "Ronald Reagan and the American Public Philosophy." Conference on the Reagan Presidency. University of California, Santa Barbara, March 27–30, 2000.

Hewlett, Sylvia Ann. *Creating a Life: Professional Women and the Quest for Children.* New Haven: Hyperion, 2002.

Historical Statistics of the United States: Colonial Times to 1957. Washington, DC: Department of Commerce, Bureau of the Census, 1960.

Hochschild, Jennifer L. *Facing Up to the American Dream: Race, Class, and the Soul of the Nation.* Princeton, NJ: Princeton University Press, 1995.

Hofstadter, Richard. *The American Political Tradition and the Men Who Made It.* 1948. New York: Vintage Books, 1989.

Hoover, Herbert. *American Individualism.* New York: Doubleday, Page, 1922.

Hume, David. "Idea of a Perfect Commonwealth." In *Hume's Moral and Political Philosophy,* edited by Henry D. Aiken, 373–85. Darien, CT: Hafner Publishing, 1970.

Huntington, Samuel P. *American Politics: The Promise of Disharmony.* Cambridge, MA: Harvard University Press, 1981.

Jackson, Robert Max. *Destined for Equality: The Inevitable Rise of Women's Status.* Cambridge, MA: Harvard University Press, 1998.

James, William. *Pragmatism.* New York: Meridian Books, 1955.

Jefferson, Thomas. *The Papers of Thomas Jefferson.* Edited by Julian P. Boyd. 28 vols. Princeton, NJ: Princeton University Press, 1950–2000.

———. *Notes on the State of Virginia.* New York: Norton, 1954.

———. *Thomas Jefferson: Writings.* Edited by Merrill D. Peterson. New York: Viking Press, 1984.

———. *Works of Thomas Jefferson.* Edited by Paul Leicester Ford. New York: G. P. Putnam's Sons, 1904–1905.

Johannsen, Robert W., ed. *The Lincoln-Douglas Debates.* New York: Oxford University Press, 1965.

Johnson, Lawrence Jeff, et al. *Key Indicators of the Labor Market.* Geneva: International Labor Organization, 2002.

Johnson, Lyndon B. *Public Papers of the Presidents of the United States: Lyndon B. Johnson.* 10 vols. Washington, DC: Government Printing Office, 1965–1970.

Karabell, Zachary. *A Visionary Nation: Four Centuries of American Dreams and What Lies Ahead.* New York: Harper Collins, 2001.

Kazin, Alfred. *F. Scott Fitzgerald: The Man and His Work.* Cleveland: World Publishing, 1951.

Keller, Morton. *Regulating a New Society: Public Policy and Social Change in America, 1900–1933.* Cambridge, MA: Harvard University Press, 1994.

Kelly, Lawrence C. "The Indian Reorganization Act: The Dream and the Reality." *Pacific Historical Review* 44 (August 1975): 291–312.

Kennedy, John F. *Public Papers of the President of the United States: John F. Kennedy.* 3 vols. Washington DC: Government Printing Office, 1962–1964.

Kerber, Linda K. *Women of the Republic: Intellect and Ideology in Revolutionary America.* Chapel Hill: University of North Carolina Press, 1997.

Keyssar, Alexander. *The Right to Vote: The Contested History of Democracy in the United States.* New York: Basic Books, 2000.

Kirkland, Edward Chase. *Dream and Thought in the Business Community, 1860–1900.* 1956. Chicago: Ivan R. Dee, 1990.

Lazarus, Emma. "The New Colossus." 1883. In *The Poems of Emma Lazarus,* 1:2. New York: Houghton Mifflin, 1889.

Levy, Frank. *The New Dollars and Dreams: American Incomes and Economic Change.* New York: Russell Sage Foundation, 1998.

Lienesch, Michael. *New Order of the Ages: Time, the Constitution, and the Making of American Political Thought.* Princeton, NJ: Princeton University Press, 1988.

Lincoln, Abraham. *Abraham Lincoln: His Speeches and Writings.* Edited by Roy P. Basler. New York: World Publishing, 1946.

———. *Collected Works of Abraham Lincoln.* Edited by Roy P. Basler. 9 vols. New Brunswick, NJ: Rutgers University Press, 1953.

———. *Complete Works of Abraham Lincoln.* Edited by John G. Nicolay and John Hay. 12 vols. New York: Lamb Publishing, 1905.

Lindsey, Lawrence B. *The Growth Experiment: How the New Tax Policy Is Transforming the U.S. Economy.* New York: Basic Books, 1990.

Lippmann, Walter. *Drift and Mastery.* 1914. Madison: University of Wisconsin Press, 1985.

Lipset, Seymour Martin. *American Exceptionalism: A Double-Edged Sword.* New York: Norton, 1996.

———. *The First New Nation.* New York: Anchor Books, 1963.

Lockridge, Kenneth A. *A New England Town: The First Hundred Years.* New York: Norton, 1970.

Madison, James. *Letters and Other Writings of James Madison.* Edited by William C. Rives and Philip R. Fendall. Philadelphia, 1867.

Maier, Pauline. *American Scripture: Making of the Declaration of Independence.* New York: Knopf, 1998.

Malcolm X. *Malcolm X Speaks: Selected Speeches and Statements.* Edited by George Breitman. New York: Norton, 1970.

Mansbridge, Jane J. *Why We Lost the ERA.* Chicago: University of Chicago Press, 1986.

Matthews, Jean V. *Woman's Struggle for Equality: The First Phase, 1828–1876.* Chicago: Ivan R. Dee, 1997.

McConnell, Grant. *The Decline of Agrarian Democracy.* Palo Alto: University of California Press, 1953.

McCoy, Drew R. *The Elusive Republic: Political Economy in Jeffersonian America.* Chapel Hill: University of North Carolina Press, 1980.

McCusker, John J., and Russell R. Menard. *The Economy of British America, 1607–1789.* Chapel Hill: University of North Carolina Press, 1985.

Melville, Herman. *White Jacket, or The World in a Man-of-War.* 1850. New York: Holt, Rinehart and Winston, 1967.

Milkis, Sidney M. *The President and the Parties: The Transformation of the American Party System Since the New Deal.* New York: Oxford University Press, 1993.

Miller, John J. *The Unmaking of Americans: How Multiculturalism has Undermined America's Assimilation Ethic.* New York: Free Press, 1998.

Miller, Perry. *Errand into the Wilderness.* 1956. New York: Harper and Row, 1964.

———. *The New England Mind: From Colony to Province.* Cambridge, MA: Harvard University Press, 1953.

————. *The New England Mind: The Seventeenth Century.* Cambridge, MA: Harvard University Press, 1939.

Miringoff, Marc, and Marque-Luisa Miringoff. *The Social Health of the Nation: How Is America Really Doing.* New York: Oxford University Press, 1999.

Morgan, Edmund S., ed. *Puritan Political Ideas: 1558–1794.* Indianapolis, IN: Bobbs-Merrill, 1965.

Morris, Edmund. *Dutch: A Memoir of Ronald Reagan.* New York: Modern Library, 1999.

Myrdal, Gunnar. *An American Dilemma: The Negro Problem and Modern Democracy.* New York: Harper and Brothers Publishers, 1944.

Paine, Thomas. *Major Writings of Thomas Paine.* Edited by Philip S. Foner. Secacus, NJ: Citadel Press, 1948.

Parrington, Vernon. *Main Currents of American Thought.* New York: Harcourt, Brace, Jovanovich, 1927.

Patterson, Orlando. *The Ordeal of Integration: Progress and Resentment in America's "Racial" Crisis.* Washington, DC: Civitas Counterpoint, 1997.

Perkins, Edwin J. *The Economy of Colonial America.* 2nd ed. New York: Columbia University Press, 1988.

Peterson, Merrill D. *The Jeffersonian Image in the American Mind.* New York: Oxford University Press, 1962.

————. *Thomas Jefferson and the New Nation: A Biography.* New York: Oxford University Press, 1970.

Phillips, Kevin. *The Cousins' Wars: Religion, Politics, and the Triumph of Anglo-America.* New York: Basic Books, 1999.

————. *Wealth and Poverty: The Political History of the American Rich.* New York: Broadway Books, 2002.

Philp, Kenneth R. *Termination Revisited: Indians on the Trail to Self-Determination.* Lincoln, NE: University of Nebraska Press, 1999.

Pocock, J. G. A. *Politics, Language, and Time: Essays on Political Thought and History.* New York: Atheneum, 1973.

Porte, Joel, ed. *Emerson and His Journals.* Cambridge, MA: Harvard University Press, 1982.

Porter, Glenn, and Harold C. Livesay. *Merchants and Manufacturers: Studies in The Changing Structure of Nineteenth-Century Marketing.* 1971. Chicago: Ivan R. Dee, 1989.

Rather, Dan. *The American Dream: Stories from the Heart of Our Nation.* New York: Harper Collins, 2001.

Reagan, Ronald. *Public Papers of the Presidents of the United States: Ronald Reagan.* 15 vols. Washington, DC: Government Printing Office, 1982–1991.

Reichley, A. James. *The Life of the Parties: A History of American Political Parties.* New York: Free Press, 1992.

Remini, Robert V. *Andrew Jackson and His Indian Wars.* New York: Viking, 2001.

Rifkin, Jeremy. *The Age of Access.* New York: Penguin Putnam, 2000.

Rodriquez, Richard. *Brown: The Last Discovery of America.* New York: Viking, 2002.

Roosevelt, Theodore. *The New Nationalism.* New York: Outlook, 1910.

Roosevelt, Franklin D. *The Public Papers and Addresses of Franklin Delano Roosevelt.* 13 vols. New York: Random House, 1938.

Rosenberg, Gerald D. *The Hollow Hope: Can Courts Bring About Social Change?* Chicago: University of Chicago Press, 1991.

Rossi, Alice, ed. *The Feminist Papers from Adams to de Beauvoir.* New York: Columbia University Press, 1973.

Rush, Benjamin. "An Address to the Inhabitants of the British Settlements in America Upon Slave-Keeping." 1773. In *From Many, One,* edited by Richard C. Sinopoli, 247–54. Washington, DC: Georgetown University Press, 1997.

——. *Letters of Benjamin Rush.* Edited by Lyman Henry Butterfield. Princeton, NJ: Princeton University Press, 1951.

Ryan, Mary P. *Womanhood in America: From Colonial Times to the Present.* New York: New Viewpoints, 1975.

Ryscavage, Paul. *Income Inequality in America: An Analysis of Trends.* Armonk, NY: Sharpe, 1999.

Samuelson, Robert J. *The Good Life and Its Discontents: The American Dream in the Age of Entitlement.* New York: Vintage Books, 1997.

Schlesinger, Arthur M., Jr. *The Age of Jackson.* Boston: Little, Brown, 1953.

——. *History of American Presidential Elections, 1789–1968.* New York: McGraw-Hill, 1971.

Schwartz, Bernard. *A History of the Supreme Court.* New York: Oxford University Press, 1993.

Schwarz, John E. *Illusions of Opportunity: The American Dream in Question.* New York: Norton, 1997.

Schwarz, John E., and Thomas J. Volgy. *The Forgotten Americans: Thirty Million Working Poor in the Land of Opportunity.* New York: Norton, 1992.

Scott, William B. *In Pursuit of Happiness: American Conceptions of Property from the Seventeenth Century to the Twentieth Century.* Bloomington: Indiana University Press, 1977.

Siemers, David J. *Ratifying the Republic: How Anti-Federalists Helped Found the American Regime.* Stanford, CA: Stanford University Press, 2002.

Simpson, Alan K. *Puritanism in Old and New England.* Chicago: University of Chicago Press, 1955.

Sinopoli, Richard C., ed. *From Many, One: Readings in American Political and Social Thought.* Washington, DC: Georgetown University Press, 1997.

Smith, Rogers M. *Civic Ideals: Conflicting Visions of Citizenship in U.S. History.* New Haven, CT: Yale University Press, 1997.

Steele, Shelby. *A Dream Deferred: The Second Betrayal of Black Freedom in America.* New York: Harper Collins, 1998.

Stevenson, Adlai E. *The Papers of Adlai E. Stevenson.* Edited by Walter Johnson. 8 vols. Boston: Little, Brown, 1976.

Taylor, Graham D. *The New Deal and American Indian Tribalism.* Lincoln: University of Nebraska Press, 1980.

Tocqueville, Alexis de. *Democracy in America*. New York: Vintage Books, 1954.

Tolles, Frederick B. *Meeting House and Counting House: The Quaker Merchants of Colonial Philadelphia, 1682–1763*. New York: Norton, 1963.

Turner, Frederick Jackson. "The Significance of the Frontier." 1893. In *From Many, One*, edited by Richard C. Sinopoli, 86–91. Washington, DC: Georgetown University Press, 1997.

Vogel, David. "The 'New' Social Regulation in Historical and Comparative Perspective." In *Regulation in Perspective*, edited by Thomas K. McCraw, 155–85. Cambridge, MA: Harvard University Press, 1981.

Washington, George. *George Washington, Writings*. New York: Library of America, 1997.

Webster, Daniel. *The Papers of Daniel Webster: Speeches and Formal Writings*. Edited by Charles M. Wiltse. 15 vols. Hanover, NH: University Press of New England, 1974–1989.

Weisberger, Bernard A. *America Afire: Jefferson, Adams, and the Revolutionary Election of 1800*. New York: William Morrow, 2000.

Wilson, William Julius. *The Declining Significance of Race: Blacks and Changing American Institutions*. Chicago: University of Chicago Press, 1978.

———. *The Truly Disadvantaged: The Inner City, the Underclass, and Public Policy*. Chicago: University of Chicago Press, 1987.

Wilson, Woodrow. *Constitutional Government in the United States*. New York: Columbia University Press, 1908.

———. *The Papers of Woodrow Wilson*. Edited by Arthur S. Link. 69 vols. Princeton, NJ: Princeton University Press, 1966–1994.

Wise, John. *A Vindication of the Government of New England Churches*. Boston: J. Allen for N. Boone, 1717.

Wolfe, Alan. *One Nation, After All: What Middle-Class Americans Really Think About*. New York: Penguin Books, 1998.

Wood, Gordon S. *The Radicalism of the American Revolution*. New York: Knopf, 1992.

Woodward, Bob. *The Agenda: Inside the Clinton White House*. New York: Simon and Schuster, 1994.

Wuthnow, Robert. *Poor Richard's Principle: Recovering the American Dream Through the Moral Dimension of Work, Business, and Money*. Princeton, NJ: Princeton University Press, 1996.

Index